For

David and Eti
and Shirah, Daniel, and Navah

with affection

Foreword

ONE could not select a more appropriate and comprehensive volume to launch the series "English in the International Context" than *The English Language Today*, edited by Sidney Greenbaum. This inaugural volume aptly captures the vital issues which concern the researchers, teachers, and teacher trainers in English in every country where English is used and taught, whether natively or non-natively.

What are the goals of this series? One key motivation for its initiation is to provide thorough, data-oriented descriptions of the uses, usages, and users of English across cultures and languages. In planning the series, and in inviting the contributors for the future volumes, we are involving scholars from every area of the world to demonstrate the multicultural and multilingual nature of the English-using speech fellowships. The series will focus on linguistic, sociolinguistic, literary and historical topics related to the spread and uses of English.

In the future volumes, we propose to include two types of works written for a general readership interested in the "English studies", as this term is understood in its broader implications: first, studies related to varieties of English specific to particular regions, including Africa, South Asia, Southeast Asia, and so on; and secondly, theme-oriented studies which cut across native and non-native varieties of English, such as discourse strategies and styles, grammatical studies, studies concerned with "mixing" and "switching" with English, and variety-specific or comparative lexical studies. The literary aspects of what may be termed the "literatures in English" will primarily focus on the stylistic characteristics of such texts. The other dimension of World Englishes—the impact of English on other major world literatures, languages, and cultures— is also within the scope of this series. In fact, this aspect has not yet been fully researched and we welcome contributions in this area.

This initial volume brings to the forefront the most debated concern of the day: the attitudes toward changing uses and usages of English. Even in scholarly and professional meetings, both in the Western and non-Western countries, the debate on this topic very rarely is characterized by equanimity, pragmatism, or linguistic realism. Such discussions often reflect judgements and biases which do not necessarily show any awareness of how human languages work. They do, however, touch the most delicate linguistic chords—those of linguistic attitudes.

The thirty-one instructive and provocative papers included in this volume, therefore, have important theoretical, applied and pedagogical implications. They represent the major English-speaking areas of the world, and are written by professionals who are well recognized for their contributions to English studies as linguists, teachers, literary specialists, or academic administrators. They certainly have one thing in common: their concern for English studies and their experience in the "real world" where English is used. The section on "Personal Reactions" is very stimulating from this perspective, for it introduces a dimension normally ignored in scholarly publications. The discussions are not restricted to the U.S.A., Australia, Canada, and New Zealand; rather the issues are seen in a broader global context, especially in the five papers in Section IV (Attitudes and Usage: English in the World Context).

This volume is of interest not only to linguists and sociolinguists. It has direct relevance to classroom teachers, textbook writers, lexicographers, and language planners. The emotional reactions this topic generates are clearly seen in the frequency with which related issues are discussed in the press, in public debates, and in official documents in such diverse sociolinguistic settings as the U.S.A., India, Singapore, Britain and Kenya, to name just a few. Wherever there are users of English in the world, attitudinal questions are alive.

I am, therefore, grateful to Sidney Greenbaum for commissioning contributions on a topic which has more than just linguistic significance; it has social and educational importance, as well, and it transcends cultural, linguistic, and national boundaries. I am particularly happy that this volume has become a flagship, as it were, of this new series.

BRAJ B. KACHRU

Preface

THIS volume was conceived at a meeting of the Commission on the English Language of the National Council of Teachers of English (NCTE), of which I was a member. I was there asked to edit a volume of papers on public attitudes to the English language in the United States. I have enlarged the scope of the book by inviting papers outlining views on the state of the language expressed in earlier periods, papers on attitudes and usage in countries other than the United States, and papers discussing the implications of current attitudes for education at various levels. All the papers except one (by Donald Davie) were specially written for this volume.

As several of the papers indicate, the state of the English language is of concern to many who are not professionally involved with the teaching of the language. The book should therefore be of interest to the general public as well as to teachers of English and students taking courses in the English language, education, or sociolinguistics.

I wish to express my gratitude for their encouragement and advice to Professor John Algeo, who was Director of the Commission on the English Language when I assembled the papers for the volume, and to Professor Braj B. Kachru, who is editor of the series of which this is the first volume.

SIDNEY GREENBAUM

ET-A*

Acknowledgements

The editors and publishers are grateful for permission to reprint the following copyright material:

BENNETT, LOUISE "Bans o' Killing", stanzas 1, 2, 8, and 9, previously published in *Jamaica Labrish*, Sangster's Book Stores, 1966.

DAVIE, DONALD "Some Audibility Gaps", previously published in *The Sewanee Review*, XC, 3 (Summer 1982), pp. 439–449.

Contents

IV. ATTITUDES AND USAGE: ENGLISH IN THE WORLD CONTEXT

V. REACTIONS: PERSONAL AND PROFESSIONAL

Contributors

John Algeo is Professor of English at the University of Georgia, a past president of the American Dialect Society, and a former director of the Commission on the English Language of the National Council of Teachers of English. His publications include *Origins and Development of the English Language* (co-authored), *Problems in the Origins and Development of the English Language*, and *English: An Introduction to Language*.

Harold B. Allen is Professor Emeritus of English and Linguistics at the University of Minnesota. He has written and edited books on the English language, particularly on American dialectology. He has served as president of the American Dialect Society, the National Council of Teachers of English, and Teachers of English to Speakers of Other Languages (TESOL).

Richard W. Bailey is Professor of English Language and Literature at the University of Michigan and a member of the Executive Council of the American Dialect Society. Recent publications include *English as a World Language* (co-edited).

Morton W. Bloomfield is the A. Kingsley Porter Professor Emeritus, Harvard University, Cambridge, Massachusetts. His publications include *Language as a Human Problem* (co-authored) and *A Linguistic Introduction to English* (co-authored).

John B. Carroll is a William R. Kenan, Jr. Professor of Psychology emeritus at the University of North Carolina at Chapel Hill. His publications include *The Study of Language, Language and Thought, The Modern Language Aptitude Test, Language Comprehension and the Acquisition of Knowledge* (co-edited) and *The Teaching of French as a Foreign Langue in Eight Countries*.

Robert Cooper is Associate Professor at the Hebrew University of Jerusalem, where he holds appointments in the School of Education and the Department of Sociology. His publications include *The Spread of English: the Sociology of English as an Additional Language* (co-authored) and *Language Spread: Studies in Diffusion and Social Change* (edited).

Donald Davie is Andrew W. Mellon Professor of Humanities at Vanderbilt University. His principal publications have been of poetry (*Collected Poems 1950–70, 1972*; and *Collected Poems 1971–83*). His contribution to this volume was originally an address given in 1978 to the South Atlantic Modern Languages Association in Atlanta, Georgia.

Lester Faigley is an Assistant Professor of English at the University of Texas at Austin. He has published essays on how writers compose, discourse analysis, the evaluation of writing, and writing pedagogy. He is co-author of two recent books, *Evaluating College Writing Programs* and *Assessing Writers' Knowledge and Processes of Composing*.

Edward Finegan is Professor of English and Linguistics and co-director of the Center for the Study of Literacy and Language Use at the University of Southern California. He is the author of *Attitudes toward English Usage: The History of a War of Words* and chairs the Committee on Usage of the American Dialect Society.

Ofelia García is an Assistant Professor in the Bilingual Education Program at the City College of New York. Her publications include several sociolinguistic studies of Spanish in the United States and articles on bilingual education of Hispanics.

Anne Ruggles Gere is Associate Professor of English at the University of Washington and Director of the Puget Sound Writing Program. Her publications include *Language, Attitude and Change* (co-authored) and *Writing and Learning*.

Manfred Görlach is Associate Professor in the Department of English, University of Heidelberg. His publications include *A History of the English Language* and *Introduction to Early Modern English* (both in German), and *English as a World Language* (co-edited). He edits the journal *English World-Wide* and the monograph series *Varieties of English Around the World*, both devoted to forms and functions of English.

Sidney Greenbaum is the Quain Professor of English Language and Literature at University College London and the Director of the Survey of English Usage. His publications include *A Grammar of Contemporary English* (co-authored) and *Acceptability in Language* (edited).

Robert Ilson is Associate Director of the Survey of English Usage at University College London. His publications include *Studies in English Usage* (co-edited).

Braj B. Kachru is Professor of Linguistics in the Department of Linguistics, University of Illinois at Urbana-Champaign. His publications include *The Other Tongue: English Across Cultures* (edited), *The Indianization of English: The English Language in India*, and *The Alchemy of English*.

William A. Kretzschmar, Jr., is Assistant Professor of English at the University of Wisconsin-Whitewater. He is editor of *Journal of English Linguistics* and assistant editor of the *Linguistic Atlas of the US and Canada*. His publications include translations, articles, and reviews on linguistic and medieval topics.

L. W. Lanham was formerly Head of the Department of Phonetics and Linguistics in the University of the Witwatersrand, South Africa, and is now Director of the Institute for the Study of English in Africa in Rhodes University, Grahamstown. His recent publications are on English in Africa, including *The Standard in South African English and its Social History* and *Language and Communication Studies in South Africa* (co-edited).

Raven I. McDavid, Jr., is Professor Emeritus of English and Linguistics, University of Chicago, and editor-in-chief of the Linguistic Atlases of the Middle and South Atlantic States and the North-Central States. His publications include Mencken's *The American Language* (co-edited abridgment), *Dialects in Culture, Varieties of American English*, and *The Mirth of a Nation: America's Great Dialect Humor* (co-edited).

Allan Metcalf is Professor of English at MacMurray College, Jacksonville, Illinois, where he is also publisher of *The Daily Other*, the only small-college daily newspaper in the U.S. He revised the stylebook for *The Cornell Daily Sun* (Cornell University) in 1960 and wrote a stylebook for *The Other* in 1978. He is also Executive Secretary of the American Dialect Society.

Susan Miller is Director of the University Writing Program and an Associate Professor of English at the University of Utah, Salt Lake City, Utah. She has published articles in rhetoric and composition theory and *Writing: Process and Product, Writing with a Purpose* (7th ed., co-authored), and *Rescuing the Subject: Rhetoric and the Writer* (forthcoming).

Julia Penelope is an Associate Professor of English at the University of Nebraska (Lincoln) where she teaches courses in Stylistics, Semantics, and Linguistic Theory. Her research has concentrated on manipulative uses of the English language, and her articles on doublespeak and sexist uses of English have appeared in *College English* and *Papers in Linguistics*.

Ian Pringle is the head of the Department of Linguistics at Carleton University, Ottawa, and an Associate Professor of English and Linguistics there. His publications include *Reinventing the Rhetorical Tradition* and *Learning to Write: First Language, Second Language* (both co-edited) and *A Historical Source Book for the Ottawa Valley* (co-authored).

Randolph Quirk is the Vice-Chancellor of the federal University of London. Until 1981 he was the Quain Professor of English Language and Literature at University College London. Sometime research fellow at Yale University, his books include *The English Language and Images of Matter* (Oxford University Press) and *Style and Communication in the English Language* (Edward Arnold).

Janice Redish is Director of the Document Design Center at the American Institutes for Research in Washington, D.C. She is a co-author of *Writing in the Professions* and *Guidelines for Document Designers*.

John R. Rickford is Assistant Professor of Linguistics at Stanford University, and Editor of the newsletter of pidgin-creole studies, *The Carrier Pidgin*. His publications include *A Festival of Guyanese Words* (edited) and *The Guyanese Creole Continuum* (in press). He is currently working on a book and several papers exploring the relationship betwen sociolinguistic variation, mobility, and change.

Konrad Schröder is Professor of English Education at Augsburg University. He has written extensively on the history of foreign language teaching in German-speaking countries.

Jerrie C. Scott, an Associate Professor of English and Linguistics at the University of Florida, is currently (1983–84) a Postdoctoral Research Fellow at the Center for Applied Linguistics in Washington, D.C. Her publications include "Black Dialect and Reading: Which Differences Make a Difference?" and "Black Language and Communication Skills: Recycling the Issues."

R. Baird Shuman is Professor of English, Director of Freshman Rhetoric, and Director of English Education at the University of Illinois, Urbana-Champaign. Among his recent publications are *The Clearing House: A Closer Look* (edited), *Education in the 80's: English* (edited), *Elements of Early Reading Instruction*, and *Strategies in Teaching Reading: Secondary*.

James Sledd is Professor of English at the University of Texas. His publications include *Dr. Johnson's Dictionary* (co-authored), *A Short Introduction to English Grammar, Dictionaries and THAT Dictionary* (co-edited).

Geneva Smitherman is Director of the Linguistics Program, Professor of Speech Communication and Senior Research Associate, Black Studies, at Wayne State University in Detroit, Michigan. Her publications include *Talking & Testifyin: the Language of Black America* and *Black English and the Education of Black Children and Youth* (edited).

James Stalker is Professor of English at Michigan State University and Director of the English Language Center. His publications include a special edition of the *International Review of Applied Linguistics* (co-edited), which includes his paper "A Reconsideration of the Definition of Standard English," and "Reader Expectations and the Poetic Line" in *Language and Style*.

Elizabeth Closs Traugott is Professor of Linguistics and English at Stanford University. Her publications include *A History of English Syntax, Linguistics for Students of Literature* (co-authored) and *Papers from the Fourth International Conference on Historical Linguistics* (co-edited).

Janet Whitcut was formerly senior research editor in the Longman dictionary and reference book department. She has worked on various Longman dictionaries, including the *Longman Dictionary of Contemporary English*, and has published, lectured, and broadcast a good deal on English usage and neologism.

I: *Issues and Implications*

SIDNEY GREENBAUM

A NARROW conception of English language studies focuses on the description of the English language as a formal system at a particular period (synchronic studies) or on the changes in the formal system from period to period (diachronic studies). For example, we can describe the rules for forming questions in present-day English or trace the changes in the formation of questions from earlier periods till today, in either instance without considering how questions are used. A broader view takes into account the uses of the language or of a variety of the language in social contexts. Social contexts may be conceived at a lower (micro-) or higher (macro-) level of abstraction. The study of the micro-level is concerned with the use of linguistic expressions or forms. It includes such matters as the communicative force of linguistic expressions when uttered in particular types of situation (according to the situation *Why don't you shave?* may be a genuine inquiry or a request for action) or the language variation that correlates with particular types of situation (*Is it not time for dinner?* is a variant in formal style for the more usual *Isn't it time for dinner?*). The study of the macro-level, on the other hand, deals with the range of functions available to the language as a whole or to a variety within the language.

A full consideration of the social contexts in which English is used requires also an understanding of linguistic attitudes, which involved evaluations of, and beliefs about, the language, varieties of the language, and specific linguistic features. These attitudes influence linguistic choices and reactions to other speakers.

English has come a long way from its obscure beginnings in the southern part of an island off the European continent. From the middle of the fifth century and for the next hundred years, waves of invading tribes of Angles, Saxons, Jutes, and Frisians brought their Germanic dialects from Europe to more comfortable settlements in Britain, driving the Celtic-speaking Britons westward to Wales and Cornwall. Isolated from other Germanic speakers, the settlers subsequently acknowledged their dialects as constituting a separate common language that they called English. A thousand years later a mere six million people spoke English, almost all of them confined to England. Now English is a world-wide language. About 300 million people speak it as their mother-tongue, and there are as many – if not more – for whom it is an additional language.

Transplanted mainly through British colonies, English has survived the political independence of the colonies and their cravings for linguistic independence. In some former colonies, notably the United States, English has remained the mother tongue of most of the inhabitants despite massive immigration of speakers of other tongues. In those countries where it is predominantly the mother tongue, it caters for the full range of functions for which language is used today: from casual conversation to philosophical argument, from poetry to technical manuals, from prayer to communication between pilot and control tower, from popular songs to business memoranda. In most of the colonies where the English-speaking settlers were always in a minority, for example India and Nigeria, English has been retained as a second language, politically attractive as a neutral language where no one native language is generally acceptable; it is often designated legally as an official language and is used internally for a variety of functions – particularly for government, law, and education, and for communication between speakers who have no other language in common, but also increasingly for literature. For most other countries – not only in the Third World but also in developed countries such as Russia – English is the primary foreign language, eagerly studied for access to Western science and technology, for international commerce and tourism, or for international economic and military aid. It is a major language of diplomacy and international conferences. In much of the world, a knowledge of English is required for many of the best jobs.

The unparalleled status of English as an international language reflects the economic and technological power of the English-speaking countries, predominantly the United States. A radical shift in power would undoubtedly result in the eventual displacement of English as the paramount international language. Even so, it will remain the national language of many countries where the majority of the population now speak it as their first or second language.

English has not always served the full range of language functions for those who spoke it as a mother tongue. There were earlier periods when English encountered competition within its original homeland in England from other languages, which displaced it for certain functions, or in some regions of the country, or among particular social classes. Indeed, for most of its history it has not been the normal language for serious writing. As late as the end of the sixteenth century scholars doubted whether English was fit for learned writing, arguing that its syntax and vocabulary were deficient for that purpose, that it was unstable and open to wide variation, and that it could not match the rhetorical and stylistic effects of Latin. If English was to be used for law, medicine, science, and other scholarly functions, its deficiencies had to be remedied. During the Renaissance period conscious efforts were made to expand the vocabulary of English and to experiment with a range of styles, provoking considerable controversy over what should be accounted appropriate usage. By the end of the Renaissance period there was no longer any doubt that English was, or could be made, adequate for intellectual discourse. And by the end of the seventeenth century, after a period of augmentation and refinement, English was considered to be in good shape. By that time too, there had been considerable movement towards the standardization of English spelling, syntax, and vocabulary.

In the eighteenth century, new concerns developed about the language. Most of the learned agreed that English had reached a near-perfect stage in its progress, having been purified of its inconsistencies; they now feared that unless changes were prevented it would deteriorate and become corrupted by the uneducated and half-educated. Moreover, writers were worried that changes in the language would render their works unintelligible to future generations. Eighteenth-century writers engaged in public debate on linguistic propriety, taking into account appropriateness to both social status and to rhetorical requirements. By the nineteenth century social propriety was the main issue, and a tradition had been established as to what constituted good language; it was claimed to be derived from the usage of the best writers and speakers after that usage was subjected to the tests of logic and the decisions of eighteenth-century writers who were accepted as authorities on language. This authoritarian approach emphasized correctness in language, and some writers went so far as to claim that good language reflected good character, introducing a moral argument for their precepts.

The prescriptive tradition of the nineteenth century has continued into the twentieth century. In addition, popular writers of this century have inveighed against misuses and abuses of language. Language, it was pointed out, can be employed to confuse, mislead, stimulate desires, and arouse fear or hate. The mass media enable the messages of politicians and advertisers to reach vast audiences, multiplying the dangers of manipulation through language, and the public must therefore be made critically aware of the devices that can distort their thinking and arouse their feelings. Linguistic engineering, it has been argued, can be employed to improve language use as well as to corrupt it. Most recently, attention has been drawn to the bias against women in some vocabulary and grammatical forms of the language, a bias that may subconsciously influence behaviour and attitudes, and attempts have been and are being made to engineer changes that will counter that bias. In the United States at least, there is increasing sensitivity to the effects of sexist language.

We have so far assumed that there is one English language. But does it make sense to talk about *the* English language? After all, there are differences between the language used, for example, in the United States and in England. If we agree that these two countries speak national varieties of a common language, it is because the populations of the two countries want to recognize them as such, despite the occasional assertions of linguistic independence for the American Language. Similarly, Indian English and Nigerian English are beginning to gain recognition as independent national varieties, rather than as deviant versions of British English, because of the changing attitudes of their speakers to their own varieties and to other varieties, attitudes that now express greater acceptance of local variation from British norms. The institutionalization of non-native varieties is viewed with alarm, however, by those who fear their sharp divergence from native standard varieties.

Within each national variety of English there are varieties that correlate with differences in region, socio-economic class, or ethnic group, and levels of education. When clusters of language features are recognized by their speakers or by others as distinctive for separate populations, the varieties containing the clusters come to be seen as separate varieties or dialects of the language: American English and Canadian English, Appalachian and Cockney dialects, Black English and Jewish English, standard English and non-standard English. Language differences may similarly be recognized as correlating with differences in sex or age. We associate specific language features with particular groups even though such features may overlap varieties, perhaps varying only in the relative frequency of their use. Some features stimulate positive or negative reactions (often intense), reactions that are reflected in attitudes to their users.

Is the English Language dying? In some obvious sense, our language is thriving. English has many more speakers than at any previous time in its fifteen centuries of existence, and the number of speakers is likely to increase in the foreseeable future. In that respect, our language is very much alive.

Is the English language disintegrating as a result of its international dispersion? Will it go the way of Latin, developing into languages that are as mutually unintelligible as French and Spanish? Certainly, there are problems of comprehension between national varieties, as indeed there are between varieties within one country. Even within the boundaries of England, local pronunciation differences may impede communication. And English pidgins and creoles are often completely unintelligible to outsiders. But the written public language remains a neutral variety that is in general comprehensible to all educated users of English, despite minor variations in the different national standards. Convergence between the national varieties and mutual intelligibility are in modern times facilitated by the mass media and by the personal contacts that are encouraged through the relative ease and cheapness of international transport. And the growth of public education at secondary and college levels is likely to maintain a common written language. Nevertheless, present trends indicate that local variation in speech will persist, a diversity that some regret and others applaud.

In addition to variation according to national and group affiliation, language varies according to use. We differentiate between what is appropriate for particular situations. Speech and writing, casual style and more formal styles, and occupational uses such as in legal documents, academic articles, newspaper reports. Attitudes on appropriateness vary and they may change. Witness the growth of the plain English movements, contemporary sensitivity to sexist language, the extended use of taboo words, the encroachment of informal styles in contexts that previously required more formal styles, the attacks on the obfuscations of advertisers, politicians, and the military. Within the standard written varieties there are disputed usages, some of them considered by certain educated writers to stigmatize their users as uneducated, unintelligent, or even morally reprehensible.

Attitudes to language varieties and appropriate uses provoke popular writers on language to pose rhetorical questions, the responses to which are often simplistic, if not uninformed. Is the standard language deteriorating, corrupted by ignorance and contamination from non-standard varieties? Are we turning into a nation of illiterates? Will America be the death of English? The anxieties that arouse such questions are genuine and cannot be dismissed. For language is a precious possession: intensely personal in its uniqueness (since each person's language is unique to some extent) and as the medium for our private thoughts, yet at the same time our major means of communicating with others. Many resent changes that conflict with lifetime practices and judgements or that are felt to obstruct communication.

Similarities in language reinforce social cohesion, differences may be socially divisive. Our attitudes affect our image of ourselves and of others – enhancing or undermining our sense of linguistic security, promoting solidarity with some and hostility toward others. Language prejudices impinge on our everyday lives, determining in part our attitudes to other individuals and to other groups. Language attitudes influence public policy on education, on the teaching of English and other languages. Greater understanding may not eliminate prejudices, but it may serve to moderate them by making us aware of them and of their effects. We can learn to restrain our private prejudices from directing our public behaviour.

This book is a contribution to the greater understanding of language attitudes: attitudes to English and other languages, to varieties of English, and to disputed usages in English. Section II provides a historical perspective by reviewing attitudes in earlier periods in the light of the state of the language at the time. Section III reports on and evaluates language attitudes in three countries – chiefly the United States – where English is predominantly the mother-tongue. Questions of disputed and divided usage are raised because of their important effect on attitudes. Section IV provides a contemporary perspective by examining attitudes to English by speakers of English as a second or foreign language. Section V presents a variety of views on the current state of the English language in the United States and on implications of current language attitudes for the teaching of English at various levels.

The topics discussed in this book impinge on public policy in various ways; for example, legislation on bilingualism and plain English, and decisions by legislators and administrators on the content and methods of English language courses in public educational institutions and on the testing of English language proficiency of teachers and students. Attitudes to the standard English dialect, to non-standard English dialects, and to other languages influence our behaviour and attitudes to those with whom we communicate in our daily lives but who do not speak as we do. In particular, such attitudes affect vitally all teaching where English is the medium of instruction, determining in great measure the progress of students, whose use of English may differ conspicuously from that of their teachers.

As we might expect, the papers in this volume convey somewhat divergent views on the state of the English language today. All the authors are professionally involved with the language in various ways. They express their concerns for the language and their reactions to the attitudes of others from professional as well as personal points of view.

II: *Historical Background*

Introduction

SIDNEY GREENBAUM

THE papers in this section provide a historical dimension to the topics treated in this book. Attitudes to the English language and to questions of usage are viewed within the contexts of political, social, and cultural history.

The paper by Richard Bailey describes how the English language spread through official government action from its original area of settlement in England to other parts of the British Isles, despite the resistance of the Celtic speakers of those areas. Nevertheless, ethnic identification has remained strong among the Celtic peoples of the British Isles. Only Cornish has failed to survive as a mother-tongue. The other Celtic languages – Welsh, Irish, and Scots Gaelic – serve to this day as mother-tongues for minorities within Wales, Ireland, and Scotland, and have won increasing popular esteem and official acceptance within this century, particularly in Eire through government intervention. Furthermore, Scotland and Ireland have developed independent national standards of English; both Scots and Irish (or Hiberno-) English have some characteristic features in grammar and vocabulary that differentiate them from the English of England, though the differences are most conspicuous for pronunciation, as in Welsh English.

The other papers in this section review, in chronological order, assessments of the state of the English language from its beginnings to the present time. William Kretzschmar discusses the struggle of English during the Middle Ages for acceptability as the language of general use in England, in competition with the vernaculars of Scandinavian and French and with Latin for intellectual pursuits. Manfred Görlach devotes his paper to the crucial Renaissance period, during which a standard variety was developed that could displace Latin as the written language. The paper by James Stalker traces the development of prescriptive attitudes towards English in the eighteenth and nineteenth centuries. Finally, Randolph Quirk reflects on the twentieth-century interest in language engineering, focusing on the influential writings of George Orwell.

7

Chapter 1

The Conquests of English

RICHARD W. BAILEY

LANGUAGE and the attitudes associated with it seem at first glance to be closely connected to the uses of power and authority. Simply stated, this apparent truth reflects continuing historical trends: migrations spread a language to new territory, where it enjoys the same esteem in which its speakers are held; political ascendancy elevates the language of the emerging powerful group; the young imitate and master the language of those whose positions they hope to assume in adult life.

Yet by accepting this idea uncritically, we fail to encompass the exceptions to it: preservation of minority languages despite promotion by the majority community of its language; retention of "accents" and "nonstandard" dialects by persons who fully acknowledge and endorse the linguistic models espoused by academies, schools, and respected individuals. In our desire to understand language variety, we need to recognize just how complex and even contradictory the connection may be between language attitudes and language use, between public ideals and personal behavior.[1]

In exploring attitudes toward the English language, we find lively and sometimes acrimonious debates about the merits and defects of its varieties. Often these arguments are based on simplistic polarities: a "standard" opposed to "dialects," clarity and grace against jargon and obfuscation, precision and complexity versus vagueness and laziness. Within these internecine arguments about English, the relation of language and authority is thinly veiled, and most of the testimony that survives from the past was composed by those in power (or by their agents) to justify the usage of the powerful and to denigrate the language behavior of the powerless rustics, the unlettered and uncivil folk. For the most part our attention is drawn to the arguments that eventually prevailed. Too seldom do we give sympathetic understanding to those who have attempted to prevent the spread of any variety of English whatsoever and to maintain an indigenous language against the force of English linguistic expansionism.

This question has been neglected for an obvious reason. Arguments *against* the use of English are seldom conducted *in* English unless the writer or speaker is obliged to reach an audience through the language he or she wishes to decry. When these voices from the past are so little heard, we tend to believe that the spread of English as a world language was inevitable and that the new language was readily accepted wherever the advantages of English civilization were made known.

We can begin our investigation by noting some of the circumstances that are normally associated with the spread of languages into new territory. In many cases, linguistic dispersion has been supported by military conquest, a balance of trade favoring the speakers of the new language, and cultural imperialism. In almost every instance, the conquered eventually adopt the language and customs of the conqueror, and only rarely do those in a position of power give up their own language for another.[2] Whenever a language seems attractive, those who consider adopting it need to be persuaded of the benefits they will derive from the arduous effort to do so. Sometimes the motivating force is the supposed superiority of the new language, its intrinsic virtues. More commonly, the change is the result of economic and cultural attractions, industrialization, urbanization, greater prosperity, or a new religion.[3] In many cases, a multilingual culture will flourish, and the old and new languages coexist, differentiated by the domains of their use. Such multilingualism may continue for many generations, as Latin, for instance, persisted for liturgy and learning in medieval and renaissance Europe. These various correlates of language choice are difficult to distinguish as we attempt to understand how a new language is adopted, what role it will play in the culture to which it is introduced, and why some languages eventually triumph at the expense of others.

In this essay, I will examine only one aspect of this complex problem: the role of official government action in establishing a place for English in the British Isles and in promoting its use when it came into conflict with the other vernaculars employed from the twelfth to the seventeenth centuries. Official language policies, we shall see, have had a relatively minor influence on the spread of English – much less important than past or present language planners have hoped.

Official, legislative, or quasi-legislative support for English emerged only as simple forms of social organization gave way to more complex and bureaucratic ones. When Germanic tribes from the continent of Europe began to invade southern Britain early in the fifth century, they did not pass laws or enter into treaties to promote the use of their language or to discourage the use of the languages native to central and southern England. Instead, they conquered and expelled the inhabitants who spoke those languages to the remote reaches of their territory. When the Vikings subsequently arrived, they came first as raiders and marauders. Only in the ninth century when the Danes and Norwegians began to settle the territory between the river Tees in the north of England and the Welland in the east-central part of the country – an area known as the Danelaw – did their linguistic influence begin to be felt and English gained Scandinavian loan words as a consequence of language contact. Still, there is no evidence of official action by a ruler or a court to influence the choice of language in multilingual settings. When a permanent record was required for some purpose, "natural" selection of languages meant that the local vernaculars were used for domestic consumption – including literary works – while Latin was employed for documents or inscriptions that were designed to have enduring value or to reach an international audience of readers. With the invasion of southern England by speakers of Norman French in 1066, however, the choice of languages became a matter for governmental decision and official action.

The century and a half following the Norman Conquest was a period of transformation crucial for the subsequent history of English. Surviving records and testimony present an obscure and conflicting image of the roles of language during that time, and modern scholarship has produced a variety of theories to explain the competing roles of English, Norman French, and Latin. As far as we can now tell, the Normans did relatively little to promote their own language in the countryside, but the king's court, the major religious communities, and the great estates centered around the fortified manors were all sources of French influence. Monastic life, in particular, was dominated by French-speakers, though the normal written language and the language of the liturgy in such communities was Latin. The kings and their feudal lords were universally French, and many of them spent time on their continental lands and married other French-speakers. After 1080, legal documents were no longer prepared in English, and soon thereafter other records – most particularly the chronicles of events – were kept in Latin rather than English. The choice of language, however, was closely linked to domain of language use and to social class. Speakers of Norman French probably numbered between 10,000 and 20,000 in a population of 1.5 million, but they occupied the positions of power at the court, in the church, and in the urban centers (Berndt, 1965, p. 147). Anglo-French literature flourished for the entertainment and edification of courtiers, but some of this literature shows the influence of native English forms and thus suggests a degree of bilingualism in the generation after the Conquest. The great mass of the population, however, remained unilingual in English, and the ordinary affairs of trade and agriculture continued to be transacted in English.

By the middle of the twelfth century, a balance among the three languages of England seems to have been reached. Latin was used for record-keeping, for learned works in history and theology, and in the liturgy of the church. French grew less usual in routine transactions except among the retinue of the king and among the most powerful of the aristocracy; it was, however, the language of the legal system, itself largely occupied with disputes among the king and his courtiers. English was still the most common mother-tongue but was not much used as a written language except to record homilies and sermons that could be preserved and circulated for the clergy who preached to the laity.

A decisive event that upset the balance among these languages was the conquest of Normandy by Philip II of France in 1204. This victory isolated the Norman French rulers of England from their continental lands and thus encouraged the use of English by the aristocracy in England. Philip's victory is rightly regarded as decisive for the re-emergence of English (in a form much influenced by French) as the language of the powerful in England, though it seems likely that the political separation of English from France merely hastened a process that was already moving toward completion. Throughout the period since the Conquest, English had always been the majority language, and its use as a spoken language reflected local rather than national or international norms. A temporary setback to the re-emergence of English occurred when Henry III of England (1216–1272) brought yet more French-speakers from his domains in the south of France and appointed them to important positions. But the barons of England resisted and compelled Henry to accept the Provisions of Oxford (1258) by which he was obliged to renounce claims to his French territory and to expel the supporters he had imported from France. Significantly, these "Provisions" were disseminated in English, the first act of government promulgated through English for more than a century and a half.

Political separation from France, however, did not end the use of spoken and written French in England. French came more and more to be regarded as the language of government records, and by 1300 it had virtually replaced Latin in most official documents – writs, charters, and petitions to Parliament. Not for another century did English gradually come to be accepted for such purposes, and such was the weight of tradition that law French did not entirely disappear for centuries to come.

Beginning in 1348, the massive plague known as the Black Death spread through England, eventually claiming more than a third of the population. Death, no respecter of persons, helped to accelerate the decline of French by speeding the demise of the minority ruling class who used it and thus hastened the rise of English both as a spoken and as a written language. The balance among French, Latin, and English is revealed by an act adopted in 1362 during the reign of Edward III (1327–1377) requiring that "all pleas which shall be pleaded in any courts whatsoever, before any of his justices whatsoever, or in his other places, or before any of his other ministers whatsoever, or in the courts and places of any other lords whatsoever within the realm, shall be pleaded, shewed, defended, answered, debated, and judged in the *English* tongue, and that they be entered and inrolled in *Latin*" (36 Edward III 15). It did not seem contradictory to those in authority that English should be mandated for the oral language of court proceedings and Latin for the written record of decisions while the law setting forth these requirements was enacted in French.

The preamble to Edward's law provides useful insight into the rationale behind the change it mandated. "Great mischiefs," it asserted, arose from general ignorance of the laws, statutes, and customs that were compiled in French, since by the mid-fourteenth century, French was "much unknown in the said realm." Other countries were seen as better governed because their laws are "learned and used in the tongue of the country." Requiring the courts to use English in conducting the business of justice would keep citizens from "offending the law" and help them to "better keep, save, and defend [their] heritage and possessions."[4] From a modern perspective, it seems entirely reasonable that proceedings at law should be conducted in the vernacular, but this principle has not been generally applied in the United Kingdom even to this day.

Turning our attention to the frontiers of English authority, we see how the hegemony of English power helped spread the uses of English into bordering domains. In Cornwall in the far southwest of the country, the Cornish language sustained a vital oral tradition with occasional and minor uses of it in written form. Cornwall's political independence virtually ceased in the mid-tenth century. English rule separated it from the Breton on the continent and from the Welsh to the north, thus isolating the Cornish-speaking community from the related Celtic languages of these two regions. When the Normans extended their power westward, they assumed control of the lands and mines but did little to induce the people of Cornwall to adopt their language.

Speakers of Cornish were too few and too powerless to assert their claims to the use of their language for institutionalized education, legal proceedings, and other routine matters of civic life. Only as Cornish speakers verged on political power did the question of their language for such official purposes arise. When Henry Tudor (1485–1509) returned from exile in Brittany to defeat Richard III and to assume the throne of England in 1485, he was assisted by a large rebel army from Cornwall and Wales. Some of his supporters from those two regions were awarded positions of authority, but "they adopted the English language, manners and clothes and many of the Welsh who returned to Wales were nicknamed *Sais* (Englishman)" (Ellis, 1974, p. 53). A subsequent insurrection against taxation brought some 15,000 rebels from Cornwall to a battlefield near London where Henry's soldiers dispersed them; shortly thereafter, Cornish peasants joined Perkin Warbeck's ill-fated rebellion against the king and his government, and they too were defeated. As a recent historian of the Cornish language writes: "The 1497 insurrection had thrust Cornwall forward into the gaze of the English administration in an unfavorable light. It was the beginning of the end of Cornwall's separate existence" (Ellis, 1974, p. 57).

Cornish did not rise to official notice in laws recognizing or regulating language. Only with the passage of the Act of Uniformity in 1549 requiring that church services be conducted in English according to the rites of the new Book of Common Prayer did the use of Cornish become the subject of political dispute, and once again Cornish people attempted to assert their rights through rebellion. The language issue was embedded in a "Supplication of the Commons of Devon and Cornwall," a document mostly devoted to the desire of the petitioners to retain the Latin liturgy and the theology of the mass that were abolished by the new prayer book. In replying to these demands, the Duke of Somerset dismissed with a sophistical argument the view that Cornish speakers had any serious claim to a liturgy in their own vernacular:

And where ye saie certein Cornishmen be offended because they haue not their s[er]uice in Cornish for somuch as thei vnderstand no English. Whie shulde they nowe be offended more when they vndersand it not in English then when they had it in Latin and vnderstode it not? And whie shulde not yow all the rest than be gladde and well pleased that haue it in English, that ye do vnderstand. Yf they haue just cause to be greved that haue it in the tongue the which they do not vnderstand. But we are enformed to be veray fewe or no townes in Cornewall but ye shall find more in them that vnderstand English then that vnderstand Laten. And therefore they be yet in better case nowe than the[y] were bifore (Rose-Troup, 1913, pp. 435–436).

[A modern English paraphrase of this argument would be stated approximately as follows: "And you say some Cornish people are offended because they do not have their service in Cornish since they do not understand English. Why should they be more offended now when they do not understand it in English than when they had it in Latin and did not understand it? Shouldn't all of you who do understand English be glad and satisfied to have the service in English? It may be that they have just cause to be aggrieved who have the service in a language they do not understand, but we are informed that there are few or no towns in Cornwall where there are more people who understand Latin than understand English, and therefore the people are generally better off now than they were before."]

From the viewpoint of Cornish speakers, of course, Latin was long familiar and no threat to their accustomed usages; English meant protestantism and the further political ascendancy by the court of England, both of which they resisted vigorously. Their desire was to have services in a language other than English, and either Latin or Cornish would allow them a measure of independence. With the failure of this, the last of the Cornish rebellions, the attempts to make Cornish an officially recognized language were effectively thwarted, and the English liturgy became an effective instrument in anglicizing the region.[5] An early nineteenth-century historian, John B. C. Whitaker, regarded this controversy with considerable bitterness: "This act of tyranny was at once gross barbarity to the Cornish people and a death blow to the Cornish language."[6]

The extension of English was less effectively furthered by official action to discourage the Welsh language. In Cornwall, the vernacular declined when the national government refused to take steps to support religious and educational institutions conducted in the Cornish language. In Wales, a much more populous area and one then still little influenced by English, sterner measures were imposed. With the Acts of Union of 1536 and 1542, Welsh-speakers could only gain access to law courts if they were willing to seek justice in English. Even more significant is the provision in the Act of 1536 that "from henceforth no person or persons that use the Welsh speech or language shall have or enjoy any manner office or fees within this realm of *England, Wales*, or other the King's dominion, upon pain of forfeiting the same offices or fees, unless he or they use and exercise the *English* speech or language" (27 Henry VIII 20).

The only persons likely to be awarded "office or fees," of course, were anglicized Welsh people or English appointees, and thus the statute did little to disseminate the use of English among the majority of the population. Contrary to the policy used in Cornwall, the government in London supported protestantism by passing an Act for the Translation of the Bible and the Divine Service into the Welsh Tongue in 1563. Church politics thus was given primary attention and the politics of English a distinctly secondary role, with the consequence that the use of Welsh in religious services helped to maintain the language.[7]

The severity of official action against other languages seems to have increased with the distance from London, and particularly strenuous efforts were made to maintain English at the expense of Irish. English-speakers first settled in Ireland early in the twelfth century as retainers of the Normans who imposed the feudal system on the Irish peasantry. Since English was not supported from above – the Normans used French in the castles and towns – these English-speakers were rapidly assimilated to the Irish language and customs. In 1366, at the same time that Edward III was making English the language of judicial proceedings in England, a parliament in Kilkenny issued an edict to regulate the behavior of those English who had forsaken "the

English language, fashion, mode of riding, laws, and usages" thought fit for English people. These so-called Statutes attempted to suppress intermarriage (as well as "fostering of children, concubinage or amour") and stated that all English people – those descended from English immigrants – should use the English language and abandon the Irish language and the Irish surnames that many of them had adopted. The penalties imposed for disobedience were severe: loss of land and property, or, if the persons not complying with the statutes had no land, imprisonment.[8]

These laws had little effect on the use of English in Ireland, however, and while most of their provisions were reconfirmed under Henry VII in 1485, those concerning the use of English were rescinded since by that time the language was little used in Ireland except in small enclaves in the extreme south of the country and among a few of the educated who lived in towns and cities. With the Reformation, Irish became strongly identified with catholicism, even though its use was only occasionally and inconsistently supported by the bishops. While Henry VIII required protestant clergy to preach in English and to provide schools for the instruction of the young in that language (28 Henry VIII 15), his efforts seem to have had little success in promoting the use of English in family, commercial, or civic life. Late in the sixteenth century, English travellers found that persons who were able to speak English refused to do so since the language implied allegiance to a foreign power and protestantism (Bliss, 1977, pp. 7–8). Only with the settlements fostered by James VI and I early in the seventeenth century in the north of Ireland, strengthened subsequently by an aggressive program of colonization under Cromwell, did English become firmly established in Ireland.

In Scotland, the spread of English proceeded differently. After their defeat at Hastings in 1066, the survivors of the English royal family fled to Scotland and sought the assistance of the Gaelic-speaking rulers of that country in their efforts to regain control of England from the Norman conquerors. While these attempts were unsuccessful, the Scottish king (encouraged by his English wife) readily adopted English customs, and he and his immediate successors gave preferential treatment to speakers of English in the church and through grants of land. Thus English, in a distinctly northern form, came to be the language of the court and of government in the central and southern parts of the country.[9]

Only in the highlands and islands of the west and northwest did Gaelic continue as the dominant language. These regions maintained their historic independence from the rulers of eastern and central Scotland until the accession of James VI of Scotland to the English throne in 1603. As a later historian has noted, James "appears to have had a perfect mania for rooting out Celtic subjects and re-placing them with settlers of Anglo-Saxon descent" (Mackenzie, 1974, p. 239), a policy that affected both Ireland and the Gaelic-speaking areas of Scotland.

Following a successful military campaign in the northwest of Scotland, James imposed upon the clans the Statutes of Iona in 1609. Among other provisions, these regulations required:

everie gentilman or yeoman within the saidis Ilandis or ony of thame having children maill or femell and being in goodis worth thriescoir ky, sall putt at the leist thair eldest sone or, having na childrene maill, thair eldest dochtir to the scuillis in the lawland and interteny and bring thame up thair quhill they may be found able sufficientlie to speik, read and wryte Inglische" (*Collectanea*, p. 120).

[A modern English paraphrase of this portion of the Statute can be rendered as requiring "every gentleman or yeoman living in any of the Islands, having male or female children, and owning property worth sixty cattle or more, shall send his eldest son (or, having no male children, his eldest daughter) to school in the lowlands and maintain and bring them up there until they are able to speak, read, and write English."]

Like the Statutes of Kilkenny, this requirement had little immediate effect on Gaelic or on the imposition of English in northwestern Scotland.

A subsequent action in 1616 by the Privy Council establishing schools in the Gaelic areas of Scotland was more effective. Once again it identifies protestantism – "the trew religioun" – with the use of English, but goes further in associating English with "civilite, godlines, knawledge and learning." Hence the Council required that "the vulgar [i.e. 'common'] Inglishe toung be universallie plantit, and the Irishe language [or Gaelic], whilk is one of the cheif and principall causis of the continewance of barbaritie and incivilitie amongis the inhabitantis of the Ilis and Heylandis . . . be abolisheit and removit."[10] Subsequent governmental actions continued to discourage the use of Gaelic in western Scotland and aided the spread of English throughout that country.

These historical events reveal a relatively consistent pattern by which successive governments used political power and influence to speed the acceptance of English. Some of the most effective techniques depended upon the allocation of resources: financial support for churches and schools conducted in English; prohibitions against public (or sometimes even private) aid for institutions employing the minority vernaculars. Other methods were a consequence of more assertive policies: loss of freedom and property as a penalty for not using English; denial of political preferment to those who would not adopt the language. It would be a mistake, however, to exaggerate the effectiveness of these policies and to conclude that they reflect a consistent imperial impulse and an effective method of undermining the use of the other languages of the British Isles. Almost certainly, the practice that was most successful was merely neglect, a failure to support the minority languages as vehicles for the cultural and economic transformation of the society during the period we have examined. It would be likewise wrong to assume that the adoption of English much mitigated sectarian and regional differences. Today, language and nationhood are widely identified with each other, but nationalism is not an ancient idea, and people who give up their language may not necessarily regard themselves as less attached to their communities than before they made the change. One evidence, perhaps, for the continued role of local identities is the persistent desire of present-day English-speakers to identify themselves as Cornish, Welsh, Irish, or Scots however personally remote they may be from those geographical communities. The attitudes, in short, persist even where the language change has taken place. And despite successive cultural transformations, only Cornish is now extinct as a mother-tongue; the remaining language communities – Welsh, Irish, and Scots Gaelic – survive as diminished but still vital centers of culture and speech.

The spread of English through official action is an important part of the history of attitudes toward the language. Once English had re-emerged as the language of the powerful, English-speakers found it natural to demand that the other languages of the areas under their political influence or control be suppressed and discouraged. Yet even the most severe measures did not have immediate effect, and the degree of success of these attempts required a measure of acquiescense from those who did not acquire English as a mother tongue. Language shift, then, is ultimately a matter of personal choice, and in Britain, the responses of anglicization ranged from enthusiastic acceptance of the new language to outright rejection of English.[11] Of course government policies do make a difference. But so do the cultural and other political institutions that play an important part in the choice of language (or one of its varieties).[12] Technology and the sources of wealth also have a share of influence. But ultimately we are obliged to examine individuals and the choices they make. Some choices are inspired by the influence of power and authority, but others result from a complicated pattern of interaction between individuals and their communities, the aspirations that they discourage or promote. Language change and language shift, then, take place through individuals making willing choices among alternatives, not solely through the force of external circumstances or the exercise of political power.

Notes

1. The essay that follows belongs to the *macro-level* of the sociology of language; see Greenbaum (1977). As he there explains, "the macro-level concerns attitudes towards the acceptability of a language or of a variety within a language, whereas the micro-level concerns the acceptability of specific linguistic features" (p. 1).
2. One of these rare cases is found in the history of English: the abandonment of Norman French by those who ruled England after the Norman Conquest. As we will see later in this essay, this shift from French to English is especially interesting since French was associated with refinement and prestige. Writing in 1597, William Harrison described the medieval linguistic setting in this way: "In the court also [the English tongue] grew into such contempt, that most men thought it no small dishonor to speake any English there. Which brauerie tooke his hold at the last likewise in the countrie with euerie plowman, that euen the verie carters began to wax wearie of there mother toong, & laboured to speake French, which as then was counted no small token of gentilitie. And no maruell, for euerie French rascall, when he came once hither, was taken for a gentleman, onelie bicause he was proud, and could vse his owne language, and all this (I say) to exile the English and British speaches quite out of the countrie" (reprinted in Bolton, 1966, pp. 17–18). Modern scholarship has shown that the enthusiasm for the Norman French and their language was by no means as widespread as Harrison suggests; if it cannot be shown that plowmen and carters learned French, his description is probably accurate enough for the immediate retainers of the king and the feudal lords. Similar cases of the dominant group adopting the language of the dominated include the "Franks in France, the Langobards in Lombardy, the Norsemen in Southern Italy and Russia, the non-Slavic Bolgars in Bulgaria, the Hittites in the late Hittite Empire, the Mongols in Western Asia, [and] the Dalmatians in the republic of Ragusa" (Dressler, 1982, p. 434).
3. I have illustrated these trends in present-day English in Bailey (1983). For an argument based on the intrinsic virtues of English, see Halliday (1975).
4. While the use of English for judicial records became gradually more common, it was not until 1733 that Parliament passed a law prohibiting the use of French and Latin in legal

records. Significantly this same law also forbade the use of "any other tongue or language whatsoever" (6 George II 6), including, of course, Cornish, Welsh, and Scottish Gaelic.

5. English liturgy was also influential in speeding the decline of another Celtic language of the British Isles, Manx. Spoken on the Isle of Man in the Irish Sea, Manx survived until the twentieth century only as the language of rural farms since successive domination by Scandinavians, Scots, and English had long made another language prominent in government.

6. Quoted by Ellis (1974, p. 63). A. L. Rowse credits Nicholas Udall with the "excellent suggestion that the new form of service should be turned into Cornish" (p. 287), but the work of Udall's he cites does not support his opinion that this idea was seriously regarded. Udall admonishes the petitioners for making a demand of their sovereign rather than a "humble and godly request"; had the desire for Cornish been expressed as a petition rather than a demand, Udall writes dismissively, "I doubt not but the King ... would have tendered your request, and provided for the accomplishment of your desires" (Pocock, 1884, p. 172). Since they had chosen to organize a military campaign against the king, their request could not be honored.

7. For additional background, see the works by Agnew and by Mathias. Subsequently, Welsh was intermittently used for the dissenting denominations (e.g. Baptists and Methodists) that did not attract large numbers of the fully anglicized gentry. After the beginning of the seventeenth century, Welsh bishops of the Anglican church sometimes provided clergy able to conduct services in Welsh, but the normal practices were to assign the "livings" to absentee English-speakers while services were conducted by resident curates in Welsh and to make use of Welsh service books and the New Testament (both published in Welsh in the mid-sixteenth century). Official support for English at the expense of Welsh was provided in the mid-nineteenth century when Parliament authorized any ten persons who could provide a building and a stipend for a clergyman to petition for services conducted in English (26–27 Victoria 82). In the courts, Welsh-speakers were first allowed to use their language in 1942, and then only if they could claim "any disadvantage by reason of [their] natural language of communication being Welsh" (quoted by Lewis, 1973, p. 196). Following passage of the Welsh Language Act of 1967, anyone could demand that legal proceedings be conducted in Welsh without the constraint of proving a "disadvantage," and in the 1970s Welsh nationalists occasionally exercised that prerogative. See also Hechter (1975, pp. 164–205).

8. See Curtis and McDowell (1943, pp. 52–59). Once again these statutes were recorded in French.

9. For further information on the spread of English in Scotland, see Romaine (1982).

10. Quoted from Masson (1891, vol. 10, p. 671). A modern advocate of Gaelic calls this act "totalitarian" and cites in support of that description a United Nations resolution that defines *genocide*, in part, as "any deliberate act committed with the intent to destroy the language, religion, or culture of a national, racial, or religious group" (Campbell, 1950, p. 115). Efforts to eradicate a language have in some settings been carried out with even more brutality, though with a similar rationale, than has been the case in Scotland; see Sadler and Lins (1972).

11. Despite official edicts and economic allurements, writes one advocate of Welsh, the English "could never prevail upon [the Welsh people] to submit to that *most ignominious badge of slavery*, the language of the conquerers" (Whitaker as quoted by Polwhele, 1806, p. 4; my emphasis). For more recent views, see Betts (1976) and MacKinnon (1974).

12. In those places where one of the Celtic languages was abandoned for English, the variety of English chosen was regularly regarded as a "purer" form than the nearby dialect. This opinion arises from speech influenced by prestige norms in second-language learning, and one result of the "purer" English is the maintenance of the linguistic and cultural boundaries of the community. Hence Cornwall remains, even with the universal use of English, dialectally separate from neighboring Devon and Somerset; similarly, rural Ireland, where English was more recently adopted, is characterized by a different English from that of the towns and cities; the Highlands of Scotland remain linguistically different from the Lowlands even though in both English is the dominant language (see Russ, 1983 and Barry, 1982).

References

AGNEW, JOHN A. (1981) "Language shift and the politics of language: The case of the Celtic languages of the British Isles." *Language Problems and Language Planning*, **5**, 1–10.

BAILEY, RICHARD W. (1983) "Literacy in English: An international perspective." In *Literacy for Life: The Demand for Reading and Writing*, ed. Richard W. Bailey and Robin Melanie Fosheim. New York: The Modern Language Association of America, pp. 30–44.

BARRY, MICHAEL V. (1982) "The English language in Ireland." In *English as a World Language*, ed. Richard W. Bailey and Manfred Görlach. Ann Arbor: The University of Michigan Press, pp. 84–133.

BERNDT, ROLF (1965) "The linguistic situation in England from the Norman Conquest to the loss of Normandy (1066–1204)." *Philologica Pragensa*, **8**, 145–163.

BETTS, CLIVE (1976) *Culture in Crisis: The Future of the Welsh Language*. Upton: ffynon Press.

BLISS, ALAN J. (1977) "The emergence of Modern English dialects in Ireland." In *The English Language in Ireland*, Diarmaid Ó Muirithe. Dublin: The Mercier Press, pp. 7–19.

BOLTON, W.F., ed. (1966) *The English Language: Essays by English and American Men of Letters, 1490–1839*. Cambridge: Cambridge University Press.

CAMPBELL, JOHN LORNE (1950) *Gaelic in Scottish Education and Life*. Edinburgh: W. & A. K. Johnston Ltd.

Collectanea de Rebus Albanicis: Consisting of Original Papers and Documents Related to the History of the Highlands and Islands of Scotland. Edinburgh: Thomas G. Stevenson, 1857.

CURTIS, EDMUND, and R.B. McDOWELL, ed. (1943) *Irish Historical Documents, 1172–1922*. London: Methuen & Co.

DRESSLER, WOLFGANG U. (1982) Review of *Language Death* by Nancy Dorian. *Language*, **58**, 432–435.

ELLIS, P. BERRESFORD (1974) *The Cornish Language and its Literature*. London: Routledge & Kegan Paul.

GREENBAUM, SIDNEY (1977) "Introduction." In *Acceptability in Language*, ed. Sidney Greenbaum. The Hague: Mouton, pp. 1–11.

HALLIDAY, F.E. (1975) *The Excellency of the English Tongue*. London: Victor Gollancz.

HECHTER, MICHAEL (1975) *Internal Colonialism: The Celtic Fringe in British National Development, 1536–1966*. London: Routledge & Kegan Paul.

LEWIS, ROBYN (1973) "The Welsh language and the Law." In *The Welsh Language Today*, ed. Meic Stephens. Llandysul: Gomer Press, pp. 195–210.

MACKENZIE, W.C. (1974) *History of the Outer Hebrides* [1903]. Edinburgh: Mercat Press.

MASSON, DAVID, ed. (1891) *The Register of the Privy Council of Scotland*. Edinburgh: H.M. General Register House.

MacKINNON, KENNETH (1974) *The Lion's Tongue: The Story of the Original and Continuing Language of the Scottish People*. Inbhirnis: Club Leabhar.

MATHIAS, ROLAND (1973) "The Welsh language and the English language." In *The Welsh Language Today*, ed. Meic Stephens. Llandysul: Gomer Press, pp. 32–63.

POCOCK, NICHOLAS, ed. (1884) *Troubles Connected with the Prayer Book of 1549*. Camden Society n.s. vol. 37. London: Nichols & Sons.

POLWHELE, R. (1806) *The Language, Literature, and Literary Characters of Cornwall*. London: Cadell and Davies.

ROMAINE, SUZANNE (1982) "The English language in Scotland." In *English as a World Language*, ed. Richard W. Bailey and Manfred Görlach. Ann Arbor: The University of Michigan Press, pp. 56–83.

ROSE-TROUP, FRANCES (1913) *The Western Rebellion of 1549*. London: Smith, Elder & Co.

RUSS, CHARLES V.J. (1983) "The geographical and social variation of English in England and Wales." In *English as a World Language*, ed. Richard W. Bailey and Manfred Görlach. Ann Arbor: The University of Michigan Press, pp. 11–55.

ROWSE, A.L. (1969) *Tudor Cornwall: Portrait of a Society*. New York: Charles Scribner's Sons.

SADLER, VICTOR, and ULRICH LINS (1972) "Regardless of frontiers: a case study of linguistic persecution." In *Man, Language and Society*, ed. Samir K. Ghosh. Janua Linguarum, ser. min. 109. The Hague: Mouton, pp. 206–215.

Chapter 2

English in the Middle Ages:
The Struggle for Acceptability

WILLIAM A. KRETZSCHMAR, JR.

THE medieval period in Britain, A.D. 450–1500, saw one upheaval after another. Germanic mercenaries dispossessed their British hosts. The Scandinavians settled great tracts of the east and north but achieved political control only briefly; their Norman relations later achieved that control but did not settle extensively. When the Church arrived it conquered not territory but the souls and intellectual life of the people. At the period's close Caxton imported the printing press and revolutionized what people read. Each upheaval, whether political, intellectual, or technological, brought with it linguistic challenges. Conquest and incursive settlement juxtaposed different vernacular languages, forcing people to choose how to communicate. Intellectual development also presented a choice, since Latin was the prime medieval medium for study and doctrine. Widespread access to printed texts brought a growing late-medieval awareness of variation in English to a crisis. Each challenge but the last made survival the real issue of acceptability – whether English could compete with other vernaculars in general use or with Latin for intellectual purposes. The question of acceptable practice within the language had to wait until it was certain that English had endured.

Competition between Vernaculars

The English language is not native to Britain. The inhabitants of the island at the time of Roman occupation spoke several languages, mainly members of the Celtic language family. After the Romans finally withdrew early in the fifth century, the dominant group, the British, employed a small number of Germanic troops to help defend them from marauding Celtish and Pictish tribes. The Germanic dialects spoken by the mercenaries were recognized as one language, called "English" in vernacular records,[1] and the mercenaries themselves came to be called "the English." These troops in time revolted, brought over reinforcements from the Continent, and began a century and a half of warfare with the British. The English did not aim simply to control British territory; they pushed British groups westward with every bloody victory so that zones of settlement became almost exclusively British or English. Borders and hatred prevented interaction between the cultural groups. Loanwords, the chief measure of linguistic acculturation for this period, show that the English adopted little except for place names (e.g.

Thames, Kent) from the Old British language – *bin* and *crag* are the only British loans still in use today in the common English vocabulary. Germanic military success established English not as the dominant but as the only vernacular in most of Britain. The remnants of the British people took their language, the ancestor of Welsh and Cornish, in flight to the hills and forests of the far west.

Scandinavian attacks upon the English posed a more complex linguistic problem than the English slaughter of the British. Legend has it that Danish groups may have begun to settle in Lincolnshire and East Anglia at the same time the English arrived; the famous predations of the Vikings began some three centuries later. In the ninth century Scandinavian armies captured the northeastern half of Britain (the Danelaw). Danish kings even held the English throne for a short and turbulent period (1016–1042). However, these conquests did not establish Old Norse in place of English. Scandinavian armies, though cruel, did not entirely displace local populations, and the Danish kings adopted much from prestigious English culture when they came to power. Settlement, not the sword, enforced the Old Norse challenge to English.

The linguistic conflict took place on homesteads and in towns of the north and east. Large numbers of Scandinavians moved in amongst the English who had been overrun. The immigrants usually chose to band together, so scattered concentrations of Danes and Norwegians coexisted with the English, who in many areas still formed the majority. Where more new settlers arrived than English remained, Old Norse would have been the preferred language. Unfortunately, not enough evidence survives to document precisely the advance of Old Norse upon English, but we can reconstruct the situation by looking at Norse influences now present in English. Hundreds of common words such as *sky*, *plow*, *sick*, *law*, *raise*, and *take* were borrowed into English, showing just how intimately speakers of the two languages must have associated; everyday words could not have been borrowed in such numbers without very close language contact. In pronunciation, the consonant cluster *sk-* is characteristically Norse, and Norse influences produced such pairs of words as *skirt/shirt* and *scrub* ("oak")/*shrub*. Although different meanings have evolved for each member of the pairs, originally the same in meaning, the fact that both members of each pair survived with separate pronunciations testifies to the acceptability in the period of both the Norse and the English pronunciation systems. Old Norse also affected the grammatical structure of English, the aspect of a language least susceptible to outside influence. Old Norse was responsible, at least in part, for the usage of the conjunction *that*, for the third person present singular ending of verbs, and even for the third person plural pronouns (*they*, *their*, *them*). English accepted all of these influences and loans, but it survived. The similarity of Old Norse and English as members of the Germanic language family and the bilingual culture induced by settlement patterns worked changes in English until the flood of Scandinavian immigrants finally slowed after the Norman Conquest. If Scandinavian armies had succeeded in overrunning the southern half of Britain, allowing still more settlement, English might not have endured at all.

The Norman Conquest in 1066 created a linguistic situation equally complex but essentially the reverse of the Old Norse–English conflict. William the

Conqueror quickly took control of all of England, but his success did not bring about substantial Norman settlement. Only the nobility changed; Normans replaced Englishmen in all high positions of church and state within 30 years after 1066. This tiny minority, about 200 in the highest ranks and perhaps a few thousand imported supporters, made the Anglo-Norman dialect of Old French the language at court, while English became the tongue of illiterate peasants. Acceptability became a social issue, since power and wealth could only be acquired or approached in French. The Norman line kept a firm grip on the English throne despite uncertain fortunes in maintaining their continental possessions. In 1300 Robert of Gloucester described the situation still obtaining ever since the Conquest:

> Thus England came into Normandy's hand,
> And the Normans could speak nothing but their own speech
> And spoke French as they had at home, and had their children taught it,
> So that the lords of this land who come of their blood
> All keep that speech that they brought from home;
> Unless a man knows French people think poorly of him,
> But low-born men keep to English, still to their own speech.[2]

Upwardly mobile Englishmen had to learn French, yet even the low-born could not avoid being affected by it.

The lesser gentry and men in the towns were at the crux of the language conflict. At the top, leaders could afford to ignore English; they could hire translators when needed but normally they surrounded themselves with French-speakers. After the Conquest no English king spoke English until Edward I (who died in 1307). Even the bishops could not converse with their flocks, though in time the percentage who could increased, especially following the command of the Fourth Lateran Council (1215) to preach in the local vernacular. In country manor houses, however, the local lords had to employ English retainers and use the English to work the land. Even though French quarters and streets sprang up in the towns to accommodate imported French artisans and merchants, these tradesmen had to communicate with their patrons' laborers as well as with their patrons. Some men, whether native speakers of French or English, became bilingual, but the weight of the adjustment fell on the low-born. As with Scandinavian linguistic acculturation, too few records remain to document the earlier stages of the process in detail, but we can reconstruct it. There are thousands of French loanwords in the everyday English vocabulary. Many loans created word pairs reflecting plain English versus French luxury: *pig, hog, sow* versus *pork, bacon* (one raised it in English but ate it in French); *stench* versus *scent, odor*; *white, red, yellow* versus *color, ivory, scarlet, ruby, russet, tawny, saffron. Chapman* gave way to *merchant*, and while the *smith* and *cobbler* often *worked* at their *crafts* for *peasants, nobles employed* the *farrier, carpenter, mason, chandler, tailor, jeweler,* and *minstrel*. French affected English syntax and grammar less than Old Norse had – the social division operated with the greater difference between the languages to limit this most difficult kind of influence – yet we do find some set phrases built on the French pattern, for instance *take leave, subject to, by heart*. This mixture of French and English vocabulary, both nouns and verbs, together with English syntax enabled English workers to meet the linguistic needs of the French controlling commerce. English may have yielded to the pressure entirely had not those in control themselves begun to use English.

By the fourteenth century the social division between language was well on its way to breaking down. In 1204 King John lost Normandy, and in 1244 the King of France demanded that lords holding land on both sides of the Channel choose to keep either their English or their Continental estates. Those who chose England were cut off from frequent contact with Continental French-speakers and could no longer as readily import French artisans or retainers. Families who lived away from court seldom had the chance to speak French with anyone outside their immediate household. It became easier and easier, over time, for even the local gentry to resort to English for daily use. By the mid-thirteenth century manuals for instruction in French had begun to appear so that men isolated from court could learn the language of the highest culture and nobility. At the same time popular romances and religious works, based on French models, began to be written in English:

> It is right that Englishmen understand English,
> Those who were born in England.
> A lord may use French,
> But everyone knows English.
> I have seen many nobles
> Who could speak no French.
> (*Arthour and Merlin, c.* 1325)

Although the poet feels compelled to justify writing in English, the times required that he and others like him try to cope with the loss of French as a native language. The greatest number of common French loanwords came into English during this time, as people struggled to adjust their means of communication to fit contradictory demands: the continuing use of French at the highest levels of power and culture, and the increasing adoption of English by those remote from court. The tide turned in popular usage, in favor of English.

Competition in Cultivated Usage

St. Augustine brought Christianity to the English in 597, and brought as well all of the benefits of education, classical culture, the monastic system, and, above all, Latin. Germanic culture was oral and traditional; whatever "civilization" the British had absorbed from the Romans the English had swept away along with the British themselves. The Church, then, was the source of literacy as well as salvation. Education meant training in Latin grammar – the elements of the language, but also study of Latin literature and the Church fathers as models for writing and interpretation. The monasteries provided repositories in which written records could be preserved, some in the vernacular but most in Latin, and scriptoria in which manuscripts could be copied and culture thus transmitted through the ages. Latin was not preferred in learned use, it was universal; no other language could even compete with it.

After the onset in the ninth century of frequent Viking raids which destroyed many monasteries and disrupted the Latin educational system, Alfred the Great (d. 899) promulgated sweeping educational reforms which included a major effort to make English translations of Latin texts:

> So completely had (learning) declined in England that there were very few on this side of the Humber who could understand their services in English, or even translate one word from Latin into English. . . . Therefore I think it advisable, if you agree, that we also (like the Greeks and Romans) translate those books which are most necessary for men to know into the language that we all understand . . . and that all the youth of England, those born of free men who have the means and who may apply themselves to it, be set to learning, as long as they may not enter another occupation, until they can read English writing well; afterwards, that we teach Latin to those whom we deem worthy to continue and to go into orders.
>
> (*Preface* to Alfred's translation of Gregory's *Pastoral Care*)

Alfred intended not only to restore wisdom and teaching but to reverse the educational process. Literacy was his primary goal; the use of English was a convenience in achieving it, leaving Latin for advanced students. Alfred's translation effort quickly made available for the first time in English, among manuscripts which have survived, the *Dialogues* and *Pastoral Care* of Gregory the Great, Boethius' *Consolation of Philosophy*, Orosius' *History*, and Bede's *Ecclesiastical History of the English People*. Learned English texts of many kinds appeared in the course of the next century and a half. For instance, Byrhtferth's *Manual* was a commentary on the Latin *computus*, a medieval scientific text, prepared by the author especially for parish priests.

Not everyone entirely approved of using the vernacular as a learned language. Ælfric (who wrote his works about 1000) composed a series of homilies and translated a collection of saints' lives, yet he was unconvinced about making too much accessible in English. He wrote his homilies in the vernacular in part to correct errors he saw in other religious texts which had received English translations. Of his saints' lives Ælfric wrote:

> I do not promise, however, to write very many in this tongue because it is not fitting for very many to be translated into our language in case the pearls of Christ might be had in disrespect. Therefore I remain silent about the *Lives of the Fathers*, since it contains many subtleties which ought not be set before the laity and which we ourselves cannot completely understand.
>
> ("Latin Preface," *Catholic Homilies*)

A knowledge of Latin implied some sophistication, and Latin texts both had distinction in the public eye and could control the spread of information because of their limited audience. Ælfric appreciated what a lack of sophistication and a loss of distinction might cause if the wrong texts were translated. Apparently there were many who agreed with him, for Latin remained the primary learned language even though English had made some advances. The number of manuscripts in English from this period, regardless of subject, cannot match the number in Latin.

The Norman Conquest completely wiped out the use of English as a cultivated language – for centuries. Latin kept its preferred status and education still began with Latin grammar, but French became widely acceptable as the vehicle for statecraft and law, history, poetry, and religious works. Most of the brilliant French literary achievements of the twelfth century were written in England, not in France. The nascent bureaucracy in government used Latin in its paperwork, but the exceptions were in French, not English. The *Rolls of Parliament* were recorded in French, officially until 1362, in practice until about 1450. French was used in English courts until the eighteenth century. Befitting its new status, French became the medium of instruction for learning Latin and was the second language of the developing English universities.

English only slowly came back into cultivated usage alongside Latin and French. Popular religious works were some of the first to be translated into English after the Conquest, some as early as 1200, to serve those same outlying gentry who were at the focus of the vernacular language conflict. As late as 1340 Dan Michel felt he had to explain his use of English in his *Ayenbit of Inwyt (Prick of Conscience)*:

> Now I think you should know how it happens
> That this book is written in the English of Kent:
> This book is made for unlearned men,
> For father, for mother, and for other kin,
> To protect them from all manner of sin.

His book is not a learned disputation, but it is addressed to a literate public; it is aimed at the more cultivated of those living away from court. In the fourteenth century many authors explain their use of English as of a common medium: some people know Latin, others French, but everyone knows English. "Everyone" did not mean peasants, but only those who had enough standing to desire cultural improvement or entertainment but not enough to acquire it in French. Official recognition of English came later. It was 1362 before Parliament declared that the business of law and government be conducted in English, longer still before there was general compliance. Also at mid-century were the first movements toward using English as the medium of instruction in Latin grammar – a tremendous change, opposed at first in the universities; Englishmen no longer had to learn French before they could even begin to become truly educated. Great cultivated poetry in English reappeared at the end of the fourteenth century, the age of Chaucer, as did translations from Latin or French such as Boethius' *Consolation of Philosophy*, now translated by Chaucer as it had been before by Alfred the Great. It had taken over 300 years for English to regain the acceptability in high culture that it had begun to achieve before the Conquest. In 1400 it had to compete with French as well as Latin, but at least it could once again compete.

The fifteenth century saw cultivated usage swing towards English as a second language after Latin. Great numbers of French works were translated into English, marking the change from a literate public reading in French to one reading in English. Caxton catered to the demand for translations of French works fashionable on the Continent, often acting as translator as well as printer. However, time had taken its toll: since English had for so long been unacceptable for cultivated purposes its vocabulary had not developed sufficiently to translate terms and concepts from Latin or French. In the preface to his translation of Virgil's *Aeneid* Gavin Douglas (who died in 1522) writes:

> Beside Latin our language is imperfect,
> Which in some part is the cause and the reason
> Why the ornate beauty of Virgil's verse
> Cannot be found in our tongue,
> For there are in Latin many words
> That have no translations in our speech
> Unless we diminish their meaning or gravity,
> And even then they are hardly well explained. . . .
> Again touching the penurity of our tongue,
> In comparison with Latin, I mean,
> That is known to be the most perfect language,
> I might as well take my time
> Looking for two different, appropriate terms
> For *arbor* and *lignum* in our speech
> Without, at the same time, using any circumlocution.
> Even so, quite often by 'aboutspeech'
> And by similar words we have to compile our rhymes.

Terms for new concepts could be borrowed or made (note "circumlocution" and "aboutspeech" above), but did not yet exist. Authors and translators readily took words from Latin and French, sometimes leaving untranslated whatever had no convenient English equivalent. Usage had to determine which of these aureate terms would remain in the language. Eventually English did gain the flexibility to compete on equal terms with Latin and French. The struggle over vocabulary continued into the Renaissance and even beyond, but that authors and readers were willing to struggle is powerful evidence of the demand for cultivated works in English.

Internal Variation and the Development of a Standard

English has never been uniform; it began as a collection of Germanic dialects. The language underwent tremendous changes during the Middle Ages, and at any given time the English of one region differed substantially from that of another. Remarkable as it may seem, given our modern delight in disputes about grammar and in accents, variation from place to place or from time to time elicited little comment from medieval authors. English scholars argued endlessly about barbarisms in Latin, but variety in the vernacular was accepted as a matter of course. Authors simply wrote vernacular texts in their local dialects; manuscript copyists adjusted unfamiliar dialectal forms to fit their own dialects – or left them alone – as it pleased them. There were no authorities as there were for Latin, and thus no basis for acceptability.

Before the Norman Conquest the West Saxon dialect was the closest thing to a standard for written English. The first major centers of culture in England were at York and Jarrow in the north, the homes of Alcuin and Bede, and at Canterbury, St. Augustine's original seat. The Northern and Kentish dialects gained some prestige, but their influence was cut off, as the supply of manuscripts was cut off, when the Vikings destroyed the monasteries and churches and burned their libraries. Cultural centers developed in the southwest, the only area free from attack, to carry on the copying of old texts and the production of new ones. West Saxon thus became dominant in large part by default, although the dialect had some reason for prestige as the speech of the English court, and it developed greater reason with the progress of Alfred's programs for education and translation. There is little evidence, however, that any one of the dialects ever had much influence on any other in the spoken language. Even in written English dialectal preference depended mainly on where the scribe was writing, and if any period author ever did discuss regional variety or preferred dialectal forms, his remarks have perished.

The Norman Conquest put a stop to almost all writing in English. With the only conservative force now removed, the changes in English which had been occurring slowly suddenly accelerated: English lost its inflections; it became more susceptible to foreign influences; and it became more regional than ever, especially since Englishmen themselves had fewer opportunities to travel across regional boundaries. Chroniclers began to talk about English shortly after the Conquest, but only as a language which the new aristocracy did not speak.

The major exception to the silence about regional differences in English was William of Malmesbury's short passage, written in the twelfth century, on the harsh character of northern speech as compared to southern. Two centuries later Ranulph Higden repeated his words, and when John Trevisa translated Higden's Latin chronicle late in the fourteenth century, he supplemented Malmesbury's account only slightly:

> Englishmen from the beginning had three kinds of speech, Southern, Northern, and Middle speech (in the middle of the land) . . . yet by mixing and meddling first with the Danes and afterwards with the Normans, the country's language is corrupted in many ways, and some men use strange 'wlaffyng, chyteryng, harryng, garryng, and grisbyttyng.' . . . It is a great wonder that the English tongue is separated in three parts, for men of the east agree more in pronunciation with men of the west, as it were under the same quadrant of heaven, than men of the north with men of the south. Thus it is that Mercians, the men of middle England, partner to both ends as it were, better understand the side languages, Northern and Southern, than northerners and southerners understand each other. All the language of the Northumbrians, especially those at York, is so sharp, 'slyttyng and frotyng,' and unshapely that we southern men can scarcely understand it.

There were some other comments on the language during the fourteenth century as English once again gained currency as a written language, but usually along the same lines: southern writers complained about northern speech, and northern writers about southern. Dialectal differences were great enough for some authors to speak of "translating" northern texts into southern English, or southern into northern. Nonetheless, these scattered comments express irritation more than they call for change. Chaucer's statement is typical:

> And because there is such great diversity
> In English and in the writing of our tongue,
> I pray God that no one 'myswrites' you (his book)
> Nor 'mysmeters' you because of faults in the language.

> And wherever you are read, or spoken aloud,
> I pray God that you be understood.
>
> (*Troilus and Criseyde*, Bk. 5)

Chaucer knows about dialect differences and recognizes that these differences can be problematic; the best he can do is to hope for the best as his book is carried to different regions. In 1400 there was no standard or accepted authority, either for spelling (so that people would not "myswrite") or for pronunciation (so that people would not "mysmeter").

At the end of the fifteenth century the time and means had come for beginning to set up a standard. Chaucer's English was already antiquated owing to rapid change in the language: the Great Vowel Shift was radically altering English pronunciation (e.g. *root* no longer rhymed with *wrote*), and the growing use of English as a learned and cultural medium was forcing its vocabulary to expand by leaps and bounds. It is worthwhile to quote at length from Caxton's cogent analysis of linguistic acceptability in his time:

> ... some gentlemen had lately blamed me, saying that in my translations I used strange terms which common people could not understand, and asked me to use old and home-grown terms in my translations. I was eager to satisfy everyone, so I took an old book and read some of it: the English was so rough and broad that I could hardly understand it. My lord, the Abbot of Westminster, then showed me some documents written in Old English ... and certainly it was written so that it was more like Dutch than English: I could neither translate nor understand it. Our language in current use is far different from that which was spoken when I was born – we Englishmen are born under the domination of the moon, which is never steadfast but ever wavering, waxing one season and waning another.
>
> And that common English spoken in one shire varies from that spoken in another. Recently it happened that two merchants were aboard ship in the Thames to set sail for Holland, and, lacking any wind, they went ashore to seek refreshment. One of them, named Sheffield, a cloth merchant, went into an inn and asked for food, and particularly he asked for eggs. And the hostess answered that she could speak no French. The merchant was angry since he too could speak no French, but he wanted eggs. She could not understand him. Finally, the other merchant said that he wanted 'eyren,' and she understood him perfectly. Alas, what should a man write now, 'eggs' or 'eyren'? It is hard to please everyone because of diversity and change in language.
>
> These days every man of any reputation in his country will say what he needs to, using such terms and constructions that few men will understand them. And some honest and famous scholars have asked me to write using the most curious [i.e. aureate] terms that I can find. Thus, between plain, rough, and curious, I stand confused.
>
> ("Preface" to *Eneydos*)

Caxton saw variation in language as a serious problem, not a mere irritant, because he expected wide distribution of his printed texts. That very distribution throughout England of Caxton's books, incorporating the variety of language he chose, provided a benchmark against which other writers and printers could measure themselves. Coupled with the recent normalization of writing practices in Chancery, that benchmark became authoritative:

> ... during the crucial period between 1420 and 1460 ... the essential characteristics of Modern Written English were determined by the *practice* of the clerks in Chancery, and communicated throughout England by professional scribes writing in Chancery script, under the influence of Chancery idiom. When Caxton returned to England in 1476, he established his press not in London, but in Westminster, under the shadow of the government offices where Chancery Standard was by that time the normal language for all official communications.[3]

English at last had influential models for acceptable practice in writing. In speech regional differences remained strong; neither printing nor bureaucratic government had enough influence, yet, to go that far. Even written English still needed centuries to become as regular as it is today. By the end of the medieval period, however, English had met the challenge of competing vernaculars, it had won its way into cultivated usage, and it had finally become subject to the issues of linguistic acceptability that we discuss today.

Notes

1. The term "English" derives from the name of one Germanic group, the Angles, although the reason why the language and people were named after this group and not another remains obscure. The first written records in English date from about 700, more than two centuries after it was in spoken use. English in the Middle Ages is customarily divided into two distinct periods: Old English, from about 500 to about 1100; and Middle English, from about 1100 to about 1500. The terms have been omitted from this paper to emphasize the essential continuity of English.
2. Robert of Gloucester, *Chronicle*, ll. 7537–7543. I have freely translated or modernized all passages from Latin and Old or Middle English. Full references for cited passages may be found in any of the many histories of English, e.g. Albert Baugh and Thomas Cable, *A History of the English Language*, 3rd ed. (Englewood Cliffs, NJ: Prentice-Hall, Inc., 1978).
3. John Hurt Fisher, "Chancery and the emergence of standard written English in the fifteenth century," *Speculum*, **52** (1977), 898–899.

Chapter 3

Renaissance English (1525–1640)

MANFRED GÖRLACH

THE period from the Reformation to the outbreak of the Civil War is one of the most important and most complex periods in the history of attitudes to the English language.[1] It should not be confused with the period of Early Modern English, which is usually said to extend from 1500 (or perhaps 1450) to 1700 (Barber, 1976; Görlach, 1978). Earlier dates, however, are relevant to some extent: the establishment of Chancery English from 1430 onwards (Fisher, 1977), the loss of almost all regional features in written English after 1450 (which induced McIntosh and Samuels to terminate their great Survey of Middle English Dialects at 1450), the printing of English books from 1476 onwards, and the establishment of Humanist Greek and Latin at Oxford and Cambridge in the late fifteenth century. All these were important conditions for the development of markedly different attitudes, as was the emergence of a rich and influential upper middle class in the rapidly expanding London of the fifteenth century. But reflections on the form, functions, and state of the English language are few before the time of Elyot, Ascham, and Wilson, and become legion after 1530, to be reduced to a trickle in the times of Cromwell, when people had more urgent problems on their minds. When statements on attitudes become frequent again after 1660, they reflect a new situation:

1. Latin had ceased to be the medium for instruction in grammar schools and for scholarly books.
2. There was growing discontent with Latin as a grammatical model of linguistic perfection, and there were attempts at replacing it by the logical construct of a universal language.
3. There were fresh efforts at "correcting and ascertaining" the English language by means of an academy, to be modelled on the Académie Française (founded in 1635). To deal with such matters a committee of literati was set up in 1665 within the Royal Society.
4. A more distanced view of Elizabethan English – sometimes nostalgic, sometimes unfairly critical – came to be the general pattern from Dryden to Johnson.[2]

These later tendencies spread in a modified and often attenuated form to what was later to become a part of the U.S.A., where the nucleus of an English-speaking society existed by 1660.

The central and most important part of this period almost coincides with the reign of Elizabeth I. The years 1550–1620 saw not only the flowering of poetry (Spenser, Sidney) and of drama (Marlowe, Shakespeare, Ben Jonson), but also of critical writing: on rhetoric (Wilson, Ascham, Peacham), on literary theory (Sidney, Fraunce, Puttenham, Campion, Daniel) and on English grammar – mostly confined to writings on spelling and reform of the orthography (Hart, Bullokar, Mulcaster) and on lexicography (Bullokar, Cawdrey). It is no coincidence that this period (which also excelled in other aspects of culture, such as music and painting) saw the establishment of England as a world power: the Armada was defeated in 1588, the East India Company was chartered in 1600, and Jamestown was founded in 1607. The power of England is reflected, from 1575 on, in a growing confidence in the value of the English language (*vis-à-vis* Latin).

The Status of English

The problems affecting the status of English in the sixteenth century were similar to those of other major European vernaculars. Latin in its rediscovered classical form was a well-ordered language; it was well equipped for all registers including various literary uses and forms, and the domains of law, scholarship, and science; and it had great international prestige, and was in widespread use in written and spoken form among the learned, who naturally derived their ideas of what a language should be like and could be made to do from classical Latin. English, on the other hand, was neither homogeneous nor provided with explicit norms: there was no fixed orthography, no printed grammar, no dictionary. Its vocabulary and syntax were thought deficient and unsuited to the expression of complex arguments in such fields as medicine and science. The attitude criticized by Hoby (1561) was widespread: "Our learned men hold opinion that to have the sciences in the mother-tongue hurteth memory and hindereth learning," an argument that is taken up and refuted in Mulcaster's point 6: "It [English] will let ['hinder'] the learned community" (1582: 257). Nor could English provide the rhetorical and poetical beauty demanded in various handbooks of rhetoric. Whether it could ever develop sufficiently to meet such demands remained in doubt throughout most of the sixteenth century. If its deficiencies were to be overcome, it would be only through the efforts of the best writers making a deliberate choice of English as their medium of expression. Mulcaster's "Why not all in English?" (1582:163) was still a necessary question in the late sixteenth century, and for Milton in 1642 writing a national epic in English meant doing "Things unattempted yet in Prose or Rhime" (*Paradise Lost*, line 16). A number of writers complained that writing in Latin (which provided a ready-made terminology and an appropriate style) would have been much easier for them; to quote a less well-known statement (Skeyne, 1586:A2r, writing in Scots on cures of the pestilence):

> And howbeit it become me rather (quha hes bestouit all my Zouthe in the Sculis) to had vrytin the samin in Latine, Zit vnderstanding sic interpryses had bene nothing profitable to the commoun and wulgar people . . .

> ["Although it would have suited me better (who spent all my youth in the schools) to have written the same in Latin, understanding such an enterprise would not have been useful for the common and uneducated people. . . . "]

The qualities of English are often described in negative terms as "not eloquent, inelegant, rude, gross, barbarous, barren, base, vile" at least until 1570–1580, when growing national consciousness and confidence paved the way for positive evaluations, such as Mulcaster's of 1582. Writers now judged the qualities disparaged above as "plain, honest, unadorned"; sometimes English is even praised as being superior to Latin in its fullness of sound, in its copiousness as a result of extensive borrowing, in its economy derived from Germanic monosyllabic words, and in its age and noble descent.

A new feature from 1525 onwards was that at least some scholars were concerned to promote a standard of English writing. Having experienced the well-ordered grammaticality of Latin on all levels from orthography to text structure (treated under "rhetoric"), humanists such as Elyot, Ascham or Wilson knew that they had to prepare English for wider functions by "fining" and "augmenting" it. Some of the best writing in the Renaissance was written with an educational bias, with the desire to let those without the grace of Latin participate in humanistic culture. But the problem remained that more energy was spent (some would say, wasted) on perfecting the pupil's *Latin* style and grammar, proper English being only mentioned if Latin was not in reach of the pupil, as in Elyot (1531:121f.):

> nourises ['nurses'] . . . that speke none englische but that which is cleane, polite, perfectly and articulately pronounced. . . .

As late as 1693, Locke can still say:

> To speak or write better Latin then English may make a man be talked of. . . . This I find universally neglected, and no care taken anywhere to improve young men in their own language, that they may thoroughly understand and be masters of it.

Under these circumstances, it is no wonder that the influence of Latin on everything linguistic and stylistic and on criteria of correctness was overwhelming, and sometimes stifling. The term "grammar" was generally understood to refer to Latin grammar (if English is discussed, the explicit purpose is most often to facilitate the learning of Latin through a proper description of the mother tongue), and was confined to the treatment of cases, concord (grammatical agreement in number, case, and gender), and rection (the ability of the verb to take certain types of objects). The larger linguistic units were dealt with by rhetoric and logic: grammar was defined as the *ars recte dicendi* (" the art of correct speech"), and rhetoric as the *ars bene dicendi* ("the art of good style"), with the rules of rhetoric including statements on grammatical errors. Since the diversity of the grammatical structures of Latin and English was either not acknowledged, or was interpreted as a deficiency on the part of English, many descriptions of English were influenced by Latin grammar in that they looked for distinctions absent in English (such as cases), neglected categories absent in Latin (such as aspect, functional word order, or *do*-periphrasis), or misinterpreted seemingly corresponding categories (as in the tense systems). Stylistic judgement, too, was largely dominated by reference to Latin authors: arguments (and counter-arguments) concerning the proper use of archaisms, loanwords, neologisms, the choice of an appropriate style in accordance with the tenets of classical decorum were repeatedly supported by a small set of quotations from Cicero, Horace, and Quintilian.

Usage and Correctness

Whereas the social pressures to conform to "educated" speech must have been enormous in the sixteenth century, the fact that no grammars or dictionaries were available for guidance produced widespread uncertainty. There are early statements to the effect that the educated speech of Londoners should be taken as a model (Hart, 1569: 21r). Although speaking about the proper language for the *poet*, Puttenham's (1589, p. 120) detailed advice on what to use and what to avoid can be taken as advice on what was to be regarded as "standard" in general. He recommends using the language "spoken in the kings Court" and avoiding the speech of

   (a) the people in the "marches and frontiers" and "port townes" (because of language mixing);
   (b) the universities (because of Latinate diction);
   (c) rural areas;
   (d) the lower classes ("of a craftes man or carter, or other of the inferiour sort") regardless of region;
   (e) the old poets ("for their language is now out of vse with vs");
   (f) "Northern-men . . . beyond the riuer of Trent" (because even the well educated show some interference from the northern dialect).

These statements make it clear that few acceptable uses were left for regional English. Only northern speech, which some thought to be purer even than the "courtly" southern speech, enjoyed a certain prestige. It occurred in print only in literary stereotyping, such as in Spenser's *Shepheardes Calender*, which induced Gil (1619, p. 18) to stress that poets were free to some extent to use dialect:

> Dialecti poetis solis ex scriptoribus concessae; quibus tamen, exceptâ communi, abstinent; nisi quod rythmi, aut jucunditatis causâ saepiuscule vtuntur Boreali; quia suavissima, quia antiquissima, quia purissima, utpote quae majorum nostrorum sermoni proxima.

> ["Of all writers, only poets are permitted to use dialects; yet they abstain from using them (except for general use), unless they use the Northern dialect, quite frequently for the purpose of rhythm or attractiveness, since that dialect is the most delightful, the most ancient, the purest, and approximates most nearly to the speech of our ancestors."]

Scotland was exceptional. As a consequence of political independence from the fourteenth century onwards, the language of the court began to be standardized on the basis of Edinburgh speech. Many features and functions of sixteenth century Scots thus suggest that "the auld leid" should be classified as a language, a language that never fledged. This failure was partly due to the persisting prestige of southern English, which heavily influenced the language of Scots poetry from the beginning. Even Gavin Douglas, in his introduction to Virgil's *Aeneid* (1515), after claiming that he was "kepand na sudron bot our awyn langage" ("retaining no Southern (English) but our own language") went on to stress that he had to borrow words "quhar scant was Scottis" from Latin, French, *and* English. Towards the late sixteenth century, especially through the impact of the English Bible, the status of Scots was undermined from both within and without; the printed standard came to be associated with English, leaving for Scots mainly the spoken domains. This uncertainty is exemplified by the semi-Scots writings of James VI, who as James I of England took pains after 1603 to avoid whatever Scots features his language still displayed.

Quintilian expressed his view of language as *sermo constat ratione, vetustate, auctoritate, consuetidine* ("Language is based on reason, antiquity, authority and usage") (I.O., I.6.1). He assigned the greatest weight to the last factor: *Consuetudo vero artissima loquendi magistra, utiendumque plane sermone ut nummo, cui publica forma est* ("Usage however is the surest pilot in speaking, and we should treat language as currency minted with the public stamp"); that sentence was taken by Ben Jonson as the motto for his *Grammar*. Quintilian added the often-quoted parallel *ergo consuetudinem sermonis vocabo consensum eruditorum, sicut vivendi consensum bonorum* ("I will therefore define usage in speech as the agreed practice of educated men, just as where our way of life is concerned I should define it as the agreed practice of all good men") (I.6.45). All statements of sixteenth-century English writers on the subject make it plain that usage cannot be based on a majority decision; they require that the speaker (as Puttenham advises the poet) "shall follow generally the better brought vp sort, such as the Greekes call *charientes* men ciuill and graciously behauoured and bred." In the same chapter Puttenham refers to Horace's famous dictum *usus quem penes arbitrium est & ius & norma loquendi*, which he translates without comment as "when vse and custom will/ onely vmpiers of speach, for force and skill."

At a time when this usage was not homogeneous, such an appeal to custom was somewhat premature. Cicero and Quintilian had been in a position comparable to that of the English writers of the eighteenth century when Dr Johnson still complained that he found the English language "copious without order, and energetick without rules" (1755). Statements like the following cannot, then, be taken at face value, but must be interpreted on the basis of what the authors actually did. Mulcaster (1582:Пj) claims: "I have ... planted my rules vpon our ordinarie custom, the more my frind, bycause it is followed, nowhere my fo, because nowhere forced," and Ben Jonson wrote his Grammar "out of his observation of the English Language now spoken, and in use."

Although the battle between reason ("logical rules of grammar") and usage was not as one-sided as it was in the 18th century, Leonard's statement (1929, pp. 15 f.) holds true for much of the Renaissance, too; he found an

> explicit appeal to custom – variously interpreted as cultivated speech, the usage of the best writers, and 'what sounds best' – and its actual repudiation in practically all cases.

Levels of Language

1. *Pronunciation and orthography*

"Correct" pronunciation is a major concern of the age because variation must have been very noticeable, and some pronunciations were highly stigmatized. Even Puttenham (who was concerned with the *written* language a poet should use) singles out for criticism sociolects of the lower classes, "for such persons doe abuse good speaches by strange accents or ill shapen soundes, and false ortographie" (1589, p. 120). From Hart onwards, the standard of the schools appears to have been quite well defined. With regard to Gil's attacks on Hart, Dobson (1968, vol. I, p. 85) remarks: "in the later sixteenth and early seventeenth centuries there was in existence a standard of correctness of pronunciation which was apparently jealously maintained, especially by schoolmasters." However, even careful phoneticians of the period carried over into their prescribed forms undetected peculiarities of their idiolects: "Each of them represents his own pronunciation and takes little account of any other . . . Gil . . . went further, not merely to ignore, but to deny the existence of, certain pronunciations that were not his own" (Dobson, 1968, vol. I, p. 195). Another of the more important grammarians, William Bullokar, "certainly spoke a form of English more coloured by dialect and vulgarisms" (Dobson, 1968, vol. I, p. 116).

This influence of the schools appears to have delayed some phonetic developments, especially where the schoolmasters could point to spelling distinctions. They generally assumed that the best sort of spoken English was that which came closest to the written standard:

1. The distinction between the sounds representing ME /ε:/ and /e:/ in words like *meat* and *meet* had been lost in colloquial and lower-class speech around 1500, but schoolmasters insisted on distinguishing such words until the late seventeenth century.
2. [ç, x] in words like *night* and *naught* must have been silent in most southern dialects from the fifteenth century onwards, but orthoepists insisted that an equivalent of *gh* was heard until the early seventeenth century.

Although excessive dependence on the written form was criticized (ridiculed in Shakespeare's Holofernes), this did not detract from the prestige and relative stability of school pronunciation – until the disorders of the Civil War swept it away.

As regards orthography, "custom" meant the practices that had developed with generations of printers (almost exclusively located in London), though some scholars like Hart insisted on the priority of "reason", i.e. a logical relationship between sounds and letters with no exceptions even on grounds of etymology. It soon became clear that there was no chance of a systematic spelling like Hart's being implemented in Elizabethan England, and scholars like Mulcaster who sought a compromise won the day (cf. Barber, 1976, p. 120). As Hart points out, a "logical" orthography would not only have made the learning of English easier for foreigners, but it would also have facilitated the acquisition of standard pronunciation without the help of a teacher by "the rude countrie English man, which may desire to read English as the best sort vse to speake it" (1569: 4v).

2. Forms and inflections

Little regulating remained to be done in this field, and few controversial issues (such as the proper form for "wrote" – *writ, wrote, wrate*) continued to be debated by men of learning. But the treatment of two topics by Ben Jonson may serve to illustrate the variability of usage, and the conflict between what grammarians postulated and what they did.

The genitive case and *of*-construction had in the sixteenth century been complemented by the form *my father his house*. Although criticized by grammarians, this construction was felt to be acceptable in certain environments, especially for nouns ending in /s/. Ben Jonson was against the practice, yet a number of instances are found in his plays, even in the title of his *Sejanus His Fall*. The comparison of adjectives also remained to be regulated. Although forms agreeing with Modern English practice predominated, instances of *more wild, learnedder*, and *most unkind*, etc., were quite frequent in Early Modern English, and the last usage was even praised by Ben Jonson as a kind of Atticism in the English language.

3. *Syntax*

Comments on Early Modern English syntax are few, partly because syntax (in the modern sense) was not felt to form part of grammar, and partly because attempts to devise rules for English that conformed with the rules for Latin grammar were doomed to failure. It is significant that discussions about the choice of the proper relative, the position of the "preposition," the use of tenses, etc., are mainly found from Dryden onwards (who criticizes his predecessors, especially Ben Jonson and Shakespeare, for "errors" in such areas).

4. *Style*

The sixteenth century provides an array of fashionable styles, all considered "best usage" and valuable stylistic models in their time, but most of them were soon forgotten, some after a period of exaggerated use:

1. Styles illustrating the capacity of English for copiousness by excessive duplication and repetition:

> What condygne graces and thankes ought men to gyue to the writers of historyes? Who with their great labours/ haue done so moche profyte to the humayne lyfe. They shewe/ open/ manifest and declare to the reder/ by example of olde antyquite: what we shulde enquere/ desyre/ and folowe: And also/ what we shulde eschewe/ auoyde/ and vtterly flye. For whan we (beynge vnexpert of chaunces) se/ beholde/ and rede the auncyent actes/ gestes/ and dedes: Howe/ and with what labours/ daungers/ and paryls they were gested and done: They right greatly admonest/ ensigne/ and teche vs: howe we maye lede forthe our lyues.

> (J. Froissart, *The Chronycles*, 1523: Ai)

2. Texts overloaded with neo-Latin, often introduced unnecessarily ("ink-hornisms"), as evident in the mock letter in Wilson (1553: 86v–87r, quoted in Baugh and Cable, 1978, pp. 218 f.):

> An ynkehorne letter. Ponderyng, expendyng, and reuolutyng with my self your ingent affabilitee, and ingenious capacitee, for mundane affaires: I cannot but celebrate and extolle your magnificall dexteritee, aboue all other. For how could you haue adepted suche illustrate prerogatiue, and dominicall superioritee, if the fecunditee of

your ingenie had not been so fertile, & wounderfull pregnaunt. Now therfore beeyng accersited, to suche splendent renoume, & dignitee splendidious:

(Th. Wilson, *The Arte of Rhetorique*, 1553: 86v–87r)

3. Ciceronian imitations of the Latin period, which crammed an entire argument with all possible ramifications into one sentence (the sentence thereby becomes coextensive with the paragraph, as in Bullokar, 1580: 1v):

> Which fower and twentie letters, are not sufficient to picture Inglish spéech: For in Inglish spéech, are mo distinctions and diuisions in voice, then these fower and twentie letters can seuerally signifie, and giue right sound vnto: By reason whereof, we were driuen, to vse to some letters, two soundes, to some, thrée soundes, hauing in them no difference, or marke, in figure or fashion, to shewe how the same double, or treble sounded letters, should be sounded, when they were ioined with other letters in wordes: which was very tedious to the learner (though he coulde speake and vnderstand perfectly Inglish spéech by nature and continuall vse) much more tedious was it, to them of another nation not aided by such vse: when our writing and printing, nothing agréed, in the seuerall names of our letters, vnto the sounding of them in our wordes: whereby our spéech was condemned of those strangers, as without order, or sensibilitie: whereas the fault was in the picture, (I meane the letters) and not in the spéech: which fault, the strangers did not perceiue, much lesse could they remedie it, when we our selues, some contented with a custome thought it could be no better, some perceiuing some fault, knew not the remedie, some knowing some remedie (as touching their owne iudgement and contentation) thought it hard to be altered, because that the great volumes alreadie in print, should be more than halfe lost, if they could not be vsed, by such, as learned first the amended writing and printing: and som are so enuious that nothing is well, but their owne doings: and some are so ambitious, they would haue no knowledge but in themselues, and haue dominon ouer vertue, not vsing vertuous waies themselves, but hindering the vertue of others.

(W. Bullokar, *Booke at Large*, 1580: 1v)

4. Lyly's euphuistic style, which was profusely ornamented with alliteration, isocola (clauses of equal length and structure), far-fetched similes and metaphors, or Sidney's Arcadian style, both demonstrating that the "honny-flowing Matron Eloquence" (1595: K4r) had found a home in Britain:

> Thou art héere in *Naples* a young soiourner, I an olde senior: thou a straunger, I a Citizen: thou secure doubting no mishappe, I sorrowful dreading thy misfortune. Héere mayst thou sée, that which I sigh to sée: dronken sottes wallowing in euery house in euerye Chamber, yea, in euerye channell. Héere mayst thou beholde that which I cannot without blushing beholde, nor without blubbering vtter: those whose bellies be their Gods, who offer their goods as Sacrifice to theyr guttes: Who sléepe with meate in their mouths, with sinne in their hearts, and with shame in their houses. Héere, yea, héere, *Euphues*, mayst thou sée, not the carued visard of a lewde woman, but the incarnate visage of a laciuious wantonne: not the shaddow of loue, but the substaunce of lust. My hearte melteth in droppes of bloud, to sée an harlot wyth the one hande robbe so many cofers, and with the other to rippe so many corses. Thou art héere amiddest the pikes betweene *Scylla* and *Caribdis*, ready if thou shunne *Syrtes*, to sinke into *Semphlagades*.

(J. Lyly, *Euphues*, 1578: 4v)

5. Archaic diction mixed with provincialisms to create a poetic diction as cultivated by Spenser, but rarely found in prose:

> Syker, thous but a laesie loord,
>   and rekes much of thy swinck,
> That with fond termes, and weetlesse words
>   to blere myne eyes doest thinke.
> In euill houre thou hentest in hond
>   thus holy hylles to blame,
> For sacred vnto saints they stond,
>   and of them han theyr name.
> S. Michels mount who does not know,
>   that wardes the Westerne coste?
> And of S. Brigets bowre I trow,
>   all Kent can rightly boaste:
> And they that con of Muses skill,
>   sayne most what, that they dwell
> (As goteheards wont) vpon a hill,
>   beside a learned well.
>
> (E. Spenser, *The Shepheardes Calender*, 1579: 26v ("July"))

6. Plain style as found in Bible translations and Puritan writings, whose authors frequently feel called upon to defend the lack of adornment by equating truth with unambiguous plain style.

Although all this variability seemed to be well regulated by the classical rules of decorum – good usage was the fit between subject matter and the corresponding type of English – the excesses illustrate how much the age was still groping for "custom" in this important field.

The first major criticism is found in Bacon, whose definition of "delicate learning" (when "men began to hunt more after wordes, than matter", 1605: 18r) is in conspicuous contrast to Ascham's belief that only a polished style will make a perfect human being (1570: 46r). Bacon's criticism influenced the development of the style favoured by the Royal Society and Dryden, which came to be the basis for modern English prose.

5. *Vocabulary*

It was obvious that the vocabulary had to be augmented if English was to be used for new domains such as various types of scholarly discourse, but Renaissance writers also felt the need to expand the vocabulary in order to provide for copiousness and rhetorical beauty. The vocabulary was augmented in various ways: loans from classical languages and from French, loan translations, new coinages exploiting native patterns of word formation, reviving old words that had become obsolete since Chaucer, or applying old words to new concepts and thereby expanding their meaning. But the lack of a dictionary to guide writers as to what words already existed in the language and the delight many of them found in coining new words led to an exuberance and duplication rarely found in later, better-ruled, periods.

Both loans and new coinages may be labelled "neologisms." Many writers paid lip service to the classical rule *ut novorum optima erunt maxime vetera, ita veterum maxime nova* ("in the case of old words the best will be those that are newest, just as in the case of new words the best will be the oldest") (Quintilian, I.O., I.6.41), expressed by Gellius (I.10) as *tamquam scopulum vitari debes verbum infrequens.* Compare also the formulations by Wilson (1553: a ii): 'beware . . . of straunge wordes, as thou wouldest take hede and eshewe greate roches in the sea" and by Gascoigne (in Smith, 1904, p. 52) "eschew straunge words, or *obsoleta et inusitata.*" Such sentiments are repeated in the eighteenth century, as in Pope's "Alike fantastic, if too new, or old" (*Essay on Criticism,* line 334).

The great prestige Latin enjoyed gave plenty of occasion for overdoing the Latinization, and the inappropriate use of unnecessary and unintegrated Latin words (inkhornisms) was widely criticized. This criticism does not make scholars such as Elyot, Ascham, Wilson, or Cheke "purists" in the modern sense: they reacted against fashionable trends among the half-educated. The frequency of ironic malapropisms in Elizabethan drama and the success of dictionaries that explained "hard words" to the uneducated (or even, like Cockeram's dictionary of 1623, also provided learned words for simple concepts) make it clear that strict avoidance of foreign words would have been impossible to enforce.

The fashion for archaizing speech in the Chaucer tradition possibly had even less impact than "purism": through Spenser it established a tradition in English poetry, but such words never achieved any wider currency. The question of how to deal with loanwords and archaisms was settled through use, which largely ignored the views of those who commented on contemporary practices.

Attitudes towards Linguistic Change

Although there are a few reflections on linguistic change before 1500, they become frequent only from about 1570 onwards. Poets and other writers grew increasingly concerned about the permanence of their work, if the English it was written in was itself so changeable. Change in English was one argument against translating the Bible, and one reason why Bacon translated his *Advancement of Learning* into Latin (1605, 1623). Waller summarized this concern in the words: "Poets that Lasting Marble seek,/ Must carve in Latin or in Greek;/ We write in Sand. . . . " Writers not only saw Chaucer's poems becoming less and less intelligible, they were also aware of the decline of Greek and Latin from the classical perfection of the Golden Age to silver and brass forms. Believing in the grammatical homogeneousness, stability and purity of Ciceronian Latin, they felt increasingly called upon to work for an equivalent norm in English, especially after 1580 when the conviction grew that English had been "fined" enough to have reached a perfection worth preserving. The major thrust of such thinking, however, came after 1660, when there was also a growing concern about "corruption," a concern based on the mistaken assumption "that the literary language of some earlier classical age is more 'correct' than the current colloquial language; and that the 'purity' of a language is maintained by the educated and 'corrupted' by the illiterate" (Barber, 1976, p. 122).

Notes

1. Much of the following is condensed and rephrased from Görlach (1978: an English version is in preparation, to be published by Cambridge University Press); I also owe a great deal to other treatments of the English language in the period, of which chapter 8 in Baugh and Cable (1978, pp. 199–252) and Barber's (1976) comprehensive and well-written book deserve special mention. For stylistic and other improvements I am grateful to Sidney Greenbaum and Helen Weiss, who read the draft and made valuable suggestions.
2. Whereas Dryden thought elegance in English poetry to have started with Waller, Pope later credited Dryden with just this refinement, the Renaissance meriting only the dubious praise of unpolished genius: "Just as Augustus Rome, so Dryden found English brick, and left it marble."

References

ATKINS, J.W.H. (1947) *English Literary Criticism: The Renascence.* New York: Barnes & Noble.

BACON, SIR FRANCIS (1605) *The Advancement of Learning.* London.

BARBER, CHARLES (1976) *Early Modern English.* London: Deutsch.

BAUGH, ALBERT C. and THOMAS CABLE (1978) *A History of the English Language,* 3rd edn. Boston: Routledge.

BULLOKAR, WILLIAM (1580) *Booke at large . . .* London.

DOBSON, E.J. (1968) *English Pronunciation 1500–1700,* 2nd edn. Oxford: Oxford University Press.

DOUGLAS, GAVIN (1962) *Virgil's Aeneid Translated into Scottish Verse* (1515), ed. C. F. C. Coldwell. Scottish Text Society III, 25.

ELYOT, SIR THOMAS (1532) *The boke named the Gouernour.* London.

FISHER, J.H. (1977) "Chancery and the emergence of standard written English in the fifteenth century." *Speculum,* **52,** 870–899.

GIL, ALEXANDER, *Logonomia Anglica.* London 1619, 2nd edn. 1621.

GÖRLACH, MANFRED (1978) *Einführung ins Frühneuenglische.* Heidelberg: Quelle & Meyer.

HART, JOHN (1569) *An Orthographie.* London.

JOHNSON, SAMUEL, "Preface to *A Dictionary of the English Language*" (1755), in W. F. Bolton, ed. (1966) *The English Language,* I. Cambridge: Cambridge University Press, pp. 129–156.

JONSON, BEN (1640) *English Grammer,* in *Works.*

LEONARD, S.A., (1929) *The Doctrine of Correctness in English Usage 1700–1800* (University of Wisconsin Studies in Language and Literature 25). Madison.

MULCASTER, RICHARD (1582) *The First Part of the Elementarie.* London.

PUTTENHAM, GEORGE (1589) *The arte of English poesie.* London.

QUINTILIAN, M. FABIUS, *Institutio oratoria,* ed. L. Radermacher. Leipzig: Teubner, 1959; ed. with an English translation by H. E. Butler, 4 vols. London: Heinemann; Cambridge, Mass.: Harvard University Press, 1920.

SIDNEY, SIR PHILIP (1595) *An Apologie for Poetrie.* London.

SKEYNE, GILBERT (1586) *Ane Breve descriptiovn of the Pest.* Edinburgh.

SMITH, G. GREGORY, ed. (1904) *Elizabethan Critical Essays.* London: Oxford University Press.

WILSON, THOMAS (1553) *The Arte of Rhetorique.* London.

Chapter 4

Attitudes Toward Language in the Eighteenth and Nineteenth Centuries

JAMES C. STALKER

ALTHOUGH attitudes toward language have remained relatively consistent throughout the last 2000 years, the eighteenth century is different in that it marks the beginning of widespread public consciousness and discussion about language. In *ca.* 100 B.C. Dionysius of Thrax noted in his *Art of Grammar* that the Greek language of his day had changed from that of the more ancient writers whom he valued, and expressed his fear that further changes would render the ancient writers increasingly unreadable. Latin writers such as Horace and Quintilian in their roles as poet and historian discussed language, both expressing the opinion that the language of common use was the base upon which writers should build in their own writings. Somewhat later, Donatus wrote a grammar for school use and Priscian wrote an 18-volume description of Latin in order to preserve the language for the future.

The medieval period is marked by a concern with the correctness of Latin usage, but next to no concern about the usage of the vernacular languages, beyond the assumption that Latin was the legitimate language for serious written works and that the vernaculars were necessary for the daily lives of the uneducated but unsuited to serious intellectual matters. Through this period, as into the Renaissance, attitudes toward language were expressed, but only by scholars, philosophers, and teachers. We have no surviving written records of public discussions of attitudes toward language. The fact that the vernaculars developed into their modern forms is the best evidence that the languages were widely and persistently used, and we can speculate that nobles and peasants recognized that they spoke different versions of the same language, but if discussions about the goodness or badness of peasant versus noble usage occurred, it seems not to have appeared in print.

The mid- and late seventeenth century ushers in a change that set a new course in language discussion. Probably the two major causes of this change were the rise of the middle class and the increased literacy rate. Vernacular language ceased to be primarily oral during the late Middle Ages when Boccacio, Chaucer, and others wrote serious artistic works in the vernaculars, and laws and serious scholarly discussions appeared in the native vernaculars. These developments set the stage for the Renaissance, which is partly defined by the rapid development of the use of vernacular languages in print. Print literacy grew and books became cheaper, and as books became cheaper, demand for schooling in the vernaculars led to a wider public concern over the state of the language.

In addition, the increased literacy and increased demand for books opened a new profession, or perhaps expanded its opportunities. During the Medieval period, writers had a primary occupation to which their writing was subordinate. They were churchmen who wrote in praise or explanation of God; or they were functionaries in the court or government, and thus had the leisure to write. However, during the late seventeenth and eighteenth centuries, writing became a distinct profession, and writers did not have to be something else first. They were supported through patronage, or they simply made enough from their writing to be able to continue to write.

We have then two factors converging, or growing out of the same historical sources: an increasingly literate audience with the education and time to be concerned about the state and usage of the language that has become increasingly important in their lives; and a growing number of people who make their economic lives through supplying books, newspapers, pamphlets, stories, plays, poems to this literate audience, and for whom language has ceased to be a casual concern but rather has become the medium through which they exercise their trade. Couple this literacy and the people who supply it with the increasing possibility of class mobility, and we have a fertile bed for the seeds of linguistic concern – and insecurity – to grow.

As Görlach[1] points out, the purity and consistency of English were among the primary linguistic concerns of the English Renaissance. There was much discussion about the heavy lexical borrowing that was popular at the time and whether the borrowing contaminated the purity of English, and the first grammars often focused on the wide variation in spelling. Although these concerns were certainly not resolved by the eighteenth century, they were replaced by broader issues, among them the effects of change on the language. Swift's "Proposal for Correcting, Improving, and Ascertaining the English Tongue" addressed this issue in 1712, and it is still under discussion today. Swift and his successors, in reading the *Chronicles*, Chaucer, Shakespeare, and others, saw in English what Thrax saw in Greek – older works were becoming increasingly difficult to read because the language had changed. They also looked forward and speculated that their own writings would be inaccessible to future readers. In their professional pride as writers, they wished to prevent further change, which from their perspective they quite legitimately perceived as detrimental to the longevity of their works.

Change itself was bad enough, but the changes English was undergoing were generally regarded as a decline from near perfection. In his "Proposal" Swift set the date of perfect English at 1642. Johnson regarded pre-Restoration English as "the wells of English undefiled" as he tells us in the preface to his dictionary (289). Dryden had his doubts about the perfectability of English, but did regard the language of his time as better than Shakespearian English. The preservation of eighteenth-century English would serve two purposes – the pragmatic one of maintaining the usefulness of works produced in the era, and the altruistic one of maintaining the language in a state as near to perfection as imperfect man could achieve.

Stabilizing language had another purpose as well. Greater social awareness coupled with greater social mobility (in part the result of increased literacy) unsettled the clear assignment of social status on the basis of language. Money and power were no longer clearly associated with a particular dialect. In order to re-establish language use as a means for social assignment, the eighteenth century turned to propriety. Discussions of rhetorical appropriateness had long specified that certain styles of language were appropriate for certain forms of discourse, and now we find that certain forms of language are appropriate for certain class levels. Although we must acknowledge that certain forms of discourse and certain class levels were accorded higher value than others, we must also recognize that some writers in the eighteenth century knew that these assignments were in some measure the function of happenstance and not inherent in the language or the people. For example, Samuel Johnson discusses the issue of inherent goodness or badness of language in the *Rambler*, in which he says that the distaste we hold for a particular word or phrase is a result of the association of that word with a particular group of people rather than an inherent feature of the word or phrase itself (214). Lowth says much the same thing in his discussion of sentence final prepositions (141).

Of course, if one wished to stabilize the language, one must decide which language to stabilize. That of the best writers and speakers was the obvious and most popular choice, followed by that of persons of the better social classes, but certainly not the language of the lower classes. However, even though no one seriously questioned that some group, generally upper class, would be the standard-setting group, there were some problems that needed resolving. For example, should English become more like Latin or be left to its own forms and devices? The majority view was generally that it was a pity that English had diverged so widely from Latin, but there was little help for it. Some attempts were made to improve English by Latinizing it (e.g. by Dryden, Lowth, and Johnson), but most people concerned with the state of the language implicitly accepted Priestly's view that English should not be, indeed could not be, Latinized and were content to continue the practice of describing English syntax in Latin terms, but to otherwise let it remain as English.

The real problem was to determine just whose language was going to set the standard. Priestly was in favor of letting the common usage dictate standards for writers, but his was a lone voice. Most people were concerned that some particular group be selected, and then their usage be set as the standard after being subjected to the scrutiny of reason and logic. Lowth rejected the double negative on the grounds that it was both illogical and out of fashion among the better classes (139). But just what constituted reason and logic was no clearer then than now. Lowth disagreed with Swift on whether English was "irregular and capricious" (vii), Priestly disagreed with both, and Johnson decided that because no one could agree, he would decide what was standard, so he wrote a dictionary and a grammar to settle the whole matter.

Perhaps one of the more interesting implications of this discussion was that anyone who could write and then gain a publisher and an audience had a right to express an opinion on language and its use. In *Protean Shape*, Tucker details the many and varied views on language, not simply the language of the best writers and speakers, but the language of sailors, women, foreigners, almost anyone who used language. The range of forums was equally amazing, from *The Adventurer* and *The Babler* through more well-known journals such as *The Spectator* and *The Tatler*, through books specifically on language such as Lowth's grammar and works such as *The Reverie: or, A Flight to the Paradise of Fools*, and letters to the *Gentleman's Magazine*. Although we are most familiar with the pronouncements on the language of writers such as Dryden, Pope, Johnson, and Swift, virtually anyone could speak his piece. Priestly is remembered today for his scientific endeavors, and that was indeed his primary area of study, but he too wrote a grammar. Lowth was a clergyman, and there were numerous anonymous letter writers as well as others about whom we know only their name (Tucker, 161). In short, what constituted good or bad, appropriate or inappropriate, logical or illogical language was open for public debate. Although professional writers seem to have been accorded special status, perhaps because they used language as a carpenter uses a hammer, anyone who could pen an acceptable letter could offer a comment in the public press on linguistic propriety.

The attitude that decisions about linguistic propriety were in the public domain did not last into the nineteenth century. The elitist view inherent in the eighteenth century social propriety gradually overpowered linguistic and rhetorical propriety as the century wore on. Furthermore, as the study of English became a staple of schooling, public views on language, although still tolerated, gave way to a more authoritarian view; language experts presented themselves who had the last word on language – what it was and how it was to be used. The experts were of two sorts, the successors to Lowth, those who wrote grammar texts for school use, and the newly important philologists, those for whom the study of language was a science, not a matter of determining propriety.

This second group was represented during the eighteenth century, but not in the fashion we have come to expect in our own century. Perhaps the most well-known philologist of the eighteeenth century, and one who well represented the spirit of language attitudes in that century, was Horne Tooke. Tooke's approach to explaining the development of language rested on a philosophical system akin to others of the century which derived current language complexities from primitives based on natural human functions. For Tooke, these primitives were discovered (or invented, many would maintain) on the basis of pure speculation. That is to say, Tooke himself decided, with the aid of his philosophical system, what the primitives must have been, and how they underlay current linguistic forms. Where the Grimm brothers and their English counterparts later in the eighteenth century and into the nineteenth based their studies on the principle of developing theory out of data, Tooke developed his theory out of philosophy. Data which did not fit was simply ignored or rejected as unfounded.[2] In this sense, Tooke, Johnson, and Lowth were kindred eighteenth-century souls; each more or less arbitrarily established himself as an authority, and through force of will and circumstance compelled recognition of his authority. None felt the need to moderate his views on the basis of consensus or the real data of language.

Fortunately for the study of language, Tooke's influence in philological circles waned in the latter part of the century as the continental philologists overwhelmed the world of language study with elegant theories which explained not only the linguistic documents on hand, but which also proved to have high predictive value – newly found documents confirmed the theories they were developing. However, although their studies became increasingly sophisticated and powerful through the nineteenth century, the philologists had virtually no influence on the public. For the philologists, the study of language became removed from the social and rhetorical concerns of the eighteenth century, and thus became an abstract and objective study. They came to recognize that objectively there was little difference in the inherent quality of different varieties of language, whether current variations in dialects or variations over time in older and newer forms of the language. Quite the contrary, variations in linguistic form held an inherent value to the student of language because they provided a broader base from which to draw comparative data, and thus were extremely useful for developing theories and testing them.

Perhaps the greatest legacy of the nineteenth-century philologists was the study of language from an objective point of view, a view that has been adopted by twentieth-century linguists. Although there is no evidence to point to a direct line from Priestly to modern-day linguists, the philologists worked from the viewpoint which Priestly expressed and thus maintained that line of inquiry.

However, the line of inquiry that influenced the public was that of Lowth's descendants, the pedogogical grammarians – Kirkham, Murray, Brown. Each of these repeated Lowth's original statement that the study of grammar was to enable the writer or speaker to use English with "propriety and accuracy." But, whereas Lowth's propriety included rhetorical propriety as well as social propriety, the grammarians of the nineteenth century gradually lost the rhetorical strand and concentrated on the social, although the dicta were frequently, if not usually, couched within a rhetorical framework, and were used to supply rules for correct and appropriate compositions. In the preface to his dictionary, Johnson complained that there were no authorities for good usage in English as there were for other languages, a complaint that Swift had made 50 years earlier and that Lowth echoed in the introduction to his grammar. Lowth's grammar and Johnson's dictionary were published in order to fill this void, and they successfully did so. By the early nineteenth century when both books had been through several editions, they had become the authorities that the language had been missing and, in so doing, they quelled public discussion over what constituted good and appropriate language. They became the tradition that answered the question.

Lindley Murray's *English Grammar Adapted to the Different Classes of Learners* is in effect an updated and expanded edition of Lowth's grammar. In the introduction to the 1819 edition, he excuses himself for not providing sources with each quotation and instead gives a blanket acknowledgement: ". . . the authors to whom the grammatical part of this compilation is principally indebted for its materials, are Harris, Johnson, Lowth, Priestly

Beattie, Sheridan, Walker, and Coote" (5). Furthermore, in defining purity of style, he says that writers must abjure "words and phrases that are . . . used without proper authority" (255). He defines propriety as "the selection of such words as the best usage has appropriated to those ideas, which we intend to express by them: in opposition to low expressions, and to words and phrases which would be less significant of the ideas than we mean to convey. Style may be pure . . . and may, nevertheless be deficient in propriety: for the words may be ill chosen, not adapted to the subject nor fully expressive of the author's sense" (256). Lowth's rhetorical propriety can still be seen in this last sentence, but the match between form and sense must be based on "the best usage." By 1839, Samuel Kirkham tells us that "the best speakers and writers" supply "the standard of grammatical accuracy in the use of . . . language" (17). Although he does state as well that "language is conventional . . . and *varied* for the purposes of practical convenience" and that we should "take the language as it *is*, and not as it *should be*, and bow to custom" (18), it is clear that the custom to which we will bow is that of the best writers and speakers. He says, "Grammar teaches us *how to use words in a proper manner*" (18), not effectively, not according to custom, but properly.

In his 10th edition of *The Grammar of English Grammars*, Goold Brown makes it abundantly clear that young scholars must study grammar so that when they speak or write they may choose a style appropriate to the subject and the audience, and leave "the critic no fault to expose, no word to amend" (95). In the summary to his chapter on the "Grammatical Study of the English Language," Brown expresses a new dimension in attitudes toward language. He says, ". . . as the vices of speech as well as of manners are contagious, it becomes those who have the care of youth, to be masters of the language in its purity and elegance, and to avoid as much as possible every thing that is reprehensible in thought or expression" (101). Linguistic form has clearly become a measure of "goodness" in a very nearly religious sense. Bad language does not simply obscure meaning or is ill-adapted to the subject under consideration, but is a window into your quality as a human being. The mid-eighteenth-century linguistic impropriety has become the mid-nineteenth-century linguistic vice.

On this basis, absolute rules of correctness become the order of the day. Lowth's rules of propriety were often couched in a relativistic context, that is the rule provided the correct usage for a particular context. Grammar texts in the nineteenth century provided rules that were correct in all contexts, or perhaps more accurately, contexts in which the rules were not applicable were contexts to avoid. Thomas Harvey's *A Practical Grammar of the English Language* incorporates "Cautions" in each chapter. In the section on adjectives, he tells his readers "Do not use *them* for *these*, *this here* for *this*, or *that 'ere* for *that*" (55). In the section on conjunctions, he writes, "Do not use *like* or *with* for *as*, *but* for *than*, *that* for *why* or *without* for *unless*" (131). Alonzo Reed and Brainerd Kellogg retain some of the eighteenth-century relativism when they comment on the distinction between *O* and *Oh* that "This distinction, however desirable, is not now strictly observed, *O* being frequently used in place of *Oh*" (51). Later in the century prospective teachers are expected to recognize errors in decontextualized sentences (Thompson). There is a right way and a wrong way, and by implication, teachers will pass this knowledge on to their students.

The eighteenth and nineteenth centuries shared two major assumptions about language – there were proper and improper uses of language, and it was not only legitimate but necessary that an authoritative person or group establish which usages were proper and improper. However, in the eighteenth century we find considerable public discussion of who the authorities should be, and an acceptance of a fairly broad range of writers on language. The eighteenth century had no language authorities; they were searching. The nineteenth century accepted the most eloquent or most popular linguistic spokesmen of the eighteenth century as authorities; they were no longer searching. As a result, public discussion of questions of divided usage was not so broadly based as in the eighteenth century. The authorities decided among themselves which usage would bear the stamp of approval. There was as well a shift from the more relativistic view of language use as a question of "propriety" to the more absolute view of "correctness."

Notes

1. Görlach, Manfred. "Renaissance English (1525–1640)," pp. 30–40 this volume.
2. See Hans Aarsleff, *The Study of Language in England*, for an excellent discussion of Tooke's role during this period.

References

AARSLEFF, HANS (1967) *The Study of Language in England, 1780–1860*. Princeton, N.J.: Princeton University Press.

BROWN, GOOLD (1851) *The Grammar of English Grammars*, 10th edn. New York: William Wood and Company.

DRYDEN, JOHN (1969) *Troilus and Cressida; or Truth Found too Late*. London: Cornmarket Press.

HARVEY, THOMAS W. (1868) *A Practical Grammar of the English Language*. New York: Van Antwerp, Bragg & Co.

JOHNSON, SAMUEL (1977) "Preface to *A Dictionary of the English Language*," eds. Frank Brady and W. K. Wimsatt. Berkeley, California: University of California Press.

KIRKHAM, SAMUEL (1839) *English Grammar in Familiar Lectures*, 105th edition. Baltimore: Plaskitt and Cugle Publishers.

LOWTH, ROBERT (1763) *A Short Introduction to English Grammar*, 2nd edn., corrected. London: A. Millar and R. and J. Dodsley.

MURRAY, LINDLEY (1819) *English Grammar Adapted to the Different Classes of Learners*. New York: E. Goodale and S. K. Gilman.

PRIESTLY, JOSEPH (1967) *The Rudiments of English Grammar*. London: T. Becket, P. A. DeHondt and J. Johnson.

REED, ALONZO and BRAINERD KELLOGG (1886) *Higher Lessons in English: A Work on English Grammar and Composition*. New York: Clark & Maynard, Publishers.

SWIFT, JONATHAN "A Proposal for Correcting, Improving, and Ascertaining the English Language." *Readings in English Prose of the Eighteenth Century*, ed. Raymond Macdonald Alden. Boston: Houghton Mifflin Company, 1911.

TUCKER, SUSIE I. (1967) *Protean Shape: A Study in Eighteenth Century Vocabulary and Usage*. London: University, The Athlone Press.

THOMPSON, ALBERT H. (1885) *The Teacher's Examiner*. Chicago: Albert H. Thompson.

Chapter 5

Natural Language and Orwellian Intervention

RANDOLPH QUIRK

DESPITE the form of my title, my purpose is less to comment on George Orwell, *né* Eric Arthur Blair, than to reflect upon the interest in reforming and manipulating natural language that we predominantly associate with Orwell. Not that I do not believe the time ripe for a revaluation of Orwell, especially in view of the undue reverence in which he is held as a serious thinker on social and linguistic matters. It is indeed not so much the quality or originality of his writing upon language that justifies his place in my title as the fact that the journalist in him, and the artist in him, seized upon the tenor of thought around him and articulated it into imaginatively arresting and memorable form.

The "thought around him" was that brought to bear upon a generation of philosophers, psychologists and linguists by the new evidence that the times has produced of the power that could be exercised by propaganda. More broadly: of the risks people ran through a linguistic inadequacy which on the one hand disabled them from expressing themselves fully and accurately, on the other hand disabled them from achieving a proper understanding of or critical response to what they heard or read. The 1920s and 1930s bore horrifying witness to the ease with which people could be misled by commercial advertisers and political demagogues alike.

Awareness of the dangers inherent in language, "the loaded weapon" (cf. Bolinger, 1980), is not a modern revelation. One of the chief impediments that Francis Bacon saw to the *Advancement of Learning* and hence of mankind itself was the too ready dislocation of words from meanings, the "Pygmalion's frenzy" in which people were too ready to be moved by words themselves without thought to what "weight of matter" they connoted (I. iv). It became indeed commonplace in the seventeenth and eighteenth centuries to speak (as Locke did) of people supposing "Words to stand also for the reality of Things" (*An Essay Concerning Humane Understanding*, III. ii). It is a theme which reaches an intellectual climax in Jeremy Bentham (*Theory of Fictions*) and the scepticism is made publicly indelible by Bentham's contemporary Goethe, whose Mephistopheles says (*Faust* I. 1900 ff.):

> where concepts fail,
> At the right time a word is thrust in there.
> With words we fitly can our foes assail,
> With words a system we prepare,
> Words we quite fitly can believe.

It is this tradition that was revived and publicised by the critics of natural language in the interwar years of this century, along with the ideas of how designed intervention could make language a more adequate (as well as a safer) tool for human use. For although historians of linguistics, with their attentions elsewhere (as in Aarsleff, 1982), in general ignore the craft of language engineering and design, this too has a long and distinguished history. In view of the philosophic scepticism we have mentioned, it would indeed have been astonishing if there had not been a comparable degree of thought given to how the shortcomings and dangers could be offset. In fact the traditional assumption (presumably as ubiquitous as it is timeless) was that, just as folk believed language to have been finitely "created," so they believed that it could be readily revised, recreated, or replaced. This latter corollary had been given learned and earnest consideration in Britain from the sixteenth century. One tradition of work was devoted to "improving" the specific language English (especially for religious and nationalistic reasons), and this tradition, today institutionalized as "language planning," has been enthusiastically applied to several European and Oriental languages, especially during and since the nineteenth century: German, Norwegian, Irish, Hebrew, Bahasa Indonesia, Chinese, to name but a few (cf. Quirk, 1982, ch. 4). Another tradition was to be more radical. The vision of regaining a pre-Babelian state of universal linguistic grace was given a fillip in the West with the "discovery" of Chinese and the idea not only therefore of a charactery, but a system of oral signs also, that might be firmly anchored in "matter" (cf. the reference to Bacon above) and hence be universal: a linguistic base for international communication. John Wilkins' *Essay Towards a Real Character* (1668) was a more fundamental proposal than most that have been made. But whether the design has been for an entirely new language (such as Esperanto) or for a modification of an existing one (such as Basic), the principle has been the same: rational design, formal control, objectivity, universality.

With these traditions of diagnosis, prophylaxis, and prescription a small number of dedicated twentieth-century scholars were deeply imbued. The perils of mankind at the mercy of propaganda were proclaimed (and enthusiastically exaggerated) in America by "General Semanticists" such as Count Korzybski and their popularizers like Stuart Chase, in Britain by C. K. Ogden and others associated with the "Orthological Institute." Some of their most impressive examples were drawn from the warped language of extremist politics, especially the crude hate-instilling, fear-engendering, thought-inhibiting speeches of Hitler and other Nazi leaders, to a lesser extent the patent inversions of truth emerging from the Moscow "show-trials" of the period. Less blood-chilling in their warnings and more modest in their prescriptions were the dozens of "plain language" advocates: the Fowler Brothers, A. P. Herbert, Eric Partridge, Ivor Brown, to name some in 1930s Britain alone (and though they were widely read in other English-speaking countries, they could of course be matched with an even longer list of writers in the United States).

Within the whole ferment of linguistic criticism, it was to this last type of "plain English" advocacy that Orwell was drawn, rather than to the more radical thinking associated with Ogden. And in a quite simple-minded way at that. His essay, "Propaganda and Demotic Speech," reveals "his belief that political liberty and simplicity of language are closely linked" (Crick, 1980, p. 324; cf. Orwell and Angus, 1968). As late as 1946, when the essay "Politics and the English Language" appeared in *Horizon*, his thinking was a shade less naïve but no more adventurous, original or indeed unconventional. Despite the acclaim it had and continues to have (homage, no doubt, to one recognized in his own time as a great prose writer, praised in fact by many as the greatest living), it is at best "sensible." It is wholly (though silently) derivative, and the entire piece is little more than an expansion of the five maxims set forth on the first page of the *King's English* by the Fowler brothers in 1906. Ironically, the maxim "prefer the Saxon word to the Latin" (one of the features which suggests verbatim adoption from the Fowlers) impinges upon the purity concept being implemented contemporaneously in Nazi Germany (cf. von Polenz, 1967), and it is perhaps indicative of Orwell's sociolinguistic naïvety that he fails to note the ideological implications in English "Saxonism" (cf. Simon, 1961).

Yet a year before this essay, *Animal Farm* had already been published, implying a great deal more sophisticated insight into the way politics can infect the English language. Indeed the oft-quoted "some are more equal than others" demonstrates that it is precisely the simple, familiar words that can be most easily twisted – in this case from absolute to gradable (cf. Quirk and Greenbaum, 1973). In the same year as the *Horizon* essay, however, it is fair to say that he rises above its stale stylistic "rules" in a vigorous polemic directed at J. D. Bernal. Though apparently not able to formulate his insight with linguistic precision, he attacks Bernal's English as 'pompous and slovenly" not on aesthetic grounds but because of the connection he perceived "between totalitarian habits of thought and the corruption of language."

It is not clear whether Orwell would have glossed this last nominalization as "the fact that language is corrupt" or "by making language corrupt." Nor is it clear whether Orwell realized that abstract deverbal nouns had precisely the propensity to neutralize and thus obfuscate such essential differences – though C. K. Ogden of course knew well enough (as did Bentham before him) and he had tried to instruct Orwell in the philosophy underlying Basic English four years earlier. (It is of some interest to note that the papers of both men are in the library of University College London, a few yards from where Ogden lived and Orwell died.)

What is clear from the attack on Bernal is that Orwell was on the way to conceiving of "Newspeak". This obviously reflects the climate of opinion associated with the "General Semanticists" discussed earlier, and reflects at least as obviously the devices (and even the criticisms) of Basic English. But we note that Orwell is as silent on his debt to Ogden as he was to the Fowlers in his "Politics and the English Language".[1] In fact, Newspeak can be seen as a satire on Basic almost as much as it is on totalitarian propaganda machinery, and it is likely that Orwell never appreciated Ogden's claims (none too plausible, in all conscience) that the severely limited lexicon on which he insisted forced the user to liberate his mind from preconception and vagueness. Newspeak had the converse goal, just as Ogden's critics said that Basic would have the converse effect.

The Orwell conception is savagely Swiftian in its brilliance, and its impact has been understandably devastating. The rapidity with which general currency was given to items like *doublethink* (and *Newspeak* itself) adequately demonstrates the way in which the public imagination was caught, the extent – one might say – to which the public were given the instant conviction that such linguistic engineering was both plausible and deeply sinister.

In fact, of course, the intellectual framework displayed in the principles of Newspeak (Orwell, 1949, Appendix) is very weak and indeed damagingly inconsistent. I am not thinking of the paragraph which purports to explain why "euphony outweighed every consideration" but is soon describing "a gabbling style of speech, at once staccato and monotonous," the words having "harsh sound and a certain wilful ugliness," though this is not untypical of the way Orwell is himself guilty of *doublethink*. It is of a piece with the rigorous control in Newspeak over "exactitude of meaning" when Orwell wishes to stress one aspect of linguistic oppresion; but, in stressing another aspect, he says that words had "the special function . . . not so much to express meanings as to destroy them."

What is more serious is that it is essential to the theory of Newspeak that limiting the number of permissible *words* automatically limits the number of possible *thoughts*. Without saying so, Orwell is thus making the claim that there is no such thing as metaphor: it is enough to say that *rat* refers only to the familiar rodent, and users of Newspeak are apparently *ipso facto* precluded from even the creative possibility of using *rat* to mean people who are as reprehensible as rats. In this, of course, we can accuse Orwell of no more than a naïvely inadequate understanding of language and the human mind. But a couple of pages later we are introduced to a whole series of words which turn out to be *inherently* euphemistic, ironical or metaphorical. Thus *prolefeed* is not what the workers *eat* but what is contemptuously "fed" to them by way of "spurious news."

Neither the fears of the General Semanticists nor the proposals to engineer away the grounds for such fears are thus seriously tested by Orwell.[2] For a later generation, which has seen successfully proscribed a form like *inflammable* in case it be misunderstood as "no danger of burning," and which is digesting such engineered forms as *chairperson* and *Ms*, how much more (or less) intellectually plausible is Anthony Burgess's explicit "reply" to Orwell, *1985*?

Orwell's fictive world of 1984 was dominated by the immediate past: not only the potentiality of propaganda and thought-control that I have discussed, but everything from the sordid austerity and the Crippsian puritanism to the perverted slogans. "Ignorance is Strength" is less a prediction of the future than a nightmare from the past: a Nazi deathcamp proclaiming "Arbeit macht uns frei." Burgess's account is less a rejection of Orwell's judgment than a revaluation based analogously upon the trends and dangers as they are perceived by someone writing thirty years later. It is a different "extended metaphor of apprehension" (Burgess, 1978, p. 51), as had been Huxley's *Brave New World* fifteen or sixteen years earlier. And there are plenty of other examples.

The syndicalist chaos in Tucland the Brave is a more plausible Britain of

1985 than the Airstrip One of *1984*, with its science-fiction efficiency. Bev corresponds to Winston (onomastically too: Beveridge? Bevan? Bevin? "big names when I was born"), but he is faced with a predicament more familiar to us than was that of Winston to the post-war readers of Orwell. And while Worker's English corresponds to Newspeak in having official status, this too is more familiar. As a man both extraordinarily proficient in foreign languages and not unacquainted with linguistic theory (he is sharply unlike Orwell in both respects), Burgess adjusts his vision of "WE" to extrapolations of what his knowledge and observation tell him can actually happen to real languages in real societies. One might say that Worker's English is to Black English as Newspeak is to Basic or one of the other carefully artificial languages engineered in the first half of this century, a point to which I shall return presently.

WE is like Newspeak only in being grossly "simplified," with a grammar and vocabulary reduced so as to "achieve the limitations appropriate to a non-humanistic highly industrialised society" (Burgess, 1978, p. 221). But the "economies" correspond to the lowest common denominators already to be found in the loosest demotic speech: *ain't* combining the role of *isn't* and auxiliary *hasn't* for example: "He ain't there and he ain't been there."[3] Since "WE is not concerned with the abstractions of philosophy or even science", the lexicon can be comfortingly vague, with encouragement of items like *wotsit*, freely supplemented with four-letter intensifiers. Hamlet's "take arms against a sea of troubles, and by opposing end them" is paraphrased in WE as "get stuck into what's getting you worried and get it out of the way and seen off."

So far, in fact, from being a language deliberately engineered with sinisterly scientific care, WE is little more than an application of the principle *communis error facit ius*. It is less a design than an institutionalization of what exists: and Burgess specifically represents it thus: "The primary aim . . . was less the imposition, under political or syndicalist pressure, of the language of the dominant social class on the rest of the community than the adaptation of an existing form of English to the fulfilment of a traditional language planner's aspiration." The horror of Burgess's vision is in fact its precise correspondence to the principles adopted by the least radical (but well attested) form of linguistic engineering: the principles that produced PTH in China and Nynorsk in Norway.

It is noteworthy that most recent "possible worlds" in fiction represent a similar implicit dismissal of the perils of wholly artificial language systems. Esmé Dodderidge's *The New Gulliver* is typical in giving linguistic form only a minor and (as in Burgess) a reactive rather than an ergative role. In her Capovolta, language is not designed to keep men down: it merely reflects woman's supremacy. The generic reference pronoun is feminine ("Everyone must do her duty"); "bitchy" behaviour is not recognised, but "doggy" behaviour is. Language is a natural reflex and not contrived to produce the reflex. The unconscious, unthinking acceptance of such language is thus seen as socially more serious than (to retain the women's lib context) such documents as the 1978 Board of Education Report in Ontario recommending (i.e. deliberately engineering) "an inclusionary language policy," formally proscribing such expressions as *mankind, man in the street,* and *man-made* (to be replaced by *humanity, the average person,* and *synthetic* respectively).

In other words, conscious language engineering like this or the now well-established restricted form of English used internationally in air naviga-tion is no longer as threatening to the artistic imagination as uncontrolled drift or (worse) the active encouragement of populist imprecision. It is natural drift into unthinking shiftlessness that alarms Burgess. Significantly, on the very first page of the novel the point is made that nobody can be held responsible for the obstetric treatment that resulted in Bev's child being moronic: " 'Nobody's fault,' Dr Zazibu had said. 'Medicine must progress, man.' " We are transported back to the savage anger of Charles Dickens at the Circumlocution Office and the irresponsibility of mid-nineteenth-century capitalism: the title *Little Dorrit* was chosen only after Dickens had abandoned *Nobody's Fault.* In consequence, the implication of *1985* is not that we want less language engineering but more: even if it has no greater ambition than to be supportive of those who – like the Fowlers and A. P. Herbert and Robert Graves – pull the forelock of respect for the *mot juste* and for delicacy of linguistic distinctions.

Notes

1. There is an unacknowledged debt also to Lancelot Hogben. In "Politics and the English Language", it happens that he takes Hogben as an outstanding example of one who uses English badly, but his illustrations of Hogben's sloppiness are taken not from the well-known *Mathematics for the Million* but the very little known *Interglossa*. This is an exercise in linguistic engineering that seeks to out-Basic Basic. The ingenious if ill-developed reduc-tionism of *Interglossa* cannot but have contributed to the ideas underlying Newspeak.
2. He is, to be fair, more sophisticated in his observations on what linguists would now call "lexicalization." He argues that the telescoped compounds of Newspeak had the "conscious purpose" of "cutting out most of the associations" that would cling to the component parts, and he illustrates the point from outside Newspeak. Thus in contrast to the full associations invited by "Communist" and "International," *Comintern* "suggests merely a tightly-knit organisation and a well-defined body of doctrine."
3. The satirical solemnity with which such trivialities are mentioned is in sharp contrast to the comparable trivialities in Newspeak: the replacement of *shall* by *will* is not trivial to Orwell for whom this was part of the "correct" and "pure English" ethos he had imbibed and continued to preach in his non-fiction.

References

AARSLEFF, H. (1982) *From Locke to Saussure.* London: Athlone.
BOLINGER, D.L. (1980) *Language – The Loaded Weapon.* London: Longman.
BURGESS, A. (1978) *1985.* London: Hutchinson.
CHASE, S. (1938) *The Tyranny of Words.* London: Phoenix House.
CRICK, B. (1980) *George Orwell: A Life.* London: Secker & Warburg.
DODDERIDGE, E. (1980) *The New Gulliver.* London: J. M. Dent.
HAYAKAWA, S.I. (1941) *Language in Action.* New York: Harcourt, Brace, Jovanovich.
HOGBEN, L. (1943) *Interglossa.* Harmondsworth: Penguin.
KORZYBSKI, A. (1933) *Science and Sanity.* Lakeville, Conn.: Institute of General Semantics.
OGDEN, C.K. (1932) *The Basic Words: A Detailed Study of their Uses.* London: Orthological Institute.
ORWELL, G. (1945) *Animal Farm.* London: Secker & Warburg.

ORWELL, G. (1949) *Nineteen Eighty-Four*. London: Secker & Warburg.
ORWELL, S. and ANGUS, I. (1968) *The Collected Essays, Journalism and Letters of George Orwell*. London: Secker & Warburg.
QUIRK, R. (1982) *Style and Communication in the English Language*. London: Arnold.
QUIRK, R. and GREENBAUM, S. (1973) *A University Grammar of English*. London: Longman.
SIMON, I. (1961) "Saxonism Old and New," *Revue Belge de Phil. et d'Hist.* 39, 687–735.
VON POLENZ, P. (1967) "Sprachpurismus und Nationalsozialismus," B. von Wiese and R. Henss (eds.), *Nationalismus in Germanistik und Dichtung*. Berlin: Erich Schmidt, pp. 79–112.

III: *Attitude and Usage: U.S.A., Britain and Canada*

Introduction

SIDNEY GREENBAUM

THE papers in this section report on, and evaluate, language attitudes in three countries where English is predominantly the mother-tongue. Most of the papers deal with the United States, where the majority of native speakers of English now live. But there are also papers dealing with the situation in the British Isles, which have the second largest concentration of native English speakers, and in Canada, where there are competing influences from American and British varieties of English and where there are conflicting claims by French speakers.

The papers on the United States cover a wide range of topics. Reviewing feature articles and letters from the public in the popular press, John Algeo notes that worry about the correct use of language is focused on vocabulary rather than on grammar, while there seems no concern about good style. James Stalker analyses views on the state of the language expressed by a group of popular writers who maintain that the language is dying; their views represent a traditional anxiety to preserve what was regarded as correct usage in a previous period and an attitude that resists language change. Anne Gere claims that the public is alienated from its language, an alienation reflected in its anxieties about language and in its reliance on popular critics of language. Julia Penelope argues that accusations of language abuse, commonly voiced by popular writers on the English language, are misdirected; she considers the major abusers to be politicians and bureaucrats who use the language to obfuscate and deceive. In his review of elicitation experiments, Edward Finegan shows that unconscious attitudes to speech differences heavily influence our judgment of the character and ability of others, some features of language variation evoking stereotype evaluations. Lester Faigley analyses the views on writing by college-trained employees, concluding that they had a broader conception of good writing than is found in the traditional classroom or popular media.

Attitudes, explicit or implicit, of official bodies are discussed in several papers, which also indicate, where relevant, differences from earlier attitudes,

ET-C*

practices, or policies. Allan Metcalf reports on the guidance on language usage given to journalists by the press style books; as he points out, the 80 million daily newspapers in the United States provide the main reading matter for the country's reading public. John Carroll examines the standards of usage in language tests that are specifically concerned with the testing of English usage; he notes that test constructors are constrained by the realities of the marketplace, since they generally intend their tests to be used nationwide and over a period of several years. Janice Redish discusses the plain English movement that began in the 1970s and has received government support; she reviews the official actions at federal and state level to ensure that documents are intelligible to lay consumers and employers. Harold Allen details the attitudes conveyed by the National Council of Teachers of English through its resolutions, reports, and publications; fierce controversy was aroused, and still continues, over a 1972 resolution adopted by one of the NCTE's constituents that asserted the students' right to their own language, which was widely interpreted as a call to teachers to renounce their duty to teach standard English. Finally, Ofelia García assesses public attitudes and official policies to bilingualism in the United States today within the context of past policies; majority public opinion is opposed to permanent bilingualism, which it considers to be un-American.

The three remaining papers invite comparisons between the situation in the United States and that of the British Isles and Canada. Worries about American economic and cultural influence are reflected in the concern over the intrusions of Americanisms or supposed Americanisms, which are thought to be polluting the native varieties; there is no comparable concern in the United States over Briticisms or Canadianisms. In her review of British attitudes, Janet Whitcut emphasizes the importance attached to differences of accent as well as of dialect in British consciousness. Robert Ilson contrasts a variety of usage problems in British and American English; the differences in prescription are greatest for pronunciation and least for grammar. Ian Pringle's paper highlights the desire of Canadians to assert their linguistic independence from their powerful neighbour. He also outlines the struggle of French Canadians for linguistic independence from the English majority in Canada.

Chapter 1

The Mirror and the Template:
Cloning Public Opinion

JOHN ALGEO

THE interest of the public in language and the attitudes of the public toward linguistic usage are easy to discover in the popular press. Feature articles, columns, and letters from readers all show what aspects of language the reading public is interested in and how the public reacts to those aspects. A newspaper or a news magazine does not print articles that are of no interest to its readers, nor does it voice opinions that are shared by none of its subscribers. Or if it does do so often, it does not continue long to publish. The press is a mirror held up to reflect the face of the public.

The press is also a powerful influence in shaping our lives. It reflects the public's interests and attitudes, but in addition the press is a major force in creating those interests and forming those attitudes. Will Rogers is quoted as having said, "All I know is what I read in the newspapers"; and more recently another entertainer, turned politician, uses newspaper clippings to buttress his domestic policies and cites the *Reader's Digest* as his authority in foreign affairs. What people know and think about language is to a great extent molded by what they read in the popular press. If the press is a mirror, it is also a template, producing multiple reproductions of the views it espouses. It records, but it also creates or, perhaps one should say, clones those views.

Because the press has this dual role of reflecting and forming popular attitudes, what it has to say about language is worth paying attention to. The clippings on which the following observations are based have not been gathered in a systematic fashion, being rather the result of desultory reading and random collection. Nevertheless, they doubtless are typical of what a systematic survey would turn up. The prejudices and interests of the collector inevitably shape a collection, and so it certainly is with the clippings dealt with below. Nevertheless, what they show about popular knowledge of and attitudes toward language is real and is noteworthy, not least as a caution.

It is clear that a sizable portion of the reading public is interested in language, and especially in words: their meaning, their origin, and their correct use. Not all, or even a majority, of the public's attention is focused on correctness and rules of usage. Much of the interest in language is relatively dispassionate. Language is fun. It is surprising. It is worth knowing about.

The origins of words are a perennial subject of interest. A feature story describes Teddy Roosevelt's refusal to shoot a bear cub on the grounds that it would have been unsporting to do so; the story is illustrated by an old political

57

cartoon from the *Washington Post* depicting the President's magnanimity, and it describes the subsequent marketing of toy cubs as *teddy bears* (*Chicago Tribune*, 26 Dec. 1977, pp. 2–5). Many readers of the article probably know that teddy bears are named for the first Roosevelt in the White House, but it is unlikely that they know the events in detail. Such etymological stories fall into the ancient genre of origin tales (for example, stories explaining "How the snake lost its legs" or "How people came to wear clothes").

The etymologized terms are often less familiar ones than *teddy bear*. They may be old-fashioned words like *madstone*, "stone reputed to prevent or cure hydrophobia," or recent additions to the vocabulary like *downsize* (which an AP report attributes to Bernard Shapiro, chief of staff of the joint congressional committee on taxation, in comments about the auto industry's plans to reduce the size of their cars).

Popular etymologizing often involves popular etymologies. Occasionally articles discuss the folk versus the real or unknown origin of a term such as *tinker's damn/dam* or *posh*. But more often the folk etymology is reported as unassailable fact. A reader from Jersey City writes to a syndicated feature, "Glad You Asked That," to inquire about the origin of the phrase *rub the wrong way*. The answer is confidently given that the expression derived from the irritation felt by an Elizabethan lady of the house when her servants polished the floor by rubbing against the grain. No maybes or perhaps about it. Or another reader writes to "Dear Abby" to tell her about the origin of *wop*: "When the Italian immigrants came off the boat, those without papers had signs around their necks with the letters 'WOP,' indicating they were 'without papers.' It was just a way of separating the Italians with papers from those without papers" (*Athens Banner-Herald*, 22 Sept. 1982, p. 17). There is no gainsaying such certainty of misinformation.

Quite apart from their history, rare and unusual words are of popular interest in themselves. *Reader's Digest* readers are assured, "Of Course There's a Word for It" (May 1981, pp. 108–109), the words in question being *aglet, anatomical snuffbox, berm, bollard, calk* (not a misspelling of *caulk*), *cissing, dingbat* (in typography, not as in Archie Bunker's usage), *dottle, duff, flews, harp* (on a lamp), *kerf, kick* (in a wine bottle, not in its contents), *philtrum, pintle, schizocarp, snath, snood* (on a turkey), *tang* (on a knife blade, not as in imitation orange juice), and *zarf*. Books on words, especially unusual ones, like Paul Dickson's *Words* (Delacorte, 1982) or Susan Kelz Sperling's *Poplollies and Bellibones: A Celebration of Lost Words* (Potter/Crown, 1977) get appreciative reviews.

New words, which may be rare and unusual for many readers of the popular press, get their share of attention too. Makers of new-word dictionaries, such as the G. & C. Merriam *6,000 Words* and the several versions of the *Barnhart Dictionary of New English*, are sources for newspaper articles about such neologisms as *cop opera*, "television series about policemen," *soap therapy*, "discussion of soap operas as a technique in psychotherapy," *cybersport*, "electronic games," and *telecopter*, "helicopter equipped with a television camera." A lot of attention goes to the perennially favorite acronym, ranging from such worrisome old standbys as SALT (Strategic Arms Limitation Talks) and MARV (Maneuverable Re-entry Vehicle) to such insouciant newcomers as JLP (Just and Lasting Peace, in the Middle East) and PLK (Plucky Little King, Hussein of Jordan).

Being by their nature more or less new, vogue words come in for a good deal of attention. Some of it is dispassionate curiosity, as in the newspaper article headed "Nation's charities sprint to cash in on the 'thon' fad" in the *Chicago Tribune* (10 July 1978, sec. 2, pp. 1, 4), Chicago being apparently as thonny a town as one is likely to find in these United States. There are *walk-a-thons, bike-a-thons, jog-a-thons, dance-a-thons, teeter-totter-a-thons, Monopoly-a-thons, weight-a-thons, kiss-a-thons*, and more.

However, many observations on vogue words note their existence mainly to disapprove of them. Bureaucratese, psychobabble, weasel words, nukespeak, and the like are targets of journalistic complaint, much of it intensified by the recent foraging of Edwin Newman and his tribe on the fields of voguish vocables. A favorite game is "Chinese Menu," in which the player chooses at random one item from each of three columns of words to produce such with-it concoctions as *non-attitudinal interface modules, socio-economic binary optimization*, or *cross-societal cognant syndromes*, these examples being products of the *non-directional generative matrix* in a column by John Keasler (*Atlanta Journal/Constitution*, 18 Sept. 1982, p. B-2). Readers are seldom perturbed by vogue words, often perhaps not themselves being sufficiently in vogue to be aware of their existence. It is rather the professional writer and reporter who is likely to engage in Hunting the Wild Bromide, as Herbert Gold has termed the sport (*Newsweek*, 5 Feb. 1979, p. 11).

Jargon, kept in its place – that is, out of sight of the Wild Bromide Hunters – is often a fit subject for "human interest" comment in the press. CB lingo (*10-4, good buddy*), gambling jargon (*juice* "bookmaker's commission"), and sports-reporting cliches (*grid classic, fine fettle, roll up a score*) are all worth feature stories from time to time. So is headlinese, typically regarded by the press with the sort of tolerant amusement that one saves for one's own peccadillos. Favorite causes for comment are the ambiguous headline ("LOT OF WOMEN DISTRESSING"), the cute headline ("PRICES SOAR, BUYERS SORE, COW JUMPS OVER THE MOON" for a story on rising meat prices), and the laconic headline ("QUIZ 8 IN AX FEST"), all examples cited by Richard Conniff in the *Smithsonian* (July 1982, p. 140).

However, the jargon of the privileged classes, such as doctors and lawyers, is fair game for complaint. In fact, such professionals are so honored in our society that they may begin to regard themselves with the honor they are accorded in television's prime-time soap operas. Then they seem to fear that to speak in nonmedical or nonlegal style is to appear ordinary, unprivileged, and mortal. Hence the doctor who talks about *cephalalgia* instead of a *headache* and the lawyer who says *forthwith* for *now* deserve the drubbings they get from Lee May and William Safire (*Atlanta Constitution*, 12 Dec. 1979, p. A-5, and 29 July 1977, p. A-5, respectively).

If linguistic pomposity is a cause for journalistic innocent merriment, so is the malapropism and the Gracie-Allenism. Robert L. Steed (*Atlanta Constitution*, 10 Sept. 1982, p. A-5) has commented on "a mute question" and a person who is "very well traveled – a voyeur," as well as on those who "just bit the tip of the iceberg" or who find themselves "up a tree without a canoe."

Other aspects of the vocabulary that evoke interest include trademarks, especially the invention of new ones like *Rondo* (a soft drink), *Baxil* (a detergent), and *Nativa* (a baby food) or the threatened commonization of successful ones like *Monopoly*, *Sanka*, *Kleenex*, *Band-Aid*, *Xerox*, and *Coca-Cola*. Names make good copy, especially unusual personal names, like *Starlight Cauliflower* and *Travalious Martinous Teekarei Campbell*, although the origins of local placenames are also popular. The attention given to words is too diverse to illustrate all its aspects, which include commentary on word play, propaganda, taboo and euphemism, sexism, gobbledegook, and slang.

Newspapers and magazines pay a good deal of attention to dialect variation, Black English, bilingualism, and foreign languages; to gestures and sign language; to writing systems and spelling; to the psychology of language, thinking, intelligence, and animal communication; and to dictionaries and their making. But judging from the abundance of the evidence, usage variation and correctness is a special concern of those who write for the popular press and of those who read it. If America, in Edwin Newman's portentous phrase, is to be the death of English, the cause is more likely to be smothering with attention than neglect.

Comments and questions on usage turn up with some frequency in the "Dear Abby" column of Abigail Van Buren, a reliable guide to the concerns of our fellow citizens. Occasionally readers write to her with linguistic questions. They are sometimes old chestnuts, like whether *I feel bad* or *I feel badly* is correct (characteristically, the questioner thinks the latter "sounds better"). Abby straightens out her correspondent in short order: "In response to 'How do you feel,' the correct response is, 'I feel bad.' (Unless, of course, you feel good.)"

Occasionally the questions are more original. One correspondent has wondered "for years" about the difference in use between *Excuse me* and *Pardon me*. Abby explains that, although "some years ago" the former was used in asking for permission to leave a room and the latter as an apology for a minor breach of etiquette, today they are "interchangeable, unless, of course, you are referring to what Gerald Ford did for Richard Nixon." (Abby's other comment, that *pardon* "sounds a tad more elegant" because of French *pardonnez-moi*, overlooks the equally French *excusez-moi*. Had she been Nancy Mitford, she might have explained instead that both are non-U for *Sorry* – U-speakers never ask to be excused or pardoned, though they may acknowledge a twinge of regret, even if they don't feel it.)

Some letters complain about the language of the correspondent's relatives. The "Caring Mother-in-Law" who moans about the atrocious grammar of her son's new wife (*We seen* and *Him and me went*) is gently advised not to offer grammar lessons. On the other hand, a daughter-in-law writes about her ex-school-teacher mother-in-law, who red-pencils the husband's letters and returns them to him. "LeRoy and I are both college graduates, and we know as much about writing as his mother," complains the wife. "Should we tell her to go jump in the lake?" Abby answers, "If you and LeRoy knew as much about writing as his mother, you would tell her to go jump INTO the lake. If one jumps 'in' the lake, it indicates that he was already in the water before he jumped." In the eternal war between mothers- and daughters-in-law, Abby's sympathies are clear. She may have been a Princess once, but she has all the instincts of a Momma now.

Generally when readers write in to bemoan the state of the language and offer their own bugaboos, Abby's response is appreciative. Thus one beldam avails herself of "Dear Abby" to teach the world that *presently* can only mean "soon, before long" and never "at the present time," for which the correct word is *currently*. Abby's answer is that she bets many readers "who are currently saying 'presently' when they mean 'currently' will be mending their ways presently."

Some of Abby's linguistic advice is gratuitous. When she is asked which is more important for getting ahead in the world, "WHAT you know or WHO you know," Abby can't resist a schoolmarmish quip: "It's neither. It's WHOM you know."

Abby is herself taken to task for solecisms in her column. The editor and publisher of the *Daytona Beach Morning Journal* chides Abby for quoting Emerson as having said "Pay every debt like God wrote the bill" instead of "as if." The sin, in editorial eyes, is not so much misquotation as bad grammar, and Abby is duly penitent.

On the other hand, when another reader scolds her for spelling *insure* when she should have spelt *ensure* ("buy insurance" versus "make sure"), Abby points out that *Webster's New International Dictionary* (the unassailably correct Second Edition, not the permissiveness-purveying Third) lists the words as synonyms. So Abby doesn't always knuckle under. Other readers sometimes defend her, with fervor, if not with common sense. When Abby was charged with having committed a "grammatical error," a champion wrote in to out-sniff her critic by pointing out that he should have written "error in grammar" since there can be no such thing as a "grammatical error." The champion is a self-acknowledged "teacher of English, NOT as some say, 'an English teacher.'" Such high standards of pettifoggery are seldom maintained by today's schoolmarms.

Readers of the popular press do not flood their favorite publications with letters on usage, but there is a steady trickle. One of Ann Lander's correspondents with the signature "In Need of Earmuffs" doesn't see why there is a lot of fuss about a TV commentator saying "Febyooary" when all around us we hear (and doubtless often see) such "non-words and atrocious usage" as "cold slaw," "sherbert," and "realator" (*Atlanta Journal/Constitution*, 30 July 1978, p. F-4). Misspellings, for example *Artic* in a headline, will evoke letters of protest, as will a split infinitive ("to no doubt compare notes"), both of which linguistic sins are linked by one exasperated correspondent to the liberal political bias of the peccant columnist (*Atlanta Constitution*, 2 Mar. 1978, p. A-5).

A favorite bugaboo is *irregardless*, which must vie with *ain't* for a record as the word whose existence is most widely denied. A letter writer to the *Saturday Review* (17 Mar. 1979, p. 6) complains of the former word and of the grammatical construction "Being that it was raining . . ." while complimenting Goodman Ace for a column about grammatical errors: "It has long been my contention that Americans abuse their own language more than any people in the world. There is no excuse! I don't know what the solution is, but I was certainly glad to learn that I am not the only one who notices these blatant mutilations of our tongue." The sentiment is typical of those who write letters to editors about usage, as is the fact that the writer himself inexcusably abuses the language with what some of his fellows would regard as a blatant mutilation, namely, the omission of *other* from "more than any other people in the world."

It is, however, characteristic of usageasters (as Thomas Clark has dubbed the tribe) that each of them has an idiosyncratic little list of offenses and that each is oblivious of most of the offenses on all the other little lists. If, as a usageaster once suggested, all the offenders against such lists should be taken out and hung, any possible survivors would doubtless find the world quite lonesome, as empty of usageasters as of the rest of us.

Goodman Ace is not the only *Saturday Review* columnist to unburden himself of observations on usage. Most professional writers seem to develop the itch from time to time and, perhaps because of the continual need to meet a deadline whether or not they have anything to say, give in to the urge to scratch. Goodman Ace's fellow SRer, Thomas H. Middleton, scratches a lot in his column "Light Refractions." Other nationally known columnists who turn regularly or occasionally to linguistic usage to fill a void are William Safire, James J. Kilpatrick, Sydney Harris, and the Great Pettifogger himself, John Simon. Edwin Newman has come close to making a career of scratching. In addition there are such less known national or regional columnists as Carole Ashkinaze, Celestine Sibley, Leo Aikman, and Jimmy Townsend.

Local writers are happy to join the parade. John Raymond, the Book Review editor for the *Atlanta Journal and Constitution*, also writes a column called "That's Life," which frequently treats matters of usage. Even such a modest small-town newspaper as the *Athens* (Georgia) *Banner-Herald* highlights correctness and usage, which are addressed from time to time by its publisher, Robert Chambers; its executive editor, Hank Johnson; its associate editor, Rick Parham; its city editor, Jon Hunt; its sports editor, Blake Giles; and assorted guest columnists from the university faculty.

The very cartoons of the popular press preach us sermons on usage. One in *The New Yorker* (22 Mar. 1982, p. 161) shows a becoated woman with arms akimbo and luggage packed addressing her husband, who is watching television with his feet on a footstool and his hand around a beer can: "You could care less? Don't you mean you couldn't care less? That kind of crummy English is why I'm leaving."

What are the usage items that are noted, lamented, and corrected in the popular press? A complete list from even a brief observation of a few publications would be too long to print here. The following are typical examples only.

By far the greatest cause of linguistic concern in the popular press is the confusion of homophones (*wreckless/reckless*), of near homophones (*flaunt/*

flout – a *bête noire* of every card-carrying usageaster), of variant forms of the same stem (*healthy/healthful*), and of near synonyms (*podium/lectern*). In the quite unscientific sample on which these remarks are based, 36 percent of the items commented upon as matters of correctness are of this type. A command of the mother-tongue and mastery of its correct use depend, it would seem, to a large extent on the user's ability to distinguish words that are similar in either form or meaning.

To tell similar words apart is no very demanding task, even when the distinctions advocated are unrealistic ones. For example, *pom-pom* is said by one usageaster to be properly used only for a type of cannon, whereas the ball of fibers waved by cheerleaders or the chrysanthemum flower is properly a *pompon*. Such advice ignores the fact that current dictionaries record both forms (unhyphenated) with the second meaning, as well as the fact that *pompom* is the form used overwhelmingly by persons who actually wave the objects at football games and who might be expected to know what they are called.

In general, popular worry is focused on matters of lexis rather than of grammar. Redundant and unnecessary expressions are another cause of significant concern, accounting between them for an additional 35 percent of the items commented upon. Examples of redundant expressions are *completely destroyed*, *most unique*, *true fact*, and *personal opinion*, in which the first words are said to add nothing to the meaning of the second ones. Examples of wholly unnecessary expressions (according to the usageasters) are *basically*, *in other words*, *it goes without saying*, and the currently favorite *you know*.

Another lexical concern is the pronunciation of such words as *defense*, *knew*, and *nuclear*. We are advised to shun the pronunciation "DEEfense," a regionalism that has been popularized by sports announcers. We are also urged to say "nyoo" rather than "noo," although the former is a minority regionalism in the United States, Americans overwhelmingly using the supposedly wrong form, which is part of a general sound change that deleted the *y*-sound after alveolar onsets. For the last word, we are cautioned against "nu-cular," an unetymological and unorthographic pronunciation favored by some presidents of the United States and many members of the Congress, despite the fact that it is said by *Webster's Third* to occur chiefly in substandard speech – two facts that are not necessarily incompatible.

Other lexical questions involve idioms, meanings, and alternative forms of a word. Should one use *predominately* or *predominantly*? The former has been in use since the sixteenth century, and the latter since the seventeenth century although it is certainly now the more common form in edited English. The latter is also the form preferred by the usageaster who raised the question, not because it is more common today, but because it is "right." The mark of the usageaster is that questions of divided usage are settled by appeal to an absolute standard that the usageaster alone knows.

As matters of meaning, we are told not to use *enormity* in the sense "enormousness" and not to say "He had his arm blown off" unless we mean that he ordered the mutilation himself. Idioms like *live audience* (for a television program) are criticized as illogical, since there is no "dead audience," although most persons who hear the expression doubtless understand it to mean that at least some of the laughter and applause accompanying the program was produced by an audience in the filming studio and not all of it dubbed in later.

These lexical questions – pronunciation, alternative forms, meanings, and idioms – account for about 14 percent of the usage items discussed in the popular press. Thus lexical items receive a lion's share of 85 percent of attention, and grammatical items a meager 15 percent. For journalists, columnists, and their readers, language is mainly vocabulary. The greater mysteries of syntax and morphology are reserved for the few.

Among those greater mysteries are the following questions. Should one use the nouns *contact* and *loan* as verbs? Which are the proper past tense forms of *hang* and *sneak*: *hung* or *hanged*, and *snuck* or *sneaked*? May one use a preposition at the end of a sentence or split an infinitive? May one say "I don't think so"? (Of course not – it's illogical for "I think not," answers the usageaster.) Which is the correct pronoun in "It is we/us" and "to my sister and me/I/myself"? Which is the correct verb in "the media is/are"?

Nearly a third of the grammatical usage problems were from one column dealing with the language of reports by police officers. How can one correct "One of the officers called out for the youths to halt three or four times"? What is wrong with "The police handed out stolen property forms"? (The answer is the ambiguous constituent structure of the last noun phrase.) What is wrong with "In firing another shot, Jones was struck by Brown's bullet and killed" when it was Brown that fired the other shot? (This item was cited for the dangling gerund, but its real problem is its evasive passive, used to avoid saying outright that officer Brown killed Jones: "In firing another shot, Brown struck Jones with the bullet and killed him" is unproblematic.)

The American public has a great deal of guidance to correct English, or at least to correct vocabulary, for grammar seems to be regarded as a minor problem and stylish writing to be a thing unheard of. How, with all that guidance, can we have gone so wrong, as we apparently have, judging from the tone of the complaints in the popular press? With such mirrors, why do we not see our linguistic sins more clearly? With such templates, why is our grammatical propriety not better formed?

Perhaps the fact is that Americans enjoy instructing one another, take pleasure in preaching, and find it easier to complain about *irregardless* and occasionally about split infinitives than to deal with the more complex and intransigent problems of government, economics, militarism, intolerance, and crime. Whatever its explanation may be, the attention the popular press gives to questions of linguistic usage is noteworthy both as a reflection of that opinion and as a formative influence on it. It is a phenomenon of our time.

Chapter 2

Language as Symbol in the Death-of-Language Books

JAMES C. STALKER

ALTHOUGH they do not agree with each other on all matters linguistic, there is a group of language critics, including John Simon, Edwin Newman, William Safire, and Richard Mitchell, who express the opinion that the English language is dying. Because their books and articles generally arouse highly emotional responses that are strongly negative or positive, but rarely anything in between, they are obviously touching something deep within us that calls for more than simple dismissal or unconsidered acceptance of their morbid view of language. When we step back and look carefully and objectively at their books that tell us that the English language is on the verge of death, and consider that view in the context of the facts of language change, we find interesting internal inconsistencies and run head-on into conflicts between fact and belief. Most obviously, the use of English by the very people who announce its imminent death would seem to imply that it retains enough vigor and clarity to remain an effective communication medium, and is not so near death as they claim. If the language is so near death, is in such a sad state of disrepair, it would seem reasonable that the decline of English should be chronicled in another language – Latin perhaps, or French, or Russian, some language that has not been destroyed by constant abuse.

But let us allow them a less extreme position, one which holds that the language is not on the verge of death, but is moving toward that verge, a position that the language is being progressively crippled by abuse. Then we should expect some agreement among these writers on changes which they believe handicap the language. But we can find no such agreement. The fact is that surveys of opinions, by these writers and others, contained in standard dictionaries, dictionaries of usage, and other discussions of usage show that the editors, writers, and their sources do not agree on which items should be included, let alone come to a consensus on their acceptability.

If the death-of-language proponents use English to explicate the death of English, cannot agree on what constitutes good or bad change in the language, and all too often ignore or deride objective studies of language usage, then what are they really trying to say? What do they want their readers to take away from the discussion other than the questionable conclusion that English is dying, or at the very least sliding into senility? Most obviously they want to reaffirm our obligation to use language clearly because it is a medium of communication. But the death-of-language writers have another purpose in their writings – to demand correct use of language because it is a symbol that we are not merely human, but rather at an advanced stage of development, and in that capacity language requires reverence, and conscious attention and maintenance. At a different level, they also want to reaffirm that correct language indicates high social status and on a larger scale, a healthy society.

The belief that correct language use indicates high social status is generally quite clear in the death-of-language books, but is not always completely overt. John Simon (1980, p. 12) blames the deterioration of language only on a vague group, the "common man", and believes that because "social classes hardly exist anymore" the only way we can tell the cultured (not to be confused with educated) from the uncultured is through "the language they use" (53). In fact, Simon is not repudiating social class; he is retaining language use as the only defining criterion of high social status and is excluding money and power. Many studies by linguists over the past several years confirm that language does indeed function as one of the criteria for assessing social status, so Simon is right, language does bear this symbolic function. The legitimate arguments on this topic are whether language *should* serve as a symbol of social status, and whether the correctness items listed in usage books are in fact the linguistic features listeners use in making social judgments. These arguments are open to proof from research, but will probably never be settled because they are really arguments about more complex levels of linguistic symbolism and can only be settled after we understand what we are really arguing about.

The death-of-language writers see a clear connection between the health of a society and the quality of the language it uses. Robert Burchfield (1980), chief editor of the Oxford dictionaries, offers one view of this connection. "People think that the language is being corrupted, because they are looking for something that accounts for the falling away of the quality of life in the West. . . . They're looking for an explanation, and what better one than that the language is being misused by other people" (71). When we see a decline in the quality of life, we can explain it simply by pointing to a decline in the quality of some pervasive aspect of society, such as language.

In *Strictly Speaking*, Newman (1974) explains that "the decline in language stems in part from large causes" and that one of those large causes is the greater voice that minorities have won for themselves in determining the course of the society. "People who felt oppressed by society organized to enforce their demands either for the first time or with greater success than ever before – blacks, Indians, Chicanos, women, homosexuals, lesbians, prison inmates, welfare recipients" (22). These people bargained with society over what they wanted out of our society, and in conjunction with the so-called "youth movement" of the sixties and seventies, discredited the established opinions. Newman explains that "The effect was almost beyond measuring, and we still do not know its full extent, but we do know that when age, experience, and position were discredited, there was a wholesale breakdown in the enforcement of rules, and in the rules of language more than most. . . . [C]orrect and relatively conventional language was widely abandoned by those in revolt" because the revolutionaries wished to disassociate themselves from the establishment (24–25). Newman concludes that "language lies to hand not only as a symbol of change but as its instrument" (25). Incorrect language is the cause of undesirable change, and it records changes caused by other forces as well.

John Simon agrees with Newman, and says that language used by a sick part of the culture is a carrier of disease, so will infect other parts of the culture should they adopt the sick language (xvi–xvii). In other words, "Abuse of language . . . leads . . . to a deterioration of moral values and standards of living" (59). This general view, that language determines our way of thinking, is a variation of the Sapir-Whorf hypothesis with the addition of value judgments about which segments of our society are "sick" or "well." Although researchers have shown that language and culture are deeply interrelated, they have not been able to prove or disprove the belief that language causes a change in the culture. Perhaps to the extent that the language a culture uses reflects the concerns of that culture, the things its members talk about, the death-of-language writers are right – language is symbolic of the concerns of the culture. But the step to assuming that language is symbolic of the health of the culture depends entirely on the value-laden assumption that a culture, or a part of a culture, that we do not like cannot have a robust and vigorous language, or conversely, that language that does not follow our rules is bad, so the people who use it are bad as well.

These assumptions derive from yet another level of language symbolism. Ultimately, the language and society argument is not really over your linguistic and social values versus my linguistic and social values, over which variety of English represents the best aspects of our society. The argument is over how language and language use symbolize our essential humanness, or more precisely, which kind of language and which language use separate us most clearly from the baser animal world and, more important, from our own baser selves. In discussing our primitive versus our rational selves, C. G. Jung, with his theories of the dialectic of the conscious and unconscious halves of the human psyche, is an enlightening person to consult. In *Symbols of Transformation*, Jung (1976) expresses the opinion that "speech and fire-making represent primitive man's victory over his brutish unconsciousness and subsequently became powerful magical devices for overcoming the ever-present 'daemonic' forces lurking in the unconscious" (169). Apart from whether the death-of-language writers would accept Jung's version of the unconscious, it is clear in their writings that the death-of-language writers agree with Jung that language is what makes us human. For Richard Mitchell (1979), "Language is the medium in which we are conscious. The speechless beasts are aware, but they are not conscious" (5). Jung also says that the use of language requires "attention, concentration, and inner discipline, thereby facilitating a further development of consciousness" (169). And again the death-of-language adherents agree that careful, considered use of language leads not only to clarity, but also to improvement in our thinking, thus by implication to a state more clearly, and upwardly, distant from our subhuman ancestry. Mitchell (1979) puts it this way:

For most of us, the rudimentary skills of language we all have even before we go to school are to intelligent discourse what "Chopsticks" is to music. The aim of education is to make those rudimentary skills into the medium of thought.

The possession of language, like the fact of birth, makes us human beings. Neither the language nor the birth is by itself enough to make us civilized human beings (214–215).

On these points, I think we could agree with both Jung and the death-of-language writers. But all we have agreed on is that we must be responsible users of the language; we must do our best to nurture the communicative efficiency of speech, of language. We have not agreed that the language must fit a particular form.

The insistence of the death-of-language writers on a particular form of language, on a language defined by specific correctness rules, in the face of a great deal of evidence (Creswell, Fries, Leonard, Meyers, Roberts, Ryan) questioning the accuracy or utility of those rules, suggests that for them correctness serves some other purpose than insuring clarity and further development of the human consciousness, and often this other purpose is given as manners or elegance. Consider this quotation from *Paradigms Lost.*

> Bad grammar is rather like bad manners; someone picking his nose at a party will still be recognized as a minimal human being and not a literal four-footed pig; but there are cases where the minimal is not enough (111).

Bad manners, hence bad grammar, are equivalent to being minimally human, only slightly higher on the evolutionary scale than a pig, that symbol of the completely uncouth and unacceptable in our nature which constantly threatens to escape from control. And throughout the death-of-language canon we find the enduring theme that if we do not follow the traditional rules of language use, and do not decide which feature list defines correct language, we will, finally, be reduced to a subhuman state where our only language will be "vague grunts, y'knows and other whatchamacallitis" (Stone, 102). Jung gives us this insight into the manners and elegance argument. "Incorrect performance and use of the rite [in this case, speech] cause a . . . regression which threatens to reproduce the earlier, instinctual, and unconscious state" (168). Or as Simon puts it, if we do not use *between you and me* instead of *between you and I* "there will soon be no more communication between you and me" (21). A loss of distinction between *fulsome* and *full* is a step toward chaos (101). That is, for the death-of-language writers, following traditional rules is the correct performance that insures that we will not lose our civilized society or our advanced state of humanity.

It would seem possible to define the correct performance and use of language as clear and appropriate use, and of course this is one of the classic definitions of standard English, the one often labeled "permissive" or "anything goes." Under this definition, as long as we attempt to exploit the resources of our language to the fullest to insure clarity of communication, and to multiply its resources, we are engaging in the correct performance of the ritual of language use and "thereby facilitating a further development of consciousness" as well as insuring the maintenance of our civilized state.

But for the death-of-language camp, clear and appropriate communication is obviously not enough. In *Paradigms Lost*, Simon asks why we must follow rules of usage if the meaning is clear. His first answer is to deny the assumption and to say that usage aids clarity, seemingly assuming that not following a usage rule inevitably causes loss of clarity. But in discussing an example from Anthony Burgess to support his position, Simon writes, "the ambiguous, and thus objectionable, construction does not quite obscure the meaning" (100). Such a statement undermines his assumption that incorrect usage inevitably leads to ambiguity, and raises the obvious question, "Why must we abide by a formal usage rule if it does not clarify the meaning?" Jung specifies that in a ritual performance, "the rules of the ritual must be scrupulously observed if it is to have its intended magical effect" (168). Defining the "rules of the ritual" as a set of correctness rules enables us to determine relatively easily whether the language in use is "scrupulously observing" those rules. Clarity and appropriateness are much more difficult "rules" to pin down than pronoun case or word distinctions. Thus, in order to use the ritual of language to reaffirm and develop our consciousness, our humanity, in order for the ritual to have its magical effect, we must, according to the death-of-language writers scrupulously abide by given formalized rules, because following the rules is a correct ritual demonstration that we are civilized humans who are further removed from our emotional, instinctual, less human selves than people who do not follow the rules.

When we recognize that all language use is fundamentally a symbolic representation of our humanity and that the argument focuses on which kind of language use is correct performance of the ritual, we can begin to see that the death-of-language writers are self-ordained priests who define and interpret the rules of ritual language use for us. As priests they determine who has the right to partake of the gift of language and who does not. Simon, as usual, puts it eloquently.

> Language, I think, belongs to two groups only; gifted individuals everywhere, who use it imaginatively; and the fellowship of men and women, wherever they are, who without being particularly inventive, nevertheless endeavor to speak and write correctly. Language, however, does not belong to the illiterate or to bodies of people forming tendentious and propagandistic interest groups, determined to use it for what they (usually mistakenly) believe to be their advantage (24).

On the face of it, language belongs to whoever has it and is using it; so it is clear that Simon is not talking about who can speak or write; he is talking about language as a symbol of high human attainment. "Correct" language serves to mark those who satisfy Simon's criterion, adherence to a formalized system of usage rules, as more than "minimally human." The others, those to whom language does not belong, those who ignore his rules, are non-human, or at best minimally human, because they are engaged in incorrect performance of the ritual.

We must consider, at least in passing, the validity of assessing the basic intent of the death-of-language writers with a depth psychology system. Are we giving them more credence than they deserve, that is, are we attacking a mouse with an elephant gun? From a linguist's perspective, the death-of-language writers too often either disregard or are ignorant of objective studies of language change and language use, so their opinions are uninformed, thus trivial, and consequently easily dismissed. However, today's death-of-language writers continue a tradition that has been active in England and America for at least 300 years, and stretches back even further in other European languages. In other words, these contemporary writers espouse a view of language that cumulatively is elephantine in size, and although it is relatively easy to demonstrate that their major tenet, that language is dying, is patently false, such demonstrations have never stilled their pens nor decreased the numbers of their agreeing readers. Thus the triviality of their position is only apparent; they must be striking some deeper concern of the human psyche than surface language form.

We can also ask whether these writers really believe that language is dying and that abiding by correctness rules is the only curative. Perhaps they simply display opinions that they know will sell their columns and books, but do not themselves believe what they write. Even if they were opportunistic hucksters peddling a product they knew to be shoddy but saleable, we would need to consider why the product is so saleable. In short, it makes no difference whether they believe what they write because so many readers do believe the view is valid. Sincere or not, they embody a view of language that has been continuous and pervasive in Western European language discussions for many, many years, but the reasons for the longevity of the view have never been satisfactorily explained. Given the objective data on language change, there is no reason to even entertain the notion that language is dying. Given the data on language use, we must recognize that language is not always used well, but that seems only to justify better education in language use, not deep concern about its viability. Even though the death-of-language viewpoint is often trivial and uninformed, and even if the death-of-language spokesmen do not really believe what they write, their works embody a very serious human concern which is symbolically realized through language form and use.

The conclusion which we must advance based on this brief Jungian analysis is that when we are writing or talking we are engaged in a fundamental symbolic ritual that marks us as human, and we are aware, albeit unconsciously, that language production *is* a ritual act, and furthermore that the ritual must be performed correctly. The conflict between the death-of-language writers and those who oppose them stems in part from a disagreement over the definition of "perform correctly," not over whether we should perform correctly. Both recognize the importance of the correct performance of the ritual. That conflict alone generates a fair amount of heat, but the greater conflict arises from the dual function of language – it both maintains and develops consciousness. With their focus on a relatively rigid view of correct performance, the death-of-language writers stress the maintenance function of the ritual, while other groups who focus on a more dynamic definition of correct performance stress the development function. In any case, argument about correct performance will inevitably be charged with high emotion because it awakens us to the history of our language as a "powerful magical device."

References

BURCHFIELD, ROBERT (1980) "The English language is changing, not going rotten." *U.S. News & World Report*, 15 Dec 1980, pp. 71–72.

CRESWELL, THOMAS J. (1975) *Usage in Dictionaries and Dictionaries of Usage*. Publication of the American Dialect Society, Nos. 63–64. University, Alabama: University of Alabama Press.

FRIES, CHARLES C. (1940) *American English Grammar: The Grammatical Structure of Present-day American English with Especial Reference to Social Difference or Class Dialects*. New York: Appleton-Century-Croft.

JUNG, C.G. (1976) *Symbols of Transformation*, trans. R. F. C. Hull. Bollingen Series. Princeton, N.J.: Princeton University Press.

LEONARD, STERLING A. (1932) *Current English Usage*. English Monograph No. 1. Chicago: National Council of Teachers of English,

MEYERS, WALTER E. (1972) "A study of usage items based on an examination of the Brown Corpus." *College Composition and Communication*, **23**, 155–169.

MITCHELL, RICHARD (1979) *Less than Words Can Say*. Boston: Little, Brown & Company.

NEWMAN, EDWIN (1974) *Strictly Speaking*. New York: Warner Books.

ROBERTS, PAUL (1952) "Pronominal *this*: a quantitative analysis." *American Speech*, **27**, 170–178.

RYAN, WILLIAM (1969) "Where has all the usage gone?" *American Speech*, **44**, 129–134.

SAFIRE, WILLIAM (1980) *On Language*. New York: Times Books.

SIMON, JOHN (1980) *Paradigms Lost*. New York: Clarkson N. Potter, Inc./Publishers,

STONE, MARVIN (1979) "Due dismay about our language." *U.S. News & World Report*, 23 April 1979, p. 102.

Chapter 3

Public Opinion and Language

ANNE RUGGLES GERE

ANYONE who has a telephone is aware of public opinion polls. Just as the family gathers around the dinner table the phone rings, and someone from Houston wants to take a few moments to ask about household cheese preferences. Twenty minutes later, after being asked to complete advertising jingles, make discriminations between competing brands, explain buying patterns, and supply information about family income, race and education, the unfortunate person who said "I'll get it" returns to cold lasagna. Or the telephone beckons the gardener to race, dropping the trowel behind a bush where it will remain until fall, tripping over the garden hose and nearly breaking an ankle, against one, two, three, four rings in order to answer the question: "If the election were held today would you vote for John Glenn or Walter Mondale?" Meals, work, sleep, coherent thoughts, and love-making of citizens in this country are interrupted by pollsters calling to inquire about voting preferences, consumer products, and public issues.

Citizens who supply information to public-opinion polls might well ask what lies behind these intrusions into private life. One answer is that it is big business in this country to find out what people think about candidates, brands of beer or public housing. A number of large corporations exist to supply information about public opinion to political parties, corporations, and others whose decisions are shaped by what the public thinks. George Gallup and Louis Harris have been joined by similar groups whose primary function is to find out what people think. Through carefully developed sampling techniques, public-opinion pollsters can, for a price, help you identify a market for your product, assess your chances of winning an election, or tell you what percentage of the population approves of the word "hopefully."

Although public opinion polls are relatively new in our society (the early ones got their start shortly after World War II), they wield considerable power and are likely to become even more influential as special interest groups play a larger part in national events. The importance of public opinion polls was particularly apparent in the 1980 presidential election to those of us who live on the West Coast. As I drove to vote I learned that Carter had already conceded the election because, even though returns were not complete in many states, the predictive power of public polls was precise enough to assure his defeat. It didn't matter that I and thousands like me had not voted yet; the pollsters were in charge of the election.

In 1981 Sidney Blumenthal claimed that activities in the Reagan White

House were directed by pollsters also.[1] Richard Beal, a pollster, *not* a speech writer, had a major role in writing the State of the Union Message. Beal's power with the president stemmed from his ability to quantify public views on given issues. According to Blumenthal, "Ronald Reagan is governing America by a new strategic doctrine – the permanent campaign. He is applying in the White House the techniques he employed in getting there" (p. 43). Reagan's aides – Deaver, Meese, and Baker – depended heavily upon "communications specialists" such as Richard Wirthlin, head of Decision Making Information; Richard Beal who assessed polls by Louis Harris, George Gallup, and other pollsters; and Robert Teeter, head of Market Opinion Research. Blumenthal asserted: "Unlike the old politicos who talked of party bosses delivering the goods and mobilizing the party faithful, Reagan's men converse about 'open windows' (the relative openness of public opinion to Presidential initiatives), 'targets of opportunity' (events or issues that can be quickly taken advantage of), 'sequencing' (the timing and order of a series of actions), [and] 'resistance ratios' (the degree to which the public accepts Reagan and what he is doing)" (p. 43).

If telephone inquiries are any indication, businesses emulate national government in allowing public opinion to shape policies. Public opinion, then, has considerable influence in many areas of our society. One area, however, where public opinion has little influence is language. No one calls to ask what people think about "hopefully." It is not that opinions about language are absent in our society; they are ever-present. Television talk shows, magazine articles, and books all contain opinions on language, but they are not opinions of the general population.

The whimsical columnist Russell Baker has described commentators on language as the English Mafia, a Mafia dominated by three families. The heads of these families, according to Baker, are "Edwin (Dry Laugh Eddie) Newman, William (The Funster Punster) Safire, and John (The Enforcer) Simon,"[2] and they have divided language into three areas. Newman terrorizes writers who commit tautology, redundancy, and ambiguity; Safire admits or rejects words into accepted usage and punishes those who deviate from his selections; and Simon polices English grammar where he raises "brutal welts on the egos of fast-buck writers who try to palm off a bogus 'which' instead of an officially certified 'that' when introducing the reader to a restrictive clause."[2] Baker notes that the big three are not alone in the English Mafia because many other arbiters of language are trying to muscle their way into the lucrative territory of publishing and television appearances.

Baker's humor, as usual, contains more than a grain of truth, for it is the powerful and influential, not the common person, whose opinion on language is offered to the public. Consider, for example, the usage panel of the *American Heritage Dictionary*. Opinions of this panel provide ratings of questionable words included in the dictionary. For example, the word "finalize" is accompanied by the information that 90 percent of the panel oppose it while 10 percent favor it. "Insignias," on the other hand, is acceptable to 56 percent of the panel. This summary of opinion is designed to provide guidance to dictionary users uncertain about language. However, panel members are not drawn from the general public.

Typical of the 136 individuals on the usage panel are Isaac Asimov, Theodore Bernstein, William F. Buckley, Jr., Walter Kerr, Margaret Mead, Katherine Ann Porter, Stewart Udall, Mark Van Doren, and William Zinsser. While many panel members polled for this dictionary may have credibility as arbiters of language, none of them can be described as members of the general public. The prominence which brought them to Houghton Mifflin's attention disqualified them from the ranks of average citizens. The usage advice in the *American Heritage Dictionary* may be based on a poll, but it is not a poll which would receive approbation from Louis Harris. Professional pollsters know better than to base their predictions on opinions of prominent people alone.

Even professionals in language study tend to rely on opinions of exceptional rather than ordinary people. For instance, in 1938 Sterling Leonard developed a list of 230 items containing usages such as "Do it like he tells you," "We will try and get it," and "It was good and cold." Leonard submitted this list, not to the general public but to linguists, asking them to rank the items as established, disputable, or uncultivated. More recently, W. H. Mittins *et al.* produced an inventory of language usage and sought professional responses to it.[3]

This line of research has been extended in recent years to investigate responses of employers and teachers to items of usage. Edward Anderson, for example, played tapes of interviews with speakers of standard and non-standard English and asked employers to indicate whether or not they would hire the speakers whose speech they heard.[4] Maxine Hairston submitted a 67-item questionnaire containing usages such as "A person who knows french and german will get along well in Switzerland" and "Our companys record is exceptional" to eighty-four professionals whose occupations included attorney, physician, business executive, and engineer. Implicit in Hairston's results is the fact that the individuals in this group, many with hiring capacities, would be reluctant to employ or promote someone who used questionable usages.[5] Researchers such as Orlando Taylor, Frederick Williams, and Bruce Fraser measured teachers' responses to statements about Black English, to children's speech samples and videotapes of speakers, and to adult speakers from six dialect groups.[6] These studies revealed that while teachers claim to value variation in language they assume stereotyped attitudes toward the language of identifiable ethnic groups.

The common feature in all these studies is their attention to the more powerful people in society; the employers, not the employees, and the teachers, not the students, were the ones consulted. Although the motives and results were different from the work of the English Mafia or the *American Heritage Dictionary* usage panel, these studies cannot be described as sampling the opinions of the general public. Where language is concerned, then, public opinion, the response of men and women representing all areas of our society, has not been given attention. Ours is a culture which seeks public opinion on issues ranging from whether a woman should be nominated to the Supreme Court to whether liquid soap is preferable to bars of soap, but does not want to know what people think about their language.

I have taken this long to report that there are no public-opinion polls because I think some serious implications radiate from this fact. All of these implications center on the issue of alienation from language. Our culture values people's opinions on politics, consumer goods, and many other issues, but on questions of language only the views of "experts" count. Accordingly, many people feel their language is alien from them.

An experience common to most English teachers provides anecdotal verification of our population's alienation from language. When English teachers tell new acquaintances what they do for a living, the response is often "Oh, I'd better watch my grammar," or "Oh dear, now you'll start correcting what I say," or – worse still – an abrupt end to the conversation as the person, who has come to associate English teachers with an incomprehensible standard of correctness, moves away. Implicit in this scenario is the view that language is "other," that it is something to guard against rather than participate in.

A similar form of alienation from language appears in the telephone calls received by many college English departments. My department, for example, has never advertised language consulting to the general public, but a number of calls come in each month. These calls, from people of all ages and positions, seek precise answers to questions of usage, punctuation, and spelling. I have taken my share of these calls over the years, and what impresses me in these conversations is not the substance but the manner. Most of the callers describe their dilemma in clinical terms as if to create as much distance as possible between themselves and the language in question. I thought I was imagining some of this until I read of a grammar hotline instituted in another college English department. The directors reported that many of their callers "betray an anxiety whose intensity is another of the surprises we have puzzled over . . ." and they say they "pause a bit when someone calls [Illinois] from Michigan to ask a spelling or a word usage that would be readily available in an abridged dictionary."[7] Although the authors see no relationship between callers' anxiety and failure to answer relatively simply questions for themselves, I think both characterize people who feel alienated from their language. This sense of alienation from language makes them simultaneously anxious and unwilling and/or unable to take action on their own behalf.

More empirical validation of the alienation theory is offered by the work of William Labov. Labov, whose work provides an exception to the general rule of relying on "expert" opinion, has investigated public opinion on language among distinct populations. On Martha's Vineyard, Labov looked at relationships between attitudes and language and found striking differences between natives remaining on the island and outsiders or those who left the island. In New York City, Labov and his associates asked informants to respond to taped selections of speech and explain how they felt about their own speech and the speech of others. Labov's methodology is noteworthy because it introduced sociological techniques; working people from the Lower East Side of Manhattan provided responses for the New York study, and they were carefully categorized according to occupation, education, and income. This approach comes close to the methods of public-opinion pollsters even though the sample is not broad enough to be representative of the whole nation. Labov's findings are even more noteworthy because they suggest considerable linguistic alienation among ordinary people. One of the things Labov found in the New York study was a difference between the way people speak and the way they feel they should speak. For example, informants stated that the initial [th] should be pronounced [θ] but often produced an [d] in words such as "thing" and "then." In his examination of subjective views of language, Labov found considerable linguistic insecurity; those interviewed claimed not to like their own language. Labov writes: "The term 'linguistic self-hatred' is not too extreme to apply to the situation which emerges from the interviews." I contend that this linguistic self-hatred is a symptom of a general alienation from language which afflicts much of our population.

Perhaps the most compelling and pervasive evidence of the general public's alienation from language manifests itself in public response to what Russell Baker calls the English Mafia, the "experts" who publicize their opinions on language. A characteristic form employed by the English Mafia is exhortation. Exhortation is a rhetorical form which deals in description rather than argument, it relies primarily on style, and it makes extensive use of the verb "be". Here is an example of Newman's descriptive style: "The Anglican Digest, reporting on the death of the Bishop of Western North Carolina, notes that he had been consecrated in 1948 and priested in 1936. I wonder when he was postulated and noviced."[9] William Safire relies on "is" as he describes language which offends him: "Again, union terminology is in the air: With unionized air carriers, the term 'customer-service representative' is usually applied to people who provide special services on the ground like writing tickets or meeting mean little kids. . . . "[10] John Simon exhorts his audience to adhere to nineteenth-century standards: "Ignorant, unnecessary change, producing linguistic leveling and flatness, could be stopped in its tracks by concerted effort. The fact that this has not often happened in the past is no excuse for the present. We have acquired a set of fine, useful, previously unavailable tools, culminating in the Oxford English Dictionary and a number of excellent treatises and handbooks on grammar. While, that is, grammar was still concerned with form, not transformation; 'transformational grammar' as the new trend calls itself, is indeed one of the aberrations of the academic bureaucracy."[11]

As these excerpts demonstrate, the English Mafia concerns itself with describing rather than making a coherent argument about language; it focuses on examples of language from the present rather than past or future; and, as Newman's "postulated and noviced," Safire's definition of special services on the ground, and Simon's play with the term "transformational grammar" show, the English Mafia relies heavily on style. It is exhortation, then, which the general public in this country responds to so favorably, buying books written by the English Mafia, purchasing magazines which contain their articles, and watching them on television.

The general public's alienation from language accounts for the popularity of exhortation by the English Mafia, and rhetoricians provide an explanation of how the state of alienation creates a hospitable climate for exhortation. Rhetorician Kenneth Burke, for example, has analyzed Hitler's successful unification of the German people against the common "Jewish Devil" as an example of identification between speaker and audience through exhortation. When people lack a common world view or a frame of reference they can be described as alienated, and the state of alienation makes them particularly vulnerable to exhortation. Burke explains this in terms of the German people: "Hitler was not offering people a rival world view; rather he was offering a world view to people who had no other to pit against it."[12] Burke's point is that Hitler's audience was sufficiently alienated from the social structure to accept exhortation about Jewish people, and I argue that much of our society is alienated from its own language, alienated enough to accept the exhortations of the English Mafia.

The English Mafia succeeds not because of its wit or wisdom or impeccable credentials, but because most people in this country feel estranged from their own language. When William Safire mocks the language of the airlines or when John Simon decries linguistic change, few people muster a competing viewpoint because they have no common view based on their sense of owning their language. Indeed, the proclamations of the English Mafia are welcome to many people because these pronouncements offer the false hope that there may be a common view after all. Like Hitler, the English Mafia offers a world view to people who have no other.

One of the more alarming consequences of public alienation from language is the public use of language to obfuscate and deceive. Annually, groups such as the NCTE's Committee on Public Doublespeak find no shortage of politicians and advertisers and other public figures who use language in dishonest ways. This is a society where the neutron bomb can be called an "anti-personnel weapon" and napalm can be referred to as "selective ordnance," and few people will ask questions. Likewise, advertisers can make vague and misleading claims about their products, and few people raise an objection. If people felt language belonged to them, if the sense of alienation were removed, the need for groups such as the Committee on Public Doublespeak would diminish because people would insist that *their* language be used with integrity and honesty.

In his book *Language – The Loaded Weapon* (New York: Longman, 1980), Dwight Bolinger makes a similar claim, arguing that the way to remove language pollution is to talk about language itself. Bolinger urges that public ownership of language be asserted, that everyone take possession of our common symbolic system rather than leaving it to minority control. Bolinger speaks of the media, specifically, as the minority which has the monopoly on language, but I would add to the list self-styled and actual experts to whom the general public assigns responsibility for language, groups such as the English Mafia and teachers of English. Bolinger closes his book with this admonition:

> To make a beginning, language must take its place alongside diet, traffic safety, and the cost of living as something that everyone thinks about and talks about. "Tell me how much a nation knows about its own language," writes John Ciardi, "and I will tell you how much that nation cares about its own identity" (p. 188).

Bolinger's plea that people accept language as their own is not a new one. In 1755 Samuel Johnson urged that people note language changes around them and "make some struggles for our language."[13] Through the years various other students of language have taken essentially the same position, so

Bolinger's statement does not differ in kind from many which have preceded it. However, it does differ in degree because the extent of language abuse is much greater today than in previous generations. The growth of the media in recent decades has exacerbated the problem of equal access to public language beyond anything Johnson or even someone living at the beginning of this century could have imagined.

There are, of course, no easy ways to decrease the general public's feeling of alienation from language. The process of changing attitudes is slow and complex, but all who care about language can play a part. English teachers can work to restore language to their students, and all of us can help give language a more prominent place in place consciousness. We can encourage discussions of language. We can hold courts, officials, businesses, and one another accountable for what we say and how we say it. We can show that language is no one's personal domain, that it belongs to everyone.

Perhaps one of the most effective ways to convince the general public that it shares ownership in our common language is to go directly to that public with questions. The expertise of public-opinion pollsters could turn to questions of language as easily as it accommodates questions of gun control or spirituality. Just as pollsters on spirituality do not instruct their informants that they should or should not be born again, so pollsters on questions of language would seek information rather than give it. Imagine the scenario: Telephones ring in homes of average citizens across the country, and the voice on the other end says "May I have a few minutes of you time? I'd like to ask you a few questions about language. Do you prefer the term 'daylight saving time' or 'daylight savings time'? How do you respond to the use of 'contact' as a verb, as in 'I will contact you next week'?"

Notes

1. Sidney Blumenthal, "Marketing the President," *The New York Times Magazine*, 13 Sept.1981, pp. 42–45.
2. Russell Baker, "The English Mafia," *The New York Times Magazine*, 26 Apr. 1981, p. 29.
3. See Sterling Leonard, "Current usage in grammar," originally published in Albert H. Marckwardt and Fred G. Walcott, *Facts about Current English Usage*, New York: Appleton-Century, 1938, and W. H. Mittins, M. Salu, M. Edminson, and S. Coyne, *Attitudes to English Usage*. London: Oxford University Press, 1970.
   Copies of these surveys are reproduced in Anne Ruggles Gere and Eugene Smith, *Attitudes, Language and Change*. Urbana, IL: NCTE, 1979.
4. Edward Anderson, "Language and success." *College English*, **43** (Dec. 1981), pp. 807–817.
5. Maxine Hairston, "Not all errors are created equal: Nonacademic readers in the professions respond to lapses in usage." *College English*, **43** (Dec. 1981), pp. 794–806.
6. See Orlando J. Taylor, "Teachers' attitudes toward Black and Nonstandard English as measured by the Language Attitude Scale," pp. 174–201; Frederick Williams, "Some research notes on dialect attitudes and stereotypes"; and Bruce Fraser, "Some 'unexpected' reactions to various American-English dialects," all in *Language Attitudes: Current Trends and Prospects*, Roger W. Shuy and Ralph Fasold (eds.), Washington, D.C.: Georgetown University Press, 1973.
7. Janice Neuleib and Maurice Scharton, "Grammar hotline," *College English*, **44** (Apr. 1982), pp. 413–416.
8. William D. Labov, *The Social Stratification of English in New York*, Washington, D.C.: Center for Applied Linguistics, 1966, p. 239.

9. Edwin Newman, *Strictly Speaking*, Indianapolis: Bobbs Merrill, 1974, p. 39.
10. William Safire, "On language." *The New York Times Magazine*, 4 Oct. 1981, p. 10.
11. Quoted in Jim Quinn, *American Tongue and Cheek*, New York: Pantheon Books, 1980, p. 32.
12. Kenneth Burke, "The rhetoric of Hitler's battle", *The Philosophy of Literary Form*, New York: Random House, 1937, p. 187.
13. Samuel Johnson, *Dictionary of the English Language*, London, 1755, reprinted in Diane Bornstein, *Readings in the Theory of Grammar*, Cambridge, MA: Winthrop Publishers, 1976, p. 33.

Chapter 4

Users and Abusers:
On the Death of English

JULIA PENELOPE

ON ANY given day of any year, I can pick up my local newspaper and, predictably, find yet another syndicated columnist bemoaning "abuses" of the English language and its imminent degeneration. If I'm seriously interested in exposing myself to nonsense about our language, I can go to my local bookstore and peruse John Simon's nostalgic *Paradigms Lost* or Edwin Newman's suave *A Civil Tongue*. My expectations will not be disappointed, and for that I am properly grateful. From these writers and others I will hear that the English language is being "abused," as though language were a sentient being, a woman or a child, or a static, concrete object, purposely constructed for some uses but not for others. Language has many uses: communication (sometimes), discommunication (lying, obfuscation, diversion), the creation of certain kinds of art, the expression of feelings, the description of perceptions. To assert, as many do, that putative "errors," or suggested changes, or nonsensical or garbled utterances constitute "abuses" of language is, I think, to misconstrue the issues in such a way that only some approaches appear to be feasible. That is, if we think of some uses or changes in the language as "abusive," we will then endeavor to stop the people we believe to be responsible from continuing such usage; if we describe language as though it were a human being in need of protection, we will believe that defending the language from other people is a reasonable behavior to engage in. Our descriptions of language both define and limit the ways in which we perceive uses of language. If we believe that there are "abuses" of language, it is possible to define other people as the "enemies" of language, and ourselves as the "protectors" of language. Having adopted such a metaphorical approach to language, it is but a small step to elevating our own views and seeing ourselves as noble, courageous, and involved in a battle against evil people who seek only the destruction of "our" language. The result is war, and what might have been reasoned argument degenerates into a test of verbal brutality.

If we are to understand the reigning confusion surrounding English usage, we must first reveal some of the conceptual, social, and political structures that make talk about linguistic "abuses" sound reasonable. In this article I will discuss and illustrate one of the major metaphorical concepts we use to think about English, LANGUAGE IS A WOMAN, and the ways in which it supports the chivalric view of English as a victim in need of protection. I will argue that many of those who see themselves as masters and protectors of

English are guilty of using the language deceptively to promote their own interests and prejudices. Elitism, the need to see oneself as superior to other human beings, which has various manifestations, among them sexism, racism, classism, and ageism, promotes prescriptivism, the idea that language use can and should be dictated by putative "masters" of it. I will show that those who accuse other speakers and writers of "sloppy" thinking and criminal abuses of language are among the least responsible users of the resources of English. Doublespeak, the linguistic manifestation of doublethink, is being used to trivialize and ridicule the claims of other speakers of the language. If we are concerned about working to promote better ways of communicating with each other, I think we must begin by confronting the fact that it is the powerful, not the powerless, who are responsible for the discommunicative uses of English that are proliferating.

Language is a woman

As both Schön (1979) and Reddy (1979) have argued, the metaphorical constructs we use to frame our analyses of problems determine, and thereby limit, our understanding of those problems, As Lakoff and Johnson (1980) have observed, the metaphors we select have a dual effect on our perceptions: they foreground some of the aspects of an event but simultaneously hide other features or variables that may be equally significant. The two metaphorical concepts that underlie claims about linguistic "abuses" are: LANGUAGE IS A TOOL and LANGUAGE IS A WOMAN. The LANGUAGE IS A TOOL metaphor, for example, defines language as an inanimate, made object, like a knife or a shovel, for which some uses are appropriate and others are inappropriate. The metaphor highlights the assumption that language is an object that people use, while it downplays other features of language, e.g. language is not concrete or tangible, it is abstract and intangible; language does not have a predetermined shape or form, it is constantly changing. The metaphor enables us to ignore some aspects of language, and to focus on other aspects that may or may not be helpful to our thinking about language.

The metaphorical concept LANGUAGE IS A WOMAN is similar to the LANGUAGE IS A TOOL metaphor insofar as it enables us to objectify language, to treat it as something outside of us, but it also structures our thinking about language as a human behavior in a variety of ways. Equating language with female human beings transfers specific cultural attitudes toward women to language. Thus, for example, we come to think of language as an object, as helpless, as a victim, as something preyed upon, as having, at some point, a phase in which it is "pure." Who among us, for example, would hesitate to speak metaphorically of the "mother-tongue"? It seems "fitting" to many people because male grammarians have regarded language as their *property*, an object uniquely their possession to govern and "protect" since the seventeenth century. As Uriel Weinreich (1971) pointed out, linguists have failed to account for the fact that "reference (especially by men) to lovingly handled objects by means of *she*" is a productive process in English. Morris Bishop (1982), for example, closes his prefatory essay in the *American Heritage*

Dictionary by saying, "Let us then try to make good choices, and guard and praise our lovely language and try to be worthy of her" (p. 21).

Once language has been thought of as "lovely," an adjective frequently applied to females, the pronoun *her* seems natural enough. But other descriptions of language based on the concept of LANGUAGE IS A WOMAN follow quickly, and less satisfyingly, once we have countenanced the chivalric perspective inherent in Bishop's choice of words. Bishop himself exploited some of the consequences of the metaphor when he ridiculed the prescriptive grammarians: "Pure English lived in perpetual danger of deflo-ration by the impure" (p. 17). Bergen Evans (1982), commenting on the difficulty most of us have distinguishing words and things, then talks about the "witchery of rhythm" and how people are "seduced by" slogans (p. 6). If we have trouble telling the difference between words and things, using female terms to describe language will lead us to accept dangerous assumptions about our language and how we can establish a relationship with our linguistic behavior.

John Simon provides one example of the extreme lengths to which the metaphorical concept, LANGUAGE IS A WOMAN, can be taken and the views about language that follow from it. In his Introduction to *Paradigms Lost* (1980), Simon continually equates the English language with the female sex and, as a consequence, describes his perceptions of English in sexual terms. He mentions writing a poem that was "enamored of its language, of the words that intoxicate anyone who gets close enough to them to experience their sensuousness and aroma" (p. xi). He discusses how "English became eroticized" for him (pp. xi–xii). He claims that circumstances "made" him "confound poetics with erotics" (p. xii), and uses phrases such as "the seductive power of style" and "a love affair with words" frequently.

It is not a coincidence that the men who regard some uses of English as "abuses," those who believe that one dialect of English is "purer" than others, also find it easy to talk about the language as though it were a female, nor do I think the evident chivalric attitude toward language is accidental. The chivalric code described women as frail, lovely creatures in need of protection by valiant knights. Similarly, writers who isolate one or several uses of English that offend them as "abuses" tend to describe themselves as the "protectors" of the "purity" of the English language. Once one has mounted a charger and gone in search of dragons to be slain, there are plenty to be found. (For a more detailed discussion, see Penelope, 1982.)

Linguistic elitism

As I've suggested, at least some of the contemporary furor over so-called "abuses" of the English language has been created by the way men conceive of the language and their relationship to it, but there is more to the situation than that. The idea of linguistic "purity" is nothing new. The harbingers of imminent linguistic doom are not, as so many of them believe, a twentieth-cen-tury phenomenon. Generations of Hellenistic schoolmasters, beginning in the second century B.C., fretted over the use of words that had not been hallowed by Classical Greek sources, and maintaining the "purity" of Sanskrit motivated the grammars of Vedic scholars. Prescriptivism, in one form or another, has been a motivating factor in the creation of Academies in Europe and the grammars they endorse, and it remains the primary justification for the many handbooks of English usage that compete for the dollars of native and non-native speakers alike. What is it about the notion that languages "decay," "decline," or "degenerate" that makes it so appealing, in spite of its disreputable history of unfulfilled predictions? Why do some people persist in their efforts to promote one dialect of English and to denigrate others?

Linguistic purism, the desire to proscribe certain terms and usages, frequently finds its staunchest defenders among the economically and socially privileged members of society. After all, it is a commercially attractive product. But purism, like other -isms, has political as well as economic origins. The issue is not really whether or not linguistic change will occur; even John Simon and Edwin Newman are quick to assert their grudging tolerance of *some* linguistic change. The real questions are: which changes are acceptable in whose language, and which methods will be approved, by whom and on the basis of what kinds of justification? The issue is power, who has it and who doesn't; who wants it and who wants to keep it. That is the unlovely fact.

Underlying the rhetoric that urges a prescriptive approach to English one can detect a note of fear, a sense of being threatened. Those writers who believe that they have attained an adequate or even good mastery of the stylistic potential of the English language feel some pride in their accomplishment, not without justification. I suspect that some of their fear is aroused by the prospect, which they see as inevitable, that, once the distinctions between "good" and "bad" ways of speaking and writing are lost, they will also lose the basis for their claims to superiority in comparison to the language use of other people. I hear something akin to panic in the tone of prescriptivists when they write about the "decline" of English, but identifying the source of the malaise is a difficult task.

Writers committed to maintaining the *status quo* lament the loss of the *shall/will* distinction, the confusion of *like* and *as*, the "misuse" of words like *flaunt* and *disinterested*, the overuse of adjectives like *heavy* and *fantastic*, and the substitution of *chairperson* and *congressperson* for *chairman* and *congress-man*. These examples represent a mixed bag of dislikes, all of them ultimately a question of which people are entitled to decide what constitutes "good" usage. Douglas Bush, writing in the *American Scholar* (June 1972), claimed that we need to be as concerned with the pollution of language as we are with other kinds of corruption: ". . . because common violation of traditional usage is an ugly debasement of our great heritage, partly because sloppy English is a symptom and agent of sloppy thinking and feeling and of sloppy communication and confusion" (p. 238). Although Bush is willing to grant that language changes, he still maintains that "acceptance of the perpetual process does not or should not mean blind surrender to the momentum or inertia of slovenly and tasteless ignorance and insensitivity." Changes in language, he asserts, "should be inaugurated from above, by the masters of language (as they often have been), not from below" (p. 244).

The repeated use of the adjective *sloppy*, the phrase "ugly debasement," the blatant accusation of "slovenly and tasteless ignorance and insensitivity," reveal the strength of the emotional response to what Bush regards as "errors" in language use. But others have even stronger claims to make for the seriousness of threats to the language. Stefan Kanfer (1972, p. 9) calls feminist linguistic innovations "a social crime – one against the means and the hope of communication." L. E. Sissman (1972, p. 32) includes feminist suggestions for language change among his examples of "Plastic English," calling them "something cheap and strange . . . something continuously and permanently deformed." Hoffman (1982) has gone so far as to suggest that one of the rules for what he calls "Dawsonese" (a dialect spoken at Dawson College in Canada) is: "Never use the word 'man' " (p. 10). His argument for including such a rule as an example of doublespeak illustrates how easily suggestions for changing the language by one group or another can be derided and trivialized by those who are unwilling to concede their own interests in the linguistic *status quo*.

> In Dawsonese there will be no equality for women until all vestiges of "male chauvinism" are expunged from "sexist" language. Words such as "chairman," "spokesman," "manhour," and "manhunt" denote discrimination. There can be no distinctions, not even those dictated by nature. In a land where French holds sway, and even the male mouse parades as *la souris*, all of this is rather odd. "Personhunt" and "personhole" may placate the purists. They may fall victims to "personslaughter." (p. 10.)

The conceptual dipsy-doodles and convolutions in such diatribes are difficult to follow, especially if one is familiar with the arguments advanced by feminists for removing sexism from our usage. Briefly, feminists concerned with sexist attitudes have focussed attention on the ways in which specific words and phrases make women in decision-making positions invisible (e.g. *chairman, congressman, spokesman*), or which draw undue attention to a female practitioner of some professions as an anomaly (e.g. *lady doctor, woman lawyer, sculptoress, authoress*) (Nilsen *et al.*, 1977). Others have commented on the omnipresence of both *man* and *he* as pseudo-generics, the use of explicitly masculine terms to refer to "all people," when the vocabulary of English provides numerous ways of talking about humanity if that is what one is really talking about. Historically, the word *man* had ceased to be the generic it is in most Germanic languages by the end of the Old English period (*ca.* A.D. 1100), and *he* was not "officially" declared to be generic until 1795 (in Murray's grammar). In 1850, an Act of Parliament made the use of *he* in British legal language a law (Bodine, 1975; Stanley, 1978). Other scholars have drawn attention to the many derogatory terms for women that exist in our vocabulary (e.g. *bitch, virago, termagant*) and the ways in which specifically female terms acquire derogatory connotations (e.g. *girl, nun, madman, fishwife*) (Schulz, 1975; Stanley, 1977). This research indicates that the English language has changed during the centuries of its use, and that it has come to reflect a masculinist bias as time has passed. Given the nature of these arguments, it makes no sense to speak of "expunging" "male chauvinism" from "sexist" language, because sexist terms are in the language because of male chauvinism. One cannot remove male chauvinism *from* sexist language. Hoffman has purposely distorted the relationship asserted by feminists. Furthermore, the terms cited by him do not "denote discrimination"; they make it easier because they foster the assumption that women don't, and therefore can't, hold positions of responsibility and power. To argue that feminists are trying to ignore distinctions of biological sex by suggesting sex-neutral terms, then to support that assertion by using an example from French of *grammatical* rather than biological gender, is doublethink/doublespeak of the most pernicious sort. The final irony lies in the author's accusation that feminists who desire specific linguistic changes are "purists." If feminists wish to change the language by substituting non-sexist terms, we are attacking the "purity" of the language (Simon, Bush, Kanfer, Sissman); for the same reason, we are also "purists" (Hoffman). Either way, we are being told that we don't have the right to "tamper" with our language.

But it's not just women who are being castigated for attempting to change English. John Simon, one of the more prolific defenders of linguistic "purity," has also dismissed Black English as an acceptable dialect in an essay that attacks the CCCC's statement on the Students' Right to Their Own Language. Both the mode and the method of his arguments are dubious.

> As for "I be," "you be," "he be," etc., which should give us all the heebie-jeebies, these may indeed be comprehensible, but they go against all accepted classical and modern grammars and are the product not of a language with roots in tradition but of ignorance of how language works. It may be a regrettable ignorance, innocent and touching, one that unjust past social conditions cruelly imposed on people. But it *is* ignorance, and bowing down to it, accepting it as correct and perhaps even better than established usage, is not going to help matters. On the contrary, that way lies chaos. The point is that if you allow this or that departure from traditional grammar, everything becomes permissible – as, indeed, it has become, which is why we are in the present pickle. (1977, p. 68.)

Simon's liberal use of phrases like "heebie-jeebies" and "present pickle" is, I gather, a ploy to persuade us that he's no linguistic fuddy-duddy. He is, however, a racist, among other things. There's no mistaking the condescending tone of the phrases "regrettable ignorance" and "innocent and touching," but there's something more insidious about the statements made by men like John Simon: their assertions are *false*. As frequently as they use the word *ignorance* to describe their perceptions of the language of other people, their justifications for such name-calling are founded on their own ignorance. John Simon, for example, says that his examples of Black English "should give *us all* the heebie-jeebies" (my emphasis). Similarly, Douglas Bush mentions "our great heritage." *Who* is included in the *we* of *us* and *our*? Not me. Not the Blacks, or the people of the Third World. Simon's first *all* is intended to include his readers, but at that point I absent myself. His second use of *all*, when he claims that the structures of Black English "go against *all accepted* classical and modern grammars," exposes his own ignorance about the history of grammars and the development of modern grammars. What does he mean by "classical"? Grammars of Greek and Latin? Well, certainly, one would not expect to find a discussion of Black English in a grammar of Classical Latin (a language that *is* dead, by the way). Of modern grammars, we have a plethora. Is he referring to the grammars produced by modern linguists? Does he, perhaps, think that the only grammars being published are the school handbooks that more nearly reflect his own prejudices? (In fact, linguists interested in social dialects have described parts of the rule system for Black English. See, for example, J. L. Dillard [1972] and Bentley and Crawford [1973].)

John Simon's ignorance is neither "innocent" nor "touching," for he reveals more clearly his lack of information the more he says. He asserts that the constructions of Black English "are the product not of a language with roots in tradition but of ignorance of how language works." This claim is steeped in ethnocentrism, as well as racism. First, it is clear that the "tradition" to which Simon implicitly refers is the Anglo-American grammatical tradition; it is not the tradition of Black speakers. Second, some scholars have claimed to have found the origins of specific Black English structures in the languages spoken by the people of Africa when they were brought as slaves to this country. Certainly, the enslaved people brought with them their own culture and traditions. Third, when Simon says that such usage can only be the "product" of "ignorance of how language works," he is treating the English language as though it were the only language, or some sort of prototype for linguistic systems in general. Yet, his assertions are based on "ignorance of how language works." (My use here is generic.) John Simon knows nothing about language in general, and he has no interest in discovering anything useful about how the structure of the English language works.

We must find a way to cut through the confusion of charges and counter-charges, the inflated rhetoric of doom and disaster, the ill-founded apprehensions and misinformation that such writers feed upon. For example, it is simply inaccurate to use words like *decay*, *degenerate*, *decline*, *deteriorate*, *corrupt*, and *die* when we talk about the "state" of the English language in the latter twentieth century. As a language, English is alive, of that fact there can be no doubt. A language may be said to be *dying* when its speakers have dwindled significantly in number; it may be said to be dead when there are no living speakers to use it, to keep it "alive." To say that English is "deteriorating," "decaying," "declining," or "degenerating" is to assume, without factual evidence, some prior, earlier stage of the language that was "healthier," somehow "better" than the language in its present stage. The word *decline*, for example, implies a movement downward from some unspecified *higher* point, while *corrupt* presupposes not only that the language was "purer" at some previous date, but that it is a thing, something that has an existence distinctly independent of the minds of the people who speak it.

Doublethink/doublespeak

Yet, something has gone awry with the uses of the English language. There is that grain of truth amidst the hue and cry that gives the alarmists whatever credibility they may have. It is apparent that, from the position they have elected to maintain, these men can only see feminists, Blacks, and other powerless groups as the perpetrators responsible for the "decline" of what they regard as *their* property, the English language, and it is their proprietary attitude toward English that is most offensive to those of us who try to work consistently and competently with language issues. Language is not the preserve solely of the rich and the educated; it is not the unique possession of just those who have privilege and a place in the popular media to have their say.

The irony of the situation lies in the fact that the very men who are protesting feminist suggestions for removing sexist attitudes from our use of English, the same men who deny that Black English is as deserving of respect as their "standard" English dialect, are also guilty of contributing to the problem they claim to deplore. Views on what is wrong with contemporary uses of English are the product of ignorance, but it is not the ignorance of feminists or Blacks or the poor, it is the ignorance of those arrogant enough to set themselves up as arbiters of usage. It is the ignorance of those who feel no compunction about ignoring the facts about language structure that linguists have been working with for years, who use specious arguments about the structure of English to advance their own cause. In order to make their arguments seem plausible, they are willing to engage in name-calling, obfuscation, omission, and exaggeration; they engage in appeals to authority (their own), they pass off *non sequiturs* as the very substance of logic and reasoning, and they will beg every question they purport to address. In short, these men are using English in a way that we have a name for: *doublespeak*.

What is *doublespeak*? D. G. Kehl (1982, p. 152) has defined the phenomenon in a way that most clearly reflects my own understanding of it: ". . . double-speak [is] pretentious and dishonest, seeking less to *express* than to *impress* . . . Basic to doublespeak, the linguistic manifestation of Orwell's doublethink and often the cloak for the doubledeal, is incongruity. It is the incongruity between what is *said* – or left *unsaid* – and what really *is*, between word and referent, between *seem* and *be*. It is the incongruity between what language is supposed to do – communicate – and what doublespeak does – obfuscate."

We are, indeed, surrounded by linguistic malfeasance, but focusing attention on Black English, or the sex-neutral terms urged by feminists, or the tendency to confuse *disinterested* with *uninterested* is little more than a diversionary tactic. Most people have ceased to worry about their language use because we daily witness the way in which media figures successfully divorce words from their referents. The language use of the decision-makers denies any connection between the word and the reality to which it is supposed to point. I don't worry about the rhetoric of the oppressed, the victimized, the poor; I worry about how Alexander Haig, Ronald Reagan, James Watt, and Margaret Thatcher use the English language to advance the economic and political interests of those who believe that a nuclear war can be "won," that sucking oil out of the earth's crust promotes "progress," that keeping Haitian refugees in concentration camps protects "freedom," that using the economic resources of the United States to support the war machine is more important than providing food and shelter to the poor and the unemployed people of this nation. Compared to Ronald Reagan and the military establishment, John Simon, L. E. Sissman, and Douglas Bush are merely well-intentioned, badly informed bunglers tilting at windmills. But I must emphasize that such writers explicitly cast their lot with the powerful when they assert that people on the bottom of the social hierarchy have no "right" to their language use, and urge us to accept only language changes from the "top."

Doublespeak provides immediate and ample rewards to those in a position to use it to protect themselves and to disguise the purposes of their actions. In a sense, certainly not the one in which he intended his remark, de Tocqueville was right when he linked "the deterioration of language with the growth of democracy" (Hoffman, p. 9). But it is not, *per se*, the "struggle for equality" that robs words of their meaning; it is the struggle *against* equality that inspires the most malicious uses of English. The politicians, government bureaucrats, and the vested interests of the military/industrial complex promote distortions of meaning and intention; they will tell the public any lie to protect their positions. The following examples illustrate, in a variety of contexts, the many ways in which the subtleties of English can be exploited by those whose decisions affect our lives.

1. The events that led up to a $300,000 Nuclear Regulatory Commission fine against Nebraska Public Power District were the result of a "communication gap" and not lying, an NPPD official says. . . . Jones said NPPD staff "gathered information that allowed them to make the statements they made to the NRC." He said the district doesn't feel it made false statements "in the manner that they're accusing us of." . . . The area that was not covered by a warning siren would have been a very small proportion of the rural population, Jones said.
(As reported in *The Lincoln Journal*, 8/10/82, p. 1)

2. There was World War II, the Korean conflict, and the Viet Nam era. . . .
(Jeanne Kirkpatrick, Memorial Day speech, 1982)

3. [Watt] emphasized that even with the sale of the 200,000 acres identified in the preliminary reports, "there will be massive land owned by the federal government for probably ever."
(As reported in *The Lincoln Journal*, 5/22/82, p. 2)

4. Decreasing federal and state support portends a period of retrenchment though more people seek mental health services during bad economic times, Grabow says.
"The ship is sinking, but land is in sight. It has lush forests and coconuts and dancing girls. What I see is a much better future. There's no question we'll make it to land because we have such strong local support," Grabow says.
(As reported in *The Lincoln Star*, 1/29/82, p. 7)

5. "You know, I aim to try and tap that great American spirit that opened up this completely undeveloped continent from coast to coast and made it a great nation, survived several wars, survived the Great Depression, and we'll survive the problems we face right now."
(Ronald Reagan's victory speech on his election to the U.S. Presidency, 11/4/80)

6. If we spend our time quibbling over how the tax cut is going to be distributed, rather than how it will help the economy's growth, we'll fail to pass an economic measure that's needed in this country.
(David Stockman, 2/24/81)

7. A member of the Red Army was encountered and neutralized by using gunfire.
(Government statement issued on Dozier's recovery)

8. We have a – scenario in a developmental mode.
(Alexander Haig)

9. "I do think it is an important leadership question and all Republican members of Congress should realize that it [the tax bill] is important to the president's program, important to the party and important to success in the fall elections,' Speakes said. 'Because that is the only way we're going to get recovery."
(As quoted in *The Lincoln Journal*, 8/16/82, p. 1)

10. "I never use the words Republicans and Democrats. It's liberals and Americans."
(Interior Secretary James Watt, as reported in *The Lincoln Journal*, 1/30/82, p. 1)

11. The other day when a major bank in New York, Manufacturers Hanover, reduced interest rates, I thought it was very interesting that the man in charge said that they were reducing them because of a feeling of public obligation that so much of our present problem is psychological. And I think it is. And I think that some of what's going on in the Congress has held back the psychology change that is needed. And this is why I believe, in addition to the Constitutional amendment being a very practical way of getting us out of a situation that has seen us have 19 deficits in the last 20 years, would be the psychological effect that would indicate that the Government is really determined to end this kind of runaway spending and have some fiscal integrity and common sense.

(Reagan's statements to the press, as reported in *The New York Times*, 7/29/82, p. 12)

Linguistic malpractice endangers our lives in so many areas that it's hard to know who to watch from one hour to the next. An official with the NPPD acknowledges "false statements," calls them a "communication gap," but assures us that only a "very small proportion of the rural population" might have been killed. Jeanne Kirkpatrick demonstrates her skill at euphemism. How quickly they think we forget! Interior Secretary Watt buries a caveat in the middle of the adverbial compound *forever*. Do you believe him? Grabow, admitting that the "ship" of mental health services is "sinking" during a time when they're most needed, nevertheless promises us "lush forests, coconuts and [of all things!] dancing girls." What if we can't swim? Reagan revealed his racism the night of his election when he apparently forgot that this continent was inhabited by many different cultures when his forefathers arrived and raped and burned and pillaged their way from one coast to the other. Was this continent "completely undeveloped"? No, it just hadn't yet been subjected to the material excesses of our culture. Stockman urges us to quibble over how the tax cut will "help the economy's growth." We should ignore the poor and the elderly and the disappearing middle class who derived little, if any, benefits from the measure. Our government tells us an enemy was "neutralized by using gunfire." Was it suicide, then? Haigspeak we managed to spot immediately, as soon as he started making statements to the press. Whose "recovery" is Speakes worried most about? That of the Republican Party, those "Americans" Watt talks about? What about the rest of us? Reagan describes our economic situation in a way that sounds familiar: "If you believe in fairies, clap your hands!" (Courtesy of Bobby Lacy.) My dwindling buying power is my fault because I don't believe in Reaganomics.

Uses of language such as these should make us gasp with horror, but, I fear, most of us barely hear them these days. I think we're inured to doublespeak because we don't think we have the power to stop it. Maybe we don't. But this is the kind of language use that not only produces despair and apathy but denies the existence of real and present dangers and urges us to accept the illusions perpetrated by politicians instead of undertaking a radical restructuring of our society. There are no "abuses" of language, but there certainly are a variety of ways in which the language is used to abuse people, whether it's racist language, sexist language, or political doublespeak. If we are going to expend our energies struggling to maintain (or recover) the integrity of meaning that is possible in our uses of English, let's understand first who the manipulators are, what they have to gain, and all that we have to lose. What our latter-day prescriptivists please to call a "civilization" hasn't yet collapsed as a result of our usage of English. Perhaps we just haven't given it enough time to do so; perhaps the suicidal negligence of a species obsessed with death will decide our fate. In that case, whoever is still alive can lament the death of English.

Note

1. I would like to express my gratitude to Debbie Alicen and Elizabeth Binhammer, who read and commented on earlier versions of this article, and to the students in my Composition and Reading classes, Fall 1982, whose class discussions helped me to identify the metaphorical concept, LANGUAGE IS A WOMAN. All errors of fact and interpretation remain, however, my own.

References

BENTLEY, R. and SAMUEL D. CRAWFORD, eds. (1973) *Black Language Reader*. Glenview, Ill.: Scott, Foresman & Co.

BISHOP, M. (1980) From the preface to *The American Heritage Dictionary*, "Good usage, bad usage, and usage." Reprinted in Boltz and Seyler, pp. 14–21.

BODINE, A. (1975) "Androcentrism in prescriptive grammar: Singular 'they', sex-definite 'he', and 'he or she'." *Language in Society*, **4**, 129–146.

BOLTZ, C.J. and D.U. SEYLER, eds. (1982) *Language Power*. New York: Random House.

BUSH, D. (1972) "Polluting our language." *American Scholar* (June), pp. 238–247.

DILLARD, J.L. (1972) *Black English*. New York: Random House.

EVANS, B. (1963) "The power of words." from *A Word-A-Day Vocabulary Builder*. New York: Random House. Reprinted in Boltz and Seyler, pp. 2–7.

HOFFMAN, G. (1982) "Jargon in Canada." *Quarterly Review of Doublespeak*, VIII, 3 (May), 9–10.

KANFER, S. (1972) "Sispeak: A msguided attempt to change herstory." *Time* (23 Oct.), 79.

KEHL, D.G. (1982) "The doublespeak of Academia." In *Speaking of Words*, eds. James McKillop and Donna Woolfolk Cross. New York: Holt, Rinehart & Winston, pp. 151–156.

LAKOFF, G. and M. JOHNSON. (1980) *Metaphors We Live By*. Chicago: University of Chicago Press.

MURRAY, L. (1795) *English Grammar*. Facsimile edition published by Scolar Press in *English Linguistics, 1500–1800*, ed. R. C. Alston.

NEWMAN, E. (1976) *A Civil Tongue*. Indianapolis: Bobbs-Merrill.

NILSEN, A.P. *et al.*, eds. (1977) *Sexism and Language*. Urbana, Ill.: National Council of Teachers of English.

ORTONY, A., ed. (1979) *Metaphor and Thought*. Cambridge: Cambridge University Press.

PENELOPE, J. (1982) "John Simon and the 'Dragons of Eden'." *College English*, **44**, 8 (Dec.), 848–54.

REDDY, M.J. (1979) "The Conduit Metaphor – A case of frame conflict in our language about language," in A. Ortony, pp. 284–324.

SCHÖN, D.A. (1979) "Generative metaphor: A perspective on problem-setting in social policy," in A. Ortony, pp. 254–83.

SCHULZ, M. (1975) "The semantic derogation of Woman," in Thorne and Henley, pp. 64–75.

SIMON, J. (1980) *Paradigms Lost*. New York: Clarkson N. Potter.

SIMON, J. (1977) "Playing tennis without a net." *Esquire* (Oct.), pp. 66, 68, 70.

SISSMAN, L.E. (1972) "Plastic English." *Atlantic* (Oct.), pp. 32, 34, 37.

STANLEY, J. (1977) "Paradigmatic woman: The prostitute." *Papers in Language Variation*, eds. David L. Shores and Carole P. Hines. Birmingham, Ala.: University of Alabama Press, pp. 303–321.

STANLEY, J. (1978) "Sexist grammar." *College English*, **39**, 7 (Mar.), 800–811.

THORNE, B. and N. HENLEY, eds. (1975) *Language and Sex: Difference and Dominance*. Rowley, Mass.: Newbury House.

WEINREICH, U. (1966) "Explorations in semantic theory," in T. A. Sebeok, ed., *Current Trends in Linguistics*, vol. III (The Hague: Mouton). Reprinted in *Semantics*, eds. Danny D. Steinberg and Leon A. Jakobovits. Cambridge: Cambridge University Press, 1971, pp. 308–328.

Chapter 5

Unconscious Attitudes Toward Linguistic Variation

EDWARD FINEGAN

THE most interesting linguistic discoveries of the past two decades, some would argue, are the systematic correlations between linguistic and non-linguistic variation. We now know – in detailed ways not suspected earlier – about patterned co-variation between linguistic features and such non-linguistic parameters as socioeconomic status, race, ethnic affiliation, sex, age, and situational formality. Of course, it has long been known that pronunciation and vocabulary differ regionally. For example, "r-dropping" is associated with New York City and parts of New England and the South, but not with the Midwest or West. Similarly, in different parts of the United States, *hero*, *submarine*, *poor boy*, and *hoagie* are used to refer to the same kind of sandwich.

Sometimes linguistic characteristics of groups of speakers come to be so closely associated with those speakers that their occurrence in a speech sample conjures up other characteristics of those speakers. In other words, features of language variation come to be associated with the non-linguistic character- istics with which they co-vary. New York speech suggests New Yorkers, Black Vernacular English suggests Black speakers, and so on. Further, people associate sets of characteristics with different social groups, and speech cues can (and usually do) call forth the stereotyped traits. If I think of New Yorkers as being generally brusque or gruff, I'm likely to judge someone speaking like a New Yorker as being brusque or gruff. A great deal more is suggested to American viewers by Archie Bunker's speech than the simple fact that he resides in New York City.

When, in the late 1960s, three groups of college students were asked to evaluate tape recordings of speakers of six American dialects, they readily rated the speakers on fifteen traits, including intelligence, friendliness, education, ambition, honesty, trustworthiness, and considerateness. The three groups of judges – Black students at a southern Black college, White students at a northern university, and White students at a southern university – could distinguish the various dialects, and all three rated speakers of "network" English (the kind used by network announcers) most highly. On all fifteen traits, the southern Blacks and the northern Whites gave first place to the network speakers, while the southern Whites awarded them first place on twelve traits. As to the least favored speech varieties, Blacks and Whites differed in their attitudes. Blacks rated educated White southern speakers least favorably, while the northern and southern White judges rated southern Black speakers least favorably. Speech styles, thus, are not necessarily uniformly pleasing to all groups within a society.[1]

Even languages themselves can come to evoke stereotypical characteristics. Hearing two Germans conversing does not create the same impressions on Americans as hearing two French speakers or two Spanish speakers.

Similarly for different professions. As children recognize from an early age, doctors, nurses, and patients talk differently; given hand puppets for these medical roles, children exhibit surprising mastery of certain salient differences among doctor talk, nurse talk, and patient talk.[2] And the characteristic jargon of the legal profession is distinctive enough to have been dubbed "legalese." In the course of everyday social interaction, we tend to develop a repertoire of ways of speaking, each appropriate to the groups with which we associate, and we come to recognize social varieties of English, just as we recognize regional dialects and professional registers. Americans, in fact, generally do well in judging the socioeconomic status of a speaker after hearing just a few seconds of speech.

Compared to the conscious judgments made in, say, letters to the editor such as those John Algeo describes elsewhere in this volume, less conscious linguistic attitudes are more subtle and potentially more important in the workaday world. The linguistic variation that is the object of concern in letters to the editor and in newspaper columns and best-selling books is almost always variation between alternate forms that have received attention in classrooms and school grammars – who/whom, like/as, (ir)regardless, ain't, split infinitives, and the like. With this small arsenal of divided or "debatable" usages, we consciously judge ourselves and others. Aware that these variants are telltale – and armed with two centuries of grammatical dogma – parents and teachers, as well as the Edwin Newmans and John Simons among friends and fellow newspaper readers, guard the avenues of language, seldom letting pass an unwelcome locution without a warning or rebuke. Like the ancient tribe of Gileadites, who used the pronunciation of the Hebrew word shibboleth to distinguish between themselves and their enemies (the Ephraimites pronounced it sibboleth), modern guardians have their own shibboleths by which to distinguish friend and foe.

Thus, we are conscious of some language differences among us, and of our evaluations of them. But there is a good deal of variation that we are not aware of. Sociolinguists have uncovered a remarkable degree of variation in the linguistic repertoire used within a speech community and even by a single speaker, but most people remain largely unaware of such variation, even as their own chameleon-like speech takes on the coloring of the situations in which they are talking – to whom, about what, in what circumstances, and so on. The mastery of these complex varieties and their appropriate social and situational allocation come quite naturally and unconsciously to us. If not multilingual, we are all at least multivarietal – in a linguistic sense. And with this variation – overlapping in some ways from dialect to dialect and variety to variety in systematic ways – comes a subtle assessment that people make of the speaker behind the speech variety. Nearly all of us tend to make judgments about other people's personality, intelligence, educational level, and more –

sometimes solely on the basis of a small speech sample. We do it on the telephone; we do it when we hear people on the radio; and we do it in face-to-face interaction.

One helpful tool in the investigation of these unconscious attitudes is what social psychologists have called the matched-guise technique. Using audio tapes of perfectly bilingual speakers – Canadians who speak both English and French natively – researchers disguised the fact that they were asking subjects for their judgments about the same person. What were really uncovered, therefore, were the respondents' attitudes toward speakers of French and English. Predictably, English speakers in Montreal judged a set of English guises to be more intelligent, taller, better looking, kinder, more ambitious, more dependable, and having more character than the same speakers in French guises.[3] Surprisingly, however, when judged by French speakers, the results were the same! The French speakers also rated the English guises to be taller, better looking, more intelligent, and more dependable. Only for religiousness and kindness did French-speaking judges rate the French guises more favorably than the English guises; on the other characteristics, in fact, the French speakers judged the French guises more negatively than the English listeners had. The investigators viewed the pattern of results as a reflection of a "community-wide stereotype" of French Canadians as being "relatively second-rate people."

Not all groups in contact with one another exhibit such shared norms of evaluation. In Israel, for example, investigators uncovered patterns of mutual hostility when they measured the attitudes of Jewish and Arab adolescents toward one another. Boys bilingual in Hebrew and Arabic were taped and the tapes played for teenage judges unaware of the experimental structure. As one might predict, the Jewish and Arab adolescents rated the guises of their own cultures higher on characteristics of honesty, good-heartedness, friendliness, and acceptability as relatives by marriage.[4]

In perhaps the earliest investigation of subjective reactions to variable features of American English, William Labov interviewed scores of New Yorkers in the early 1960s to collect samples of their speech and probe their attitudes toward it.[5] Labov knew certain variables of the New York City sound system to be socially significant: the /r/ in words like car or beard, the initial sounds in words like them and those (versus the infamous "dem," "dat," "dese," and "dose") and thirty, three, through (versus the stereo-typical "toity-toid 'n toid" of conductors over subway loudspeakers), along with variation in the vowels of two word classes: dog, coffee, law, and bad, past, sad.

Labov found the stigmatized forms in greater use among lower socioeconomic classes than among the middle classes. Equally significant, all socioeconomic groups used more prestige forms in careful speech than in casual conversation. He documented similar patterns of social and stylistic variation for all the sounds he investigated, and he concluded that the New York City speech community is unified more by norms of evaluation than by identity of usage.

To determine subjective reactions to the pronunciation of these sound variants among New Yorkers, Labov employed the matched-guise technique.

Using an audio tape compilation of five New York women reading a total of twenty-two sentences, including one each in which none of the variables appears, he played the tape of the supposed twenty-two New Yorkers for listener-judges, asking them to assess occupational suitability. The judges were given a ranked list of jobs (ranging from television personality to factory worker) and asked to indicate on a chart which occupation was the highest the speaker could hold, speaking as she did. By varying the kind and number of variables in the sentences, Labov could control for the effects of the individual phonological variables. He compared his findings for each variable with the evaluation of the neutral utterance so as to discount whatever role voice characteristics and other background noise might play in the assessment.

The variables were not regarded identically by all New Yorkers. There was variation among the attitudes to the variables and there was differentiation between classes in evaluating them. But in general all classes participated in similar patterns of evaluation, with the lower middle class generally manifesting the greatest sensitivity. Differences existed among the responses of Jews, Italians, and Blacks, as well as between men and women. The more a stigmatized variant was used by a particular group, the more negative was that group's evaluation of the feature. Women, for example, exhibited greater stylistic variation than men in their usage for different degrees of formality, but they showed less tolerance for the stigmatized variants in the usage of others. Overall, New Yorkers viewed their own speech patterns unfavorably, and Labov concluded that they suffer from a marked linguistic self-hatred.

Respondents were also given a list of words in two pronunciations and asked which they ordinarily used and which they thought correct. The discrepancies between what a person thought correct and what was reported as his or her ordinary pronunciation was tallied as an Index of Linguistic Insecurity (ILI). Here, too, there were interesting differences among social groups. Women showed a mean ILI score of 3.6, nearly 50 percent more than the men's score of 2.1. Of the ethnic groups, Blacks showed the lowest ILI at 1.3, while the score for Jews was 2.4, and for Italians 3.8. Labov again concluded that New Yorkers manifest "a profound linguistic insecurity," especially among the lower middle class.[6] The working class showed least insecurity, the upper middle class and lower class intermediate values.

The influence that characteristics of our speech has on others is evidenced in a study of evaluations of school boys by student teachers.[7] Researchers in Montreal arranged for a sample of third-grade boys to draw pictures, write compositions, and make audio tapes of a set passage. The researchers gave the three items and a photograph of each boy separately to groups of student teachers, asking them to evaluate these four sources of information for indications of intelligence and other characteristics. Independently of one another, an average rating of appropriate characteristics could be assigned to each photo, audio tape, composition, and drawing. The researchers then devised composite boys, mixing the photos, tapes, compositions, and drawings of different boys, coupling in every case, however, a highly valued drawing with a highly valued composition. The composite boys were presented to another group of student teachers who were asked to indicate their assessment of various characteristics of the boys.

The results, disappointing as they may be from a social point of view, are not surprising. The student teachers gave significantly more weight to a boy's photograph and speech sample than to his composition and drawing in assessing intelligence. That is, in cases where the control judges had assessed a composition and drawing to be indicative of a high degree of intelligence, the student teachers evaluated the composite boy as being less intelligent if the picture and voice sample of the composite were indicative of less intelligence in the control judgments.

We do not yet have complete information on which speech characteristics influence judgments about people. Nearly all the research findings are based on reactions to variation in sound patterns, rather than in vocabulary or syntax. In fact, inquiry has focused more on the segmental phones (vowels and consonants) than on prosodic features such as intonation, speed, and pausing, though these too are thought to be influential cues.

As in several of the experimental settings discussed here, when a set passage is read by speakers, only a subset of phonological variations can be subject to evaluation by listener-judges. Thus, the New York City listeners ranked occupational suitability on the basis of variation in three consonants and two vowels, the syntax and vocabulary fixed by the passage. When relatively unconstrained speech samples are elicited, on the other hand, listeners can respond to a wider range of linguistic features. A Chicago study, for example, established correlations between the silent pauses of fifth- and sixth-grade students' speech and judgments by teachers on scales relating to "confidence-eagerness." These same teachers based judgments for scales relating to the "ethnicity-non-standardness" dimension of evaluation on such syntactic characteristics as pronominal apposition (e.g. "That boy in the boat, he's a friend of mine") and clause fragments, as well as on deviations in pronunciation (in this case, between -s and -z and between voiced and voiceless *th* – ei*th*er vs. e*th*er).[8]

The two dimensions of evaluation referred to result from a statistical procedure known as factor analysis. The Chicago teachers had rated the student speech samples along twenty-two bipolar scales, similar in structure to those used in Montreal and with the three groups of American college students discussed above. Factor analysis revealed that these rating scales were not generally independent of one another but rather that the teachers had used certain scales in the same way – that is, to judge some common, underlying dimension of evaluation, the two chief of which Frederick Williams labeled "confidence-eagerness" and "ethnicity-non-standardness." Other research in Memphis has confirmed the validity of these two underlying dimensions, around which teacher ratings cluster.[9]

We also know that different groups exhibit different attitudes toward variants depending on their own socioeconomic status, sex, age, ethnic affiliation, and so on. Thus, ratings of students done by teachers in Chicago and Memphis indicated that teacher race affected judgments of "sounding disadvantaged." White children were rated as more culturally advantaged by

White teachers than by Black teachers, and while the Black students were perceived by both groups of teachers as more culturally disadvantaged than the White students, Black teachers rated them less so than White teachers did.[10] We have not refined our techniques sufficiently to know exactly to what extent different groups may respond preferentially to different stimuli or to what extent different features of the variation are associated with particular traits of personality or social status. Nor do we know yet to what extent any measure itself reflects values of one group more than another, as, for example, a scale of job suitability "plainly reflects values which are best exemplified by speakers with a middle class orientation."[11]

More crucially, we do not know to what extent the characteristic associations of stigmatized language features can outweigh other indicators of ability or personality in job interviews, promotions, school success, and other real-world situations. So as to exclude confounding variables and facilitate researchers' goals, some of the laboratory-like experiments reported here have created somewhat artificial situations – such as judging job suitability solely on the basis of the pronunciation of a simple set passage, whereas personnel officers would have substantial additional information upon which to base a decision.

What we do know is that people are generally comfortable making an extraordinary range of social and personal judgments about others on the basis of what would appear to be the scant evidence of a few seconds of speech. In relatively unified communities like Montreal (at least in the late 1950s and 1960s when the research reported here was carried out) and New York (at least in the 1960s), the basic attitudes toward speech characteristics are shared across social groups. In other communities, such as Israel, the mutual antagonism of social groups toward one another's language reflects distinct speech communities. And with the three groups of Black and White college student judges discussed earlier, judgments were shared about which varieties were most favored but not about least favored varieties.

From existing research, some implications can be drawn. The most obvious is that speech is an important factor in the way people perceive one another. Impressions of social affiliation, personal traits, and even physiognomy and intelligence are influenced in part by speech characteristics. For some characteristics, these impressions are valid because we do indeed speak like those with whom we are socially affiliated and with whom we wish to identify. But these impressions are mediated by social stereotyping, and the characteristics of the persons making judgments can also be a biasing factor, not all social groups making identical judgments of the same speech samples. Nevertheless, there is surprising agreement about the direction of evaluation of speech samples within a speech community, different groups often exhibiting shared norms of evaluation. Finally, it is worth noting that social mobility, perhaps more than social status, is a factor in the kinds of speech one uses and to that extent in the perceptions others have of us. In studies in New York City[12] and on Martha's Vineyard,[13] socially mobile persons exhibited speech characteristics of the group they were moving toward more than of the group of current affiliation.

We might ask, then, to what extent attention should be paid to speech characteristics in native language instruction. Doubtless, people of good will may differ in their interpretation, some claiming that people can "improve" their speech and thereby enhance their perception by others. Reformers should bear in mind, though, that speech patterns appear to change spontaneously when social goals change and that perceptions of people through their speech are filtered by social stereotyping.

Notes

1. G. Richard Tucker and W. E. Lambert, "White and Negro listeners' reactions to various American-English dialects." *Social Forces*, **47**, No. 4 (1969), 463–468. Also available in Richard W. Bailey and Jay L. Robinson, eds., *Varieties of Present-Day English*. New York, The Macmillan Company, 1973, pp. 293–301.
2. Elaine A. Andersen, "Learning to speak with style: A study of the sociolinguistic skills of children." Diss. Stanford University, 1977.
3. Wallace E. Lambert, "A social psychology of bilingualism." *The Journal of Social Issues*, **23**, No. 2 (1967), 91–109.
4. Cited in Lambert (1967) from W. E. Lambert, M. Anisfeld, and Grace Yeni-Komshian, "Evaluational reactions of Jewish and Arab adolescents to dialect and language variations." *Journal of Personality and Social Psychology*, **66**, No. 2 (1963), 84–90.
5. William Labov, *The Social Stratification of English in New York*. Washington, D.C.: Center for Applied Linguistics, 1966. Much of the New York City study is also available in William Labov, *Sociolinguistic Patterns*. Philadelphia: University of Pennsylvania Press, 1972.
6. Labov, *Social Stratification*, pp. 455–481.
7. C. R. Seligman, G. R. Tucker, and W. E. Lambert, "The effects of speech style and other attributes on teachers' attitudes toward pupils." *Language in Society*, **1**, (1971), 131–142.
8. Frederick Williams, "Some research notes on dialect attitudes and stereotypes." In Roger W. Shuy and Ralph W. Fasold, eds., *Language Attitudes: Current Trends and Prospects*. Washington D.C., Georgetown University Press, 1973, pp. 113–128.
9. Frederick Williams and Associates, *Explorations of the Linguistic Attitudes of Teachers*. Rowley, Mass.: Newbury House Publishers, 1976, p. 99.
10. Williams, *Explorations*, p. 100.
11. Labov, *Social Stratification*. p. 412.
12. William Labov, "The effect of social mobility on linguistic behavior." In Juanita V. Williamson and Virginia M. Burke, eds., *A Various Language: Perspectives on American Dialects*. New York: Holt, Rinehart, 1971, pp. 640–659; repr. from *Sociological Inquiry*, **36**, (1966), 186–203.
13. William Labov, "The social motivation of a sound change," *Word*, **19**, (1963), 273–309; conveniently reprinted in Labov, *Sociolinguistic Patterns*, pp. 1–42.

Chapter 6

What is Good Writing?
Views from the Public

LESTER FAIGLEY

NOTIONS of "good writing" have been brought to the attention of the public in the past few years as part of the debate surrounding the "literacy crisis" among young Americans and the "back-to-the-basics" movement. One of the claims of those who maintain that a literacy crisis exists is that students at all levels of education do not write as well as they used to. This claim is based on the results of standardized tests of verbal abilities taken by high-school seniors, which from 1963 through the 1970s steadily plummeted. Numerous articles and broadcasts in the popular media expressed shock over this decline and pointed to causes ranging from permissive standards to television to *Webster's Third New International Dictionary*. Later the debate shifted to whether verbal skills really had declined or simply the population of students had changed. Lost for the most part in these debates was how proficiency in verbal skills should be defined, and, as a corollary, what is good writing.

The definition of what is "good" and "bad" writing is a crucial variable to discussions of skills in literacy, especially if comparisons are to be made across time. Standards often change over the years. For example, the winning time in the marathon in the 1908 Olympic Games – 2 hours, 55 minutes – would not even qualify the runner to participate in this year's Boston Marathon. The definition of good writing assumed in the popular media and by the authors of standardized tests is the opposite of Augustine's definition of evil as the absence of good. Good writing is defined as the absence of error. In the often-cited *Newsweek* article, "Why Johnny Can't Write" (8 December 1975), examples such as the following were offered as evidence of the verbal depths to which the young people of America had fallen: "It's obvious, in our modern world of today theirs a lot of impreciseness in expressing thoughts we have." A personnel official is quoted who complains that college graduates make errors formerly associated with high-school graduates. Elsewhere, the article maintains that writing instruction should focus on "grammar, structure and style."

The same definition of good writing underlies pronouncements about declining writing skills based on standardized tests scores. Standardized tests, of course, are not direct examinations of writing ability since students rarely write more than their names. Instead, they test for a student's knowledge of the conventions of usage, spelling, and punctuation. The logic runs as follows: if students can recognize errors, they are unlikely to make errors in the texts they write, thus producing "good" writing.

This essay examines whether the public's view of good writing is the same as the one assumed in the popular media. I am going to suggest that large segments of the public have a conception of good writing that is considerably broader in scope than the conception presented in broadcasts and articles such as "Why Johnny Can't Write." But before I present evidence for this belief, I will first look at where the view that "correct" writing is good writing originates.

In every writing class I teach, I begin the first day by asking students what they think good writing is. I have taught long enough to expect a pattern of responses. Recently, three graduate students and I interviewed beginning college freshmen concerning their beliefs about writing including what is good writing.[1] Below are some representative responses:

1. Being able to use words properly and organize your thoughts, things like that.
2. A developed paper. You know, with an introductory paragraph, developing the thing, and concluding.
3. Good writing is in some sort of followed order, not all jumbled up, and it has an end. I hate it when you read a book or something and it doesn't end, you know? You just read and you get the whole story and you get to the middle and its all exciting and everything, and then they just drop it, or if it has subplots and stuff, they never finish those.
4. Good writing is very formal and doesn't necessarily have stupidness things like grammar and that sort of thing.
5. I would say something that explains the question in great detail.
6. I think that good writing has to be precise. It has to have correct grammar, correct spelling and punctuation. It needs to flow, from paragraph to paragraph, from sentence to sentence, and you don't want it to get too monotonous like all simple sentences.
7. Everything has to relate from what you start on. A paragraph has to build up. What you finished with can't be completely different than what you started with. Stay with a main theme, and watch run on's and stuff like that, you know, common sense grammar.
8. Being able to express yourself so that the reader can understand what you're trying to say, what you're trying to get across to him.

All of the above responses with the exception of the last one uphold the notion of good writing expressed in the *Newsweek* article. They confirm what I have long intuited – that many students think of proper usage when asked to define good writing. Other qualities that students mention besides correctness are adequate support (examples 2 and 5), organization by structural paradigm (2 and 3), formal style (4), varied style (6), coherence (6), unity (7), and readability (8).

Two fairly obvious but important conclusions can be drawn from these responses. First, students think of good writing almost exclusively in terms of text features. The only exception among the above responses is example 8, where the writer and reader are both included in a definition of good writing. Furthermore, students think that these features are consistent across different kinds of texts. If students say that good writing is formal, they do not qualify this generalization. Their definition of good writing holds for diaries and encyclopedias, for poetry and political treaties.

Second, students' definitions of good writing reflect what students have been told good writing is. The qualities of good writing that students mention repeat definitions of good writing in widely used high-school English textbooks. For example, fully two-thirds of Warriner's *English Grammar and Composition* (Harcourt, Brace, Jovanovich, 1977), a six-volume series used in grades 7 through 12, deals with matters of mechanics and usage. Chapter headings in Warriner's books include the following: "Kinds of Usage," "Correct Agreement," "Using Pronouns Correctly," "Using Verbs Correctly," "Using Modifiers Correctly," 'Writing Complete Sentences," "Achieving Sentence Variety," and "Unity and Coherence in Paragraphs." Since the Warriner series is a statewide adoption in Texas (as well as in several other states), the similarity between students' responses and Warriner's headings is no coincidence. The continuing popularity of the Warriner series suggests that its concept of good writing is that of secondary English teachers.

The notion that good writing contains certain common properties, regardless of the type of text or purpose, has been inherent in the teaching of writing from the beginnings of composition courses in the nineteenth century. Although some of these notions, such as arrangement and unity, can be traced from classical rhetoric, precepts such as support for ideas, grammatical correctness, and paragraph structure derive from eighteenth- and nineteenth-century rhetoricians and grammarians. One of the chief proponents of the doctrine of good usage was George Campbell, a Scottish preacher and rhetorician, whose *Philosophy and Rhetoric*, first published in 1776, was printed in over thirty American editions. But the person probably most responsible for disseminating these assumptions about good writing to teachers and students in the twentieth century was another Scottish rhetorician, Alexander Bain. Bain's *English Composition and Rhetoric* appeared in England in 1866 and in the United States in 1867. By 1901, it had been reprinted numerous times on both sides of the Atlantic. It is significant that Bain chose the word "composition" to appear before "rhetoric" in his title. Unlike classical rhetoricians, who were concerned with how a speaker could convince a particular audience, Bain was chiefly concerned with matters of style and form divorced from any rhetorical context. His model for teaching writing prevailed for almost a century without serious challenge, and his influence continues to the present.

Even a cursory inspection of Bain reveals that John Warriner borrowed much more than Bain's title. Bain set out many of the ideas found in Warriner and other contemporary writing textbooks, prescriptions such as that sentences should vary in length and paragraphs should have topic sentences. The widespread use of handbooks in college composition courses also follows the tradition of Bain. The contents of these textbooks include very little besides material on style and usage.

The sources of ideas about correct usage that high-school and college students have are no mystery. The question that I want to examine is whether these beliefs about good writing persist after students have graduated. Recently, Thomas Miller and I explored this and other related questions in a stratified survey of the writing of college-trained people.[2] We wanted to know how much writing college-trained people do on and off the job, what methods of composing and what media they use, and how they conceive of good writing. A great deal of anecdotal evidence and several specialized surveys of particular occupations *suggest* writing is an important skill on the job, but no one to our knowledge had attempted to survey a cross-section of college-trained people before our effort. We obtained a sample of 200 individuals who closely fit government statistics for the kinds of occupations and employers of college-trained people. We asked these individuals to fill out a survey instrument, and we supplemented the data gathered from this instrument with interviews.

We found that the people we surveyed wrote a great deal on the job. On the average, they wrote for over 23 percent of total work time, or over one day in a five-day work week. Nearly three-fourths of the people surveyed claimed to write 10 percent of work time or more. Only four people claimed never to write while on the job. In professional and technical occupations, where over half of all college-trained people are employed, persons we surveyed wrote on the average 29 percent of total work time. No one employed in a professional or technical occupation in our survey claimed not to write on the job. People on the job not only wrote a lot, but the kinds of writing that they did were quite diverse. They used a variety of composing strategies, sometimes dictating, sometimes writing without revising, and sometimes rewriting a document through a series of drafts. They often work together in composing. Most people we surveyed (73.5 percent) sometimes collaborate with one or more persons in writing.

To gain a sense of what college-trained people think is good writing, we asked two related questions: "What should be taught in college writing courses?" and "What are the effects of bad writing at your place of work?" We analysed the content of the responses to both questions.

In answer to the first question, "What do you think should be taught in college writing courses?" *clarity* was mentioned more often than any other quality (by 43 percent of those surveyed), followed by *grammar, mechanics, and usage* (42 percent), *organization* (33 percent), *business and technical writing* (31 percent), and *brevity* (26 percent). At first glance these qualities seem similar to those mentioned in students' definitions of good writing. People frequently expressed concern for grammar and mechanics. One person said, "It must not be assumed every incoming freshman has a fundamental knowledge of English grammar and how it works." Another observed that students need to be better prepared when they come to college:

> College is too late to start teaching the language. Writing structure without adequate vocabulary or grammatical background is useless.

But when people explained what they meant by terms like "clarity," "correctness," and "conciseness," we discovered an underlying conception of good writing different from the classroom conception. Almost always these qualities were linked to the needs of the reader. Here are some specific examples of what people on the job think needs to be taught in college writing courses:

1. One should be taught to express one's ideas clearly, concisely, and briefly. Successful people in business are terribly busy and want to receive correspondence that gets quickly to the heart of the matter. Too many people are overly "wordy" and unable to take an involved, complicated subject and reduce it to the major points. Many a good idea has been killed with an overabundance of words.
2. Brief, precise written documents are essential.
3. As time continues to become more valuable, I believe that students should be taught to write letters that are to the point and composed in a short time.
4. The absolute necessity of clear, concise written communication.
5. The important distinction between academic writing and industrial communication is that academics encourage obfuscation while business deplores unclear and imprecise communication.
6. Know the object of the written product. Know the audience and write for that audience. Too many times both are overlooked.
7. How to express oneself clearly in writing in a manner that will be acceptable to the reader.
8. Communication skills should stress clear, basic ideas that get right to the point.
9. How to convey the required information as concisely as possible.
10. Greater emphasis should be placed on how to define, as specifically as possible, the reader, what is needed to tell that reader my message, and what are the objects of my document.

People on the job were concerned with correctness, but their view was much broader than simple conformity to standards of usage. Correctness was not so much an end in itself as it was a way of facilitating the reading of a written text. Furthermore, correctness extended to matters other than spelling. As one person put it, "How could a client trust that the diameters of pipe [to be used in a chemical plant] are accurately specified in a report filled with typographical errors?" In the same way, clarity and brevity were valued because they make a document easier to understand. These qualities are explained well by a person in marketing:

> Planning and organization are most important in meeting the needs of the intended reader, whether he is a client, a potential client, a regulator, or some other person. A written report or document must convey the intended message as clearly and accurately as possible in as short a form as possible. Clarity of expression permits the reader to devote most of his or her energy to the consideration of the message. The reader should not be forced to wonder what the writer intended to say.

Many people who expressed concern for the "basics" also thought that students need to know much more than the basics. They need to be able to write efficiently and effectively for different purposes and for different readers.

The second question we asked, "What are the effects of bad writing at your place of work?" threw light on why people on the job typically have broader views of good writing than students graduating from high school. People responding to this question most frequently mentioned misunderstanding (58 percent), loss of time (49 percent), and a bad public image (40 percent). Often these qualities were linked, as in the following examples:

1. Bad writing diminishes credibility, creates confusion, and slows the work process which results in decreased productivity.
2. Time is wasted in correcting bad writing. It creates a poor image of the company and misunderstandings.
3. Customers feel that bad writing reflects on the ability of the employer to get the job done.
4. Many people do not understand the instructions they are supposed to follow, thus operations are not carried out properly.
5. It can create ambiguity as to a company's responsibility in any given matter.

Responses to this question indicate that notions of good writing held by people on the job are often very pragmatic. Writing affects them directly. For example, managers are responsible for the writing produced by their employees, and managers often have to serve as editors, revising the prose of subordinates if it is poorly written. Consequently, such experiences shape the perceptions of good and bad writing among people on the job. Often a great deal is a stake in a written document. A poorly written document can cause loss of clients and even litigation, as well as adversely affecting the writer's opportunities for advancement in a particular company or agency.

The difference between what I have described as the traditional classroom conception of good writing and the conception (if our survey is valid) held by many members of the public brings into question the classroom definition of good writing and the way that writing is taught in the schools. We are now seeing the beginnings of a fundamental shift in perceptions of writing and in the way writing is taught among colleges and universities. One piece of evidence is a change in the way good writing is defined in the classroom. One recent college textbook says "the key element of good writing is that it communicates effectively and efficiently with the audience for which it is intended";[3] another observes that "no absolute standards define the goodness and effectiveness of what you write."[4]

This changing perception of good writing has led to changes in the writing curriculum. College writing courses are no longer offered just at the freshman level nor are all writing courses offered in the English department. Students at many colleges and universities take advanced writing courses that focus on the kinds of writing students will do in their professional careers. Even in freshman writing courses, students no longer exclusively write "themes." Increasing emphasis is being placed on writing for specific audiences and purposes. Many teachers now give writing assignments that simulate the kinds of writing students will do in life, an instructional technique that has been used successfully in disciplines such as business, law, and medicine for many years. Papers written for these assignments are graded according to how well they achieve the writer's purpose and meet the reader's needs, not just by the presence or absence of errors. At the heart of these changes is the rediscovery of the rhetorical tradition that dates back to classical Greece, a tradition that accommodates the roles of writer, reader, and subject matter in shaping a text. Accompanying this trend has been a return to an earlier definition of "rhetoric" without the pejorative overtones it has acquired in recent years, both as a term to describe written communication and as a discipline dedicated to the study of effective written communication.

Some people might argue that too much can be made of the public's notion of good writing. They might point out that the kind of writing discussed in the responses quoted above is writing with the purpose of informing. Writing has other purposes, such as expressing ones' emotions, solving problems, and exploring ideas. They might argue that too strong an emphasis on the informative functions of writing could cause other functions to be neglected. Nevertheless, all writers need to think of their readers and their purpose, no matter what kind of discourse. More than anything else, we learn from the public that being "correct" in writing isn't enough. Writers need to be sensitive to the reader's needs and flexible enough to use a variety of styles and forms in different writing situations. As one of the people we surveyed put it: "Students should be taught three things that cover all writing skills: that the reader will read it, that the reader will understand it, and that the reader will remember it."

Notes

1. I am grateful to Roger Cherry, David Jolliffe, and Anna Skinner for their assistance in interviewing students. The research discussed in this essay was supported by grants from the Fund for the Improvement of Postsecondary Education and the University of Texas at Austin.
2. The results of this survey are described in Lester Faigley and Thomas P. Miller, "What we learn from writing on the job." *College English*, **44** (Oct. 1982), 557–569.
3. Maxine C. Hairston, *Successful Writing*. New York: Norton, 1981, p. 1.
4. John J. Rusziewicz, *Well-Bound Words*. Glenview, Ill.: Scott, Foresman, 1981, p. 4.

Chapter 7

Newspaper Stylebooks: Strictures Teach Tolerance

ALLAN A. METCALF

BEHIND nearly every newspaper in the United States, a stylebook stands guard and lays down the law. Typically, it is a kangaroo court with a hanging judge.

Of the lawgivers, the most influential by far – though also thereby the least distinguished – is the Associated Press–United Press International joint stylebook. It is the most influential because it governs the practice of the two wire services used by nearly all U.S. daily newspapers. It is the least distinguished because it serves as a common denominator, striving for norms that will prove acceptable to thousands of editors and millions of readers across the nation.

Technology dictated the effort to establish nationally acceptable norms. The Teletypesetter, introduced in 1951, led directly to the first joint stylebook; the device automatically set AP and UPI material in type, but without the possibility of editing at the local newspaper, so AP and UPI had to agree on a uniform style that would be acceptable everywhere.

Present-day electronics easily permits local editing of wire-service copy before it is typeset, so even the smallest newspaper can afford to alter some of the joint stylebook policies to suit local tastes. Before long, individualized computer programs will undoubtedly be available to convert automatically to the local norm, as for a newspaper that spells out "ten" instead of following the joint stylebook's "10."

But there is such a thing as American newspaper style – inelegant, unobtrusive, brief – and the joint stylebook embodies it. Actually, the "joint stylebook" is two separate books, one edited by Howard Angione, titled "The Associated Press Stylebook and Libel Manual," published by AP in New York; the other edited by Bobby Ray Miller, titled "The UPI Stylebook," published by UPI in New York. Both issued new editions in 1977. The strictures are exactly the same in both books, but phrasing and examples differ. Neither version is noted for any literary or stylistic merit in its own right. This essay will generally cite the version published by the Associated Press, the older and more widely used of the two agencies.

(Except for the References at the end, this essay follows AP style, including the use of quotation marks rather than italics for titles and citations.)

The joint stylebook may be a common denominator, but it lays down the law in no uncertain terms. In the AP version, it takes 244 pages to rule on abbreviations, punctuation, grammar, spelling, names and the proper use of words – everything from "a, an": use the latter before vowel sounds, to "ZIP code": all caps for the first word, lower case for the second. Humorlessly, Big Brother is even watching "Yukon": do not abbreviate, no "Yuk"s allowed.

Judgments on words are swift and decisive. For example:

—Use "people" for "a large or uncounted number of individuals," "persons" for "a relatively small number of people who can be counted."

—"Bimonthly" is every other month, "semimonthly" twice a month.

—"Hopefully" is "in a hopeful manner. Do not use it to mean it is hoped, let us hope or we hope."

—"Disinterested" means "impartial"; only "uninterested" means that someone lacks interest.

—The past tense of "dive" is "dived."

—An acquitted defendant is not "not guilty," but "innocent," to avoid the possible crime of dropping the "not" through a typographical error.

The joint stylebook snaps out standards in spelling, too. For example:

Adviser, busing (traveling by bus), catalog, cigarette, flutist, glamour, glamorous, ketchup, long-distance (n.), no one, OK, percent, predominantly, rock 'n' roll, Sun Belt, teachers college, theater, T-shirt, TV, U-turn, worshiping.

Every word, in fact, has a single acceptable spelling. If a word is not listed in the stylebook, consult Webster's New World Dictionary, Second College Edition, and use the first spelling. Never mind that the dictionary may find more than one spelling acceptable. If the New World fails, turn to Webster's Third New International and take their first spelling. There's never a choice.

Against such strictures, the nattering nabobs of the American Heritage Dictionary Usage Panel look like pusillanimous pansies of permissivism. And yet the effect of these stern stylebooks has been anything but stultifying. The stylebooks have influenced both writers and readers to adopt enlightened attitudes toward usage – rejecting rigidity, studying informality, and accommodating to current usage, variation and change.

How can extreme strictures lead to flexibility and acceptance of change? First of all, by the nature of the strictures themselves.

Newspaper style distinguishes itself from academic and book publishers' style by its simplicity, informality and adaptability. It is a style that hides style; if a newspaper appears to be written in plain everyday English, that is no accident, but the intent of the stylebook. A conservative formality, though manifest in occasional odd rules, swims against the current.

The simplicity of newspaper style is pervasive. It may be noted in the absence of special typographical devices: °, %, #, £ are always degree, percent, No., pound. Type size and face do not change for titles or quotations. Where academic and book style gives italics or underline to a title like Nabokov's *Pale Fire*, newspapers will put "Pale Fire" in quotation marks. Even quotation marks are denied to titles of reference works and periodicals: *The New Yorker* and *Chicago Reader* become simply The New Yorker and Chicago Reader.

Capitalization is more a mark of distinction in newspaper style than elsewhere. "In general, avoid unnecessary capitals," says the AP Stylebook. "Use a capital letter only if you can justify it by one of the principles listed here." And the principles are few: Capitalize names: John, America, General Electric, and some derivatives from names: American. Capitalize titles of books, songs, and other compositions; capitalize formal titles when used immediately before a name. But do not capitalize "words that are derived from a proper noun but no longer depend on it for their meaning": french fries, manhattan cocktail, venetian blind. And when formal titles are used alone, or set off from a name by commas, they revert to lower case. Even the president and the pope are thus lowered.

Or consider the sacraments (lower case): AP style calls for the Lord's Supper, Holy Communion, Holy Eucharist – rites that commemorate the life of Jesus or signify a belief in his (lower case) presence – but also baptism, confirmation, penance, matrimony. Still respectful, but decidedly informal.

Like capitalization, abbreviation is to be used with restraint, as leading to possible difficulties for readers, although the concern for brevity and compactness does allow commonly understood abbreviations like CIA, FBI, GOP, UFO. Still, there are notable exceptions: United States and United Nations may be abbreviated only as noun modifiers; U.S.S.R. is restricted to datelines only, Soviet Union being the preferred designation; and though some months may be abbreviated when giving exact dates (Jan. 1, but April 23), days of the week must always be spelled out.

Newspaper punctuation likewise inclines to simplicity. For example, the AP stylebook warns writers to be sparing with parentheses, which "are jarring to the reader. . . . The temptation to use parentheses is a clue that a sentence is becoming contorted."

Most prominent of the punctuation rules is the instruction to omit a comma before "and" or "or" in a simple series, an injunction that can be upsetting to the novice journalist who has done well in English classes.

A decided informality appears in newspapers' use of titles. The AP Stylebook prohibits the use of Dr. for those whose doctorates are honorary and mandates the title only for those whose degree is doctor of medicine. Furthermore, the Dr. is to be used only once, in the first reference.

This brings us to the complicated matter of how to refer properly to women. It is a matter on which Americans, editors and readers alike, do not at present agree, and the common ground sought by the joint stylebook is accordingly muddy here. The Associated Press' firm but delicate position on courtesy titles deserves quoting in full:

> **courtesy titles** In general, do not use the courtesy titles *Miss, Mr., Mrs.* or *Ms.* on first reference. Instead, use the first and last names of the person: *Betty Ford, Jimmy Carter.*
>
> Do not use *Mr.* in any reference unless it is combined with *Mrs.*: *Mr. and Mrs. John Smith, Mr. and Mrs. Smith.*
>
> On sports wires, do not use courtesy titles in any reference unless needed to distinguish among persons of the same last name.
>
> On news wires, use courtesy titles for women on second reference, following the woman's preference. Some guidelines:
>
> MARRIED WOMEN: The preferred form on first reference is to identify a woman by her own first name and her husband's last name: *Susan Smith.* Use *Mrs.* on first reference

only if a woman requests that her husband's first name be used or her own first name cannot be determined: *Mrs. John Smith.*

On second reference, use *Mrs.* unless a woman initially identified by her own first name prefers *Ms.: Carla Hills, Mrs. Hills.*

If a married woman is known by her maiden last name, precede it by *Miss* on second reference, unless she prefers *Ms.: Jane Fonda, Miss Fonda.*

UNMARRIED WOMEN: For women who have never been married, use *Miss* or *Ms.* on second reference according to the woman's preference.

For divorced women and widows, the normal practice is to use *Mrs.* on second reference. Use *Miss* if the woman returns to the use of her maiden name. Use *Ms.* if she prefers it.

MARITAL STATUS: If a woman prefers *Ms.*, do not include her marital status in a story unless it is clearly pertinent.

This is a typical entry on a matter of disputed usage: detailed, decisive – and straddling the fence. It speaks with authority, commands without question or apology, suggests no exceptions. We know that Czeslaw Milosz will be plain Milosz on second reference, while Sandra Day O'Connor will be Mrs. O'Connor. The traditional distinction in treatment of the sexes prevails. And yet—

And yet the underlying attitude toward usage seems anything but traditional and authoritarian. The wire service seems eager to attune its rules to actual contemporary usage, rather than to a principled norm. For along with the instruction to give women traditional titles indicating marital status comes an ungrudging recognition of Ms. The decision on which to use, Miss, Mrs. or Ms., is to be based not on the stylebook's rule but on the woman's own preference.

Furthermore, in accord with the current implications of each title, the woman who chooses Ms. is to have the courtesy of silence regarding her marital status, if at all possible.

Thus community standards guide usage, community standards that include both the views of those who prefer the traditional usage and the views of those who would liberate women from publicly declaring their marital status.

That community standards prevail, rather than editors' whims, is confirmed by the responses to a survey of editors who attended the Associated Press Managing Editors convention in 1975, as reported in Editor & Publisher for Nov. 22, 1975. Of the 207 newspapers in the survey, 148 followed AP style in using Miss or Mrs. for women in second reference, 68 of them having exceptions such as Ms. for women who prefer it. Another 37 newspapers used surname without title for public figures such as Lynette Fromme and Patty Hearst, but often let the woman's preference guide local usage. Seventeen editors said the decision depends on the preference of the individual, considerably more than the five who were "violently unequivocally opposed to 'Ms.'"

The authoritarians seemed an endangered species. Compared with the one Arkansas editor who declared, "We will not compromise the English language to artsy-craftsy idiocy!" there were numerous statements that the policy is to do whatever the woman wants. The editor of a paper which still used only Miss and Mrs. wrote, "We hang loose on usage, which means we will play follow-the-leader when a leader shows up." According to the Editor &

Publisher article, that statement was "perhaps most symbolic of the editors' feelings."

Advocates for extreme positions on the Ms. rule are not lacking, but as in public life neither extreme has yet prevailed; the Equal Rights Amendment has failed, but fewer and fewer women are confined to the role of housewife. On the conservative side, The New York Times has refused to recognize Ms., but it gives the sexes its own style of equal treatment by using Mr. for men, as well as Miss or Mrs. for women. On publication of the revised New York Times Manual of Style and Usage in 1976, Lenora Williamson reported in Editor & Publisher for Feb. 7 the explanation of the manual's editor, Lewis Jordan: "the term [Ms.] has not been universally accepted, . . . a great many women object to it, and . . . using the term for those requesting it – as do many newspapers – might conceivably open the way for requests from various other groups for other special forms of address." None of his three reasons has to do with preventing change, deploring decay, following first principles or making language logical; they all show attention to reader response, real or imagined.

At the other extreme, a committee on professional equality of the Washington Press Club likewise advocated proscribing Ms., but for opposite reasons. As reported by I. William Hill in Editor & Publisher for May 1, 1976, the committee urged abolition of courtesy titles for both men and women, except in obituaries or for clarity. In the committee's view, Ms. is "unnecessary, uninformative and (under current practices) requiring the use of the distracting phrase 'as she prefers to be known.' "

The joint stylebook no longer requires the "distracting phrase," but it has rejected both extremes and continues to mirror current usage, calling for Ms. when the woman wants it. Whenever the status of Ms. is clarified in contemporary usage, the joint stylebook is likely to follow along.

Much the same attitude is found in rules for references to race and ethnic groups. AP style sits firmly on the fence: "Use 'black' or 'Negro,' as appropriate in the context." And though the stylebook calls for "Mexican-American" rather than "Chicano," it adds: " 'Chicano' has been adopted by some social activists of Mexican descent, and may be used when activists use it to describe themselves." Not the grammarian or lexicographer, but the person who is subject of the story, determines the exception.

The varying practices in regard to courtesy titles illustrate another factor that conduces to enlightened attitudes toward usage. No working journalist can escape knowing that stylebook standards are not uniform, and that no stylebook has universal preeminence. The situation contrasts with that which prevails for dictionaries and handbooks of usage; they have no self-imposed limits to their authority, and even if the author is modest, the reader may assume universal validity for his or her favorite dictator. Furthermore, a writer may not even be aware that a different dictionary or usage manual would have different attitudes toward matters of disputed usage; the journalist, on the other hand, learns to expect and look for differences of style from one newspaper to another. It is something like the difference between religion and politics. Individuals have a choice of religion, wherever they live in the United States, but they must abide by the laws of the place where they happen to live, and submit to different laws when they move to a different political jurisdiction.

So the reporter leaving the Associated Press for The New York Times will leave the Ms.s behind and waste no time agonizing over the change.

Editors freely compile and revise their own stylebooks, aiming not to prescribe for all civilized writing but to set a style suited to the standards of their readers. Because so much material comes from wire services, the AP–UPI joint stylebook has a pervasive influence, but hardly a newspaper exists that does not make at least a few minor adjustments to suit local taste. Major newspapers issue their own complete stylebooks; smaller newspapers publish booklets or sheets keyed to the joint stylebook, indicating local points of difference.

The State Journal-Register, for example, a Copley newspaper in Springfield, Ill., in 1979 published a 26-page booklet of additions and modifications to the joint stylebook. The majority of entries deal with names encountered locally: agencies and offices of municipal government, for example, as well as of the state in the state capital. But there are usage differences too. Courtesy titles, as might be expected, are among items receiving special local treatment. The Journal-Register omits courtesy titles for women as well as men in second and subsequent reference, except in obituary, engagement and wedding reports; there both sexes get titles, though Ms. is to be avoided.

While the joint stylebook calls for a plural verb with "couple" of persons, the Journal-Register makes it singular. The sample sentence "The couple were married Saturday" in AP style contrasts with the Journal-Register's "The couple was married."

And while the joint stylebook insists on the spelling "theater" in all circumstances, the State Journal-Register allows "Theatre" in names like Theatre Guild.

In Jacksonville, Ill., 35 miles to the west, the state's oldest newspaper uses no supplemental sheet, but it too makes exceptions to the joint stylebook in the matter of titles. Editor John Power mentioned in a recent interview the Jacksonville Journal Courier's use of Mr., as well as Mrs. and Miss, in obituaries – which used to be provided in advance by foresighted citizens. And while the AP stylebook proscribes Dr. for those who hold only honorary doctorates, the Journal Courier follows the wishes of local honorees and Dr.s them.

In one case the Journal Courier determinedly goes against local preference, referring to "Rev. William Mallotke" despite his complaint that it should be "the Rev." Power explained that the newspaper's usage followed AP style, though in fact the joint stylebook preserves one of the shibboleths of American newspaper style by insisting on "the Rev." The solemn explanation in the AP Stylebook is that "the abbreviation 'Rev.' does not stand for a noun."

This explanation of "the Rev." is typical for newspaper stylebooks – brief and unemotional. Explanations, even of items hotly debated elsewhere, are spare, sometimes to the vanishing point, and not in the least argumentative; they present what appears to be simple fact. Compare the AP Stylebook and the American Heritage Dictionary on "bimonthly" and the dreaded "ain't":

bimonthly Means every other month. *Semimonthly* means twice a month.

bi·month·ly (bī-mŭnth′lē) *adj.* **1.** Happening every two months. **2.** *Nonstandard.* Happening twice a month; semimonthly. See Usage note below. —*adv.* **1.** Once every two months. **2.** *Non-standard.* Twice a month; semimonthly. See Usage note below. —*n. pl.* **bimonthlies.** A publication issued bimonthly.

Usage: Bimonthly is rigidly restricted to the sense of *once in two months*, and *biweekly* to that of *once in two weeks*, according to 84 per cent of the Usage Panel. The remainder also accept the corresponding secondary senses of *twice a month* and *twice a week*, which are more properly expressed by *semimonthly* and *semiweekly*. An even stricter distinction exists between *biannual* (twice a year) and *biennial* (once in two years, lasting for two years). *Biyearly*, in strict usage, means *once in two years*, and *semiyearly* means *twice a year*.

ain't A dialectical or substandard contraction. Use it only in quoted matter or special contexts.

ain't (ānt). *Nonstandard.* Contraction of *am not*. Also extended in use to mean *are not*, *is not*, *has not*, and *have not*.

Usage: Ain't, with few exceptions, is strongly condemned by the Usage Panel when it occurs in writing and speech that is not deliberately colloquial or that does not employ the contraction to provide humor, shock, or other special effect. The first person singular interrogative form *ain't I* (for *am I not* or *amn't I*), considered as a special case, has somewhat more acceptance than *ain't* employed with other pronouns or with nouns. (*Ain't I* has at least the virtue of agreement between *am* and *I*. With other pronouns, or nouns, *ain't* takes the place of *isn't* and *aren't* and sometimes of *hasn't* and *haven't*.) But *ain't I* is unacceptable in writing other than that which is deliberately colloquial, according to 99 per cent of the Panel, and unacceptable in speech to 84 per cent. The example *It ain't likely* is unacceptable to 99 per cent in both writing and speech. *Aren't I* (as a variant of the interrogative *ain't I*) is acceptable in writing to only 27 per cent of the Panel, but approved in speech by 60 per cent. Louis Kronenberger has this typical reaction: "A genteelism, and much worse than *ain't I*."

Both books reach the same conservative conclusion, but the reader of the AP Stylebook will have no sense that any dispute is involved, or that morality is at stake; each statement is just another arbitrary rule to keep in mind.

The exception among newspaper stylebooks in this regard is The New York

Times Manual of Style and Usage in its revised 1976 edition. Reflecting The Times' special responsibility as the leading defense against the decay of language, editor Lewis Jordan does not spare his sarcasm. Compare the Times Manual's entries for "imply, infer" and "hopefully" with their more conventional counterparts in the AP Stylebook:

imply, infer. The Bible says that sowers are also reapers. But an exception must be made for those who sow by implying and those who reap by inferring. The current tendency to make *infer* synonymous with *imply* would destroy an essential distinction. Let us continue to use *imply* when a speaker or writer implants allusions or suggestions, and to use *infer* when a listener or reader harvests from indirect or direct statements a crop of his own conclusions. Blessings may ensue.

imply, infer Writers or speakers *imply* in the words they use.

A listener or reader *infers* something from the words.

hopefully means in a hopeful manner, and its use should be confined to that meaning: *They sought hopefully for the solution so desperately needed.* Do not use *hopefully* in this sense: *Hopefully, they will find the solution so desperately needed.* The intended meaning in such a case is *they hope to find, it is hoped* (parenthetical) or *it is hoped that* or some equivalent phrase, and one of them should be used. The foregoing, it is hoped, will clear up this troublesome matter and enable us to move on hopefully to solutions of other problems.

hopefully It means in a hopeful manner. Do not use it to mean it is hoped, let us hope or we hope.

Right: *It is hoped that we will complete our work in June.*

Right: *We hope that we will complete our work in June.*

Wrong as a way to express the thought in the previous two sentences: *Hopefully, we will complete our work in June.*

The Times' attitude of upholding a noble standard against the ravages of decay appears in the editor's Foreword, where he declares, "The intent is to give preference to that which safeguards the language from debasement: to maintain, for instance, distinctions like that between 'imply' and 'infer'; to avoid faddish neologisms like the verbs 'host' and 'author' " – and yet even this traditionalist adds, "to avoid the timeworn and the trite; to shun slang and colloquialisms in inappropriate contexts, but to use them without self-consciousness when the context is appropriate."

As might be expected, the Foreword to the AP Stylebook, by Louis D. Boccardi, makes no mention of preservation or debasement. He writes, "The orders were: Make clear and simple rules, permit few exceptions to the rules, and rely heavily on the chosen dictionary as the arbiter of conflicts." And then simply, "Language changes, and we will review entries annually, making necessary changes."

Howard Simons' Preface to the Washington Post Deskbook on Style, published by McGraw-Hill in 1978, adopts a most tolerant attitude: "Other newspapers have different rules, different audiences, different resources, different needs. But to the extent that common sense informs this stylebook, it can be useful to all."

Common sense, acknowledged arbitrariness, variation from newspaper to newspaper, attention to community norms, awareness and acceptance of change – these factors combine to encourage in the reader and user of a newspaper stylebook an enlightened attitude toward usage. Perhaps nothing contributes so much to the sense of relativity projected by newspaper stylebooks, however, as the whimsicality of some of their strictly enforced rules.

—Consider, for example, The State Journal-Register's entry for "players": "It is Cubs first baseman Bill Buckner, not Cubs' first baseman Bill Buckner. Buckner plays for the Chicago National League ball club. He is not owned by it." Such reasoning would lead to "the plays audience," "General Grants campaign," "Lincolns assassination."

—Under "police beat," The Journal-Register warns: "We have had a consistent problem in leading police beat items with figures, be it dollars stolen, value of damage, etc. This shouldn't be done.
"Wrong: '$1,650 WORTH of stereo equipment. . . .' "

No explanation, of course, why this natural approach is wrong.

—The joint stylebook, in the hard-nosed tradition of usage purists though without fuss or comment, flatly prohibits "host" as a verb. Newspaper writers continue to overlook the entry.

—In AP-UPI style, "over" is not to be used for "more than"; "following" is not to be used for "after," as in "after dinner."

The greatest idiosyncracies, however, are to be found not in a stylebook that aims at satisfying all 1700 of the nation's daily newspapers, but in the special preferences of the individual newspapers themselves. They are exemplified in this conclusion to a leaflet of "Helps for Newspaper Correspondents" issued by the Journal Courier Co. in Jacksonville, Ill., and used until retired (but not superseded) in 1980:

SPECIAL DON'TS

Do **not** abbreviate names of days; names of months, except in dates; names of states, except after the name of a city.

Do not use contractions such as **don't, isn't, wasn't, can't, aren't, weren't, didn't.**

Do not use **ladies** for **women. Lady** is a title.

Do not write **bros.** for **brothers.**

Do not use **remains** in speaking of a dead person. Use **body.**

Do not use the name of the state after names of towns in your immediate territory.

Do not use the name of the state after names of major cities.

Do not write 32 **people.** Make it 32 **persons.**

Do not use Monday **eve** when you mean Monday **night**.

Do not use **there** for **their.**

Do not write **Mr.** J. P. Jones. When using initials, omit the **Mr.**

Do not use **Messrs.** or **Mesdames.**

Do not say 45 years of age. Make it 45 years old, or just 45.

Do not write **render** a song.

Do not begin a fire story with **"The fire laddies were called out . . ."** or **"the fire bell rang at . . ."**

Do not use **at his brother, Jack Jones' home.** Make it **at the home of his brother, Jack Jones.**

Do not use **a good time was had by all.**

Do not use **sick** for **ill.**

Do not abbreviate names of persons.
Do not begin a story with the time of day or month.
Do not spell out numbers above 10.
Do not say the weather is warm. Be specific by giving temperatures.
Do not copy news from other newspapers.

On a typical day in 1981, 240 million Americans went about their business, and 80 million daily newspapers were printed to help them go about that business. Tens of thousands of reporters consulted stylebooks – or at least kept them in mind – as they prepared stories for local newspapers and the wire services. Thanks to the joint stylebook, considerable uniformity in style and usage prevailed, but it was for the most part informal and attuned to change.

References

The Associated Press Stylebook and Libel Manual, ed. Howard Angione. New York: The Associated Press, 1977.

Facts About Newspapers '82. Washington, D.C.: American Newspaper Publishers Association, April 1982.

Helps for Newspaper Correspondents. Jacksonville, Ill.: Journal Courier Co., n.d.

HILL, I. WILLIAM. "Press club recommends style changes." *Editor & Publisher*, May 1, 1976, p. 74.

The New York Times Manual of Style and Usage, ed. Lewis Jordan. New York: Quadrangle/The New York Times Book Co., 1976.

O'HARA, J.D. "Everything from Ms. to zzz." (Review of AP and UPI Stylebooks.) *Columbia Journalism Review*, Jan.–Feb. 1978, pp. 55–57.

O'HARA, J.D. "Keeping up with the Times." (Review of *New York Times Manual*.) *Columbia Journalism Review*, May–June 1976, pp. 50–52.

"Poll shows policies on Ms. usage varies [*sic*]." *Editor & Publisher*, Nov. 22, 1975, p. 28.

RAMBO, C. DAVID. "Style, like fashion, changes with the times." *Presstime*, August 1983, pp. 24–35.

"Revised Stylebook Recalls the Basics." *Editor & Publisher*, Oct. 24, 1981, p. 32. (For the *Kansas City Star* and *Times*.)

"Revised UPI–AP stylebook goes into effect October 1." *Editor & Publisher*, Aug. 27, 1977, pp. 7, 25.

Stylebook: The State Journal-Register. Springfield, Ill.: State Journal-Register, 1979.

The UPI Stylebook, ed. Bobby Ray Miller. New York: United Press International, 1977.

The Washington Post Deskbook on Style, ed. Robert A. Webb. New York: McGraw-Hill, 1978.

WHITMAN, ALDEN. "The Times issues a new manual of style." *New York Times*, Feb. 2, 1976.

WILLIAMSON, LENORA. "New York Times stylebook does not recognize 'Ms.' " *Editor & Publisher*, Feb. 7, 1976, p. 16.

Chapter 8

Standards of English Usage in Language Tests

JOHN B. CARROLL

MAKERS and publishers of standardized tests do not attempt to set or enforce standards of English usage. If they appear to do so, it is only because they seek to respond to the demands, preferences, and tastes of their clients, the purchasers and users of tests in education, business and industry, government, and the private practice of psychology.

Problems of English usage and diction are involved to some degree in the large majority of psychological and educational tests, if only in the writing of test manuals and instructions to test-takers. But in most tests they also arise in the preparation of the actual questions or "items," whenever those items are couched in, or contain, verbal expression. They also come into notice when, as in some tests, examinees are required to give verbal responses; these verbal responses (e.g. "free response" answers, or even short essays) must be evaluated, and sometimes evaluation is at least in part according to standards of languge usage.

Tests are built for many different purposes, ranging from the assessment of general intelligence, aptitude and achievement to the evaluation of a person's proficiency in some highly specific area of knowledge or skill. There are also tests of personality, interests, and attitudes that are presented in written language. Test constructors have to attend to standards of English usage and diction just as writers in any field must. In addition, they often concern themselves with matters of language simplification, readability, vocabulary control, and the like, but these will not be considered here.

I will not address the problems or attitudes of test constructors in the preparation of whatever English text may be required in tests in general, for these problems and attitudes are little different from those found in other fields of writing. I focus, instead, on tests that are specifically designed to assess knowledge and ability in the use of the English language, especially knowledge of conventions of English usage in punctuation, capitalization, wording, sentence construction, and grammatical expression.

The making and distribution of tests is a large and diverse industry. There are hundreds of test publishers, although only a handful of them dominate the market.[1] There are literally thousands of published tests, but one can count only two or three dozen widely used instruments that are concerned with the testing of English usage.[2]

In preparing this paper, I wrote to those responsible for test construction activities at six of the larger test publishing organizations, and received prompt and informative replies from each addressee.[3] I asked the test constructors to tell me how they dealt with the problem of standards of English usage and diction in preparing their tests.

Of some help, also, were the comments of test reviewers published in the series of *Mental Measurements Yearbooks* edited over many years by Oscar K. Buros,[4] which provide test users with information about the characteristics of the many tests in print, and often sharp critiques of them from both measurement specialists and authorities in various disciplines and curriculum areas.

Constraints on Test Construction

Commercial test publishers are interested in making a profit, and even non-profit testing organizations must take care that their products are well accepted and widely used. This means that test constructors must be conscious of, and responsive to, the demands and attitudes of their clients with respect to what is tested, the format of the tests, the psychometric characteristics of the test scores, and many other matters, including cost, distribution policy, etc. However idealistic or innovative a test constructor might desire to be on some particular question of test content or format, the realities of the marketplace have to be faced. In most cases, test constructors lean toward compliance with perceived requirements and preferences of potential test purchasers and users – and in education, where most tests are used, this means school administrators, teachers, and even school boards and parents.

Where educational tests are concerned, the message from all my respondents was clear and simple: "Our tests follow the curriculum." Several test constructors reported going to great pains to determine exactly, and in detail, what the English curriculum of the schools across the country actually consists of, and would be likely to be, for the next few years during which planned tests would be applicable. They reported preparing lengthy "blueprints" of tests under development, with detailed specifications of item content and coverage, on the basis of examination of current textbooks, workbooks, state curriculum guides, and the like.

Since most tests are designed to be used nationwide, a common denominator of curricular content must be found. Local variations in curriculum standards must be set aside in favor of content that is nearly universally addressed throughout the nation. As one respondent commented, however, in the case of English it is astonishing how uniform the curriculum appears to be across the nation, despite the absence of dictation from any central educational authority.[5]

Nevertheless, there are tensions. In commenting on the National Teacher Examinations in English Language and Literature, a reviewer had this to say:

> . . . what this test attempts to do, it does very well. The audience for which it is written will probably be quite satisfied with it. All of which presents this reviewer with a worrisome prospect. If used in the intended ways, the NTE English language and literature test will do its share to insure a continuing supply of the kinds of English teachers there are already too

many of. We confront here the testmaker's classic dilemma of whether tests should attempt to influence curriculum or whether they should reflect the curriculum as it exists. Those responsible for this test have opted for the latter and in so doing have significantly reduced the probability that the teaching of English will at any time soon be able to address the critical need to develop communication fluency on the part of the captives of the English classroom.[6]

Indeed, most often, the "testmaker's classic dilemma" referred to here is resolved in favor of simply testing the curriculum as it is perceived to exist. In the case of tests of English usage, this implies adopting widely accepted standards. The testmaker's only problem is to determine what those standards are. On this, I will have more to say below.

There is another major source of constraint in test construction, namely, the desired measurement characteristics of a test. In order to be acceptable for use in most contexts, tests have to be capable of being administered in relatively short periods of time (e.g. in a school period, or at most in several school periods). Thus, they can usually cover only a small portion of the content addressed – ideally, a "representative sample" of it, but they must do that as efficiently and economically as possible. A further constraint is that one usually desires a test to spread the examinees over a range of performance from high to low. Although the matter is arguable, it is considered inefficient to test content that is likely to be known either by nearly all examinees or by only a tiny minority – at least, this is true for the typical "norm-referenced" test that seeks to determine a student's standing relative to other students at a particular age or grade level. (This constraint is less likely to apply in the case of the so-called "criterion-referenced" test that attempts to assess student knowledge and performance on an absolute basis, with respect to a particular curriculum or curriculum unit.) For technical reasons, the inclusion of items that do not help in spreading examinees over a range of performance tends to decrease the reliability – the measurement accuracy – of the test scores.

In order to insure that tests have desired measurement characteristics, test constructors have developed elaborate procedures of field testing and item analysis, often carried out over a period of years. Preliminary drafts of test items are tried out on appropriate samples of students, with the object of finding out how easy or difficult the items are, or more precisely, the numbers of students who answer them according to the designated key. If the items are multiple-choice, the frequencies of answers to the several presumably incorrect choices are determined. Items are selected or revised for the final form of the test, or thrown out as unpromising, on the basis of the tryout data, which also contain information on how effectively an item discriminates between students who perform well and who perform poorly on other items in the test.

It will frequently happen that apparently quite legitimate and worthwhile items are eliminated from tests as a result of field trials and item analysis. Experience has taught makers of English usage tests that there are many points of usage that are not worth testing because they do not yield items with desirable statistics. The director of English testing at Educational Testing Service, for example, surmised that "only a tiny minority of a sample population would be found to observe the distinction between *different from* and *different than*. . . . The statistics would show that ninety-five percent of the population was guessing, and guessing the wrong answers."[7] His reply attached a long list of points that are expressly not tested in ETS's usage tests, including not only the distinction just mentioned but also, to give only a few examples, the acceptability of *center around*, *irregardless*, *kind of a*, and *try and*; distinctions between *anxious* and *eager*, *between* and *among*, *fewer* and *less*, *like* and *as*, and *which* and *that* (in nonrestrictive and restrictive clauses); the placement of *only* when no ambiguity is involved; the possessive with the gerund (as in *John['s] leaving*); and the number of the verb after *none*.

It should be noted that this list was a guide in constructing tests used at the senior high school and collegiate level; an even more liberal list (or possibly a more conservative one) might apply in the construction of tests at lower educational levels by ETS or other testing organizations. One can speculate about reasons for the poor item statistics: Were these points ones that most students know, or were they points that few students know? Is the teaching of these points so varied, inconsistent, and confused that it is meaningless or unfair to include them in a test intended for nationwide use? In any event, from the perspective of the test constructor, the main reason for not testing them comes out of item statistics, regardless of how the importance of these usage points might be viewed.

One respondent cited an experience with what he regarded as a "perfectly legitimate" test item that was answered more often correctly by students in the lower half of the test distribution than by students in the top half. Obviously, this item could not be included in the test. He also mentioned a case in which he prepared what he thought was a "perfectly honest test," only to find that it produced a "very much skewed set of scores." The editors had to "insert a number of rather insipid and sometimes obsolete uses in order to get a normal spread."[8]

Several respondents commented that they generally avoid testing points to English usage in which there is significant dialect variation, mainly on the ground that to do so could produce troublesome variations in regional norms and expose publishers to accusations of racial and ethnic bias.

Determining Standards of English Usage for Tests

Respondents were practically unanimous in stating that they sought to test for knowledge of "standard, formal written English usage." Some observed that there were occasions when informal speech could be the standard, but insisted that contexts for such items would have to be clearly evident. Most commented that they were, in general, rather conservative in the standards they adopted – perhaps not as conservative as purists like Edwin Newman and William Safire, but conservative enough to conform to the standards they felt were being observed in the majority of school curricula. In determining what those standards are, they appeal to a wide range of textbooks, writer's handbooks, style manuals, dictionaries, and books such as Theodore Bernstein's *The Careful Writer*.[9] They claim also to be alert to the writing practices observed in respected newspapers, magazines, and current general literature.

Still, as one respondent commented, "no one source is considered the authority as judgment must inevitably be used to determine the appropriateness of language within the particular testing context."[10] The implication, apparently, was that test authors have to make their own decisions when sources disagree. Another respondent pointed out that "most of the decisions in language usage testing derive from the authors of the particular achievement test," and that differences could occur from one test to another within the same testing organization.[11] Nearly all respondents mentioned the importance of item statistics in determining whether items should be retained, revised, or scrapped.

Test constructors make much use of panels of experts. Often test construction is a long-drawn-out process, involving a multi-stage review by panels of different kinds of experts – professors of English and of journalism, professional writers, and teachers, not only in preliminary stages of item writing, but also in the evaluation of field testing data and in the revision of tests after initial publication. The many types of test review make for a kind of democracy in decision making, such that many shades of opinion are taken into account, from all regions of the country. At the same time, it could be argued that the multiple review process makes for conservatism in testing usage, in that minority objections to items may be given disproportionate weight. In any case, it cannot be said that test constructors have fixed and immutable attitudes about standards of English usage that they test. They are responsive to their clients and potential test users.

The standards of English usage tested for are reflected in instructions to test takers. For example, in administering the Usage test (L-4) included in the Iowa Test of Basic Skills designed for grades 3 through 9, the teacher is to read:

> This is a test on the use of words. It will show whether you know how to use words according to the standards of correctly written English.[12]

The directions for administering the language test of the Stanford Achievement Test became somewhat less prescriptive over the years. They included the instruction, in 1964: "Decide which, if either, of the two choices in each sentence is correct in standard written English"; in 1972, "Choose the best form to write in a school paper"; in 1982, "Decide which word or group of words belongs in the blank." The chief author of this test commented: ". . . the items are labeled as applied grammar, and are in general noncontroversial at present. . . . We have tried to omit any that are not considered standard written English."[13]

The current College Board testing program includes, alongside the well-known Scholastic Aptitude Test, a test frankly labeled as a "Test of Standard Written English," and test-takers are thus clearly put on notice that they are to adhere to usage in "standard written English," whatever that may be.

What Usage Standards are Tested?

The kinds of usage standards that are tested vary somewhat depending on the population for which a test is designed. A reasonably good appreciation of what the standards are can be attained only through inspection of the tests themselves. Many will doubtless be surprised, however, at the rather elementary character of many of the questions asked – most of them, as one correspondent noted, "beneath the notice of Edwin Newman."[14] Even at higher levels, commonly tested points include such matters as the agreement of subject and verb (but usually avoiding such problem cases as *none is/are*), the correct case for personal and relative pronouns as objects of verbs and prepositions (but avoiding such problems as *It's me*), and the avoidance of adjectives like *good* and *real* as adverbs. A reviewer characterized the items in the English Expression subtest of the Sequential Tests of Educational Progress as follows:

> To turn to the test itself, the potential user should start by trying the questions on himself. He will probably find the items unambiguous and carefully framed, provided he accepts the premises of the test makers. These premises are rather conservative. The student whose classification depends on the test would do well to avoid dialect forms, to distinguish *like* and *as* with precision, and under no circumstances to label "the reason is because" as "no error." To be fair, with all the talk of correctness and effectiveness, there does emerge a half-articulated ideal of prose composition that does command respect. Aside from correctness in the sense of conformity to allegedly standard usage, what is being pushed is a type of prose which is regular, unambiguous, lucid, and therefore readable and eminently suitable for practical situations – for examinations, manuals, scholarly articles, and the more honest forms of journalism.[15]

Test constructors recognize that language changes, and over the past several decades, one can see certain trends in the kinds of grammar and usage points tested. Above all, test makers now avoid testing matters on which there is evident disagreement among language authorities, or that are obviously in transition. Although they would probably avoid splitting infinitives in writing instructions and test manuals, they do not penalize students for doing so, and the form is never, or rarely, the critical matter in a test item. Similarly, they would be inclined to substitute *unbiased* or *indifferent*, as appropriate, for *disinterested* and *uninterested* in a reading comprehension passage, and would not find it profitable to test students' appreciation of the differences in meaning involved.

This is not to say that test makers have no problems in determining standards of usage. One respondent remarked that it is "difficult to decide what should be tested as standard English, since the standards are constantly changing."[16] Another respondent cited a recent discussion in England about the capitalization of words referring to the deity, pointing out that schools would probably be slow to accept uncapitalized forms, and that "many curriculum specialists would not understand a test adopting such rules."[17]

On the whole, it may be said that test makers tend to show a strong allegiance to rather conservative but undebatable standards of written English. Their tests give high marks to students who have learned the conventions observed by the majority of good writers and editors. One respondent commented that he had read Safire and Newman "with an ironic interest, attending more to the play of intelligence and wit in their prose than to their biases or (can we say?) their standards." "As for the 'liberal linguists' you mentioned," he continued, "there are few of us that could be lumped with Labov or Fishman or Spolsky.

Some of the 'liberal-ness' of the linguists I have always felt to be more a matter of politics than of scholarship, anyway."[18]

Conclusion

Attitudes and policies of language testers on English usage are well summarized in the following excerpt from one respondent's letter:

> Through this procedure – basing the tests on the most widely used textbooks, consulting reliable published references, using outside content and bias reviewers from different areas of the country, and sorting for items with the "healthiest" statistics – we hope to test the most widely agreed-upon language usage.[19]

Test makers and publishers stand somewhere in the middle between purists and liberals on matters of language usage, perhaps a little closer to the purists than to the liberals. Because of the various constraints under which they work, it is probably too much to expect them to mount any sort of crusade in either direction away from their centrist position, and it is extremely unlikely that they would be inclined to do so, or that they would be successful in any such effort.

Notes

1. A list of more than 500 publishers of psychological and educational tests, with addresses and indications of the tests they publish, is to be found in Oscar Krisen Buros, ed., *The Eighth Mental Measurements Yearbook*. Highland Park, N.J.: Gryphon Press, 1978, pp. 1988–1996.
2. Details about these tests, and usually, reviews of them by one or more authorities, are to be found in O. K. Buros, *op. cit.* Most of them are found classified in sections devoted to achievement batteries and tests in English.
3. Listed here, in alphabetical order, are the six test construction organizations contacted, the major tests concerned with language usage that are published by them, and the individuals supplying replies to my queries (some of these individuals are not directly employed by these organizations, but are authors of tests published by them):
    The American College Testing Program publishes an English Usage Test as a part of its ACT Assessment Program designed for candidates for college entrance. Information was supplied by Cynthia B. Schmeiser, Assistant Vice President, Test Development Area, Research and Developmental Division.
    CTB/McGraw Hill publishes two widely used tests containing sections on English usage: the California Achievement Tests and the Comprehensive Tests of Basic Skills. Both are multi-level batteries designed for all grades of elementary and secondary school; most of the levels include sections devoted to English usage and language structure. The organization also publishes an Educational Skills Test, designed for entrants in open-door colleges, that includes a Mechanics of Writing section. Further, it has developed and made available criterion-referenced Writing Proficiency Programs, described as a diagnostic-prescriptive approach to the teaching of expository writing at Grades 9–13. The programs include components designed to assess students' writing skills. Responses to my queries were received from Dr. Donald Ross Green, Director of Research, and several editors of tests, including Arnold W. Seibel, Editor, Criterion-Referenced Instruments, Test Development Department.
    Educational Testing Service publishes numerous tests designed for various levels of elementary, secondary, and higher education. The most important among these involving the testing of language usage are the Test of Standard Written English, for college entrants; the CLEP (College-Level Examination Program) General Examinations: English Composi-

tion; The CEEB (College Entrance Examination Board) Achievement Test in English Composition; and the National Teacher Examinations: English Language and Literature. It has also been responsible for preparing the Sequential Tests of Educational Progress, a multi-level achievement battery designed for grades 4 to 14, each level of which includes a section on English Expression. An extensive reply to my queries was received from Dr. Robert J. Jones, Chairman, Humanities, College Board Test Development.

The Psychological Corporation publishes a large variety of psychological and educational tests; however, test construction and research are conducted chiefly by outside authors, with follow-up research done in-house. Its Differential Aptitude Tests, a battery designed for high school counseling and vocational guidance, contains a section on Language Usage. Information was received from Dr. Jerome E. Doppelt, Director, Measurement Division, and from David O. Herman, Senior Project Director, and Marjorie Wolper, Senior Editor. In addition, replies were received from Dr. Irving Balow, University of California at Riverside, author of the language sections of the Metropolitan Achievement Tests, an achievement battery for elementary and secondary schools, and from Dr. Eric F. Gardner, Syracuse University, senior author of the Stanford Achievement Tests, and Dr. William W. West, University of South Florida, a consultant who has prepared language tests in the Stanford Achievement Test series (as well as tests for other testing organizations).

Riverside Publishing Company, a subsidiary of Houghton Mifflin Company, is a prominent publisher of psychological and educational tests. Important and widely used tests involving sections on English usage are the Iowa Tests of Basic Skills, an achievement test battery designed for grades K through 9 developed at the University of Iowa; the Tests of Academic Progress, for grades 9–12; the College English Placement Test; and the Purdue High School English Test. Information was received from Dr. Edward C. Drahozal, Senior Research Consultant, Test Development and Research.

Science Research Associates publishes several tests that have sections concerned with language usage: the SRA Achievement Series, for grades 2–12; the Iowa Tests of Educational Development, for grades 9–12; and the National Educational Development Tests, for grades 9–10. A response to my queries was received from Marlene C. Semple, Project Editor, Test Development.

4. The latest of these yearbooks was cited in note 1. Earlier volumes in the series have been appearing since 1935. With Buros's death in 1978, publication of the series is to be continued by the Buros Institute of Mental Measurements at the University of Nebraska. A further useful source of information is O. K. Buros's *Tests in Print II* (Highland Park, N.J.: Gryphon Press, 1974); also, reviews of tests in English have been assembled in a special volume, *English Tests and Reviews*, from the same editor and publisher, 1975.

5. Letter to author from Eric F. Gardner, Syracuse University, 2 August 1982.

6. Quoted from a review by Roger A. Richards, Berkshire Community College, in O. K. Buros, ed., *The Eighth Mental Measurements Yearbook* (Highland Park, N.J.: Gryphon Press, 1978), p. 144.

7. Letter to author from Robert J. Jones, Educational Testing Service, 3 August 1982.

8. Letter to author from William W. West, University of South Florida, 11 August 1982.

9. The list of references cited by my respondents is too long to reproduce here. Among the more frequently mentioned references were the following (which, except for general English dictionaries, I cite in what appears to be the latest edition):

Dictionaries
   The American Heritage Dictionary
   Webster's Third New International Dictionary
   Webster's New Collegiate Dictionary

Usage dictionaries
   Bergen Evans & Cornelia Evans, *A Dictionary of Contemporary American Usage* (New York: Random House, 1957).
   Margaret M. Bryant (Ed.), *Current American Usage* (New York: Funk & Wagnalls, 1962).
   Henry W. Fowler, *A Dictionary of Modern English Usage* (2nd ed., rev., New York: Oxford University Press, 1965).

Writers' handbooks

T. M. Bernstein, *The Careful Writer: A Modern Guide to English Usage* (New York: Atheneum, 1975).

T. M. Bernstein, *Miss Thistlebottom's Hobgoblins: The Careful Writer's Guide to the Taboos, Bugbears, and Outmoded Rules of English Usage* (New York: Farrar, Straus & Giroux, 1971).

John C. Hodges and Mary E. Whitten, *Harbrace College Handbook* (8th edit., New York: Harcourt Brace Jovanovich, 1977).

Frederick C. Crews, *The Random House Handbook* (2nd edit., New York: Random House, 1977).

Wilma R. Ebbitt and David R. Ebbitt, *[Perrin's] Writers' Guide and Index to English* (6th edit., Glenview, Illinois: Scott Foresman, 1978).

Style manuals

A Manual of Style (Chicago: University of Chicago Press, 1969).

American Psychological Association. *Publication Manual* (2nd edit., Washington, D.C.: American Psychological Association, 1974).

Textbooks and grammars

Hans P. Guth & Edgar H. Schuster, *American English Today* (New York: McGraw-Hill, 1975–1977).

Raymond W. Pence and D. W. Emery, *A Grammar of Present-day English* (2nd edit., New York: Macmillan, 1967).

Robert C. Pooley, *The Teaching of English Usage* (Urbana, Illinois: National Council of Teachers of English, 1974).

John E. Warriner and Francis Griffith, *English Grammar and Composition* (New York: Harcourt Brace Jovanovich, 1977).

10. Letter to author from Cynthia B. Schmeiser, American College Testing Program, 10 August 1982.

11. Letter to author from Marjorie Wolper, The Psychological Corporation, 27 July 1982.

12. *Teacher's Guide for Administration Interpretation and Use, Levels 9–14, Iowa Tests of Basic Skills* (Boston and Iowa City: Houghton Mifflin, 1979), p. 19.

13. Letter to author from Eric F. Gardner, Syracuse University, 2 August 1982.

14. Memorandum to author from Arnold W. Seibel, CTB/McGraw-Hill, August 1982.

15. Quotation from a review by John C. Sherwood, Professor of English, University of Oregon, in O. K. Buros, ed., *The Eighth Mental Measurements Yearbook* (Highland Park, N.J.: Gryphon Press, 1978), p. 145.

16. Letter to author from Marlene C. Semple, Science Research Associates, 2 August 1982.

17. Letter to author from William W. West, University of South Florida, 11 August 1982.

18. Letter to author from Robert J. Jones, Educational Testing Service, 3 August 1982.

19. Letter to author from Marlene C. Semple, Science Research Associates, 2 August 1982.

Chapter 9

The Plain English Movement

JANICE C. REDISH

FOR at least the past decade, government and private businesses have been trying to reduce the paperwork burden on themselves and their clients. Reducing this burden has two complementary aspects – eliminating some paperwork entirely and simplifying the rest. The effort to simplify the language in legal, government, business, technical, and academic documents has been called the "plain English movement."

This paper is an overview of the plain English movement as it developed in the 1970s and as it is progressing in the 1980s. In the first half of the paper, I discuss what plain English is (and isn't), where plain English applies, and what's been happening in the plain English movement. In the second half of the paper, I explore what the plain English movement has accomplished, and where resistance comes from that keeps it from accomplishing more.

1. What is Plain English?

Plain English means writing that is straightforward, that reads as if it were spoken. It means writing that is unadorned with archaic, multisyllabic words and majestic turns of phrase that even educated readers cannot understand. Plain English is clear, direct, and simple; but good plain English has both clarity and grace (to borrow the title of Joseph Williams' excellent new English textbook).

Unfortunately, many people – both opponents and proponents of the plain English movement – assume that plain English means limiting the writer to one-clause sentences with words of one or two syllables. Some people are put off by writing like that; some worry that it can't be sufficient to convey the law.

The *Quarterly Review of Doublespeak* recently reported that one airline had a plain English version of its policy on overselling seats on a sign on its counter: "We overbook. You may get bumped. We will pay you" (*QRD*, Vol. 8, No. 2, Feb. 1982). That is certainly plain English, but lawyers will be quick to point out that these ten words aren't enough to explain the legal intricacies of the policy on bumping passengers. The plain English movement says the legal document can also be put into language that ordinary people can understand – perhaps not in ten words, not in two- three- and four-word sentences, but in clear, comprehensible language.

Lawyers, in a state that requires plain English in service agreements for consumers, developed new forms that begin, "You are the client. Your name and address are ... I am your lawyer." Some lawyers worry about legal documents written in such simple language. They complain that their clients may be put off by the excessive simplicity; and they may be right. Only a test with a variety of clients will tell us if the new forms are appropriate. These forms are in plain English; but they could also be written in a more sophisticated style and still be in plain English.

The objective of the plain English movement is to have writers *communicate effectively* with their readers. The appropriate level for the writing depends in part on the characteristics of the audience and the purpose of the document. For a document to be in plain English, the people who use it must be able to

find the information they need easily, and
understand it the first time they read it.

See Figures 1, 2, and 3 below.

2. Where Does Plain English Apply?

Although the phrase "plain English" has been used primarily for legal and bureaucratic documents, interest in plain English extends far beyond government. The intent of the plain English movement – making documents easily understandable to busy readers – and the techniques that are being developed and taught by plain English writers are equally applicable to business, technical, and academic writing.

Executives are interested in plain English because clear, direct communication can save them reading time now and save them the costs of misunderstanding later. Computer manufacturers are becoming more interested in plain English as their businesses expand to reach consumers who have no training in computer technology or computer jargon.

University teachers in many fields are interested in the plain English movement because it offers an alternative to the philosophy that writing is an art that can be shown but not taught. Writing in plain English is not the same as

Figure 1

This sentence is part of the "covenants and conditions" of an installment sales agreement (a loan for a new car). The spelling and wording are reprinted *exactly* as they appear on the document.

The buyer further promises to pay the holder hereof a delinquency and collection charge for default in the payment of any instalments above recited, where such default has continued for a period of ten days, such charge not to exceed five per cent of the instalments in default or the sum of five dollars, whichever is the lesser.

A plain English version of this sentence might be:

You also promise to pay a late fee if your payment is more than 10 days overdue. This late fee will be

five percent of the amount overdue or
five dollars

whichever is less.

Figure 2

This letter, addressed to a job applicant, is not in plain English. It is much too wordy; the writer uses pompous words unnecessarily. The important message (Sorry, we aren't going to ask you to an interview) is buried in an impersonal sentence in the third paragraph (Regrettably, your candidacy was affected.)

We sincerely appreciate the time, effort and interest you took in responding to our advertisement. Moreover, we are gratified that you made us cognizant of qualifications that may be applicable to our rapidly growing company.

While the response was most gratifying, its magnitude unfortunately precludes personal contact with each candidate. In order to at least communicate in some practical manner, however, it is necessary to utilize a rather impersonal vehicle that in no way can truly express our appreciation for sharing your personal and professional qualifications with us.

Recently we have reviewed candidates' qualifications relative to the position of your interest, and have narrowed the field of applicants. Regrettably, your candidacy was affected. Accordingly, we will retain your résumé for future consideration. Be assured that complete confidence will be maintained.

We thank you for sharing your qualifications with us. Hopefully a subsequent position opening will provide us the opportunity to discuss career opportunities, in depth, together.

Sincerely.

Figure 3

These are the headings from two different agencies' versions of an application form for loans to college students. Which do you wish was the form you had to understand?

1. PRIVACY ACT NOTICE
   RIGHT TO FINANCIAL PRIVACY ACT NOTICE
   CRIMINAL PENALTIES
   NOTICE
   GUARANTEED STUDENT LOAN PROGRAM
   TERMS AND CONDITIONS OF LOANS
   GUARANTEE FEE
   ELIGIBLE STUDENT BORROWERS
   ELIGIBLE LENDERS
   ELIGIBLE EDUCATIONAL INSTITUTIONS

2. What is the guaranteed student loan program?
   Who is eligible to apply for a guaranteed student loan?
   To whom do I apply for a loan?
   How much can I borrow?
   How much should I borrow?
   What are the terms of a guaranteed student loan?
   What will my monthly repayment be after graduation?
   When should I apply for a loan?
   How do I apply for a guaranteed student loan?

crafting fiction à la Faulkner or James Joyce. The skills needed to write clear, succinct non-fiction prose or to develop useful, understandable forms can be taught; and the ability to write well is a highly valued skill in a highly competitive world.

3. What Has Been Happening? (A brief history of the plain English movement)

Before the 1970s

The plain English movement isn't really new. Stuart Chase in *The Power of Words* (1953) bemoaned the "gobbledygook" that flourished then in the bureaucracy, in the law, and in universities.

Even before the plain English movement was revived in the 1970s, John O'Hayre, an employee of the Bureau of Land Management (part of the Department of the Interior), wrote a book called *Gobbledygook Has Gotta Go*. The sixteen essays in the book still make an excellent easy-to-read text on how to write plain English.

For the writer, inside or outside of government, who wanted to write plain English, other sources were also available before the 1970s. These ranged from George Orwell's six principles in his classic essay, "Politics and the English Language," to Strunk and White's slim volume of good advice, to Rudolf Flesch's books with titles like *The Art of Readable Writing*.

What was missing before the 1970s was any mandate that lawyers and bureaucrats write so that consumers could understand. Exhortations by essayists and style books by writing specialists carried little weight against centuries of tradition. In the 1970s, the plain English movement acquired greater legitimacy through a federal commission, presidential executive orders, and new laws and regulations on the federal and state levels.

What happened to make plain English an issue worthy of new laws and regulations? Two major concerns came together to produce the plain English movement of the 1970s. One was the tremendous growth in the size of the federal government and the inordinate amount of paperwork that new government programs generated. The other was the rise in consumer activism.

Since 1970: Plain English at the federal level

Since 1970, plain English has been mandated in a few federal laws and regulations governing consumer documents. The Magnuson–Moss Act sets requirements for readable warranties. The Truth-in-Lending regulation (Reg. Z) sets requirements for language and print in credit documents. The Electronic Funds Transfer Act requires clear writing in automatic banking rules. ERISA (the Employment Retirement Income Security Act) requires readable pension plan summaries (Black, 1981, pp. 267–268). In all of these cases, the laws themselves are not models of plain English and many experts quarrel with the specific requirements. Nevertheless, the intent is to make legal documents clear to the non-legally trained consumer.

The Paperwork Commission. The concern for the amount of paperwork the government imposes on individuals and businesses led first to the Commission on Federal Paperwork. Established by an act of Congress in 1974, the Commission spent two and a half years studying the paperwork burden and recommending ways to alleviate it.

The Commission's thirty-six reports on federal programs, cross-program problems, and the impact of paperwork on people contain a total of 520 recommendations. In its *Final Summary Report* (dated 3 October 1977), the Commission estimated the cost of federal paperwork at "more than $100 billion a year or about $500 for each person in this country." The Commission concluded that "a substantial portion of the cost is unnecessary" and, moreover, that "federal paperwork hurts most those least able to fend for themselves." One of the strongest messages in the Commission's report was that the government needed to rewrite its documents into understandable language and formats that were clear to consumers.

President Carter's Executive Orders. Many of the Commission's recommendations were adopted by the Carter administration. Some were placed as requirements on federal agencies through two executive orders. In Executive Order 12044 (24 March 1978), President Carter established a regulatory reform program. One part of that program was the requirement that all major regulations "[be] written in plain English and [be] understandable to those who must comply with [them]."

President Carter also issued an Executive Order requiring agencies to reduce the burden that forms put on individuals and businesses (EO 12174, 30 November 1979). Again, the agencies were to reduce burden in two ways – by only using necessary forms and by keeping necessary forms "as short as possible . . . elicit[ing] information in a simple, straightforward fashion." EO 12174 also required each executive agency to prepare an annual paperwork budget, not in terms of dollars, but in terms of the hours required to comply with its requests for information. The Office of Management and Budget (OMB) was given the authority to review and modify the agencies' paperwork budgets.

The Paperwork Reduction Act. When he issued EO 12174, President Carter also sent proposals for a paperwork control program to Congress. Part of that program was to put the provisions of EO 12174 into law and, furthermore, to extend OMB's authority to agencies whose paperwork had not previously been reviewed by OMB.

The Reagan Administration. President Carter signed the Paperwork Reduction Act in late 1980, but the new law did not take effect until after the change in administrations. In the Reagan administration, the emphasis has shifted from a consumer orientation to a business orientation, from plain English to eliminating paper. On the one hand, one of President Reagan's first acts in office was to rescind both of President Carter's executive orders (12044 and 12174) in favor of an order on regulatory reform that said nothing about clear language (EO 12291, February 17, 1981). On the other hand, OMB in the current administration is taking the Paperwork Reduction Act very seriously, slashing paperwork budgets and refusing to allow agencies to collect information as they traditionally have.

The official government positions, however, have had less impact on what actually happens than the conviction of an agency's administrator. Administrators in the Carter days who had no interest in plain English paid lip service to the executive orders and did nothing. Administrators who understand that clarity in documents saves money for businesses and for the government are still simplifying their documents.

Since 1970: Plain English at the state level

Government documents. Until very recently, most of the action to improve government documents has been at the federal level. Two state legislatures, however, have just passed laws affecting state government documents. In California, beginning 1 January 1983, all state agencies will have to write their documents in "plain, straightforward language." In Michigan, all state forms that are reviewed under the new *state* Paperwork Reduction Act will have to be in plain language.

Consumer documents. Most of the plain English action at the state level has been in attempts to legislate clarity and comprehensibility in consumer contracts. Seven states now have plain English laws: New York, Connecticut, Hawaii, Maine, New Jersey, West Virginia, and Minnesota. Similar bills are pending in several states and have been introduced but defeated in others. (I'll discuss some of the objections that have caused these defeats in Section 5 below.)

The plain English laws vary somewhat from state to state, although most follow the model of the first – New York's Sullivan Law (named for its sponsor, State Assemblyman Peter Sullivan). The laws typically cover only agreements between a consumer and a person or organization acting as a business (that means a landlord as well as a bank). Leases, mortgages, service contracts, credit applications, and loan forms are typical of the documents covered. Some of the state laws don't cover insurance policies because they are covered by different laws. Some of the state laws set a maximum amount that can be involved, and that excludes many real estate documents.

Most of the state laws have only a vague definition of plain English – for example, "written in a clear and coherent manner using words with common and everyday meanings; appropriately divided and captioned by its various sections." Only New Jersey and Connecticut offer more detailed clear writing guidelines as part of the law. In New Jersey, the guidelines are for judges to consider when a case is presented. In Connecticut, the guidelines are one of two possible tests a judge may use to determine if a document is in plain English. The second acceptable test in Connecticut is a readability score.

Connecticut is the only state that sets a readability score as an acceptable test of plain English in consumer contracts. Many states, however, use readability scores as the test of plain English in insurance policies. Readability formulas are very poor measures of how comprehensible and useful a document is. They don't tell if a document is well organized or well designed. They don't consider the grammar of the sentences at all. The use of readability scores as relevant measures of plain English is a very important and controversial topic. Unfortunately, I don't have space to discuss it at length here. (See Redish, 1979, 1980, 1981; Charrow, 1979; Charrow and Charrow, 1980; Selzer, 1983.)

The plain English laws have had a beneficial effect beyond the limited scope of their technical application. They have served their purpose not by sending people to court over incomprehensible documents, but by being catalysts for change. Consumers in states that have not passed plain English laws have also often benefited, as businesses that operate in several states usually use their new documents wherever they do business.

Since 1970: Plain English in the private sector

Insurance companies began to simplify their policies in the mid-1970s even before any of the state laws on consumer credit documents were passed. By 1979, thirty states had passed or proposed laws or regulations requiring readable policies in at least some types of insurance (Pressman, 1979). Many home insurance, property and casualty insurance, and life insurance policies have now been simplified. In addition, many banks and loan agencies that are not affected by state plain English laws have seen the value of clear English for their own staff and their consumers and have rewritten their documents.

4. What Has the Plain English Movement Accomplished?

Since the mid-1970s, a handful of government documents and many insurance and banking documents have been rewritten into plain English. There are new handbooks and training programs to help writers, designers, and teachers. There has been an upsurge of interest in research on language and design. As examples appear in new fields and are accepted by lawyers and consumers, it becomes easier for other writers in the same field to follow the examples. It also becomes a little easier to persuade writers in other fields of the acceptability of simplifying their documents.

In order for a movement like plain English to succeed, we must

increase awareness of the problems that traditional documents cause,
understand what causes the problems,
develop ways to solve the problems,
apply the solutions, and
teach others how to apply the solutions.

In the past decade, work has been carried out on all of these aspects of the plain English movement.

Examples of increasing awareness: Simply Stated, the newsletter that we put out at the Document Design Center, began with a circulation of 300 in 1979 and now goes to more than 10,000 people. The Practising Law Institute courses on Drafting Documents in Plain Language in 1979 and again in 1981 drew lawyers from around the country who wanted to learn about plain English laws and how to comply with them (MacDonald, 1979; Given, 1981).

Examples of understanding the problems and developing solutions. Much of the work on understanding the problems and developing solutions has been done here at the Document Design Center where an interdisciplinary team has pulled together research from many academic fields which we apply when we analyze and rewrite documents (Felker, 1980; Felker *et al.*, 1981; Charrow, 1981). Research has shown that the *organization* of public documents is as much a problem as the length of the sentences and the difficulty of specific words. Research at Carnegie–Mellon University has shown that readers trying to make sense out of traditional legal documents translate them into scenes in which there are people doing actions. Important and relevant research is also being done in Great Britain and Europe (Wright, 1980; Hartley, 1981; Jonassen, 1982).

Examples of solutions. The examples in Figures 4 and 5 show how writers have applied the solutions to produce examples of plain English.

Examples of teaching others. Teaching others to write in plain English encompasses both retraining writers on the job and changing the curriculum in writing courses for people still in school. Workshops in clear writing are now available from many sources. Interest in "practical" writing courses has grown immensely in colleges and professional schools.

During the 1960s, many schools abolished their writing requirement; during the 1970s they expanded their writing programs. The focus of freshman English courses changed from literature to composition. Writing specialists set up labs on most campuses where students can get help in learning basic writing skills. The National Endowment for the Humanities helped establish programs linking writing specialists and subject-matter specialists on the premise that writing is a skill every discipline requires. Research about writing in non-academic settings began to change academic courses (Faigley and Miller, 1982; Goswami, Redish, Felker, and Siegel, 1981; Anderson *et al.*, 1983). Books on clear English for lawyers began to appear (Wydick, 1979; Felsenfeld and Siegel, 1978; see also the material in MacDonald, 1979 and Given, 1981). The Document Design Center is now developing a new course in clear legal writing for first year law students (see *Simply Stated*, p. 22). In the summer of 1982, eighty teachers of legal writing came to a two-day institute to learn about these materials and to get ideas for teaching future lawyers how to write in clear English.

The plain English network grows steadily. Examples of documents in plain English continue to appear. Yet all of the plain English material together represents only a small fraction of the documents in circulation. Why?

Figure 4

Plain English in legal notices (on an application form for a student loan).

The Privacy Act of 1974 allows us to require you to give your Social Security Number (SSN) in order to receive a loan. We need your SSN to identify you on our records, to keep track of your eligibility and school attendance, and to record your payments. If you do not put your SSN on the application in item 2, you will not receive a loan.

The Right to Financial Privacy Act allows the U.S. Department of Education to have access to any information about you that we keep because we have made a loan to you. If you get a loan, we will tell a credit bureau how much you have borrowed from us and whether you repaid it when you should. If you want to keep a good credit rating, you should make sure that you are never late in making your loan payments.

If you lie on this application, and get a loan that you would not have gotten if you had told the truth, you may have to pay a fine or go to jail or both.

Figure 5

Plain English in a handbook on insurance benefits:

How long will my spouse receive the Spouse's Benefit?

How long your spouse receives these benefits will depend on how much service you have at the time of your death.

If you have less than 20 years of service, then your spouse will receive payments for a period that is 2 times the length of your service. For example, if you die after putting in 18 years of service, your spouse will receive monthly benefit payments for twice this amount of time, or for 36 years.

If you have 20 years or more of service at the time of your death, your spouse will get these benefits until he or she dies.

We may require proof of age, family status, and other facts relating to any person's qualifications to receive Spouse's Benefits. All proof must be satisfactory to us.

5. Why Hasn't the Plain English Movement Accomplished More?

I have written at length elsewhere about some of the forces that keep writers from using plain English (Redish, 1983). Let me briefly review them.

The pressure of budgets and deadlines. Clear writing and consumers' problems take a back seat to all of the other pressures with which most writers in government and business must contend.

Inertia. It's easier to do what has always been done.

Fear of taking risks. If the demand for clear English is not made from or supported by the top echelon in the agency or company, writers are going to hesitate to change traditional styles.

Distance from the people who use the documents. Many documents are written and reviewed by teams of subject matter specialists, but no one represents the people who must read and understand the document. These subject matter specialists have become so familiar with the material that they can't put themselves in the place of the reader for whom the material is new and complex. In a case with which I am very familiar, a forms design team includes subject-matter specialists, data processors, and representatives of several offices in the agency that use data from the form. No one represents the client who must fill out the form, and the goal of making the form easy for the client gets lost as each member of the team negotiates to get the needs of his or her group met.

Desire to be seen as part of an elite group. Writers hesitate to give up the jargon or traditional style of the documents in their field because being able to read and write in a non-plain style is a mark of distinction to them.

Lack of knowledge of how to write in plain English. Writers follow the models they have seen and most of the documents they see in their fields are not well written. Most documents are written by people who were not trained to be writers but to be lawyers or computer programmers or doctors or insurance executives. They had little training in writing in school and what they had didn't deal with writing documents for clients or consumers.

In order to understand the sources of resistance to the plain English movement, we also have to explore some of the concerns raised by language purists, by lawyers, and by business people. If you listen to what people say in their roles as consumers, you will almost always find that they favor plain English. They want to be able to understand their leases, notices, warranties, loan agreements, and insurance policies. When they are not thinking of themselves as consumers, however, you may also detect other attitudes – attitudes that have slowed the acceptance of plain English. Let us examine a few of these negative attitudes.

Some people are concerned that plain English will lower our standards of good English. Some people worry that the plain English movement will destroy the beauty and richness of English. They think of plain English as writing down to people. They think we are catering to the "lowest common denominator" or treating people in a condescending manner by acting as if people can't handle the intricacies of legal or technical documents.

We must remember, however, that we are not talking about English literature, but about public documents. The *purpose* of the documents that we want to put into plain English is to convey critical information. To be effective, a document must reach its audience at the audience's reading level.

Sometimes this means writing very simply because the audience is not highly educated. If the purpose of a technical manual is to show army mechanics how to fix a tank and we know that most army mechanics read at a tenth-grade level, the document won't serve its purpose if we write it at a post-college level. Improving the mechanics' literacy skills is also an important goal; but, if we want the tanks fixed correctly now, the technical manual is not the place to demand reading skills that the mechanics do not have.

Sometimes it means writing in a direct, straightforward manner because the audience, although highly educated, doesn't have the time to hunt through the traditional document's disorganization and convoluted style. A computer specialist, reacting recently to a draft of a new computer manual, objected to the questions and participial forms (looking, finding, signing on) we put in the headings, to the short straightforward sentences in which we addressed the reader as "you," and to the active and imperative verbs. "Unprofessional," "juvenile," and "condescending" were her comments.

In our experience, however, these features help people. We tested the Federal Communications Commission's new marine radio regulations, which have questions as headings and plain English as the text, against the old regulations, which have single nouns as headings and text in traditional bureaucratic style. Readers who had the new rules found the information they needed more quickly, answered more questions correctly, and rated the rules easier to use (Felker and Rose, 1981; Redish, Felker and Rose, 1981).

In a test of product warranties with and without informative questions as headings, more than 90 percent of the subjects said they preferred the warranties with the question headings (Charrow and Redish, 1980). A manual that the Document Design Center helped to organize and write has won an award as the best piece of internal communications in the insurance industry. The manual explains insurance benefits to the company's employees; and we used questions as headings, personal pronouns, clear, active sentences, lots of examples, and other features of plain English in the text. Clearly, some people liked it!

Sometimes writing in plain English means translating non-standard into standard English. Even highly educated speakers of standard English do not understand the legal and bureaucratic documents they receive. They may be having problems because these documents violate the rules of current standard English.

Consider, for example, this sentence from an automobile loan form currently in use:

> The buyer shall not remove the said car from the county where he now resides without written notification to the holder hereof.

I don't think the borrower has to write to the lender every time he *drives* the car into another county, although that is what "remove" means today. I assume the borrower must notify the lender if he *moves* (i.e. changes residence). The *Oxford English Dictionary* says that the word "remove" in the meaning "change one's place of residence" was very common in seventeenth- and eighteenth-century English. It isn't used that way now by any speaker of standard American English. In plain (standard) English, the form might say:

> You must notify us in writing if you change your address.

Language changes; languages always have. We can argue about whether English today is richer or poorer for the changes, but the argument isn't going to alter the dynamic nature of language. Why should we expect speakers of standard modern English to understand vocabulary and sentence structures that were easily understood in the seventeenth century but that are not part of today's standard language?

Some people are concerned that a plain English legal document isn't going to stand up in court. Many consumers don't believe that a document can be legal without the magic and mystery of the special legal words and indecipherable phrases. Some lawyers remain skeptical that legal documents can be written in plain English and still be legally precise. Lawyers argue that many of the words in legal documents have developed their meaning over years of litigation and cannot be translated into clearer English. It is true that certain words are "terms of art" that have no common English equivalents. However, the individual words are not the major cause of incomprehensible legal documents. Poor organization and writing in the nominal style (long sentences, nouns instead of verbs, passive voice, etc.) are the problem. Moreover, according to David Mellinkoff, Professor of Law at UCLA and author of several books on legal language, most words that lawyers think are untranslatable "terms of art" *can* be defined for the lay person – and for the lawyer who does not specialize in that particular topic.

The growing number of examples of plain English legal documents that have been accepted by attorneys shows that documents can be written that are both legally accurate and understandable to non-lawyers. The irony in the lawyers' position is that most of the legal documents that my colleagues and I have helped to rewrite were, in fact, not legally sufficient or precise in the original. They had gaps the lawyers did not mean to leave. They were ambiguous in ways the lawyers did not intend.

Furthermore, failing to write in clear English can cause legal problems. Incomprehensible English has been the cause of many lawsuits. The sixth U.S. Circuit Court of Appeals ruled recently that a loan agreement violated the Truth in Lending Act because of its indecipherable language (*Simply Stated*, 22).

Some people are concerned that plain language costs a lot for little return. Opposition to plain language bills in many states has come from the businesses that would be affected. In part, they object because of the concern I've just discussed – the fear of changing proven legal language. In part, they object that the extra cost is not offset by added benefits. They argue that rewriting and reprinting documents is expensive and that consumers don't care and don't read the documents anyway. I know of no definitive study that has investigated the cost–benefit trade-off of plain English documents. Unfortunately, few businesses are in touch with their consumers' reactions to their documents – good or bad; and few have done any research on the effectiveness of their old or their new documents.

Poor documents can be very costly to businesses. Most businesses must maintain expensive operations to offset the problems caused by incomprehensible documents. They spend millions of dollars a year answering letters and toll-free telephone calls because customers don't understand the procedures for using the company's equipment or services. Computer companies, for example, are now trying to write more self-explanatory (user-friendly) manuals to cut the extremely high costs of staffing "consumer inquiry offices." Most companies also have offices just to answer employees' questions about documents they can't understand (such as their insurance benefits).

The expense of answering consumers' and employees' questions includes the cost of space, equipment, labor, manuals (in plain English?) and training for the people who answer the questions. How much of this cost could be saved by plain English documents is not yet known, but it could be substantial.

References and Resources

ANDERSON, P. *et al.* (Eds.) (1983) *New essays in technical and scientific communication.* Baywood, N.J.: Baywood Press.

BLACK, B. (1981) "A model plain language law." *Stanford Law Review*, **33** (2), Jan. 1981, 255–300.

CHARROW, R.P. and CHARROW, V.R. (1979) "Making legal language understandable: A psycholinguistic study of jury instructions." *Columbia Law Review*, **79** (7), Nov. 1979, 1306–1374.

CHARROW, V.R. (1982) "Language in the bureaucracy," in R. J. DI PIETRO (Ed.), *Linguistics and the Professions* (Volume VII in the series Advances in Discourse Processes). Norwood, N.J.: Ablex, pp. 173–188.

CHARROW, V.R. (1979) *Let the Rewriter Beware.* Washington, D.C.: American Institutes for Research (Pub. C2, 14 pages).

CHARROW, V.R. and REDISH, J.C. (1980) "A study of standardized headings for warranties" (Document Design Project Technical Report No. 6). Washington, D.C.: American Institutes for Research. Available only from ERIC (ED192341).

CHASE, S. (1953) *The Power of Words.* New York: Harcourt Brace Jovanovich.

FAIGLEY, L. and MILLER, T.P. (1982) "What we learn from writing on the job." *College English*, **44** (6), Oct. 1982, 557–569.

FELKER, D.B. (Ed.) (1980) *Document Design: A Review of the Relevant Research.* Washington, D.C.: American Institutes for Research.

FELKER, D.B. and ROSE, A.M. (1981) "The evaluation of a public document." (Document Design Project Technical Report No. 11). Washington, D.C.: American Institutes for Research.

FELKER, D.B. *et al.* (1981) *Guidelines for Document Designers.* Washington, D.C.: American Institutes for Research.

FELSENFELD, C. and SIEGEL, A. (1978) *Simplified Consumer Credit Forms.* Boston: Warren, Gorham and Lamont.

FLESCH, R. (1949) *The Art of Readable Writing.* New York: Harper and Bros.

GIVEN, R.A. (1981) *Drafting Documents in Plain Language.* New York: Practising Law Institute.

GOSWAMI *et al.* (1981) *Writing in the Professions: A course guide and instructional materials for an advanced composition course.* Washington, D.C.: American Institutes for Research.

HARTLEY, J. (1978) *Designing Instructional Text: A practical guide.* New York: Nichols.

JONASSEN, D.H. (Ed.) (1982) *The Technology of Text.* Englewood Cliffs, N.J.: Educational Technology Publications.

MACDONALD, D.A. (1979) *Drafting Documents in Plain Language.* New York: Practising Law Institute.

MELLINKOFF, D. (1963) *The Language of the Law.* Boston: Little, Brown.

MELLINKOFF, D. (1982) *Legal Writing: Sense and nonsense.* New York: Charles Scribner's Sons (hard cover); West Publishing Co. (soft cover).

O'HAYRE, J. (1980) *Gobbledygook has gotta go.* Washington, D.C.: U.S. Government Printing Office, reprinted 1980 (0-318-330).

ORWELL, G. (1978) "Politics and the English language." Reprinted in P. ESCHOLZ, A. ROSA, and V. CLARK (Eds.), *Language Awareness*, New York: St. Martin's Press. (This is a wonderful collection of readings on gobbledygook, jargon, and other language problems.)

PRESSMAN, R. (1979) *Legislative and Regulatory Progress on the Readability of Insurance Policies.* Washington, D.C.: American Institutes for Research (Pub. R1, 15 pp.).

Quarterly Review of Doublespeak, published by the Committee on Public Doublespeak of the National Council of Teachers of English, 111 Kenyon Road, Urbana, IL 61801.

REDISH, J.C. (1981) "The limitations of readability formulas." *IEEE Transactions in Professional Communication*, **24** (1) Mar. 1981.

REDISH, J.C. (1980) "Readability", in D. B. FELKER (Ed.) *Document Design: A review of the relevant research.* Washington, D.C.: American Institutes for Research, 69–94.

REDISH, J.C. (1979) "Readability", in D. A. MACDONALD, *Drafting Documents in Plain Language.* New York: Practising Law Institute, pp. 157–174.

REDISH, J.C. (1983) "Language of the Bureaucracy", in R. W. BAILEY and R. M. FOSHEIM (Eds.) *Literacy for Life: The demand for reading and writing.* New York: The Modern Language Association of America, pp. 151–174.

REDISH, J.C., FELKER, D.B., and ROSE, A.M. (1981) "Evaluating the effects of document design principles." *Information Design Journal*, pp. 236–243.

SELZER, J. (1983) "What constitutes a readable technical style?", in P. ANDERSON *et al.* (Eds.) *New Essays in Technical and Scientific Communication.* Baywood, N.J.: Baywood Press, pp. 71–89.

Simply Stated, published by the Document Design Center, American Institutes for Research, 1055 Thomas Jefferson St., NW, Washington, D.C. 20007.

STRUNK, W. and WHITE, E.B. (1978) *The Elements of Style.* New York: Macmillan, 3rd ed.

WILLIAMS, J. (1981) *Style: Ten lessons in clarity and grace.* Glenview, IL: Scott, Foresman.

WRIGHT, P. (1980) "Strategy and tactics in the design of forms." *Visible Language*, **14** (2), 151–193.

WYDICK, R. (1979) *Plain English for Lawyers.* Durham, N.C.: Carolina Academic Press.

Chapter 10

Attitudes of the National Council of Teachers of English

HAROLD B. ALLEN

PROBABLY no population group has a greater or more intensive range of concerns with the English language than do those who teach it – from the kindergarten teacher to the university professor with his graduate seminars.

Only one organization purports to represent these teachers in their continuum from the kindergarten through the Ph.D. – the National Council of Teachers of English. Founded in 1911 as a protest against the college-dominated prescriptions of literature for the schools, the NCTE has become, with its nearly 90,000 members, the largest subject-matter teachers' association in the world. Each member belongs to one of three major sections – elementary, secondary, or college. Many members belong also to internal special groups such as the Conference on English Education and the Conference on College Composition and Communication. Each section and each conference has its own national publication. Besides the various journals, however, there is a large annual output of books and pamphlets and various teaching aids. NCTE is indeed a major educational publisher. Then the Council holds an annual convention with an average attendance of about 5000 to 6000, in addition to a smaller spring convention and many workshops and committee meetings.

An immediate inference could be that such a wealth of opportunities to exchange and disseminate information must yield a large body of informed and uniform attitudes toward the language that has given the Council its name – English. But no more than in other professions does the professionalism of English teachers produce unanimity of opinion about their professional concerns. Indeed, they have even disagreed about the role of the language itself. Some of them see it as merely one leg of a tripod consisting of literature, composition, and language, but others see it as the necessary base for English literature and English composition to flourish and have their being, with the argument that without the English language there would be no English literature and no English composition.

In its more than 70 years of meetings and publications, among the members' principal concerns with the English language are these:

Bidialectalism
Bilingualism
Censorship

Dictionaries, role and quality of
Grammar, with respect to its nature, its content, methods of teaching it, and
    the effect of knowledge of grammar upon learning control of standard
    English
Grammatical terminology
Language acquisition and child language
Language, ethical use of
Linguistic knowledge, role and amount of
Names, study of
Reading and linguistics
Regional dialects
Sexism in language
Spelling, language research and the teaching of
Teacher-training in the English language
Usage
Vocabulary growth

About most of these concerns the NCTE has taken no official position,
although trends and emphases are apparent in the topics and titles of papers
read at conventions and in articles in the various journals. In recent years,
however, various social and political forces have so driven language controversies into the public limelight that the Council several times has taken official
stands by the action of its board of directors, the policy-making unit within its
complex structure.

These differences of opinion have several origins. Some are due to
differences in educational theory. Some are due to differences in political or
social outlook. And some are due to a conflict between the old and the new,
between the traditional and the modern – perhaps sometimes even between
insufficient knowledge and knowledge. There is a natural reluctance on the
part of a teacher with a long-vested interest in a particular set of language
statements and attitudes to replace the familiar by the threatening unfamiliar.
The reluctance may sometimes be re-enforced by inadequate preparation in the
English language.

As early as 1916, when scholarly attention to the English language was based
upon nineteenth-century historical linguistics, such inadequate preparation led
a convention speaker in the college section to demand that the prospective
teacher have a course in historical English grammar and one in Modern
English grammar (though not the Latinate grammar of the school textbooks).
In 1924 the late Charles C. Fries of the University of Michigan, soon to become
a Council president, led a panel of six distinguished scholars in a discussion of
what the English teacher should know about the English language and of what
English linguistics could do to help in the problem of teaching good English.

Fries, as a matter of fact, did more than any other person in NCTE's history
to arouse the Council to the value of sound linguistic knowledge in the
preparation of teachers and in the teaching of English. He was active in
forming the Committee on English Language Training for Teachers, a
committee of linguists that in 1928 insisted that every English teacher have a

course in the structure and the history of the language. Curious about the effect of this pronouncement, in 1935 he helped a Michigan graduate student obtain an NCTE grant to support a nationwide survey of teacher-training in the English language, a study which the grantee replicated in 1960. The second study was published in large part as a section of the Council's *The National Interest and the Teaching of English* in 1961, the entirety of which was subsequently printed in *The Congressional Record*. Both surveys revealed a grievous inadequacy in language preparation. As if in anticipation of such a finding, Fries years earlier had written a commercially published *Teaching of the English Language*, with a modicum of what the teacher should know about the history of school grammar rules and about acceptable standards of grammar, pronunciation, and vocabulary. He then drew upon his personal research to produce in 1940 his inductively prepared NCTE monograph, *American English Grammar*, and then in 1952 his *Structure of English*, both intended to provide additional background for the teacher.

Fries led in another field as well, with his suggestion in 1952 that prompted the first NCTE program on teaching English as a second language.

The influence of Fries and his students, two of whom became Council presidents, for years pervaded the Council's attention to its concerns with the English language. It has been an influence that at times has met with resistance from teachers admitting little relationship between the study of the English language and the teaching of literature and composition. Yet it has been a powerful influence for increased emphasis upon the crucial role of sound English language instruction in the schools and in teacher preparation.

One of the Council's first concerns with the language was that with grammatical terminology. Readers who recall from their own school days puzzling over the difference between a subject(ive) complement, predicate noun, and predicate nominative (There isn't any!) may well wish that the concern had been successful many years ago. At the first convention in 1911 a speaker complained, "In twenty-five English grammar texts there are 10 different names for the use of *good* in the sentence 'He is good,' and 18 different names for the use of *red* in the sentence 'We painted the barn red'." The following year a committee on linguistic terminology gave a lugubrious report that little uniformity could be expected. The issue simmered on the back burner for another generation, when a hopefully formed committee on linguistic terminology sponsored two meetings of linguists and authors, one at the convention of the Modern Language Association and the other at the NCTE convention. The vain hope had been that with the advent of structural linguistics both grammarians and linguists could at last agree upon terms so that the Council itself might take an official position. But they could not and would not. This is all probably to the good, for rigid enforcement of a set nomenclature could arguably stultify progress, but it doesn't help the puzzled student to be confronted now with superficially synonymous terms from traditional grammar and structural grammar and transformational grammar as he studies English structure. He can find both *subjective complement* and *predicate nominative* as synonyms as he shifts from one book or teacher to another, but then may come a cropper when he finds an apparently synonymous "NP [Noun Phrase] as the second element in a VP [Verb Phrase] when the V [Verb] is BE."

Whether such information, either from traditional grammar or from modern linguistics, is of practical value to the student in his producing good English is still an issue within the Council, although research for six decades has increasingly demonstrated that this kind of knowledge has little or no benefit as a help for a student seeking to improve his ability to use English appropriately and effectively. Convention speakers and journal writers for years struggled to find immediate practical value in the teaching of grammar, trusting, for example, that knowledge of the difference between a nominative pronoun and an objective pronoun could forever eradicate *It's me.* A convention speaker in 1924 declared that the solution was to have "not less grammar but better grammar," and a fellow-speaker on the same program demanded a "vitalization" of grammar. As recently as 1967 another speaker deplored efforts to reject traditional grammar rules by titling his paper "In Grammar's fall/we sinned all."

During the first school awareness of structural grammar in the 1950s some linguists were ready to argue that it at last would provide the practical help needed by students, but before its impact could be felt the field of linguistics was taken over by the new transformational-generative grammar. Several researchers offered hope with experiments intended to ascertain whether students' knowledge of transformational theory helps them develop skill in writing mature sentences. But the low degree of improvement realized that hope only in part. Recent research, however, shows that improvement can be much greater if only the students are not required to study transformational theory but instead simply work with writing exercises prepared as applications of the transformational rules of sentence-combining.

Although he then had in mind the structural frame of reference, this conclusion had been anticipated by Fries in 1951, when at the NCTE business meeting he succeeded in getting adopted the Council's first official position statement about the language: "The NCTE supports the scientific study of the English language, and realizing the importance of the results of that study in freeing our teaching from wasteful and harmful practices, recommends that, in the training of teachers, both prospective and in service, opportunities be provided to acquaint English teachers with the principles, methods, results, and applications of modern linguistic science."

The English language, Fries was wont to insist, is a worthy object of study in and for itself and does not need to be studied only for practical benefits. But the resolution he sponsored had important implications for both past and future classroom concerns of the Council, concerns that collectively may be looked at under the rubric of Usage.

On the one hand, this statement was a copestone to the aggregation of articles and brochures that, peaking in the 1930s in the so-called Battle of Usage, served to establish Fries's point of view that good English is essentially that of the men and women who carry on the affairs of the English-speaking people. Two important Council research monographs, Sterling Leonard's *Current English Usage* in 1932 and Albert Marckwardt's *Facts About Current*

English Usage in 1938, together with later articles by John S. Kenyon in *The English Journal* and *College English* in 1948, had effectively altered the attitudes toward usage found in college and high-school textbooks, although some elementary-school textbooks even today retain much of the traditional armory of Latinate grammatical rules.

On the other hand, in supporting the scientific study of language, this resolution was a foundation for not only extending the study of regional language variation but also for expanding the study of variation so as to include social variation in the interdisciplinary area called sociolinguistics – an area which was to older studies of usage much as chemistry is to alchemy. Fries himself had initiated the scientific study of regional speech in the United States when in 1928 he used an NCTE grant to bring together a group of linguists whose deliberations led to the extraordinary developments in dialect geography in the United States, the completion of the Linguistic Atlas of New England and of the Linguistic Atlas of the Upper Midwest and the ongoing editing of similar atlas materials in the Middle and South Atlantic States and the North Central States. NCTE's steadily growing recognition of the validity of regional dialects appears in the recent convention programs devoted to descriptions of such dialects. This enlightened attitude long ago obliterated the attitude exemplified in the published statement of a former director of speech improvement for the New York City schools, namely, that the pronunciation of final -r is "uncultivated."

But attention to social variation as a subject of linguistic analysis and study came rather as a reaction to forces outside the Council, principally to related social, economic, and political forces known as the Civil Rights Movement. In northern industrial cities the schools had received thousands of Black children speaking a variety of Southern English now generally known as Black English or Black Vernacular. Because control of only this dialect arguably handicapped these children educationally and, later, occupationally, the question of what to do about the dialect became a matter of linguistic controversy, a controversy that more than once became sharp and bitter.

Already, in 1962, NCTE had presciently anticipated the problem and even the controversy in an official resolution

> That the National Council of Teachers of English support all efforts that record our changing language accurately and completely, and that the Council, whenever distortion or misrepresentation takes place with respect to its position, inform both the lay public and members of the profession, through its own publications and other media, of its long established policy of giving voice to the diversity and breadth of viewpoint of our membership.

The voice that was heard, at meetings and in the journals, was sometimes a quarrelsome and derisive voice as Black English became the battleground for those whose diversity of viewpoint covered a wide range with sharp contrasts. At one extreme some advocated an insistence upon Standard English and the ultimate elimination of Black English. At the other extreme some demanded such recognition of Black English as a language in its own right that it was justifiably to be let strictly alone. Between the two extremes bulked most of the writers and speakers in their advocacy of varying degrees of what has come to be known as bidialectalism. Some, for example, considering Black English a separate language, wanted it taught and treated as if it were French or German. Some espoused a program in which Black speech was to be unmodified but Black students were taught control of standard written English, an approach that seems to have won the largest number of adherents. But all the disputants apparently accepted the insistence that the teacher of students speaking Black English should, as the judge in the now famous Ann Arbor case declared, acquire some insight into the nature of Black English and its cultural attributes.

This controversy has not been uniformly resolved, but an official sense-of-the house resolution passed in 1973 may possibly indicate the Council's overall position, as well as a turn-the-other cheek attitude toward the critical press. It was resolved:

> That we respond in humane, not punitive, terms to whatsoever linguistic resources our students bring with them to our classrooms; that we also respond humanely to whatever intellectual resources our journalists bring to their typewriters and microphones; and that we help both students and journalists grow from the point at which we find them, realizing that we won't help either by cutting them off or treating their efforts with less than the humane responses that should characterize our discipline.

What had drawn the critical attention of the press was a resolution passed the preceding year by the Conference on College Composition and Communication, a constituent group composed of NCTE members involved in the first-year English programs in colleges and universities. Its resolution, then, is not that of NCTE as a whole, although the distinction was not perceived or made by editorialists and commentators or even by school administrators. The resolution itself emerged from a 2-year period of discussions by members of an *ad hoc* CCCC committee, It was adopted in November 1972 by the CCCC executive committee. Subsequently there was prepared a detailed position paper detailing the reasons for the resolution and providing an ample bibliography. This position paper, entitled "Students' Right to Their Own Language", was adopted along with the resolution at a CCCC business meeting in April 1974.

The resolution reads:

> We affirm the students' right to their own patterns and varieties of language – the dialects of their nurture or whatever dialects in which they find their own identity and style. Language scholars long ago denied that the myth of a standard American dialect has any validity. The claim that any one dialect is unacceptable amounts to an attempt of one social group to exert its dominance over another. Such a claim leads to false advice for speakers and writers, and immoral advice for humans. A nation proud of its diverse heritage and its cultural and racial variety will preserve its heritage of dialects. We affirm strongly that teachers must have the experiences and training that will enable them to respect diversity and uphold the right of students to their own language.

Not surprisingly, diverse reaction appeared not only in the press but also within NCTE itself. Editorialists, self-annointed protectors of the purity of the native tongue, rushed to defend the battlements against the onslaught of the linguistic libertarians. Cooler heads within the Council suggested that, as a sociolinguistic statement, the resolution should have recognized that it is normal for languages to have elite forms and also that it presented an impractical goal for the teacher, whom it placed in a sometimes indefensible position. Nevertheless, the resolution gained a widely favorable reaction as a "humane" approach to a language and social problem of extreme complexity. But whether its precise wording still represents the views of a majority of CCCC has been questioned. After a two-year study an *ad hoc* committee charged with determining whether the resolution was still appropriate reported to the CCCC executive committee that instead of altering the resolution the Conference should request the Council itself to undertake a massive study that would extend concern beyond college composition classes to elementary and secondary schools, to teacher preparation, and to developing public awareness and cooperation respecting the relevant language and social issues. Fearing fatal internal dissension, the CCCC executive committee tabled the report instead of presenting it to the Conference at the national meeting in 1984.

A related concern with the language of a minority has led to official action by the Council. Although another organization, Teachers of English to Speakers of Other Languages (TESOL), is primarily devoted to the problems of non-English speakers in the schools, NCTE has found that it too has some involvement. The Council recognizes that the regular English teacher also has a responsibility when the classroom contains only two or three speakers of other languages, not enough to justify hiring a specialized English-as-a-second-language instructor. The Council also has felt the need to provide help to the teacher who receives students from a bilingual education program and finds them not quite prepared to progress with the native speakers. Accordingly, the executive committee has recently approved officially a position paper promising cooperation with bilingual educators and the development of aid for the teacher faced with only a handful of non-English speakers.

Another social concern with language arising from the ferment of the sixties is specifically a product of the feminist movement. Within the Council it has appeared in talks and well-documented articles and books as a protest against various aspects of sexism in language, ranging from the generic use of the masculine pronoun to the use of masculine designations for persons not necessarily masculine. So *Everyone should take their seat* is now officially blessed by the Council despite traditional grammatical rules of concord; and *chairman* and *policeman* are replaced by *chair* and *police officer*. Although some have protested that the Council, which has officially protested against censorship, actually engaged in censorship with a resolution prohibiting sexist language in Council publications, that resolution has received general approval and has influenced commercial publishers. A later resolution, however, has yielded a point in granting authors the right to use sexist terminology if a footnote is present to specify that the inclusion of the objectional locution is at the author's express request.

The Council, not through a resolution but tacitly through accepting the annual reports of the committee on Doublespeak, has taken a strong stand against deceptive and unethical use of the English language by public figures. The committee pulls no punches in its annual awards to the individual or organization most deserving of castigation for deliberately unethical language. Ronald Reagan, for example, was so chosen because of the misleading rhetoric of his presidential campaign speeches. The Doublespeak awards, needless to say, receive national publicity.

In several ways the Council's concerns with the English language during the past 20 years have been stimulated and focused through its Commission on the English Language. Created in 1961 for that very purpose, it is composed of twelve NCTE members, serving staggered terms of 3 years. Usually two or three are linguists; others are members especially involved in languge teaching in the schools. Since its establishment the Commission has been responsible for the preparation and publication of three pamphlets on American dialects and for the preparation of historical leaflets illustrating historical phases of the language, a workshop for teachers of the English language in NDEA institutes, a national conference for teachers and employers involved with speakers of Black English, the founding of the Clearinghouse Committee on Social Dialects, a disk record bearing samples of historical English and of current regional dialects, a number of programs at the annual NCTE convention, and the preparation of this collection of articles on attitudes to the English language.

Although other language concerns have not produced official action, convention papers and journal articles and other publications over the years have definitely established the National Council of Teachers of English as a leading forum for progressive proposals and experimental methods and procedures for dealing with the English language in teacher preparation and in the classroom. Its speakers and writers have advanced critical approaches in current lexicography. They have reported linguistic applications in the teaching of spelling. They have promoted the adoption of new ways of assisting language development in children. They have found educational value in the teaching of the study of names. Despite, or, more likely, because of, the encouragement of diversity among its members, the main thrust of NCTE thought and activity respecting the English language has clearly made it a principal constructive educational force.

Chapter 11

Bilingualism in the United States: Present Attitudes in the Light of Past Policies

OFELIA GARCIA

Introduction

Bilingualism in the United States has become public and controversial. The large size of the United States population that uses an ethnic mother-tongue at home is not in itself an issue. However, the daily use of non-English languages in schools, churches, newspapers, radio broadcasts, voting polls, courts and politics, has attracted many critics who argue that bilingualism is a private matter and should not be encouraged by public policy.[1] In contrast, advocates of bilingualism argue that bilingualism is a national resource that must be supported and developed by any responsible modern government.[2] This paper will briefly trace the history of bilingualism in the United States up to the present period. It will then present current attitudes from the perspective of these past policies.

The Nature of Bilingualism in the United States

Although bilingualism has a long tradition in the United States, it has always existed only at an individual level and has never been promoted as a stable feature of American society. In Joshua Fishman's terms, what is accepted in the United States is *bilingualism*, that is, the use of two languages by individuals, but not *diglossia*, that is, the enduring societal arrangement for the existence of two languages, each having its secure, legitimate and widely implemented functions.[3]

Bilingualism can result from two different situations:

(a) The second language is acquired naturally when two languages come into contact.

(b) The second language is learned in a formal situation such as schools.

This distinction between *natural* and *learned* bilingualism has great relevance to an understanding of attitudes toward bilingualism in the United States. While the first type of bilingualism constitutes a *group* process that occurs naturally in any society, like the United States, where immigration is prevalent, the second is a process of *individual* enrichment. As we will see, even learned bilingualism has been opposed in some periods of United States history. But it is natural bilingualism that has caused most of the controversy and does still today.

Bilingualism in United States History

English has never been the official language of the United States, but it has clearly been the *de facto* dominant language since the British colonists introduced it in North America.[4] We can distinguish five major periods in United States history with regard to attitudes toward bilingualism.

1. *From 1777 to 1880*

Although English was promoted by many, such as John Adams and Noah Webster, during this first period, languages other than English were widely used by the foreign ethnic minority that dominated the colonies. In fact, the political system of the new nation was legitimized in texts that used different languages. For instance, the Articles of Confederation were published in English and in German. The use of languages other than English was considered during this period an appropriate measure to integrate new immigrants into the society.[5]

2. *From 1880 to 1923*

By 1880, the previous promotion of the ethnic mother-tongues for the benefit of the government was completely restricted. This change seems to be explained by the change in the origins of the immigrants. Whereas the bulk of the immigration prior to 1880 was of northern European background, the 35 million immigrants who came to the United States after 1880 were primarily from southern and eastern Europe.[6] They were considered racially inferior and thus race and ethnicity became the predominant factors in restricting the use of non-English languages in both public and private. This practice had its antecedents in attitudes already existing prior to 1880, when the languages of Native Americans and of Africans were an exception to the promotion of ethnic mother-tongues. The fact that in 1880 the United States economy had begun to provide fewer opportunities also made it necessary to restrict linguistic rights as a means of limiting educational and economic benefits. These restrictive measures directed toward racially distinct immigrants at a time of economic hardship, coupled during World War I with mistrust of the large German minority, led to the Americanization movement that encouraged the ban on use of non-English languages. By 1923 there were thirty-four states that explicitly allowed only English as the medium of instruction in both public and private schools.[7]

3. *From 1923 to 1958*

In the famour Meyer vs. Nebraska case of 1923 (262 US 390), a Nebraska statute that prohibited the teaching of foreign languages was rendered unconstitutional. This judicial decision viewed ethnic languages also as "foreign" and thus as something to which individuals have a right as an enrichment practice. However, this decision did not recognize the language rights of the ethnic minority. Bilingualism is thus publicly seen in this period as a private practice to which all are entitled as individuals, but which is not encouraged by policy.

4. From 1958 to 1968

In the wake of Sputnik, legislation such as the National Defense Education Act of 1958 (Title VI of the Foreign Studies and Language Development, 20 USC 401 ff.) and the Fullbright–Hays Act (Section 102 (b) (6) of the Cultural Exchange Program of 1961, 22 USC 117 ff.), as well as the Foreign Languages in the Elementary School (FLES) movement, promoted bilingualism of United States citizens for defense purposes. This bilingualism was seen as the use of English plus a "foreign" language, and was indeed a change from the favorable public attitude toward bilingualism in the nineteenth century when bilingualism consisted of English plus an "ethnic mother tongue." Yet, whereas the bilingualism that was encouraged by these promotive measures was permanent (English + foreign language), the bilingualism that had been encouraged in the early nineteenth century was in the long run transitional (ethnic mother-tongue + English → English).

The 1958 to 1968 period promoted learned bilingualism at an individual level for the benefit of the United States government. However, no effort was made to promote natural bilingualism as a more expedient and less expensive measure. During this period of promotion of foreign languages, only one voice rose to encourage the maintenance of ethnic mother-tongues as important to the country at large Joshua A. Fishman.[8] His *Language Loyalty in the United States* (1966) became the first inspiration for public support of natural bilingualism, not just as a transitional phenomenon as it had existed in the nineteenth century, but as a permanent measure that would secure for the benefit of the majority as well as the minority the preservation of the ethnic mother-tongue.

5. 1968–present

Of the 226.5 million people in the United States in 1980, nearly 23 million United States residents speak a language other than English at home.[9] Almost half of these speak Spanish. Of the 11.1 million who speak Spanish at home, 8.3 million consider themselves bilingual, since they report that they speak English very well or well. Of the 11.8 million who use another ethnic mother-tongue at home, 10.3 million indicate that they speak English very well or well. Thus, of the 23 million people in the United States who use a language other than English at home, 18.6 million are bilingual.

Although the large number of people who use non-English languages at home alarms many, the use of ethnic mother-tongues in private has been tolerated throughout United States history. It is only when these ethnic mother-tongues begin to be used in public that bilingualism becomes controversial.[10] Starting in 1968, programs organized by the government as well as by ethnics themselves made bilingualism a public issue. Support for natural bilingualism in public, especially when it is government-funded, has been sharply criticized. In contrast, since learned bilingualism remains a mostly private phenomenon, it is not seen as a threat. Thus, even when the recent trend has discouraged natural bilingualism, learned bilingualism continues to be encouraged.

I. 1968–the Present. Natural Bilingualism

A. *The use of the ethnic mother tongue in public:*
Government Programs

The bilingual measures introduced after 1968, despite misinformed public opinion to the contrary, do not promote permanent bilingualism (ethnic mother-tongue + English). In effect, they only support transitional measures that accelerate the shift to English by permitting the minority to participate more fully in American society.[11] Senator Ralph Yarborough, a Democrat from Texas who proposed the original bill that later became the Bilingual Education Act, declared in the Senate on 1 December 1967: "My purpose in doing this is not to keep any specific language alive, . . . but just to try to make those children fully literate in English."[12] In the same way, the Amendments to the Voting Rights Act are not an assertion of the language rights of the ethnic minority, but rather a desire to allow the linguistic minority to participate in the democratic process.

Before we examine the prevalent attitudes toward bilingualism in the United States today, we will review the laws and judicial decisions that allow the transitional use of ethnic mother-tongues in education, elections, and other government-funded programs.

(a) *Education.* The continuing rise in the number of students with limited English proficiency in United States schools induced the government to become involved in meeting their educational needs. According to the report entitled "Projections of Non-English language background and limited English proficient persons in the United States to the year 2000" issued by the National Clearinghouse for Bilingual Education on October 1980, the total number of LEP children aged 5–14 estimated for 1976 is 2.5 million, with a drop to 2.4 million in 1980 and a gradual increase to 2.8 million in 1990 and 3.4 million in 2000.

In 1968 the Bilingual Education Act was passed as Title VII of the Elementary and Secondary Education Act (20 USC 880 b). This law, later reauthorized in 1974 and 1978, provides financial assistance to educational agencies that establish programs of instruction using native languages for children of limited English proficiency. In 1979 it was estimated that there were 300,000 children served by Title VII grants in over seventy languages.[13] The Equal Educational Opportunity Act of 1974 (20 USC 1701–1703) also supported bilingual instruction by requiring that educational agencies "take appropriate action to overcome language barriers that impede equal participation by its students in its instructional programs."

At the state level, there are now thirty-one states that have bilingual provisions which explicitly or implicitly permit school districts to offer courses in a non-English language. Yet, there are still four states – Arkansas, Nebraska, North Carolina, and West Virginia – which have English-only statutes applicable to both public and non-public schools.[14]

The federal legislation supporting bilingualism in schools has been reinforced by important judicial decisions.[15] The most important decision in this respect, Lau vs. Nichols, guaranteed the right of non-English-speaking students (in this case Chinese) to a meaningful education. Although the Supreme Court's ruling on 21 January 1974 mandated school districts to address the needs of their non-English-speaking students, it did not expressly endorse bilingual education, but proposed it as one course among many that could be taken to remedy the situation.

A task force that was set up after the Lau decision by the Office of Civil Rights issued a memorandum in 1975 entitled "Task Force Findings Specifying Remedies Available for Eliminating Past Educational Practices Ruled Unlawful under Lau v. Nichols." This memorandum, which became known as the "Lau Remedies," mandated districts with more than 5 percent minority children to set up voluntary compliance plans to include bilingual education. Although these remedies were disseminated, they were never published in the Federal register for review and comment, nor published in final form. In 1978, they were challenged in court by the Northwest Arctic School system in Alaska. Following a court order that resulted from this challenge, the proposed Lau regulations were issued by the Secretary of Education under the Carter administration, Shirley M. Hufstedler, on 4 August 1980 (*Fed. Register*, Vol. 45, No. 152). These regulations would have required transitional bilingual instruction for a minimum of two years and a maximum of five for students who spoke the non-English language better than English. As required by law, a public comment period for the proposed regulations ended 20 October, 1980, and regional hearings were held in San Antonio, New York City, Denver, New Orleans, San Francisco, and Chicago. The Education Department's Office for Civil Rights received over 4000 letters from citizens, parents, educators, and professional organizations. Many of these letters were overwhelmingly critical of the proposed regulations as being unnecessarily prescriptive.[16]

The new Republican administration that came to office in November 1980 prepared to tighten the budget of a hurting economy. The restriction of bilingualism in education became a favorite example of how the federal government could save money while giving the power back to the states. On 2 February 1981, the new secretary of Education, Terrel H. Bell, withdrew the Lau regulations that had been proposed by the Carter administration. Secretary Bell offered the following explanation: "We will protect the rights of children who do not speak English well, but we will do so by permitting school districts to use any way that has proved successful."[17]

ET–F*

There are two bills regarding bilingual education now under consideration that would further restrict the use of the non-English language in the classroom. The Bilingual Education Amendments of 1981 (S 2002), introduced by Senators Huddleston (D-KY) and Absnor (R-S.D.), limits the time a child can participate in bilingual education to one year. The Bilingual Education Improvements Act of 1982 (S 2412), developed by the present Administration, would amend the definition of bilingual education to authorize funding of a wider range of educational approaches which might not be bilingual in nature, such as English as a Second Language and immersion.

A recent "decision memorandum" authored by Emerson J. Elliott of the Education Department's Office of Planning and Evaluation said that the department's 1983 budget proposal would "reflect a new and more flexible Federal policy . . . [that] would permit the funding of any special language program that addresses the needs of English limited children."[18] Furthermore, instruction in the ethnic mother-tongue would be restricted to only those children whose dominant language is other than English. The emphasis of the new administration is clearly not on promoting natural permanent bilingualism.

This trend away from support of bilingual instruction has also been felt at the state level. For example, in 1975 Colorado had passed a stringent bilingual education law. However, in August 1981 the English Language Proficiency Act repealed the bilingual–bicultural program by limiting eligibility on language dominance (which language a child uses first and most naturally) and not on language proficiency (how well the child speaks and understands a particular language). Furthermore, the new law promoted English as a Second Language as the most desirable method of instruction.[19]

(b) *Elections*. Bilingual elections were a result of a long process that started when the Voting Rights Act of 1965 (42 USC 1973 b) eradicated the use of literacy tests. The fact that Puerto Ricans were being barred from voting was declared an injustice. Beginning in 1973, a series of lawsuits were filed. In the important case Puerto Rican Organization for Political Action vs. Kusper, the court determined that a Spanish monolingual could not cast an effective vote in an English-only election. The Voting Rights Act was finally amended in 1975, and section 203 of Title II and section 301 of Title VIII provided for bilingual elections. The law insured that any voting or registration material must be translated when 5 percent of the voting age population were members of a single-language minority group.[20] The Act is up for reauthorization in the Fall of 1982 and the controversy has become heated. It is reported that after every election, letters reach congressional offices and the Federal Elections Commission demanding repeal of non-English language ballots. Protests over the bilingual ballot are also common in radio and television talk shows. Representative Don Edwards, the Democrat from San Jose who helped write the 1975 legislation, recently stated: "The letters and comments against them are running 500 to 1. I've got 500,000 people back home, most of whom don't want it."[21]

(c) *Other government programs.* There are a number of other important government measures that encourage the use of the non-English languages in public. For example, the Court Interpreter's Act (Public Law 95-539) enacted on 28 October 1978, provides for the use of interpreters in courts of the United States. The 1980 census provided Spanish language questionnaire forms. Many government agencies which provide social-welfare benefits have also made strides in employing bilingual workers and in printing bilingual forms. Yet, rather than encouraging permanent bilingualism, all these government measures use the ethnic mother-tongues only to promote the assimilation of today's numerous non-English immigrants.

B. *The use of the ethnic mother tongue in public: Ethnic Programs*

The present bilingual policies of the United States government do not promote permanent bilingualism. They only address the communication needs of monolingual speakers of ethnic mother-tongues who are mostly first-generation immigrants. These government programs grew as outcomes of the Civil Rights Act of 1964 (42 USC Section 2000d), which prohibits discrimination "on the ground of race, color or national origin." The temporary use of the ethnic mother-tongue while the immigrants shift to English guarantees the right of those individuals to equal opportunity.

The ethnic boom that was felt in Europe in the 1960s has also influenced ethnolinguistic minorities in the United States. Second- and third-generation ethnics today have been victims of government and educational policies that discouraged bilingualism. Thus, they are now monolingual English speakers. For racially indistinct ethnics, this shift to English has been often accompanied by structural incorporation into the mainstream. During the last decade, these second- and third-generation ethnics, who are culturally, linguistically, and structurally assimilated, have begun to feel a keen interest in their country of origin and their ethnic mother-tongue. Thus, they have established socio-cultural institutions that are organized, funded, and governed by the ethnic group. The purpose of these institutions is to preserve the ethnic culture and to maintain the ethnic mother-tongue. Language Resources in the United States III, a research project being conducted under the direction of Joshua Fishman at Yeshiva University, has documented the enormous growth of ethnic publications, ethnic broadcasts, ethnic religious units, and ethnic mother-tongue schools in the United States. In 1980, Language Resources III had identified 762 ethnic publications in 48 languages, 2470 radio and television broadcasts in 59 languages, 5414 schools in 50 languages, and 7203 religious units in 41 ethnic-mother tongues.[22]

These ethnolinguistic socio-cultural institutions differ in the degree of interest that they have in maintaining the ethnic mother-tongue and in promoting permanent bilingualism. Differences in language loyalty among ethnolinguistic groups have also been identified. Yet, what is important is that in 1980, while the United States government was promoting transitional bilingualism among ethnics, ethnics themselves were succeeding in efforts to maintain their separateness and unique cultural and linguistic characteristics. There has been a reawakened interest in ethnicity and in the ethnic mother-tongue especially among ethnics who have succeeded in American society.

Attitudes toward natural bilingualism today

Editorials that appear daily in major United States newspapers vehemently oppose permanent natural bilingualism.[23] Even transitional natural bilingualism has been attacked. For example, Stephen Rosenfeld and Noel Epstein, both of *The Washington Post*, and Fred M. Hechinger of *The New York Times* have been openly critical of bilingual education. The promotion of a non-English language even as a temporary measure is seen as divisive since it emphasizes loyalty to the old country. Many critics of bilingualism in the United States feel that it would weaken national unity and would create a separatist movement similar to that of Quebec.[24] Nathan Glazer, in a paper prepared for a conference on bilingualism at the University of Southern Carolina, summarizes these arguments as follows:

> The critics seem to be saying that it was a good thing that people of many stocks were molded here into one nation speaking one language, that it would have been a worse country had this not happened, and therefore it could be a worse country because it now is happening less.[25]

President Reagan, speaking against bilingual education before the National League of Cities on 2 March, 1981, stated that it was "absolutely wrong and against American concepts to have a bilingual education program that is now openly, admittedly, dedicated to preserving their [students'] native language."[26]

The continuous influx of large number of immigrants coupled with an increased ethnic awareness is seen as a threat to the strength and cohesiveness of the United States. A Miami editor expresses this new xenophobia as follows: "People feel threatened because this was basically an English-speaking community twenty years ago and it no longer is."[27] It is precisely this threat that has encouraged Senator S. I. Hayakawa from California to propose a constitutional amendment (Senate Joint Resolution 72) to make English the official language of the United States. Hayakawa's amendment has received little support. However, most of his critics do not favor bilingualism, but feel that the amendment is completely unnecessary, since English is and will continue to be the *de facto* official language of the United States.

This restriction of natural bilingualism in the United States has also been felt at the state level. In November 1980 an antibilingual ordinance was passed in Dade County, Miami. Although the new ordinance did not repeal the 1973 resolution that made Dade county bilingual, it did cut off funds to promote any language but English, or any culture but American.

II. 1968–the Present, Learned Bilingualism

While natural bilingualism was encouraged by the government as a transitional stage and by ethnics as a permanent condition in the 1970s, interest in learned bilingualism decreased tremendously during this decade. In 1970, 24 percent of the students in the seventh to twelfth grade were studying a foreign language. By 1976, the latest year for which figures are available, the number had slipped to 17.0 percent.[28]

As the 1970s drew to a close, interest in natural bilingualism decreased, while interest in learned bilingualism increased. The President's Commission on Foreign Languages and International Studies was instrumental in promoting learned bilingualism. The recommendations issued by the Commission in November 1979 suggested the reinstatement of the foreign-language requirement and stated that language education should start earlier and last longer.[29] Two bills recently introduced by Representative Paul Simon and Senator Moynihan (H.R. 3231 and S. 1817 respectively) attempt to provide grants for foreign-language programs to improve foreign-language study for elementary- and secondary-school students.

Recently, the Modern Language Association has reported that for business and political reasons the number of students taking non-Western languages (especially Arabic, Chinese, and Japanese) has increased significantly. Richard Brod, the M.L.A.'s director of the Foreign Language program, believes that "an interest in language study will grow in the broader context of increasing attention to international concerns."[30]

It is significant to notice that as public attitudes against natural bilingualism increase, interest in learned bilingualism increases. The two forms of bilingualism have been generally perceived by the American public as being distinct. Today, whereas natural bilingualism for the minority is vehemently opposed, learned bilingualism for the majority is approved and favored.

Bilingualism in the future?

The two tendencies prevalent in the 1980s – that is, the restriction of natural bilingualism for the welfare of the minority coupled with the promotion of learned bilingualism for the welfare of the majority – have centered today's discussions about bilingualism in the future on reasonings that had been advanced by Fishman since 1966. Fishman had argued that if bilingualism is beneficial to all, the least expensive and most efficient way to promote it would be by encouraging both natural and learned bilingualism. Recent attempts to encourage bilingualism in the United States for business and defense purposes promote permanent natural and learned bilingualism for the benefit of the minority as well as the majority. The bill proposed by Congressman Henry B. Gonzalez of Texas (H:R: 4389) "to establish a National Commission for Utilization and Expansion of Language Resources" falls under this new trend. The proposed Commission would "develop a national policy for identifying, preserving, and improving our language resources as well as a program to encourage the development of language skills for use in nontraditional areas such as commerce, trade, and defense." The recent memorandum on bilingual education issued by the Hazen Foundation along with the Academy for

Educational Development also promotes this goal. This memorandum summarizes the new shift in bilingual policy as follows:

> The American public is beginning to accept the ideas of "minimum competencies" and "basic education" expected of all those growing up in the society. Language competence, including proficiency in at least one language in addition to English, could become part of the constellation of basic skills more generally expected of students. The participation of all kinds of students in bilingual education programs is a way for the worlds of foreign language instruction, bilingual education, and education for international understanding to come together as part of a general improvement in American education.[31]

Current attitudes toward bilingualism in the United States are not new. English has endured as the *de facto* language precisely because the majority has always favored it as the only link to American ethnicity. Although government programs have used the non-English languages in public, monolingualism rather than bilingualism has been the ultimate goal of the programs. Recently, second- and third-generation ethnics in the United States have joined other ethnolinguistic minorities in the world in struggling for recognition of their distinct ethnicity and language. The extensive use of the ethnic mother-tongues in government and ethnic programs has created a wave of opposition to public bilingualism in the United States. The majority of United States citizens have never favored permanent natural bilingualism, although they have allowed transitional bilingualism as a temporary stage on the way to complete shift to English.

More favorable attitudes have always existed toward learned bilingualism than toward natural bilingualism. Yet, the United States have never been successful in promoting bilingualism in schools. Although learned bilingualism is favored by most Americans as an enrichment activity, it is very difficult to achieve within a society that always equates bilingualism with disloyalty and foreignness.

Only one out of ten persons in the United States has a second language.[32] Bilingualism in the United States will remain a rare phenomenon, unless it is promoted for both the majority and the minority.

Notes

1. The following editorials in the *New York Times* repeat this majority view: "Divisive languages," 28 Oct. 1975, "Bilingual danger," 22 Nov. 1976, "The bilingual goal, in plain English," 26 Nov. 1977, "Many voices, but one language," 12 Dec. 1979, "Battle over bilingualism," 8 Sept. 1980, "In plain English," 10 Oct. 1981.
2. Joshua Fishman, *Bilingual Education: An International Sociological Perspective* (Rowley, Mass.: Newbury House, 1976), pp. 3–22, A. Bruce Gaarder, *Bilingual Schooling and the Survival of Spanish in the United States* (Rowley, Mass.: Newbury House, 1977), pp. 95–128.
3. Joshua Fishman, "Societal bilingualism: Stable and transitional," in *Language in Sociocultural Change* (Stanford: Stanford University Press, 1972), pp. 135–136.
4. The following give good accounts of past language policy in the United States: Steven A. Grant, "Language policy in the United States. Report to the Task Force on Government Relation," in *Language Study for the 1980s. Reports of the MLA-ACLS Language Task Force*, ed. Richard I. Brod (New York: Modern Language Association of America, 1980), pp. 95–105. Shirley Brice Heath, "A National Language Academy? Debate in the New Nation," *International Journal of the Sociology of Language*, No. 11 (1976); Shirley Brice Heath, "Language politics in the United States," in *Georgetown University Roundtable*

(1977), pp. 267–296; Arnold H. Leibowitz, "Language policy in the United States," in *Bilingual Education*, ed. La Fontaine, Persky, Bogubchick (Wayne, New Jersey: Avery, 1978), pp. 3–15.

5. Heinz Kloss, p. 84, Ricardo Otheguy, "Thinking about bilingual education: A critical appraisal," *Harvard Educational Review*, **52,** No. 3 (1982), 308.
6. Heinz Kloss, p. 13.
7. Arnold H. Leibowitz, "Language policy in the United States," pp. 5–8.
8. Joshua A. Fishman, *Language Loyalty in the United States* (The Hague; Mouton, 1966).
9. Provisional Estimates of Social, Economic, and Housing Characteristics, PHC 80-S1-1.
10. This attitude is characteristic of many critics of bilingualism. See, for example, Richard Rodriguez, *Hunger of Memory* (Boston: Godine, 1981).
11. For the claim that transitional bilingual education reduces ethnic mother-tongue maintenance see Joshua Fishman, "Minority language maintenance and the ethnic mother tongue school," *Modern Language Journal*, **64** (1980), 167–173, and "Bilingualism and biculturism as individual and as societal phenomena," in *Bilingual Education for Hispanic Students in the United States*, ed. Joshua A. Fishman and Gary D. Keller (New York: Teachers College Press, 1982), p. 35. See also Bruce Gaarder, *Bilingual Schooling*, p. 146; Rolf Kjolseth, "Bilingual education programs in the United States. For assimilation or pluralism," in *Bilingual Schooling in the United States*, ed. Francesco Cordasco (New York: McGraw Hill, 1976), pp. 122–140. This is also the view expressed by Hispanic leaders in William Trombley, "Overtones of politics affect bilingual policy," *Los Angeles Times*, 7 Sept. 1980.
12. Heinz Kloss, p. 37.
13. U.S. Office of Education, *Strengthening Bilingual Education*, June 1979, p. 5.
14. For an up-to-date summary of statutory and constitutional provisions at the state level and court decisions and legislation at the federal level regarding bilingual education see Tracy C. Gray, H. Suzanne Convery, and Katherine M. Fox, *The Current Status of Bilingual Education Legislation* (Washington D.C.: Center for Applied Linguistics, 1981). Also see Herbert Teitelbaum and Richard J. Hiller, "Bilingual education: The legal mandate," *Harvard Educational Review*, **47,** No. 2 (1977), 138–170.
15. Other cases which upheld bilingual education are Serna vs. Portales Municipal Schools (CANM 1974, 499 F. 2d 1147), Keyes vs. School District No. 1 Denver, Colorado (C:A. Colo. 1975, 521 F. 2d 465), Morales vs. Channon (C.A. Tex. 1975, 516 F. 2d 411). More recent cases include The Idaho Migrant Council vs. Board of Education (647 F. 2d 69 1981), Castaneda vs. Pickard (648 F 2d 989).
16. Fred M. Hechinger, "U.S. ruling fuels controversy over bilingual teaching," *New York Times*, 20 Jan. 1981. The same attitude appears in "Bilingual rules for schools draw protest from union," *American Teacher*, Oct. 1980. Also in Albert Shanker, "Can U.S. force schools to go bilingual?" *New York Times*, 24 July 1980.
17. Marjorie Hunter, "U.S. Education Chief bars bilingual plan for public schools," *New York Times* 3 Feb. 1981.
18. Susan G. Foster and Eileen White, "Policy reversal on bilingual efforts charted in memo," *Education Week*, 10 Feb. 1982.
19. J.R. "Advocates in three states struggle to keep bilingual education," *Center for Law and Education Newsnotes* (Cambridge, Mass), Jan. 1982.
20. Joan Rubin, "Spanish language planning in the United States." Keynote address at El Español en los Estados Unidos, Chicago, 3 Oct. 1981.
21. David Hoffman, "Representative Edwards caught in middle of battle over bilingual ballot," *San Jose Mercury News*, 1 Feb. 1981.
22. Joshua A. Fishman, Michael Gertner, and Esther Lowy, "The Non-English Language Resources of the United States. A Preliminary Reconnaisance." Report to the U.S. Department of Education, 1980, p. 21.
23. For examples of these editorials see note 1.
24. See, for example, "Many voices but one language," *New York Times*, 12 Dec. 1979; William Trombley, "Overtones of politics affect bilingual policy," *Los Angeles Times*, 7 Sept. 1980; "Charles McCabe himself," *San Francisco Chronicle,* 15 Oct. 1980.

25. Martin Ridge, ed., *The New Bilingualism: An American Dilemma* (Los Angeles; University of Southern California Press), p. 64.
26. Lawrence Feinberg, "Reagan denounces Carter's proposed rules on bilingual education," *The Washington Post*, 4 Mar. 1981.
27. William Trombley, "Can bilingual education do its job?" *Los Angeles Times*, Sept. 4, 1980.
28. Lee Dembart, "Mystery shrouds language skills," *Los Angeles Times*, 7 Sept. 1980.
29. Final Report of the President's Commission, MLA Newsletter, Aug. 1980, p. 1.
30. Pat Orvis, "More students learn 'exotic' languages," *New York Times*, 22 April 1980.
31. "A new direction for bilingual education in the 1980's," Mimeographed statement based on a meeting convened on 23 July 1981 by the Hazen Foundation and the Academy for Educational Development.
32. Language Usage Census (CPR Series P-23, No. 60).

Chapter 12

English, My English?

JANET WHITCUT

BRITISH people who haven't thought about it believe that the English language belongs to them, in the way Icelandic belongs to the Icelanders; to such an extent that the expression "British English" may be regarded here, outside professional circles, as a tautology. The two assertions "He speaks X, therefore he's an X" and "She's an X, therefore she speaks X," which are reasonably valid for Icelandic, have of course never been true for us. (He speaks English, therefore he's a Californian? A Jamaican? A New Zealander? She's a British citizen, therefore she speaks Welsh? Turkish? Gujarati?) Nevertheless, there is a real sense in which our relationship with English must be rather different from other people's, because we subconsciously feel that our own great-grand-parents evolved it out of their own heads, from primeval animal grunts, on that same patch of soil where our local garage now stands.

That is not to say that we are less or more concerned than anyone else about preserving its "purity." Like the rest of the English-speaking world, including the Canadians of whom Ian Pringle speaks, a lot of us believe that we do not speak or write English as well as we might. British linguists have been as unsympathetic to this belief as any other linguists, supposing it to be another manifestation of class snobbery in our class-ridden society, the setting up of shibboleths to exclude the striving masses. But in Britain in fact, as in other countries, what seems chiefly to be at issue is the maintaining of what Robert Ilson calls the High Variety of English, a "hieratic" level of language appropriate to formal discursive prose: the sort of prose in which most of this book is written, and the sort in which linguists write their own condemnations of it.

Some aspects of this High level of language are not natural to anyone's speech. If we learn, for the purposes of writing, to translate "Who'll we send it to?" into "To whom shall we send it?" we are acquiring a conventional skill, like the skill of eating corncobs without getting butter on our chins. Judgments on these matters, however, like judgments about the proper way to eat corncobs, have been very deeply entrenched for a long time in the conscious-ness of a great many educated and even semi-educated people. They were taught them at school by their teachers, who derived them ultimately from the work of a number of eighteenth-century grammarians, who based a good many of their judgments upon Latin: you can't split a Latin infinitive, so don't split an English one.

The people who make the fuss about usage – and they certainly besiege the

BBC and the serious newspapers daily on the subject – are not today chiefly worried about "vulgarisms"; the avoidance of *ain't* seems no longer to be an interesting issue, since the purists have won that battle, and the very common non-standard grammar of "we was", for instance, is never mentioned. What people mind about most, to judge from the phone-ins and the correspondence, is novelty. They were taught at school to mind about the split infinitive and the double negative, but they mind instinctively, without necessarily having been taught, if 12p in the decimal money system is referred to in speech as "twelve pee."

Of the sensitive points which Robert Ilson quotes from *The Spoken Word*, some, such as the use of *flaunt* for *flout* or *infer* for *imply*, can perhaps be classed simply as "confusions"; others, such as the use of *disinterested* for *uninterested*, reflect a natural shift of meaning (in this case back to an older meaning); others, such as the use of *data* with a singular verb, are the matter of changing grammar; while others again such as *interface*, *parameter*, and *ongoing situation*, are a question of jargon and cliché. People tend to distrust jargon, perhaps for the healthy reason suggested by Geoffrey Nunberg that they don't like to feel the specialists are taking over.

Everything I have so far said about the state of mind of the British purist is surely true of the self-appointed guardians of English anywhere in the world. What probably is particularly strong in Britain, though Ian Pringle has noticed the same thing in Canada, is the passion to preserve our language from Americanisms. We do not face, as Canadians do, the presence of the giant only a few miles away across a land frontier; but like all the nations of Western Europe we are exposed to American influence on our folkways, and of course far more than the others to American influence on our language. We have been absorbing the products of the Hollywood film industry for generations. Now, however, perhaps for political reasons as Britain's role on the world stage has declined, the last-ditchers among us who seem to have no objection to truly "foreign" borrowed words such as *ombudsman* or *aficionado* become hysterical over the infiltration of British English by American vocabulary and grammar.

True, a great deal of Americanism has been quietly slipping in unnoticed. We lash ourselves into frenzies over the use of *hopefully* as a sentence adverb, but there seems to be much less fuss over the erosion, under American influence, of the old British distinction between "do you have" (*Do you often have colds?*) and "have you got" (*Have you got a cold today?*). A British shopper is now quite likely to ask "Do you have any cauliflowers today?" and come to that to say *truck* for *lorry* and *sidewalk* for *pavement*, and to *rent* a car or a dinner jacket instead of *hiring* it. In the field of data processing we write *program* for *programme* and *disk* for *disc*.

When it comes to American pronunciations, we do get agitated: over R*Esearch*, or LAB*oratory*, or SKED*ule*. As Ilson remarks, we think that any pronunciation or word or grammatical construction that we don't like must be American, so that when we censure the purely British pronunciation *con*TROV*ersy* we unjustly call it an Americanism.

In these areas of innovation, the British purist possibly acts and will go on acting as a useful force for conservatism, retarding the pace of language change without being able in the long run to prevent it: a role often attributed in political matters to the House of Lords. It may be different in the matter of traditional judgments. Perhaps as the generation that was intensively taught old-fashioned grammar dies out, people will simply not know that there is anything the matter with the double negative because the teachers who taught them didn't know either.

Even if there is some value in controlling the hieratic level of written English, how far ought the same controls to be applied to speech? To judge from the recommendations that Robert Burchfield had to make to the BBC in *The Spoken Word*, people think that you ought to be able to speak spontaneously over the air in the way you would write. This means planning the sentence far enough ahead to avoid, for instance, not only the false concord of "Every one of those present *were* members of the union" but the regionalism of 'We want this *changing*." To be able to do that while thinking on his or her feet, the professional broadcaster must be by inheritance or schooling able to speak in the dialect called Standard British English.

This is quite different from speaking in the accent called RP, or Received Pronunciation. A dialect is strictly speaking a matter of grammar and vocabulary, while an accent is a matter of pronunciation alone. It is perfectly usual to speak in Standard British English but to pronounce it with a Cockney, Yorkshire, or Welsh accent, and many educated British people besides broadcasters do just that.

RP is the speech of a class, and like the rest of our class system it is now in decline. In 1917 the phonetician Daniel Jones defined this pronunciation as "that most usually heard in everyday speech in the families of Southern English persons whose menfolk have been educated at the great public boarding-schools." The emphasis is not only on "public schools", which implies that this was the speech of families who could afford the fees of Harrow and Winchester, but on "boarding-schools", which by drawing boys from all over the country purged their speech of regionalisms. The resultant accent, based on the educated speech of London and the Home Counties, was used throughout Britain by the upper and upper middle classes. In the early days of broadcasting, it was the accent always used in serious programmes on the air.

Things are different today. The BBC, wishing to humanize its once somewhat pompous image, uses announcers on its internal services with a wide variety of regional accents. This policy reflects a change throughout the country in the status of RP. Many upwardly mobile people have substituted something rather like RP for the local accents of their forebears, but their "neutral" speech still shows some regional variation. Many other highly-educated people will have nothing to do with RP, but lovingly preserve the speech of their own region. The children of RP-speaking families may make strenuous efforts to acquire a Cockney or Birmingham accent so as to sound like all the other kids at the disco. Too "posh" an accent is a disadvantage not only to a Labour but to a Conservative politician, for the same reason that an old Etonian may refer to his embarrassingly grand Alma Mater as "Slough Grammar School."

It has been estimated (Trudgill, 1979) that only about 3 percent of the population now actually speak RP in its pure non-regional form. It is the pronunciation always taught to foreigners, though, throughout the whole sector of the world English language industry that stems from Britain. (After all, an awful lot of people learn American English.) It is also the speech of the BBC World Service, as distinct from the internal services, and for that reason alone it must be apprehended by millions as the authentic voice of Britain.

As RP shades into the regional accents, so these shade into each other. It is impossible to say how many there are, because that depends on what distinctions you want to make, but they are certainly more numerous in a long-settled country like ours than in the newer English-speaking countries. Dialect, as we have seen, is separable from accent, and is more affected by education. Accordingly the *Survey of English Usage* at University College London, a project concerned chiefly with studying the grammar of Standard English in both speech and writing, gathers its material from what graduates say or write, on the theory that graduates use the dialect of Standard English however they may pronounce it.

Standard English, although prestigious and non-regional, is a dialect among others, and has no God-given right to be called the "English Language." The other dialects with which it jostles on these islands are rival ancient forms of English, not corruptions; they have their own organized grammar. One can of course use a "modified" form of a regional dialect, just as one can have a "slight" regional accent, with the proviso that while pronunciation is a matter of gradient, grammar and vocabulary are a matter of one thing or the other: either you say "We want this *changed*" (Southern England and Scotland) or "We want this *changing*" (parts of the Midlands and Northern England). Or one may be lucky enough to be bidialectal, which is very useful.

The British are extremely conscious of accent and dialect, and tend to judge a whole personality by speech alone, not distinguishing what is individual from what is regional. In general, like other people, they find rural dialects and accents charming and urban ones less so. The most confident rival to Standard English is educated Scots, which everybody respects.

Scottish English has its own ancient and distinguished literary and educational tradition. In its educated form today it constitutes a real Standard, the language of broadcasting and the serious Scottish newspapers, but is distinguishable chiefly as an accent rather than a dialect. The most striking feature of the accent is of course its quality of "rhoticity", the pronouncing of "r" wherever it occurs in the spelling, which Scottish speech shares with many American accents but which is absent from RP.

To educated speakers of both Scottish and Irish English, RP sounds somewhat "foreign," the language of London. Irish English continues the great literary tradition of O'Casey, Joyce, Yeats, Synge, and Beckett. It certainly constitutes a Standard, expressed in Irish broadcasting and transmitted through the Irish educational system, but is less institutionalized and more fluid than Scots. It has of course no official structure for its promotion even though the Irish Republic is a separate country; there is nothing comparable to the pronouncements by which Noah Webster in 1800 urged that spelling changes should be introduced to make American English deliberately different from its British original. The Irish national effort has gone into the promotion of the Irish language itself.

Richard Bailey has traced the history and the changing fortunes of the Celtic languages in these islands, so it remains only to say a very little about their position today. The rising tide of Celtic nationalism is one aspect of what Ofelia Garcia has called "Europe's ethnic boom": it has expressed itself differently in Ireland, in Scotland, and in Wales. In the Irish Republic, a separate country since 1922, Irish is a compulsory school subject and there are some Irish medium schools; it has been encouraged by the requirement of an examination pass in Irish for Civil Servants; it is one of the official languages of the EEC; and it is used as well as English in the flight announcements on an Irish aircraft, although the stewardesses are unlikely to be able to chat in it. It is not the language of Dublin, but is truly alive only in the Gaeltacht, the rural Irish-speaking West.

In Scotland, where Scots Gaelic is the language of the Highlands and Islands, a good deal is now being done for its standardization and for its encouragement through broadcasting and bilingual education, but it is less of a fighting issue: Scottish nationalism does not depend upon it.

The minor Celtic languages Manx and Cornish are dead, though there are some recent attempts to revive the latter.

In Wales the situation is rather different. Although some areas such as Pembroke have spoken English for centuries, and most Welsh people have had some contact with English since the Middle Ages, there were few mother-tongue speakers of English in Wales until a century or two ago: in this sense English in Wales is more recent than English in North America. Today nearly everybody can speak at least some English, but a large minority speak it as a second language. Welsh is thus the most viable of the British Celtic languages. Its mother-tongue speakers, estimated at as high as 20 percent of the population, are mostly in the north, but many of the English-speaking majority have learnt some Welsh. It is energetically promoted in the schools, and has now its own television channel, in response to impassioned demand. Signposts on Welsh roads are in both Welsh and English. Welsh English, however, is scarcely a recognizable separate form, unlike the English of Scotland, since historically it has been taught as a foreign language. Its most noticeable feature, to the outside ear, is the characteristic Welsh "sing-song" intonation, which seems to make a statement sound like a question.

The Celtic languages, though the longest established, are only one of the non-English language groups represented within this chiefly English-speaking land. They are the languages in respect of which we most energetically foster the "natural permanent bilingualism" of which Garcia speaks; and they are spoken in the more outlying parts of our islands. Even Welsh is scarcely heard in England beyond the range of Welsh television. But in the heart of our most crowded centres, in London and the great northern industrial cities, we are gradually battling out what to do for the new immigrant linguistic minorities in our midst. It is books in Gujarati and Urdu, not in any Celtic language, that you find on the shelves of a London public library.

These new citizens come particularly from South and East Asia and

Southern and Eastern Europe. They are the children and now the grand-children of refugees and immigrants who have arrived here since the Second World War. In response to recent EEC directives, part of the European Community's programme for the children of migrant workers, more is being done to teach their various minority tongues and cultures in British schools. A city school may teach Greek, to Greek Cypriots, up to the Advanced Level of the General Certificate of Education; there is increasing awareness of the problem of improving the young people's literacy in the language they speak at home. In addition a good deal of mother-tongue language teaching of Greek, Turkish, or Polish goes on in evening and Saturday classes, often organized by local churches and other bodies but with some government funding, for the benefit both of immigrants and of the children of temporary residents. There is a real concern to preserve bilingualism, especially among the new British-born generations.

Since Britain has only lately and to a fairly modest extent become a country of immigration, we do not seem to feel much concern, as Garcia says some people do in the United States, lest the promotion of non-English languages may weaken national unity; in any case, many of those immigrants whose skin colour makes them most identifiable as "foreign" are not the ones with a language problem. The East African Asians arrived with the good English they learned at school back in Africa.

In the towns, at any rate, the Local Education Authorities have English Language Centres which deploy the specialized teachers in the schools. Children who do not speak English at home spend most of the week with the rest of their age-group, and perhaps two weekly hours with a specialist English teacher, in groups graded according to fluency. Except for those who have almost no English, English medium instruction in mathematics and the sciences at any rate presents little difficulty, since the whole class must learn the new words with the new concepts.

One might hope that this up-and-coming group of bilingual speakers would be a valuable economic resource to their country of adoption, whose indigenous inhabitants have an appalling record of sloth in the learning of foreign languages. Unfortunately they do not come from the rich countries to whom we would like to sell. The Germans, it is said, "sell in English but buy in German." Despite directives from the EEC, the enthusiasm of the British Overseas Trading Board, endless conferences on the subject, and now in a period of high unemployment the urgent demands of prospective employers, the native British seem less willing than ever to learn languages properly at school. The learning of Russian, Spanish, German, and even French to any useful level has actually gone down in recent years, owing not only to cuts and staffing problems but also to a general lack of interest. In the new non-selective comprehensive schools more children learn some French, but two-thirds of them give it up at the age of 14. The result is that companies expect to have to train their employees themselves, or of course to employ a foreigner. A company which recently advertised for a Japanese-speaking switchboard operator could find nobody who was willing even to learn Japanese for the purpose, and had to bring in someone from Japan.

British English in its more or less central form goes on its course, influenced by all these rival dialects and all these other tongues with which it coexists in a crowded country. That course is further affected by the cultural movements of the wider world. Like other people, we have developed new permissiveness, new equalities, and new pruderies. Our speech is more sexually and lavatorially frank than ever, and the franker the more educated and articulate we are. It is in cultivated homes that the babies without euphemism *shit* in their pants. It is sexual frankness that lets us say *fuck*, but it is sexual egalitarianism that makes us now use the verb intransitively with a plural subject "they fucked", and transitively or intransitively with a feminine one "does she fuck?" That same egalitarianism has given rise to *Ms* in business correspondence and on official forms, to *salesperson* and *draughtsperson* in the job ads.

Our prudery, by contrast, extends continually into new areas of euphemism. From what is surely a generous social concern, the old have for a long time been called *senior citizens*, the poor have been *underprivileged*, and the stupid have been *underachievers*. We have gone through the same process as other English speakers of trying to purify our language from racial slurs, so that now there are some subjects that it is as difficult for us to talk about it as it was for the Victorians to talk about sex. A recent directive from an inner London borough discussed at some length the incidence, diagnosis, and treatment of sickle-cell anaemia among its citizenry, without once explaining that nearly all the people who get it are *black*.

If the treatises on usage do not, as Ilson remarks, discuss the fluctuating status of words like *Yid* and *fuck*, perhaps it is because their authors are reluctant to dip their feet in these deep waters. To make such judgments would entail making value judgments on their whole society.

References

BURCHFIELD, ROBERT, *The Spoken Word*. BBC, 1981.

JONES, DANIEL, *English Pronouncing Dictionary*. J. M. Dent & Sons Ltd., 1st ed., 1917.

NUNBERG, GEOFFREY, *The Case for Prescriptive Grammar*. MS., 1980.

TRUDGILL, PETER, "Standard and non-standard dialects of English in the United Kingdom: problems and policies." *International Journal of the Sociology of Language*, 1979.

Chapter 13

Usage Problems in British and American English

ROBERT F. ILSON

I. *What is a usage problem?*

Not every language problem is a usage problem. Consider the adjective *unique* (as in "a unique experience"). Many people would argue that it is wrong to compare *unique*; that is, to say "a more unique experience" or "the most unique experience I've ever had." The comparability of *unique* is a problem of usage. Now consider the adjective *atomic* (as in "an atomic bomb"). Nobody would argue that it is wrong to say "a more atomic bomb" or "the most atomic bomb of all" – because no one, in the normal course of events, would even think of saying them. The comparability of *atomic* is not a problem of usage. So the first thing required of a usage problem is that it should be a *problem*; that is, something that people actually say, rather than something they'd never dream of saying.

But that is not the only criterion that a usage problem must satisfy. Instead of *isn't*, some people say *ain't* and some (at least in Britain) *bean't*. *Ain't* is a well-known usage problem; *bean't* is not. Why is this? The reason may be that *bean't* is restricted to one or more regions of the English-speaking world, whereas *ain't* is very widespread. The pronunciation of *dispute* as *DISpute* rather than *disPUTE* may have originated in the north of England, but if it is felt to be a usage problem in British English today (as seems to be the case), that is because it can now be heard in many places. So the second thing required of a usage problem is that it should involve an item that is of fairly wide distribution, not one that is felt to be limited to regional dialect.

And a third requirement of a usage problem is that its public discussion should not cause too much embarrassment. At least that is the only reason I can think of why words in the general area of slurs and smut – words like *yid* and *fuck* – are not condemned in treatises on usage in the way that *ain't* is. Some years ago, an important British publisher wanted to find out which types of word people wanted included in dictionaries and which types excluded from them. At first it was proposed to include various examples of smut in the questionnaire, but eventually it was decided not to include them, on the grounds that their simple presence – even in a question about their appropriateness as dictionary entries – might make people refuse to take part in the market-research exercise altogether. And I think it is significant that it was never proposed to include racial or religious slurs on the questionnaire at all.

However, the three criteria for usage problems discussed so far – actual occurrence, fairly widespread occurrence, and discussability without giving offence – are really not so much reasons why some items become usage problems as reasons why other items do *not*. We may know why usage books don't discuss *bean't*. But why do they prefer *isn't* to *ain't*? Why, indeed are there usage problems at all?

II. *Why are there usage problems?*

In discussions of usage, two sorts of argument have traditionally been heard. The first has been advanced by those who think that such discussions are worthwhile, the second by sceptics.

The first argument is that some items are better than others on logical, historical, or aesthetic grounds. Thus *none is* is better than *none are* because *none* really means "not one." Or "The split infinitive in the majority of cases . . . sounds clumsy, inelegant, or even ugly. It is a question of Euphony . . . " (Queen's English Society, pp. 7–8).

The second argument is that some items, regardless of their logical, historical, or aesthetic merits, are associated with the language of the uneducated and the poor, so that those who condemn them are at one and at the same time asserting their own educational and social respectability, and adding linguistic obstacles to the educational and social ones that must be surmounted by lower-class folk who wish to join them. *Ain't* is held to be a typical class marker in this sense nowadays, though there is evidence that it has not always been so and may not be so everywhere even now.

Recently, a third line of argument has been developed in the work of Geoffrey Nunberg (1980). Although Nunberg's approach is brilliantly original, it is in some ways similar to the first argument, modified in a sociological direction. Nunberg claims that speech communities establish and maintain their identity in part by taking some particular type of discourse as central and worthy of special admiration. For some communities – in the Arab world, perhaps? – this may be the language of formal religious observance; for others, the cut and thrust of unbuttoned conversational repartee. For the English-speaking world, however, it is the non-fictional familiar essay, as exemplified by the work of Hazlitt and Lamb. The constructions recommended by the more judicious commentators on usage are, according to Nunberg, those which require the sort of moderate forethought and sentence planning appropriate to such relatively informal, yet structured, discourse. People who strive to say "*none* of the people *is* here" must remember the beginning of their sentence when they get to the middle of it; those who say "none of the *people are* here" need do no more than adjust their verb to what comes just before it.

A fourth consideration, perhaps a sociologically "laundered" version of the second, may be implicit in the notion of "diglossia", introduced by Charles Ferguson and extended by Joshua Fishman and others (see Hudson, 1981, pp.

53–57). In some communities, different language functions are assigned to different languages, or to varieties of one language so distinct from each other as almost to constitute different languages. Thus in a number of countries (Malta, for example), English is the language of higher education, while another language is used in what might be called "ordinary life." In the Arab World the Standard Arabic used for religion and higher education is so different from the various Arabic vernaculars that special instruction in it is necessary. On the whole, the English-speaking world is not like that. The English used in sermons, law-courts, and doctors' consulting rooms differs far less from the English of ordinary conversation than English differs from Maltese, or than Standard Arabic differs from its vernaculars. And yet, there may be a universal tendency in this direction, so that when English-language usage books recommend some items and condemn others, however arbitrarily, they may be responding to a need to maintain a distinction within Standard English corresponding to the High variety and the Low variety of some other languages.

III. *Usage problems in British and American English*

There are recognized usage problems in both British and American English, but are they the *same* problems? Whatever the answer, a comparison is likely to tell us something about the relation of the two varieties – and something about the nature of usage problems in general. As a point of departure for our investigation, we are fortunate in having *The Spoken Word* (1981), a booklet prepared for the BBC by Robert Burchfield, Chief Editor of the Oxford English Dictionaries. The booklet is based on a monitoring of BBC radio programmes carried out in "mid-1979" by Dr. Burchfield and several colleagues, supplemented by letters and telephone calls about usage problems received by the BBC. As is obviously appropriate in a booklet "prepared directly for broadcasters" (p. 7), the first section is devoted to pronunciation, and it is here, in an area of particularly striking differences between British and American English, that I shall begin.

Pronunciation

Dr. Burchfield lists 120 words whose pronunciations constitute usage problems, and marks 14 as "the ones that give most offence when pronounced otherwise than as" he recommends. To find out whether any of these 14 are usage problems in American English, I have compared Burchfield's treatment with that in two American dictionaries, AHD (*American Heritage Dictionary*, 1979) and W8 (*Webster's New* (Eighth) *Collegiate Dictionary, 1974*). I take disagreement between the dictionaries as evidence of at least a potential usage problem in American English.

I have tried to show the point at issue as clearly as possible, and I haven't worried very much about phonetic details:

Dr. Burchfield's list

Word (in British spelling)	Recommended	Rejected	AHD	W8	American problem?
(1) comparable	COMparable	comPARable	COMparable	COMparable	NO

Observation: Although the Canadian-American linguist Mark Aronoff (1979, p. 123) discusses both pronunciations of *comparable*, the fact that AHD and W8 give only Burchfield's recommendation suggests that it is not an American usage problem.

(2) composite	COMpozitt	COMpozight	comPOZitt	comPOZitt	NO

Observation: W8 gives the pronunciation recommended by Burchfield, but labels it *esp Brit.*

(3) contribute	conTRIBute	CONtribute	conTRIBute	conTRIBute	NO

(4) controversy	CONtroversy	conTROVersy	CONtroversy	CONtroversy	NO

Observation: The shift in stress from the first syllable of *controversy* to the second parallels an earlier development in the word *laboratory*. The pronunciation "laBORatory" now considered by Americans so characteristic of British English, is not recorded in the *Oxford English Dictionary* (1933), and had to be added in Vol. 2 of its supplement (1976). British English originally, like American English today, stressed the first syllable of *laboratory*, so that a stress-shift which British speakers take for granted in the case of *laboratory* is disputed in the case of *controversy*.

(5) deity	DEEity	DAYity	DEEity	DEEity, DAYity	YES

Here the potential usage problem for American English is the same as for British.

(6) dispute	disPUTE	DISpute	disPUTE	disPUTE	NO

(7) distribute	disTRIBute	DIStribute	disTRIBute	disTRIBute	NO

Observation: The British problems with *dispute* and *distribute* are much the same as with *contribute*. For *distribute*, W8 also enters the problematic pronunciation and labels it British, but it has no British pronunciation of *contribute* or *dispute*.

(8) government	government	goverment, govment	government	all three entered	YES

(9) jewellery	jewel-ry	jew-lery	jewel-ry	jewel-ry	NO

(10) kilometre	KILometer	kiLOMeter	both in	both in and note	YES

Observation: Though both pronunciations are in AHD and W8, I've called this an American usage problem because (1) they are given in different orders in the two dictionaries, suggesting a difference in assessment between the two books, and (2) W8 has a usage note suggesting, as Burchfield says explicitly, that the pronunciation *kiLOMeter* is based on analogy with measuring devices like *therMOMeter* rather than measuring units like *CENtimetre*.

(11) primarily	PRImarily	priMARily	PRImarily, priMARily	priMARily	YES

(12) research	reSEARCH	REsearch	both in	both in	NO

Observation: AHD and W8 give both pronunciations in the same order, but with no suggestion that one is better than the other

(13) spontaneity	spontanEEity	spontanAYity	spontanEEity	both in	YES

Observation: This is the same problem as with *deity*.

(14) temporarily	TEMporarily	tempoRARily	tempoRARily	tempoRARily	NO

Observation: This is the same problem as with *primarily*.

Conclusions: In only five of Burchfield's fourteen most egregious cases is there a recognized potential usage problem in American English. But some of Burchfield's fourteen cases can be grouped together. For the group *contribute, dispute,* and *distribute* there is no American usage problem because the pronunciation recommended by Burchfield is the only one entered as American in AHD or W8. For the group *deity, spontaneity* there is an American usage problem, because AHD gives only the pronunciation that Burchfield recommends, but W8 gives both. For the group *primarily, temporarily* there is an interesting split. *Temporarily* is not an American usage problem, because AHD and W8 give only the pronunciation that Burchfield rejects – a pronunciation that Burchfield himself calls an Americanism (1981, p. 10). But *primarily* is a potential American usage problem, because AHD gives both Burchfield pronunciations while W8 gives only the "American" one.

Vocabulary

The Spoken Word (pp. 18–25) includes a list of forty-seven words that constitute usage problems in British English. For each item I have tried to give an idea of the problem, and say whether it is dealt with in the *American Heritage Dictionary* (AHD), which prides itself on the treatment of usage. For American English I have also consulted the *Webster's New* (Eighth) *Collegiate Dictionary* (W8) and the *Oxford American Dictionary* (OAD). For additional opinions on British English I have referred to the *Collins English Dictionary* (CED), the *Concise Oxford Dictionary* (COD), the *Oxford Paperback Dictionary* (OPD), and of course the great *Oxford English Dictionary* itself (OED).

The symbol * indicates that the usage in question is, according to Burchfield, to be avoided "if possible."

(1) *agree* 'agree to, accept': *agree a compromise*
AHD: Usage note? No. *AHD: Treated otherwise*? Use not included.
Observation: Dr Burchfield *accepts* this use of *agree* plus direct object "even in formal broadcasts," but the very fact that it is on the list of usage problems suggests that some people find it questionable. It seems to be unknown in American English, but Americans should bear in mind that British speakers are just as surprised to hear Americans say "they protested the war" instead of "they protested against the war." Burchfield's entry for *agree* is out of alphabetical order, suggesting last-minute inclusion.

(2) *aggravate* *'annoy, irritate': *Your behaviour aggravates him.*
AHD: Usage note? No. *AHD: Treated otherwise*? Use labelled *Informal.*
Observation: This use of *aggravate* with a human direct object may be regarded as more of a problem in British than in American English, though it is interesting that the British OPD (1979) simply labels the relevant sense *Informal* (like AHD), whereas OAD (1980) adds a Usage note à la Burchfield.

(3) *ain't* Avoid except humorously
AHD: Usage note? Yes. *AHD: Treated otherwise*? Word labelled *Nonstandard.*

(4) *alternative* ?More than two alternatives
AHD: Usage note? Yes. *AHD: Treated otherwise*? No.
Observation: The queried usage is, according to Burchfield, "disputed by a minority of people."

(5) *anticipate* *'expect': *anticipating rain*
AHD: Usage note? Yes. *AHD: Treated otherwise*? No.

(6) *around* ?'about, approximately': *around 50*
AHD: Usage note? No. *AHD: Treated otherwise*? Use labelled *Informal*.
Observation: Burchfield's comment is: "more usual in the US than in Britain."

(7) *comprise* *'compose': *11 player comprise the team. The team is comprised of 11 players.*
AHD:Usage note? Yes. *AHD: Treated otherwise*? No.

(8) *data* Are, not *is
AHD: Usage note? Yes. *AHD: Treated otherwise*? No.

(9) *decimate* *'destroy more or less than 1/10 of' *AHD: Usage note*? No.
AHD: Treated otherwise? Sense included without comment.

(10) *deprecate* *'depreciate, belittle'
AHD: Usage note? Yes. *AHD: Treated otherwise*? No.

(11) *dilemma* *'predicament involving more than 2 choices'
AHD: Usage note? Yes. *AHD: Treated otherwise*? No.

(12) *disassociate* Replace with *dissociate*.
AHD: Usage note? No. *AHD: Treated otherwise*? No.
Observation: For AHD, *disassociate* simply *means* 'dissociate.'

(13) *disinterested* *'uninterested'
AHD: Usage note? Yes. *AHD: Treated otherwise*? Use labelled *Nonstandard*.
Observation: According to Dr Burchfield, confusion of *disinterested* with *uninterested* "attracts more unfavourable comment" than any other usage problem on this list except perhaps the use of *hopefully* discussed below. It is worth noting, however, that the oldest citation for *distinterested* in OED is in the meaning 'uninterested' (1612), that the oldest OED citations for *uninterested* are in the meanings 'impartial' (1646) and 'disinterested' (1661), that *disinterested* and *uninterested* didn't switch round to their approved meanings until 1659 and 1771 respectively, and that the spread of *disinterested* at the expense of *uninterested* is bound to be helped by the existence of the noun *disinterest* and the non-existence of a noun *uninterest.

(14) *due to* *'because of': *Play was stopped due to rain.*
AHD: Usage note? Yes. *AHD: Treated otherwise*? No.
Observation: There would presumably be no objection to the "The stopping of play was due to rain" or even "Play is due to resume shortly." Nor should there be any objection to the historian Edward Crankshaw's sentence "That this collection survives is entirely due to her" (*Observer* (London), 5 September 1982, p. 23). In all these cases *due* can be construed as an adjective modifying

stopping, *play*, and the noun clause *that this collection survives* respectively. Note, however, that when followed by a verb in a phrase like *is due to resume*, *due to* has really taken on the role of a modal expression, and *is due to* can then be compared to *is supposed to*, *is about to*, *is able to*, etc.

(15) *enormity* *'enormousness': *the enormity of their responsibilities*
AHD: Usage note? Yes. *AHD: Treated otherwise*? No.

(16) *flaunt* *'flout'
AHD: Usage note? Yes. *AHD: Treated otherwise*? Use labelled *Nonstandard*.
Observation: Despite its *Nonstandard* label, AHD provides for this sense of *flaunt* an example attributed to the (anti-prescriptivist!) American linguist Robert A. Hall, Jr.

(17) *following*: **Police have arrested someone following extensive inquiries.*
AHD: Usage note? No. *AHD: Treated otherwise*? Use not included.
Observation: There is a real ambiguity in Burchfield's example, but the general objection to this use of *following* is like that raised against *due to*. Both *following* and *due* (plus *to*) are now used as prepositions, and it is proposed that they should be restricted to adjectival use. But several *-ing*-forms are now often used as prepositions, with or without *to* (e.g. *concerning*, *including*, *owing to*, *regarding*, *respecting*), and although *following* is not entered as a preposition by AHD, it is so shown, without comment, in both the British COD (1976) and the American W8 (1974).

(18) *hopefully*: **Hopefully, they will arrive soon.*
AHD: Usage note? Yes. *AHD: Treated otherwise*? No.
Observation: In Britain, the use of *hopefully* as a "sentence adverb" (or "disjunct") is often regarded as an Americanism. But, as shown by the AHD Usage note, it is regarded with considerable distaste in America as well as in Britain. In fact the American OAD takes over without change the critical Usage note on it to be found in the British OPD. The objection may have to do with the fact that *hopefully* is here being used in the role of the non-existent **hop(e)ably*. After all, no one objects to sentences like "Regrettably, they will arrive late," which have inhibited the spread of sentences like "Regretfully, they will arrive late."

(19) *imply* *'infer'
AHD: Usage note? Yes (at *infer*). *AHD: Treated otherwise*? No.

(20) *interface*: **the science-religion interface*
AHD: Usage note? No. *AHD: Treated otherwise*? No.
Observation: the objection is to *interface* as a figurative boundary area rather than the literal one exemplified by Burchfield's "The interface of the two liquids . . ." AHD's *interface* has one definition, worded so as (in principle) to cover both literal and figurative uses. The use of *interface* as a verb, recorded in W8, does not seem to have become widely current in Britain.

(21) *ironical(ly)* *'paradoxical(ly)': *Ironically, the tortoise beat the hare.*
AHD: Usage note? No. *AHD: Treated otherwise*? No.

Observation: AHD relates *ironic, ironical,* and *ironically* to *irony,* which is defined so as to allow the adjective and adverb forms to be used in the way Burchfield rejects, though it is not clear that this was AHD's intention. Lexicographers should consider more carefully the capacity of inflected and derived forms to develop meanings not directly inferrable from their sources.

(22) *latter* *'last': *the latter of the three*
AHD: Usage note? Yes. *AHD: Treated otherwise?* No.

(23) *lay* *'lie'
AHD: Usage note? Yes. *AHD: Treated otherwise?* Use labelled *Nonstandard.*

(24) *loan* *'lend'
AHD: Usage note? Yes. *AHD: Treated otherwise?* No.
Observation: Although American AHD says that *lend* "is considered by many to be preferable to *loan* in general usage . . . *and particularly in formal writing*" (emphasis mine), the British CED (1979) says that *loan* 'lend' is "avoided by careful speakers and writers except when referring to the formal lending of money: *the bank loaned him the money.*"

(25) *militate* *'mitigate'
AHD: Usage note? No. *AHD: Treated otherwise?* Use not included.

(26) *ongoing.* Avoid especially in the phrase "*an ongoing situation.*"
AHD: Usage note? No. *AHD: Treated otherwise?* No.
Observation: The objection to this word in Britain, though strong, seems to be based on the feeling that it is overused rather than incorrect.

(27) *p* 'pence or penny' Avoid especially in speech: *"It cost three p."
AHD: Usage note? No. *AHD: Treated otherwise?* No.
Observation: For AHD, *p* can mean 'penny' but not 'pence.' Before the decimalization of British currency in 1971, the symbol for penny or pence was *d* (from Latin *denarius*), which was not used in speech. There were 12 pence in the shilling, and it was rarely necessary to refer to sums of more than 11 pence (with stress as shown). Since 1971 the pound has been divided into 100 (new) pence (abbreviation *p*). Furthermore, an amount like £1.24 is sometimes written as 124 p. Thus the word *pence* is now used far more than it used to be, and its abbreviation *p* has been found convenient in speech as well as in writing – despite objections. The greater productivity of *pence* and *p* in combinations has been accompanied by a change in stress pattern from pre-decimal 11 pence to post-decimal 11 pènce (or 11 p̀). *P* has the further advantage that it can replace both *penny* and *pence.*

(28) *parameter* *'limit, boundary, dimension': *the parameters of the situation*
AHD: Usage note? Yes. *AHD: Treated otherwise?* No.

(29) *portentous* *'pretentious'
AHD: Usage note? No. *AHD: Treated otherwise?* No.
Observation: AHD enters this sense without comment.

(30) *prestigious* 'having or showing prestige'
AHD: Usage note? No. *AHD: Treated otherwise*? No.
Observation: "Rearguard opposition to this use can now be ignored" (Burchfield). The less controversial alternative *prestigeful* does not seem to have caught on, and though recorded in the British COD and the American W8, it is not in AHD or CED.

(31) *pristine* *'fresh as if new': *a pristine layer of snow*
AHD: Usage note? No. *AHD: Treated otherwise*? No.
Observation: AHD enters this sense without comment.

(32) *protagonist* *'proponent'
AHD: Usage note? Yes. *AHD: Treated otherwise?* No.
Observation: As AHD points out, the disputed sense is probably influenced by the assumption that *protagonist* must the opposite of *antagonist*.

(33) *refute* *'deny'
AHD: Usage note? No. *AHD: Treated otherwise*? Synonym essay at *deny*.
Observation: AHD's treatment of *deny* and *refute* in a Synonym essay (along with *gainsay* and *contradict*) rather than in a Usage note suggests that the confusion of the two words is an understandable error rather than, as it were, an unpardonable sin.

(34) *responsibility*: ?*claim responsibility for* (*an act of terrorism*)
AHD: Usage note? No. *AHD: Treated otherwise*? No.
Observation: Though placed by Burchfield at *responsibility*, the objection may really be to *claim*. W8 has a Synonym note saying that the meaning element shared by *demand, claim, require,* and *exact* is "to ask or call for something as or as if one's right or due." The implication is that one *claims* something good, a prize rather than a punishment, say, and that may be why people object to the *claiming* of responsibility for a bombing or an assassination.

(35) *seasonable* *'seasonal'
AHD: Usage note? Yes. *AHD: Treated otherwise*? No.

(36) *situation*: *a crisis situation*; *a no-win situation*
AHD: Usage note? No. *AHD: Treated otherwise*? No.
Observation: Dr. Burchfield says that what causes "increasing dismay and resentment" is the use of *situation* "with a preceding noun or noun phrase . . . often in contexts where it is totally redundant . . . " The British satirical magazine *Private Eye* has run a recurrent feature devoted to particularly bad examples of phrases with *situation* in them, and it does seem (despite a Burchfield-like Usage note taken over by OAD from OPD) that such phrases have attracted more attention in Britain than in America. Far be it from me to attempt their defence, but I think at least two things can be said on their behalf. First, a "crisis situation" may really be a crisis-like situation; i.e. one that has some of the characteristics of a crisis, but to which one hesitates to apply the name. Calling it "a crisis situation" rather than "a crisis" has a downtoning, qualifying effect that may show the presence rather than the

absence of thought on the speaker's part, making the word *situation* far from "redundant." Second, the word *situation* is useful for referring to phrases without quoting them in full, as in "a chicken-and-egg situation" or indeed Burchfield's own example "a no-win situation." It would be much more cumbersome to speak of "a position (or *situation*, for that matter) in which no clear-cut victory is possible." An analogous role is played by the word *case*, as in "a case of the chicken or the egg."

(37) *thankfully*: **Thankfully, the weather was fine.*
AHD: Usage note? No. *AHD: Treated otherwise*? No.
Observation: For AHD, *thankfully* is an undefined derivative (a "run-on") of *thankful*. The problem of *thankfully* is that of *hopefully*, as Burchfield points out. Once again, nobody objects to such sentences as "Fortunately, the weather was fine," and I think that *thankfully* has suffered because it ends in *-fully* rather than *-ably*, *-ately*, or some other combination of suffixes. As Burchfield himself says, "Other sentence adverbs . . . are not objected to." Nor is there even any objection to a sentence adverb that ends in *-fully*, provided that its source is a noun that cannot also be a verb (and that is therefore much less likely to have an alternative in *-ably*): *Mercifully, the weather was fine*. One can say "I hope" or "I thank you," but not "I mercy."

(38) *transpire* **'happen'*
AHD: Usage note? Yes. *AHD: Treated otherwise*? No.

Conclusions: Of Dr Burchfield's thirty-eight vocabulary usage problems in British English, twenty get Usage notes in AHD, but eighteen do not. This is a wide discrepancy, and deserves closer scrutiny. Two of the eighteen cases ("*agree* a plan" and the use of *p* for *pence* in speech) are Briticisms unknown in America. One (*around* 'approximately') is a genuine case of a usage which is completely normal in America but considered something of an Americanism in Britain. What of the other fifteen cases (*aggravate, decimate, disassociate, following, interface, ironic(al(ly)), militate, ongoing, portentous, prestigious, pristine, refute, responsibility, situation, thankfully*)? A check of British CED shows, first, that *following* is not entered as a preposition – just as it is not in AHD. As for the other fourteen words, only *aggravate* and *refute* get Usage notes in CED! This fact gains in significance when it is realized that of the twenty cases where both Burchfield and AHD recognize a usage problem, CED has notes on nine. Turning now to Burchfield's own *Oxford Paperback Dictionary* (which is much smaller than CED or AHD), we find that of the twenty cases where Burchfield and AHD agree that there is a usage problem, OPD has Usage notes on thirteen, whereas of the fifteen cases (other than *agree, around*, and *p*) where Burchfield and AHD disagree about the existence of a usage problem, OPD does not enter *disassociate* or *interface*, does not enter a sense of *portentous* equal to 'pretentious,' and has Usage notes on *refute, situation*, and *thankfully* – i.e. on only three of the fifteen items. All this goes to show that the choice of which *potential* usage problems are *actual* usage problems is rather arbitrary. But it also shows that the usage problems agreed on by Burchfield and AHD are far more likely to be regarded as usage problems by other British commentators on usage than those treated by Burchfield but not by AHD.

Grammar

Dr Burchfield ends his booklet with a section on grammar. Although dictionaries provide Usage notes on some grammatical problems, we must really look elsewhere for an American basis of comparison. The Reader's Digest book *Write Better, Speak Better* (RD-1972) has been chosen because it claims to be comprehensive and includes "a complete dictionary of usage."

Burchfield's grammar problems are divided into three degrees of serious-ness: *** "Unacceptable uses in any circumstances," ** "Uses resisted by listeners but permissible in informal circumstances," and * "Debatable features: preferences provided":

*** *"Unacceptable uses in any circumstances"* (Burchfield)

(1) False Concord in Sentences: ****There's two birds in the nest.* ****Every one of them were here.*
RD: Treated? Yes.
Observation: The RD comments are indicated in "agreement of verb with subject" and at "there." RD seems to make the same points as Burchfield, saying at "there" that "The number of the verb is not affected by *there* but depends on the number of the subject" and, at "every," that "*Everyone* and *every one* are always singular and followed by singular verbs and pronouns." Neither Burchfield nor RD discusses the problems presented by such sentences as "Everyone has left, haven't they?," where more than one clause is involved.

(2) Classical plurals construed as singulars: *criteria, data, media, phenomena, strata*
RD: Treated? No.
Observation: RD does not discuss the problem in general. But it has an entry for *data*, including the annotated example "We have proved that *these* [not *this*] *data are* [not *is*] reliable."

(3) Failure to use the oblique case of pronouns: *between you and* ***I
RD: Treated? Yes.
Observation: It is perhaps because purists tried so hard to get people to say "It is I" instead of "It's me" that now the problem is to get them to say *me* rather than *I*! Burchfield does not discuss the use of *myself* for *me* in such sentences as "He loved and cherished my brother and myself," but RD does, under the heading "reflexive pronouns."

(4) Hanging or unattached participles
RD: Treated? Yes.
Observation: In American English, these are called "dangling participles" or sometimes "misplaced participles."

(5) Confusion of *less* and *fewer*
RD: Treated? Yes.

(6) Wrong participles:
We want this changed (not ***changing).
This needs changing (not ***changed).
RD: Treated? No.
Observation: This seems to show a significant British-American difference, the constructions rejected above representing uses more common in British regional dialects than in American ones.

(7) Inability to carry through a sentence with *one* as subject
RD: Treated? No.
Observation: Another major British-American difference. Burchfield not only provides an elaborate quotation from Iris Murdoch ("One's best hope is to get into one of those 'holes' where one's two neighbours are eagerly engaged elsewhere, so that one can concentrate upon one's plate") but says in a footnote that "In American English . . . 'one . . . his' is commonly found." Note also that in British English, the use of *one* to mean 'I' has attracted unfavourable comment as a sign of false modesty: *One got hurt when one fell off one's horse.*

(8) Confusion of *more* and *most*: ****the most interesting of the two*
RD: Treated? No.
Observation: RD's failure to condemn this construction is striking, but does not mean that it is unnoticed in American English. But what concerns RD (and OAD) more is the use of *most* as a short form of *almost*, a problem that is apparently unknown in standard British English.

** "*Uses resisted by listeners but permissible in informal English*" (Burchfield)

(9) Preposition at end
RD: Treated? Yes.
Observation: It is fascinating that both Burchfield and RD concentrate on showing when it is desirable or even obligatory to end a clause with a preposition ("What a shocking state you are *in*!"), rather than condemning the practice. This reversal of emphasis is similar to their treatment of such pronoun problems as *me* and *I* (point 3). Was it puristic hypercorrectness or a delicate sense of language play that made the learned Steven Runciman write, *à propos* of the ancestors of young Prince William, "The years to come will show after which of them he will take" (*Times Literary Supplement*, 3 September 1982, p. 949) rather than ". . . which of them he will take after"?

(10) *Like* as conjunction:
***Winston tastes good like a cigarette should.*
RD: Treated? Yes.
Observation: RD simply says: "Use *like* as a preposition; *as* as a conjunction." Burchfield is more tolerant, saying that "modern writers regularly use this construction . . ." British "small ads" (classified ads) are wont to say that things for sale are "as new" rather than "like new."

(11) Verbless sentences:
"Another sunny day. Still no letters." (I. Murdoch)
RD: Treated? No.
Observation: Burchfield says such constructions are all right in broadcasts and common in fiction. He does not mention their frequency in advertising.

(12) Use of present tense for future tense:
"At 8.30 X hunts through the BBC sound archives . . ."
RD: Treated? No.
Observation: It is difficult to understand why listeners object to this. Surely no one would object to "The train leaves tonight"? But there may be a significant difference between the two examples. Quirk and Greenbaum (1973, sec. 3.40) say that the simple present with future reference is "often used with dynamic transitional verbs: *arrive, come, leave*, etc." These verbs all suggest a change of state, the beginning or end of something. The verb *hunt* does not, nor do such other "broadcasting" verbs as *read, investigate, discuss*, etc.

(13) Emphasis on minor words, especially *a*, *an*, and *the* (also prepositions)
RD: Treated? Yes.
Observation: The RD treatment is not in its "dictionary of usage," but under the heading "the vowels in unemphasized syllables" (pp. 633–635) in an earlier discussion of "Overmeticulous pronunciation." As for Burchfield, he accepts such emphasis in "informal broadcasts" only, and then in moderation. Stressing a preposition, as in "They are standing *bŷ* their threat . . ." may be a way of giving emphasis to the sentence as a whole without focusing specifically (or "contrastively") on any major part of it, but this problem deserves far more attention than can be devoted to it here.

* *"Debatable features: preferences provided"* (Burchfield)

(14) Use of *who* and *whom*
RD: Treated? Yes.
Observation: The problem presented by such phrases as "a person who (not **'whom'*) I know *is* talented" would not arise in the more formal English equivalent "a person whom I know *to be* talented." Other languages seem not to permit the use of inflected verbs, like *is*, in such constructions as freely as modern English does.

(15) Different from/to/than
RD: Treated? Yes.
Observation: Burchfield prefers *different from* to *different to*, and rejects *different than*, which he calls "now common in American English." This is a classic case of a World-English form, *different from*, coexisting with a distinctively British variant (*different to*, not mentioned in RD) and a distinctively American one (*different than*). But *different than* is gaining ground in Britain because it alone can be followed by a clause without *what* or *how*: "different than we thought" (by contrast with "different from what we thought").

(16) Split infinitives
RD: Treated? Yes.
Observation: As with other "classics" among usage problems, both Burchfield and RD emphasize when the split infinitive is acceptable ("combining to flatly forbid hostilities") rather than when it is not.

(17) Misplacing of *only*
RD: Treated? Yes.
Observation: Here too Burchfield and RD give examples where *only* is placed "at a distance from the word or words it limits" *without* unacceptable ambiguity. It is curious that people who object to a sentence like "I only want one thing" (rather than "I want only one thing") do not object to "I just/simply want one thing." And, as Bolinger (1980, p. 6) says, "I only want one thing" can have an element of politeness that "I want only one thing" lacks.

(18) Meaningless fillers
RD: Treated? Yes.
Observation: RD's comments are in a discussion of "speech tics" on pp. 588–589. Two of Burchfield's "meaningless fillers" are distinctively British. One is *then* ("Nice to talk to you, then" or "What you going to do about it, then?"). The other is the repeated use of so-called tags with falling intonation ("I went into this shop, dìdn't I. But they were shut, wèren't they."). Sequences of such tags may be more characteristic of working-class than of middle-class speech. But British English in general has a whole range of tags and tag-like constructions that are rare or unknown in American English ("He's a real goer, is our John," or, from Mike Leigh's television play *Grown-Ups*, "When are you going to have a little baby? I can't wait, I can't."). And British English uses tags more frequently: a recent corpus-based study of modern British and American plays revealed that the British plays had *several times* as many tags as their American counterparts. Yet another of Burchfield's fillers is perhaps more characteristic of British than of American English: the use of *actually*, as in modestly polite contradiction or amplification: "Are you a teacher?" "I'm a university lecturer, actually."

(19) Wrong sequence of tense
RD: Treated? Yes.

(20) "Strengthening of *I* by . . . *myself*"
RD: Treated? No.

(21) Use of *will/would* for *shall/should*
RD: Treated? Yes.
Observation: The *shall–will* distinction has more life in Britain than in America. It is implicitly defended by Burchfield, but the RD Usage note says "Few writers today observe the old distinction . . .", implying, perhaps, that no *speakers* (of American English) do. A truly remarkable feature of the language of people who do make a *shall–will, should–would* distinction is the use of "I should" in giving advice to others, making it possible for at least some of them to say "*I* should behave *yourself* (if I were you)." The combination of *I* with

yourself is not only strange to Americans, but would, I believe, be very difficult to explain for theoreticians of grammar (such as those of Chomsky's school).

(22) Confusion of *may* and *might*
RD: Treated? Yes.
Observation: Burchfield gives no examples of this confusion, nor do the OPD entries for *may* and *might* to which he refers his readers. RD gives no examples of *may–might* confusion either. However, RD does say "In using *may* or *might*, observe the SEQUENCE OF TENSES . . ." and "*Might* is conditional." So, though it's hard to see what the problem is, it may lie in these areas. Interestingly, a local London newspaper, the *Hampstead and Highgate Express* (3 September 1982, p. 1), says, of a woman who died two days after being turned away from a hospital, that she "*may* [emphasis mine] have lived if doctors had heeded advice at an inquest four years ago . . ." I would have used *might* here.

(23) *None* plus plural verb:
**None of us are blameless.*
RD: Treated? Yes.
Observation: Burchfield says that this sort of thing "should be kept to a minimum." RD says that *none* can be "Either singular or plural, depending on the meaning." Clearly, there is felt to be a problem about *none* in both British and American English.

Conclusions: Of the twenty-three problems of "grammar" listed above, RD recognizes sixteen, and of the seven problems discussed by Burchfield but not by RD, two (wrong participles and sequence after *one*) have to do with features of British rather than American English, and two (verbless sentences and present tense with future reference) seem characteristic of professional broadcasting and hence less likely to be treated in a book, like RD's, intended for a general readership.

General Conclusions

In the three areas of language covered in our comparison, the extent of agreement between Burchfield and his American counterparts has increased steadily: 5/14 for pronunciation, 20/38 for vocabulary, 16/23 for grammar. This corresponds rather well with the notion that pronunciation is the area of obvious difference between varieties of a language (the British linguist J. R. Firth is supposed to have said that it is part of the meaning of an American to sound like one), whereas grammar is the area of the underlying similarity. It is particularly striking to consider these figures in the light of Hudson's "very tentative hypothesis" about "the different types of linguistic items and their relations to society":

> *syntax* is the marker of cohesion in society . . .
> *vocabulary* is a marker of divisions in society . . .
> *Pronunciation* reflects the permanent social group with which the speaker identifies (1981, p. 48).

If the figures discussed up to now were all I had to go on, I think I would be more impressed by the differences than by the similarities between usage problems in British and American English. But as Creswell (1975) has shown, the variation in the selection and treatment of usage problems is enormous even among books dealing with American English only, so that on balance it is doubtful whether the differences between Burchfield and the Americans are greater than the differences among the Americans themselves. And as we have also seen significant differences between Burchfield and the British CED and OPD, it is at least possible that British commentaries on usage are as different among themselves as American ones are.

In any case, something striking that has emerged from the comparison is the efforts of usage commentators on both sides of the Atlantic to "make reparation" for some of the pronouncements of their predecessors (such as those against *It's me*, end-placed prepositions, and split infinitives) which have been interpreted so as to lead to unnatural and even ambiguous sentences in the name of "correctness."

Before ending this study, I should like to mention a factor that does not show up when one counts usage problems in British and American English but is nevertheless an important part of the background. That is the way speakers of each variety view the other. In a recent study of letters to the BBC about language, David Crystal (1981) found that of the twenty most frequent complaints the fourth most frequent was "a vocabulary problem – some people hate words and phrases of American origin." Indeed, as Crystal later suggests, for some people it seems not only that if something is American they hate it but also that if they hate something they assume it's American. (This attitude is by no means universal in Britain, and it has not stopped the steady arrival on British shores of American expressions, so that lexicographers must be constantly changing their varietal labels from *American* to *Chiefly American* to no label at all.) American attitudes towards British English may be different, but perhaps not totally different: an old American *Harper Handbook* (1962, sec. 66b) advises its users to "Avoid 'fine writing' by not overusing foreign words [like *garçon* – RI] and Briticisms [like *lift* 'elevator' or *petrol* 'gasoline' – RI] " and not to "use such words too frequently or merely to convince the reader of your erudition and affected dignity." It is, however, extremely unlikely that people in Britain would associate Americanisms with "fine writing"!

In this investigation of usage problems in British and American English I have been concerned not only to *count* items, but to *account* for them. A Jewish tradition has it that God's own prayer is "May my mercy be greater than my justice." I think that people who study usage problems should be of a similar disposition: may our desire to understand be greater than our desire to condemn.

References

American Heritage Dictionary (AHD): see *Heritage Illustrated Dictionary.*
ARONOFF, MARK (1979) *Word Formation in Generative Grammar.* Cambridge, Mass: MIT Press.
BOLINGER, DWIGHT (1980) *Language – The Loaded Weapon.* London and New York: Longman.

BURCHFIELD, ROBERT (1981) *The Spoken Word.* London: BBC.

Collins English Dictionary (CED) [*Collins Dictionary of the English Language*] (1979). London and Glasgow: Collins.

Concise Oxford Dictionary (COD) [*The Concise Oxford Dictionary of Current English*] (1976). Sixth Edition. London: Oxford University Press.

CRESWELL, THOMAS J. (1975) *Usage in Dictionaries and Dictionaries of Usage.* Alabama: University of Alabama Press.

CRYSTAL, DAVID (1981) "Language on the air – has it degenerated?" London: *The Listener*, 9 July 1981, pp. 37–39.

Harper Handbook of College Composition (1962) Third Edition. By G. S. Wykoff and H. Shaw. New York: Harper & Bros.

Heritage Illustrated Dictionary of the English Language (1979) International Edition. Boston: Houghton Mifflin Co.

HUDSON, R.A. (1981) *Sociolinguistics.* Cambridge: Cambridge University Press.

NUNBERG, GEOFFREY (1980) "The Case for Prescriptive Grammar." MS.

Oxford American Dictionary (OAD) (1980) New York & Oxford: Oxford University Press.

Oxford English Dictionary (OED) (1933) Oxford: Oxford University Press.

Oxford Paperback Dictionary (OPD) (1979) Oxford: Oxford University Press.

Queen's English Society. *Some Common Errors in Spoken English. A Guide for Public Speakers.* Pulborough, Sussex: MS. undated.

QUIRK, RANDOLPH and GREENBAUM, SIDNEY (1973) *A Concise Grammar of Contemporary English.* New York: Harcourt, Brace, Jovanovich. (=*A University Grammar of English.* London: Longman, 1973.)

Reader's Digest (1972) *Write Better, Speak Better* (RD). Pleasantville, New York: Reader's Digest.

Webster's New (Eighth) *Collegiate Dictionary* (W8). (1974). Springfield, Massachusetts: G & C Merriam Co.

Chapter 14

Attitudes to Canadian English

IAN PRINGLE

I

CANADIAN English is a collection of varieties of English spread (in places very thinly) over the huge area of Canada. It is not quite like any other national variety of English. However, public attitudes to English in Canada are for the most part not very different from attitudes to English in other major English-speaking countries in the world. The English-speaking population of Canada, if they think about their language at all, tend to believe that they speak and write it less well than they should. They are confident that there is an identifiable standard of correct Canadian English of which some unknown authorities – perhaps English professors, or the people who write grammar books and dictionaries – are the guardians. Most people do not know the details of what constitutes this correct English, but those details, they are sure, are known, and fixed, and presumably therefore one can find out what they are: after all, they are enshrined in grammar books and the dictionary.

When tests are devised (usually by English professors) to demonstrate that the schools are not teaching grammar or that university students are illiterate, it is to the arcana of the international English prescriptive tradition, rather than to some specifically Canadian tradition, that the test constructors turn to find their traps. Even in tests of English as a second language, where one would suppose that there might be a place for a specifically Canadian tradition of testing, the same objects of devotion may be presented.

If in such respects Canadian public attitudes prove to be much like public attitudes elsewhere, there are nonetheless a few respects in which Canadian attitudes are much more distinctive. The first of these is simply coincidental. Canadian English is both extraordinarily various in its regional and second-language forms, and extraordinarily uniform in its urban form. Canadians celebrate (or mock) their diversity with a few well-known stereotypes of non-standard varieties of Canadian English, and also deplore the poverty of the urban variety by poking fun at some recognizable traits of its impoverished form. In principle this is not different from the Australian celebration of "Strine;" the difference in the raw material, however, makes the product different as well.

In two further respects, Canadian attitudes are much more distinctive. First, like so much of Canada's cultural heritage, Canadian views of their English have a separatist function: they serve to assert the reality of a Canadian linguistic identity which, Canadians sometimes fear, is not as obvious or even as real as they would like it to be. This they do by exaggerating the differences between Canadian and American English (which often entails disparaging American English), and by asserting that at least in some respects Canadian English is more like British English, and is therefore better. Unlike American English, British English is a good safe distance away, and so obviously different that imagining a high degree of similarity does not constitute any threat to Canadian self-images. American English, on the other hand, is so close, so omnipresent, and so similar that it is necessary to insist on whatever differences can be found or imagined.

Within Canada a related complex of attitudes interprets the role of English *vis-à-vis* the other languages of Canada, and especially French. Canada is officially bilingual, with French and English sharing the status of official languages, and multicultural, with active support for the maintenance of distinctive traits of other cultures, including their languages. Because social inequities and historical discontents often correlate with the use of a particular mother-tongue in Canada, many Canadians view the English language as an enemy which threatens the survival of their own language and culture. In areas under the jurisdiction of the Federal government, the governments of the officially bilingual provinces of New Brunswick and Manitoba, and the government of the officially monolingual French-speaking province of Quebec, this perception of English as an enemy has led to a considerable body of legislation concerned to define, defend, and sometimes extend the rights of linguistic minorities. With the exception of some of the recent language legislation in Quebec, such legislation does not in any way diminish the rights of native speakers of English. However, there is a small element of the English Canadian population which finds any defense or extension of the linguistic rights of non-English-speaking Canadians highly offensive. Their counter-attack usually refers to the manifestly monolingual destiny of North America, or to the British heritage of Canada. In addition to a distinctive separatist role *vis-à-vis* American English, therefore, Canadian public attitudes to English reveal a complex of attitudes according to which members of linguistic minorities inside Canada assert their difference from English Canadians, use the threat of linguistic assimilation as their call to man the barricades, and provoke a backlash reaction among certain elements of the English population, a reaction which justifies their fears. Canada's language legislation, which provides legal definitions of the linguistic rights of Canadian citizens, is very much a part of this complex of attitudes. In these respects, public attitudes to Canadian English are distinctive, if not unique.

II

Except for its vocabulary, Canadian English has not been much studied.[1] It is commonly believed to be remarkably uniform, at least in its urban varieties; indeed, it has been claimed that "a uniform Canadian dialect covers a larger land-mass than any other one dialect in the world."[2] Such claims, however, are impressionistic; serious studies of the English of urban Canada have been completed only for the cities of Ottawa and Vancouver. The English of rural Canada has also been little studied; however the collections of dialect data gathered in such areas as Newfoundland and the Ottawa Valley have led one observer to make exactly the opposite claim: that, with the possible exception of Scots, Canadian English is the most varied national variety of English.[3]

Beyond the variation, whatever its extent, in the English spoken by Canadian anglophones, varieties of Canadian English are spoken as a second language by most of the country's non-anglophone peoples. For sociolinguistic and economic reasons with long historical roots, a large proportion of Canada's francophone population speaks English, with varying degrees of skill, as a second language. Canada also continues to be, with the U.S. and Australia, one of the three countries in the world most hospitable to immigration, and Canadian multicultural policies officially favour the maintenance of immigrant languages, whether they were brought in the eighteenth or nineteenth century and have survived (the case, to cite just a few examples, with Ukrainian, Icelandic, Gaelic, a number of varieties of German, Kashubian) or have arrived in more recent immigrations (as is largely the case with Italian, Greek, Portuguese, Lebanese, Polish, among others). The 1976 Census of Canada lists forty-one languages or language groups still spoken as a mother-tongue in Canada (excluding the official languages and the indigenous languages); for their speakers English is usually the preferred second language of wider communication. Finally, English is the preferred second language of the majority of Canada's indigenous peoples, who speak more than sixty different languages as their native tongues.

The immense number of rural and second-language varieties of Canadian English has given rise to only three widely recognized stereotypes by which Canadians reveal that they are aware that there is something distinctive about Canadian English. Undoubtedly the oldest of these is the stereotype of the English of the Canadian French, which has been represented in Canadian English literature for more than a century, and which continues to be evoked on popular radio and television shows such as "The Royal Canadian Air Farce." In its written form, the stereotype suggests a number of phonological traits of Canadian French English, and may suggest as well a certain degree of pidginization in the syntax, though not usually to quite the extent in this example:

> "Bon!" said LeNoir, "das good. One glass he mak' me feel good. Two das nice he mak' me feel ver fonny. Three glasses yes das mak' me de frien' of hevery bodie. Four das mak' me feel big; I walk de big walk; I am de bes' man all de place. Das good place for stop, eh?"[4]

In the corresponding spoken form, the same pidginizing tendencies appear in the syntax, along with the replacement of "th" sounds by *t* and *d*, the erratic variation in *h*'s (both placed before words which begin with a vowel and dropped from words which begin with *h*), the uncertainty about *i* and *ee* sounds. In addition, *r* sounds are usually trilled and, if the performer is skilful enough, word-stress is often delayed to the final syllable, and pronounced with a marked rise in pitch. Together these traits, all of which do indeed have their origin in aspects of Canadian francophone English, unambiguously signal to English Canadians that a French Canadian is being represented.

A second stereotype represents the English of Newfoundland. The first feature is, once again, the representation of English "th" sounds as *t* and *d*, a common feature of Newfoundland dialects with a Hiberno-English background. The second is due to the fact that the same Newfoundland dialects often preserve a distinctive pronunciation of "oy" sounds which is perceived (wrongly) as being identical with the *i*-sound, as in a traditional Newfoundland folksong which many Canadian children learn in school, beginning:

> I'se the b'y that builds the boat,
> I'se the b'y that sails her . . .
> [i.e. "I'm the boy . . ."]

Together with a vague Irish cast to the vowels, these two features are sufficient to suggest to English Canadians that the speaker being represented is an uneducated fisherman from a Newfoundland outport. In Canadian popular culture, "the Newfie" occupies the role attributed to "Polacks" in American culture at the same level – Polish jokes which find their way to English Canada are recounted as "Newfie jokes." (In French Canada, however, the protagonist is often "un Anglais.")

The third common stereotype is a stereotype of a rural variety of Ontario English which is taken to represent the English of any "farmer." This stereotype has been much in vogue recently, thanks above all to the performances on radio, television, and stage and the writings of the actor Don Harron in his role of "Charlie Farquharson." In both the written and the spoken realisations, Charlie Farquharson's English is distinguished above all by the use of "yer" as a definite article, by a collection of obvious substandard features, and by malapropisms and approximations, some of which are actually amusing. In its written form, his English relies as well on a high proportion of eye dialect and misspelling, as in his account of the flight of American Loyalists to Canada after the American revolution:

> Now the Birtish General in all this too-do was yer Lord Cornhaulus – him as lost the toss when Warshinton threw the silver dollar acrost yer Potomac River. The British squares extinguished themselves on yer feeled of battle when they formed up their pantaloons and fell, never to rise agin. After the Birtish got demobbed by yer rebels and went back home, there was still a buncha Yanks down in yer States that wasn't too pro-Yanky. They was still singin' "God Save Yer King" while the rest of em was standin' up for "My Country, What's It To Thee?" . . . But the main kick yer pro-Yanky Yanks had agin yer Toree was they never did bare arms on yer 'Merken side. That made them in the eyes of Oncle Sam, nothin' better'n drafty dodges. . . . .[5]

In its oral manifestation, this dialect is clearly based on an approximation to a rural accent of a kind common in South-western Ontario.

To be sure, most Canadians do not recognize the Ontario background in this stereotype. But at least they are clear that it is no more standard than are the Newfoundland and French-Canadian stereotypes. When it comes to the more uniform English of the urban centers, it is much harder to determine what

Canadians think their English is. Almost without exception, Canadians believe (wrongly[6]) that Canadian English is uniquely characterized by the use of *eh?* at the end of sentences, or even within them.

Perhaps the only trait of Canadian English which is believed to be as uniquely characteristic as *eh?* is the fairly frequent tendency in Canadian speech to utter declarative statements with a slightly rising intonation. This feature is probably of Irish origin; it is normal in Jamaican English, and has recently been described as a feature of New Zealand English.[7] Canadians who become aware of it tend to interpret it as a sign of insecurity on the part of Canadian anglophones, as though they could not make even a straightforward declarative statement without inviting some kind of reassuring feedback. Other commentators, however, have taken it to reflect an alleged diffidence in the Canadian national character, due presumably to the fact that Canada is not taken seriously either by the British, who think it is still a colony, or by the Americans, who think of it as a wayward northern State which has not yet completely thrown off its ties to European tyrannies which real American immigrants come to the new world to escape.

Beyond the occasional recognitions of this trait, most Canadians would be hard put to say what it is that distinguishes standard Canadian English. They know that they do not sound British, whatever some Americans may think. They know, too, that Americans are wrong when they accuse them of saying "oot" and "aboot"instead of 'out" and "about." However, few know that the Canadian pronunciations of *out* and *about* are indeed a distinctive national trait, nor do many even recognize that their pronunciations of *out* and *about* have different vowel sounds from their pronunciations of *loud* and *crowd*.

On the other hand, despite what many Englishmen seem to think, Canadians are just as confident that they do not have the same accent as Americans. It is important to many Canadians to insist that Canadian English is different from American English. It has to be different, because Canadians are different.

III

In language, as in everything else, Canadians are aware of the powerful giant to the south of them, constantly exerting its influence through the strengths of its technology, the vibrancy of its popular culture, the nonchalance with which its entrepreneurs have assumed that Canada is and should be simply a freely accessible extension of American resources and markets. The economic defenses Canada has mounted againt these incessant influences have been puny (albeit irritating to some American interests). The linguistic defenses (a quiet assumption of superiority, a constant reiteration of the need to man the barricades) have perhaps been more effective – not so much in forestalling influence from the south as in reassuring Canadians that at their best they are largely impervious to it, and with care will remain so.

Admittedly there has always been a current of thought in Canada admiring the vitality and inventiveness of American English, as when F. Blake Crofton praised American boxing slang in 1901: "Americans have contributed largely to the common store of striking expressions."[8] In addition, at least some

Canadian linguists have viewed Canadian English as chiefly a descendant of the English brought to British North America by refugees from the American Revolution and their "late Loyalist" successors, somewhat modified by the important later immigrations from the British Isles and by independent developments (my own position); or at least have admitted that it is extremely difficult to clarify what is exclusively "Canadian" and what exclusively "American" in the more than a century of common North American cultural experience that preceded the Revolution, and the constant movement back and forth across the border subsequently.[9] Almost as frequently, however, Canadian linguists prefer to view Canadian English as an independent variety, whose manifest similarities to American English are due more to the coincidental fact that Irish, Scottish, and Northern English dialects were important ancestors of both varieties than to a common cultural heritage in North America or to sources in what was to become U.S. English.[10]

Outside of the academy, this belief in the direct descent of Canadian English from British English is certainly the commonest view in Canada. At its most extreme, it exaggerates the defects of "American English" in order to affirm the superiority of British-oriented Canadian English:

> We have known an "intelligent American," – that, it seems, is the term they now prefer – deny our own British origin, for, quoth Jonathon, "I swam yeow must be an American, cause you speak English, right straight along, just as I do, and Britishers can't do that, they call a jug a joog, and one gentleman when he seed me streaking off from him says, he says says he, 'Wher't be gwain?' Now that ain't English.[11]

Even when Americans and their English are not so savagely misrepresented, observers of Canadian English have always commented on the threat of "a corrupt dialect growing up in our midst" as Americanisms endanger "our noble mother-tongue."[12] In part, this threat is due to the Americans who have always been in our midst.

At least as often, the enemy within proves to be American books which find their way into Canada because of American enterprise:

> The Americans, who are masters of book-making, have pushed their dictionaries into general use, especially in Canada, with a zeal which outruns their claim, sound as it is in some respects, to be the producers of the best English dictionaries. It is manifest, however, that the conditions in the United States do not warrant this ascendency of their dictionaries.[13]

In particular, this has always been a problem in the schools, not only because of the strength of American enterprise, but also because few Canadians have produced works which can effectively compete; and not only because the language thus exemplified in schoolbooks is American English, but even more because the cultural values represented in those books are American. As early as 1836, Dr. Thomas Rolph, a prototype of the twentieth-century Canadian nationalist, was complaining:

> It is really melancholy to traverse the Province, and go into many of the common schools; you find a herd of children, instructed by some anti-British adventurer, instilling into the young and tender mind sentiments hostile to the parent state; false accounts of the late war in which Great Britain was engaged with the United States: geography setting forth New-York, Philadelphia, Boston, &c., as the largest and finest cities in the world; historical

reading books describing the American population as the most free and enlightened under Heaven; insisting on the superiority of their laws and institutions, to those of all the world, in defiance of the Agrarian outrages and mob supremacy daily witnessed and lamented; and American spelling-books, dictionaries, and Grammar, teaching them an anti-British dialect, and idiom; although living in a Province, and being subjects, of the British Crown.[14]

The surviving lists of texts used in Canadian schools early in the nineteenth century show that Rolph's description was correct: in spelling, grammar, and reading Canadian students were at least as likely to work from an American text as from a British text.[15] Moreover, when the complaints about the use of American textbooks reached such a pitch that some action had to be taken, as often as not the action that was taken was one which has remained typically Canadian: a more or less perfunctory Canadianization of some American text. Sometimes what has been involved is merely the addition of a preface and a few substantive changes; sometimes a more considered reworking of an American original; sometimes a wholesale plagiarization of an American original.[16]

Similarly, much of what Canadians read apart from textbooks is of American origin, and since the advent of radio and television much of what they hear over the broadcast media is American. The sort of double standard inculcated by this situation pervades all aspects of English usage in Canada, and is thus reflected in Canadian attitudes to their English.

In spelling, for example, the late Walter S. Avis has often pointed out that there are a small number of words (*connection, curb, jail, net, recognize, tire, wagon*) for which Canadians scarcely believe there is a British variant (*connexion, kerb, gaol, nett, recognise, tyre, waggon*).[17] Apart from these, where there are variant spellings Canadian practices are characteristically complex. In general, one could say that the more popular a publication is, the more likely it is to use American spellings, and the more learned or ostentatiously formal it is, the more likely it is to use British spellings. Thus American spellings are strongly preferred in daily newspapers, but almost without exception academic and professional journals admit only British spellings. So far as I am aware, every Ministry of Education in the country implies that children should be allowed to use either British or American spellings; however, textbooks approved for use in schools almost invariably use only British spellings, and teachers undoubtedly prefer them too. Perhaps as a result, most Canadians would agree that British spellings are better. This is an unsophisticated but quite sound sociolinguistic judgment about the roles of spelling choices in Canadian printed matter: works which consistently use British spelling want to be considered classier; works which consistently use American spelling do not care.

As for views of Standard Canadian pronunciation, the situation is still more complex. In theatre, and especially in that strand of theatre which sees itself as part of a British tradition, Canadian actors acquire remarkably plausible British accents: true Brit is the received standard of the annual Shakespeare festival in Stratford, Ontario. Moreover, many of those who have acquired such an accent maintain it in their everyday life, for in Canada, unlike the U.S., a stage British accent never signals the presence of a villain: Canadians have always had too many real Englishmen in their midst to be able to abuse British accents this way. Outside of the theatre, however, there is only a small segment of the population who are likely to try to modify their native Canadian English towards a British standard, and most of the rest of the population, if they recognize what is happening, would consider these more British accents affected.

However, the widespread rejection of a British standard does not mean that Canadians accept the Americanness of their usual pronunciations. For nationalist ends they can exaggerate any aspect of American pronunciation that is taken to be different from Canadian English. In addition, there is one shibboleth of pronunciation which Canadians use to mark their difference from Americans: the pronunciation of "u" and "ew" spellings after *t*, *d*, and *n*. Canadians think they know that Americans invariably say "toon" for "tune," "doo" for "dew," "nooz" for "news." They also believe that the British do not do these things. Consequently when they want to stress how their English differs in sound from American English, they are particularly likely to settle on these sounds. In former years many school English texts which concerned themselves with matters of elocution regularly included advice to say "news," not "nooz." The same recommendation has regularly been included in manuals of style prepared for announcers on CBC radio and television. In fact, however, a great many Canadians actually have the "oo" pronunciations as their native pronunciations. The effect of the prescription, therefore, is hypercorrection: Canadian radio and television announcers strive to put "you" pronunciations in after every possible *t*, *d*, and *n* sound, even when they are historically incorrect, saying "manyouver" for *manoeuvre* and, in order to avoid saying "the nooz at noon," announcing "the nyooz at nyoon." In addition, just to be on the safe side, they manage to insert "you" pronunciations in words such as *suit, resolute, rule*, far more often than these occur in the southern British English which they take to be their model. Such hypercorrections demonstrate once again the attitude that Canadian English is different from American English because it is more like British, and therefore better.

As for the vocabulary of Canadian English, Canadians have always objected to the presence of particular terms which they take to be invented American slang. The objects of contempt change over time. In 1857, they included such obvious abominations as *donation* for *gift, hung* for *hanged, limbs* for *legs*, and *pants* for *trousers*.[18] In recent times they have included the terminology of popular music and the metaphorical extension of computer jargon such as *interface*. Otherwise, however, Canadians are not particularly defensive about their vocabulary. Even where available research suggests that they may prefer *tap* to *faucet* or *porridge* to *oatmeal*, they do not usually think of such differences as proving that their vocabulary is British: who can be expected to know what the British call a *tap*? Moreover, where Canadians are aware of differences, they recognize quite realistically that the long-standing penetration of Canadian lifestyles by American technical expertise and commercial drive means that Canadians drive *trucks*, not *lorries*, and their cars have *fenders* and *trunks*, not *mudguards* and *boots*; their trains, where they survive, are pulled by *locomotives*, not *engines*, and followed by *cabooses* rather than *guard's vans*.

Most British terms, if not quaint, are incomprehensible: what on earth is a *guard's van*?

However, it is above all in matters of divided usage, in those traditional points of grammatical practice that are the subject of two centuries of prescriptive rulings, that Canadian attitudes are most subtle and complex. In general, as I have already noted, Canadian purism is much like the purism of the rest of the English-speaking world.

Like those of other countries, authors of Canadian grammar and composition books confidently repeat as absolute laws prescriptions which have no historical or literary justification:

> We should be especially careful to make the form of pronouns used after any part of the word "be" agree in case with the subject preceding it. We should say, for example, "It is he," since the pronoun "he" must agree in case with "it," the subject of the verb.[19]

> As auxiliaries, *shall* is used with the first person and *will* with the second and third; thus: I *shall* go, We *shall* go, but, Thou *wilt* go [sic, in 1935], You *will* go, He *will* go, They *will* go.[20]

> *Can* means "having the ability," and *may* means "being permitted." For example: My dad said I *may* go to Jane's party because I *can* drive the car now since I passed my driving test.[21]

As elsewhere, editors of Canadian newspapers occasionally select an example of what is taken to be appallingly bad English, usually from a bureaucratic or academic source, and comment at length on how standards are slipping. It is symptomatic that one of the earliest editorials attacking *Webster's Third New International Dictionary* was that of Canada's most influential and widely circulated newspaper, the Toronto *Globe and Mail*, which complained in part that "the English language has been corrupted by advertising men, song writers, masters of ceremony, sports reporters. It has been pushed into decay by lazy educators who would neither entice nor drive their students into the daily drill which is necessary to its mastery."[22]

Needless to say, the editorial team did not name editorial teams among those driving the language to decay. But in Canada as elsewhere editorial teams exemplify the linguistic corruption they deplore in others. That of the *Globe and Mail*, for example, began an editorial on Friday, 8 October 1982, with the sentence:

> Just as the ideal of even-handed justice for all can be somewhat tilted toward *he* who can afford to argue the rightness of his case, so the democratic ideal can be distorted by the disparate financial resources of election candidates. [The malevolently added emphasis is mine.]

Similarly in Canada rank amateurs occasionally decide they are authorities on matters of good usage, set themselves up on some appropriate lily-pad, and tell their names publicly to the admiring bog. I don't think there is any Canadian instance quite as egregious as that of Mr. Edwin Newman in the U.S., whose discovery that "you may not *convince to*" deserves to rank with Dryden's discovery that sentences cannot end with a preposition in English.[23] But Canada's school textbooks certainly reveal some astonishing rules: the third edition of *Mastering Effective English*, originally published in 1937 but still one of the most widely used composition texts in Ontario schools, promulgates the following rule:

So may be used as a conjunction only when it means *provided that, on condition that, in case that*. The sentence "We were walking down town, so we decided to have lunch at the Walker House" is wrong both grammatically and rhetorically . . . . RIGHT He will sell anything, so (provided that) he gets a profit out of it.[24]

In the early 1970s a now dead journalist, Mr. Norman DePoe, had a column "Speaking of Words" which was widely carried in Canada by newspapers in the Southam chain. Much of it was of this calibre:

> In the manifesto that started this series, we quoted Macbeth: "damn'd be him that first cries 'Hold, enough!' " How many times have you heard "damn'd be he"? This vacillation between "he" and "him" is further confounded when they turn up together with "who" or "whom," there being some sort of fatal tendency for one to attract the other, so that a perfectly correct "him who" turns into the incorrect "he who." (In the case of the quotation from Macbeth, the word "that" is used instead of "who," but the principle of fatal attraction still operates, so that I have heard a number of well-educated speakers insist that it should be: "Damn'd be he that first cries . . ."). A simple way to run a test on this kind of sentence is to recast it, using the word "let." Would you say "Let he be damned"? Well then, it's "damn'd be him."[25]

Editors of professional and academic periodicals share the same certainties. A few years ago one of my students, Miss Sandra Gratton, attempted to survey the attitudes of such editors towards matters of grammar and good usage. Twenty editors responded to her questionnaire. In all, they identified twenty-eight different reference works which they claimed to consult (see Table 1). Despite the low response rate, the list is, I am sure, representative. One may note the ignorance revealed in the references to "Oxford" dictionaries and for that matter to "Webster's" dictionaries: there are no grounds for inferring that the people making these claims had much awareness that there are different

TABLE 1. *Preferred Reference Works of Twenty Editors*

Fowler's *Modern English Usage*	6
Chicago *Manual of Style*	4
Webster's Dictionaries:	
"Webster's Dictionary"	2
Webster's New International Dictionary	1
Webster's Third	1
"The Merriam–Webster Dictionary"	1
Oxford Dictionaries:	
The *Oxford English Dictionary*	2
"The Oxford Dictionary"	1
The *Concise Oxford Dictionary*	1
Fowlers' *The King's English*	2
The Canadian Press Style Book	1
The *Dictionary of Canadianisms*	1
Gowers' *Complete Plain Words*	1
"Horbrace" [*sic*]	1
Maclean–Hunter Style Book	1
Roget's *Thesaurus*	1
Strunk and White's *Elements of Style*	1

"Oxford" and "Webster's" dictionaries, nor that their recommendations and authority might differ.

Miss Gratton took her survey one step further: she made up three sentences illustrating problems of divided usage, and asked the editors whether or not they would accept them. In all cases the form traditionally regarded as "incorrect" is one which Sterling Leonard judged to be acceptable on the basis of his 1932 survey and which, as A. H. Marckwardt and Fred G. Walcott showed, has a long history of acceptance in literary texts and edited publications.[26] The sentences were:

Neither author nor publisher are subject to censorship.
There have been less accidents.
The cheese was different than the one I bought before.

Of the editors who replied, only one did not condemn all three sentences as incorrect. Their replies suggested there could be no doubt: "We would not consider that any doubt enters into any of your three examples. All three would be considered ungrammatical and changed without hesitation"; "We edit to ensure correct grammar in the traditional sense. . . . We would change them all to proper English"; "There is no element of doubt about any of the three statements you give as examples, because each is quite clearly grammatically incorrect"; "Doubt arises only when there is ignorance."

There was one exception; one editor suggested that the first form might escape correction:

The first one, "Neither author nor publisher are" I might let go because this is such a common usage, one gets used to hearing it. I would probably alter it in the original copy. But if it slipped by me the first time, I might not bother to correct it on the proofs.

This hint of permissiveness is brief, however:

Actually, I don't know why there would be any doubt about the three examples you have chosen because to me they are very obviously incorrect; but then perhaps that it [sic] because I had an English education.

These editors are probably more aware of what the prescriptive rules are than are the editors of more popular periodicals and of newspapers. Their attitudes, however, are typical of the nearly universal faith.

Among academics the situation is similar. Some years ago my colleague Aviva Freedman and I attempted to take a survey of attitudes to "correct usage" among all the teaching staff of two university English departments. The questionnaire consisted of a list of sentences representing widely discussed problems of divided usage. Some were taken from literary sources; some from Leonard; some from examples of incorrect usage in widely used composition handbooks. We asked the respondents to identify the error in each sentence (a mistake: most of the target population found this request so offensive that they did not answer it all). We asked them to identify the frequency of the error in student writing at different levels, and to say whether or not they would accept the "incorrect" form.

Table 2 gives an idea of the results. Note that in every instance there were some English professors who could not identify the error. However, with one

TABLE 2. *Sample Results: Survey of English Professors*

	Frequency %				Acceptability %		
	Rare	Moderately frequent	Very frequent	Can't say	Yes	No	Can't say
6. Everyone volunteered, but they all failed to appear.	0	25	63	13	19	81	0
7. Of the two poems, the most discussed is "The Ancient Mariner."	0	50	45	5	5	95	0
8. Jane Austen now feels that it is necessary to partially clarify Frank Churchill's relationship to Jane.	0	16	74	10	17	72	11
18. Considering how little satisfaction she obtained from it, it was just a waste.	12	47	35	6	35	59	6
27. While many Canadian politicians dislike the thought of American supremacy, none of them would agree to take a more offensive stand against the U.S.	24	33	19	24	57	33	10
28. Tom's life was decadent and wealthy in those days, and his spectacular parties never had less than two hundred guests.	22	39	28	11	28	67	6

exception the vast majority of those who did identify an error judged it to be unacceptable. The sentence that escaped outright condemnation, no. 27, is actually taken from the widely used composition text mentioned above, which many of the respondents had used as a required text at various times. It explains: "In formal English, *while* is used as a conjunction only with the meaning 'at the same time' ".[27] Again, therefore, attitudes in Canada prove not to be strikingly different from attitudes in other English-speaking countries.

In addition, when Canadian authorities resort to making rulings for some purpose, they usually reveal the same kind of reliance on their personal biases as authorities elsewhere do. For example, W. S. Avis, making rulings on matters of divided usage for the guidance of Canadian high school students in the *Dictionary of Canadian English: The Senior Dictionary*, says in his discussion of *shall* and *will*:

> The usage of *shall* and *will* has never been uniform in English, although some grammarians have attempted to insist on uniformity. The general practices in the more common situations needing these words are as follows. 1. General usage. (a) *Simple future.* In speech and writing, the prevailing use in Canada, and in many other parts of the English-speaking world, is *will* in all persons. . . . This usage would appear more in printed matter if editors did not revise the copy to bring it in line with their stylebooks.[28]

On the other hand, in his discussion of the use of *they, them, their* after indefinite singular antecedents he says the following:

> *everybody, everyone.* a. Both these pronouns are grammatically singular. . . . In informal speech, the pronouns are sometimes used as collectives. A verb immediately following either of them is usually singular, but another pronoun referring back from a little distance is likely to be plural: "Everybody dresses in their best clothes." To make such expressions accord with formal written usage, it is often better to change the *everybody* or *everyone* to a more specific plural or collective than to change the later pronoun. (*Ibid.*, s.v. *everybody*.)

No doubt both pieces of advice are sensible. What I find intriguing about them is that Avis virtually admits that, owing to the nefarious habits of editors, he does not have the evidence he wants to justify the ruling he is making that *will* is acceptable in the first person for simple future time. On the other hand, I cannot believe he did not have evidence which would have justified using *they, their, them* after singular indefinite antecedents, for my own collection of citations shows that this usage is just as common, and just as standard, in printed Canadian English as it is in printed English elsewhere when the antecedent is semantically indeterminate. The only possible explanation of the inconsistency, then, must be that Avis found the use of first person *will* acceptable, but did not like the use of indefinite *they*. Despite the more scholarly tone, his practice is not different in principle from Fowler's in, for example, his acceptance of *none are* on the authority of the *Oxford English Dictionary* (s.v. *none*),[29] and his misrepresentation of the evidence of the same dictionary (which actually does not have any adverse comment on the indefinite *they*) in his discussions of *they* (e.g. s.v. *they, their, them*). Clearly Fowler himself found the former acceptable, and the latter unacceptable, made his rulings on that basis alone – and justified them by whatever evidence could be made to serve his purpose.

All in all, then, Canadian puristic attitudes are clearly similar to attitudes elsewhere. However, there is a difference, and again it is a characteristically Canadian difference. Though Canadians believe that British authorities are the most reliable, and certainly make "Fowler" and "the Oxford" their favourite reference works, their purism is in fact very American.

Canadian puristic attitudes have always been shaped by American attitudes. Ironically, the pattern probably started quite accidentally: the authorities of the Upper Canadian Boards of Education who, early in the nineteenth century, argued that Canadian students should study out of Murray's readers, spellers, and grammar rather than Webster's[30] did not know that Lindley Murray was in fact an American; they thought the English imprints made his work British. For most of the twentieth century, and increasingly in the last three decades, Canadians have taken their purism almost entirely from American sources. Composition and grammar books used in schools discuss matters of American purism, rather than British: the problem is the acceptability of *different than*, not *different to*. The similarity of Canadian attitudes to American is apparent in the *Globe and Mail*'s review of *Webster's Third*: it makes exactly the same kind of points, in the same kind of way, as the majority of the American reviews. In the collection of discussions and reviews of *Webster's Third* published by Sledd and Ebbitt,[31] the Canadian and American reviews contrast equally starkly to the common sense and learning which appear in the British reviews.

Equally, the shibboleths whose quasi-religious status is attested by the way they are passed on as revealed truth in letters to editors in Canadian newspapers, if they are recent, are typically of American origin. For example, Edwin Newman's new commandment ("You may convince that. You may convince of. You may not convince to"[32]) is more than echoed in a letter to the editor of the *Globe and Mail* (18 Nov. 1982, p. 7):

> Also incorrect is the use of "convince" in "she convinces the boy to tell someone". . . ; the right verb would be "persuade." You may convince people of [sic] the rightness of [sic] and action; you may convince them *that* they should do something; but you may not convince them *to* do anything.

Since first encountering Newman's new commandment, I have been using it as a modern example of the arbitrary and ill-informed decisions on which most of the English prescriptive tradition is based. It is apparently the case that, once a prescriptive ruling is published, it can never be retracted or invalidated. The truths revealed in eighteenth-century prescriptive grammars have continued to be passed on ever since by a process which in any other field of scholarship would have to be called plagiarism, a concept, however, which has no validity in either religion or the prescriptive tradition. *Hopefully* having been declared incorrect, no demonstration by a professional grammarian that its semantic relation to the sentence of which it is part is (like that of *frankly*) comprehensible, attested, historically and theoretically justified, no socio-linguist's proof that it is (by any sensible measure) standard, can make it correct in the judgments of the faithful; instead the commandment not to use it passes on. Accordingly since 1976 I have been predicting that within ten years I would find Newman's new commandment passed on as absolute truth, without acknowledgment to its author. In making good my prediction, the author of the letter I cite also shows how immediate the influence of American purism is in Canada.

In the same way, all the tiresome, hostile clamour about "descriptive linguistics" or "structural linguistics" which the publicity department of the Merriam-Webster Company so regrettably stirred up in the Safires, Newmans, Simons, etc., of the U.S. continues to resound in empty vessels in Canada. Consider, for example, this extract from an essay written by a Canadian high-school English department head for the journal of the Ontario Council of Teachers of English:

> It is apparent that the teaching of English is still and increasingly influenced by the discipline known as structural linguistics or modern linguistic science or descriptive linguistics. Its precepts are that language changes constantly, that change is normal, that the spoken language is basic in human life and that writing is a mere reflection of speech, that correctness rests upon usage, and that all usage is relative – with the effects in practice of downgrading the traditional rules of grammar, of denying any standards of right and wrong in speech or writing, and of a Humpty-Dumpty philosophy of usage (any word means whatever its users make it mean); in short, every student is his own egghead.[33]

All purists necessarily locate the linguistic Golden Age in the past, and for this author the period at which English reached perfection was the Augustan age.

But, alas, this Augustan spirit and intelligence has [*sic*] been undermined by those who are attracted to jargon, permissiveness, formlessness, and mindlessness – the ones who think themselves to be linguists rather than teachers of English (*loc. cit.*).

Both in the substance and the rhetoric of its charges against linguistics, this essay is characteristically American. So strong is this American orientation in Canadian purism that in those areas where standard Canadian practice resembles British rather than American practice, Canadian judgments nonetheless fall squarely in line with American judgments. For example, Canadian standard usage, like British, tolerates plural verbs after collective nouns to a much greater extent than American English, as in "The Cabinet are meeting to discuss the question," or "The National Democractic Party are leading in fourteen ridings." For years I have been asking groups of graduate students to judge the correctness of sentences such as these. I have yet to have a Canadian student judge them to be acceptable.

Nonetheless Canadians confidently use their puristic attitudes to serve the same separatist ends as their attitudes to their spelling and pronunciation: to convince themselves that their English is not the same as American English. We may illustrate the point by a final quotation from Waterston and Beattie's *Composition for Canadian Universities*. In their discussion of levels of usage, the authors say of *Webster's Third*, "*Webster's* is too 'permissive' by Canadian academic standards" (p. 178). The sniff is almost audible. Canadian standards are higher.

IV

From a national point of view, then, Canadian attitudes to English have to be discussed above all in terms of their use by Canadians to assert their differences from Americans. Within the country, however, the most important facts about attitudes to English have to do above all with the relation of English to other languages spoken in the country. Given that the country is officially bilingual and multicultural, the kinds of language contact which might occur in it are innumerable. John De Vries has suggested a taxonomy of six different kinds of bilingualism: official-official (English-French); official-immigrant (e.g. French-Italian); immigrant-immigrant (e.g. German-Polish); official-indigenous (e.g. English-Cree); immigrant-indigenous (e.g. Ukrainian-Cree); indigenous-indigenous (e.g. Cree-Inuktitut).[34] In addition it may well be desirable to make a distinction between urban immigrant languages such as Italian and Portuguese (usually the result of fairly recent immigrations and probably not likely to last for much more than a generation) and rural immigrant languages such as Icelandic, Kashubian, Gaelic, Ukrainian, Mennonite *Plattdeutsch* (typically the result of pre-1900 immigration and still persisting, though with differences by language as well as by the size of the settlements), since these two kinds of immigrant languages clearly have different sociolinguistic statuses. But although most of these kinds of bilingualism probably do exist, the actual numbers of people involved are very small. The advance reports of the 1981 census data, for example, reveal that only 1.2 percent of Canada's population reported having neither English nor French as one of their languages, compared to 15.3 percent who claimed to be bilingual in the official languages, 16.6 percent who were unilingual francophones, and 67 percent who were unilingual anglophones.

It is not surprising, then, that the very extensive research into Canadian bilingualism has focused almost exclusively on bilingualism in the two official languages. In fact it has been even narrower than that. It has looked at bilingualism in the official languages above all in terms of its effects on that part of the population that is most bilingual (namely the French-speaking part of the population) with an eye to its effects on the status of French and francophones in Canada.[35] Ever since the anglophone population started to outnumber the francophone population early in the nineteenth century, political discussions in Canada have been forced to wrestle with the consequences of English-Canadian attitudes to French and francophones. Undoubtedly these have helped to determine French-Canadian attitudes to English and to English Canadians. And yet studies of the consequences of official bilingualism for public attitudes to English in Canada are just as rare as other studies of Canadian attitudes to English.

Today, the fact of official bilingualism (of course, it does not necessarily entail personal bilingualism) pervades much of everyday life. At one level, it is manifested in the use of the two languages in almost every document emanating from a Federal Government source, from postage stamps to income-tax declarations. Owing to comparatively recent Federal language legislation enacted (in 1974) to ensure that all merchandise offered for sale must normally be labelled in French, it means that almost all merchandise sold in Canada is labelled in both languages. For an apparently sizable proportion of the English-speaking population which finds it difficult to turn a box of cornflakes around early in the morning, such labelling has led to many bitter complaints about having French "stuffed down your throat." It has also led to complaints that the reduction in the size of print required to get French and English lists of ingredients and instructions on small containers such as medicine bottles makes them really dangerous for people with poor vision. On the other hand, a good many people undoubtedly recognize that having French forced down your throat with your cornflakes, uncomfortable though that may be, is nothing compared to the discomfort and indeed danger to which unilingual Francophones were previously exposed, when the instructions for the use of medications (or for that matter fire extinguishers) were usually printed only in English.

Equally, as a kind of public enactment of its official bilingualism, Canada has a tradition of macaronic speech-making on what might be called high public occasions. In addresses to the nation on 1 July (formerly "Dominion Day," but now officially relabelled "Canada Day"), in speeches from the throne on the opening of Parliament, in the delivery of judgments in the Supreme Court, appropriate ministers and monarchs and chief justices read what is basically a single continuous text with English and French alternating, often with no discernible reason for the switch from one language to another except that the speech writer felt that it was time for the other language to have a turn.

Sometimes the results are simply embarrassing. Since French is so clearly the subordinate language in Canada, English Canadians have always found French difficult to learn, even where it has been a required subject throughout most of their education. Unless they get involved in politics, most English Canadians have no more reason to become fluent in French than upper-class Londoners have to become fluent in Cockney or Americans of the South-West to become fluent in Spanish. As for those who do get involved in politics, a few are genuinely bilingual, and more make valiant efforts to reach an acceptable level of fluency. And yet the results almost always leave much to be desired. In the kinds of judgments which ensue one can see hints of all the attitudinal complexities which surround Canadian bilingualism today. On the one hand, English Canadians are used to encountering perfectly fluent English from French-Canadians. Often their English so completely resembles Anglophone Canadian English that nothing could reveal that their first language was French. In addition, although English Canadians do have a stereotype of French Canadian English, they are for the most part quite tolerant of slightly accented or even heavily accented English spoken by a Canadian francophone. The francophones, on the other hand, tend to be utterly contemptuous of the attempts of anglophone Canadians to speak French. That they are expected to tolerate it on high public occasions from anglophones with execrable accents merely reminds them of their traditional subordinate status. And traditionally in face to face conversations with anglophones they almost invariably switch to English. Indeed, this tendency is so strong that they often try to switch to English with anyone whose French is not clearly Canadian French – a disconcerting experience for Alsatian or Vietnamese immigrants whose English may be relatively weak compared to their fluent French. With such immigrants, the tendency to switch to English betrays a long-standing provincialism which assumes that only French Canadians and the French of France can speak French (and not even the latter, if they are blond, and look Germanic). With the English, it may well constitute a separatist assertion: the use of the French language in Canada is uniquely the right of French Canadians, and a domain on which English Canadians should not trespass. And yet the fact that it is they who switch can always been invoked as yet another cause of resentment at the subordinate status granted to the minority group.

At another level, the fact that they are bilingual means that there is always a possibility, at least, of anglicism in their French. To an even greater extent, however, the very considerable English element in popular Canadian French is due to the series of events which isolated Quebec from France before the Industrial Revolution, and to the largely successful attempt of the very powerful French-Canadian clergy in the nineteenth century to protect their flocks from the twin evils of English and Protestantism by keeping as many of them as possible ignorant and isolated on farms. Consequently when the effects of the Industrial Revolution reached Quebec, they were brought by English-speaking entrepreneurs, and almost the whole of subsequent technology came to Quebec labelled in English. The anglicization of Quebec French was certainly reinforced by the need of French-Canadians to be bilingual in the twentieth century, when their subordinate status within Quebec was clearly established; however, the real roots of the anglicization are to be sought in the nineteenth century.

Because of the anglicizing tendencies, French Canada has long had a very strong puristic tradition which deprecates all English borrowings, including even those which, like *weekend* and *building*, are more or less standard in the French of France, so that *hot dogs* may be sold as *chiens chauds*.

However, the anti-English attitudes manifest in modern French-Canadian purism, and intolerance of English-Canadian attempts to use French whatever the occasion, are scarcely adequate to suggest the depth of French-Canadian resentment of English and anglophones. Such attitudes naturally had their origin in the British conquest of French Canada in 1759–60. They grew throughout the nineteenth century, as more and more Provinces (often with the connivance of the Federal government) restricted the use of French in all domains, but particularly in education, thereby revealing an assimilationist policy which was rarely articulated, but always clear. French Canadian resentment smouldered more and more intensely as a result. In the 1960s, however, a sudden drop in their previously high birthrate started to reduce the proportion of francophones in the country and aroused fears that the remainder would be completely assimilated, starting in Montreal, where the proportion of the population speaking English was growing rapidly in the city French Canadians proudly thought of as the second-largest French-speaking city in the world. Suddenly from the embers there flared a full-scale terrorist campaign aimed at effecting the separation of Quebec in order to preserve its francophone character.

In response to the resulting crisis, Prime Minister Lester B. Pearson appointed the Royal Commission on Bilingualism and Biculturalism in 1963. Its reports, and the many research studies and surveys which lay behind them, clarified the nature of the problems, demonstrated their depth, and suggested solutions.

Insofar as the suggested solutions lay within the jurisdiction of the federal government, it set about trying to provide them. The Official Languages Act of 1969 gave English and French equal rights, status, and privileges as languages of Parliament and of the Federal government. Massive and costly attempts were made to make the proportions of francophones in the upper echelons of all branches of the civil service reflect more accurately their proportions in the country. Unilingual civil servants started taking classes in the other official language, and federal funds were made available to Provinces to foster bilingual education.

The same impulses were reflected in many Provincial jurisdictions, with extensions of the rights and privileges of French Canadians in Manitoba, Saskatchewan, New Brunswick, Ontario, and Alberta. In Quebec, however, a contrary trend prevailed, inspired by fears for the survival of French. It culminated in the Charter of the French Language of 1977 (Bill 101), which was introduced by the newly elected separatist Parti Québécois government. The Charter instituted the current policy by which only children born to anglophone parents who were themselves educated in English in Quebec could be educated in English. (A subsequent ruling of the Supreme Court of Quebec has found that this aspect of Bill 101 violates the Canadian Bill of Rights promulgated in 1982.) The intention was clear: French was to prevail in the schools; given the expectation that the relatively small proportion of the population descended from anglophones educated in English in Quebec would shrink, French was to become the only language to which immigrant populations could assimilate. French was to be the language of business; tribunals were established to set guidelines and timelines by which the major enterprises were to switch to the exclusive use of French. French was to be the only language of government and the professions. Above all, French was to be the language visible on the streets.[36]

These changes have undoubtedly had a profound effect on life in the Province of Quebec. In particular, the public aspect of Quebec's metropolis, Montreal, has changed very fundamentally; it is now clear as never before that the majority population in the city is francophone, and self-confidently so. After more than a century in which they calmly assumed that the majority francophone population would switch to English at their convenience, the English-speaking population of Montreal has now had to make a choice: either to learn to function in French, or to leave. Many have, of course, chosen the latter option, and according to a recent survey some 20 percent of the remainder intend to do so as well. However, those who have elected to stay have for the most part acquiesced in the changes, and are doing their best to learn to function in French.

In other areas of the Province, the changes have not been so easy for the anglophone population to accept. Nor have they been so seemingly fair. There are a number of parts of the Province where the original settlement was anglophone, rather than francophone. This is particularly the case with the Eastern Townships region south of Montreal, with isolated communities around the Gaspé Peninsula, and above all with the Ottawa Valley. In all these areas, although the accidents of history which determine how boundaries are drawn on maps have made them parts of Quebec, anglophone settlement antedates French settlement. Today, however, the descendants of the original settlers find that they are excoriated by the Provincial government as examples of the arrogant anglophones who for two centuries have been unwilling to learn the language of the francophone majority by whom they are surrounded. Yet in the case of the Ottawa Valley communities, for example, the settlement was originally part of the Ottawa Valley Irish settlement, the cultural and familial links of the communities are with the anglophone communities of the Ontario side of the Ottawa River to the south of them, and their metropolitan centre has been not Quebec City, some 400 miles further east; not Montreal, which is nearly 200 miles away; but the national capital, Ottawa, which is within 100 miles – and is predominantly anglophone. Today such people can communicate officially with their provincial government and its representatives only in French.

It should be stressed that, unlike such dominated linguistic minorities as the Bretons or Alsatians in France,[37] the Québécois have always had a great deal of autonomy within Quebec, and could have implemented the kind of legislation now in effect at any time after 1867. Since 1840 there has been no political attempt to limit the use of French in Quebec, whatever the restrictions imposed outside of that Province. It is therefore particularly tragic that, at the very moment when English Canada, in the outpouring of belated generosity which followed the Centennial celebrations of 1967, began to move to redress past injustices, Québécois governments for the first time began to exercise within Quebec the kind of power they had always had in principle, and to use it to regulate the role of English within Quebec. The vindictiveness with which they have done so is understandable in the historical context of English-Canadian attitudes to French and the French-Canadian resentments these have maintained and fostered. But it has indubitably been vindictive.[38] The traditional hatred of English as the language of political and commercial domination, the contempt for it as the source of linguistic impurity, and the fear of it as the medium of cultural assimilation, have been used as the excuse for outright carelessness about individual rights. It is all very disconcerting to the liberal anglophone element which expects that here, as elsewhere in the world, a previously oppressed minority, having gained or assumed political power, ought to demonstrate that it has learned through its own suffering a higher standard of morality than the standard formerly applied to it.

Although they are nowhere else so extreme, the hostile attitudes towards English which are so evident in Quebec policies today are shared by many other linguistic groups in Canada. Not all: many immigrant groups eagerly promote the linguistic assimilation of their children (just as many individual Québécois want their children to be bilingual in fact, though not to have to work in English). But other immigrant groups see English as the enemy of their unique identity, much as the Parti Québécois government sees English. The multicultural policies which are supposed to help to maintain the languages and cultures of both indigenous peoples and immigrant groups in the much vaunted "Canadian mosaic" count for even less in the face of the raw power of English than do the bilingual and bicultural policies which are supposed to foster the use of English and French as second languages. Yet in no other group is the resentment of English so clear and so important as it is amongst the francophones of Quebec, and particularly their political leaders.

Not surprisingly, the vindictive intent of recent Quebec language legislation has extended the bigotry which undoubtedly exists among some English Canadians. Increasingly, letters to editors of newspapers and comments on radio talk shows display resentment of French Canadians generally, Québécois particularly, the whole attempt to legislate the status of English and French in Canada at the Federal level since 1967, the government which has enacted this legislation, and the Québécois Prime Minister and Cabinet Ministers who have been in power for most of the time since then. At its worst, the counter-reaction is extremely red-neck, seeing in this, as in the recent change to the metric system, an ongoing plot to wrench the country out of its traditional English orbit. As the title of an outrageous but very successful book has it, *Bilingual Today: French Tomorrow*. The very vehemence of the reaction seems to confirm the worst fears underlying Quebec actions.

For a majority of the population of English Canada, however, the reaction is much milder. For some, a feeling of betrayal (again familiar in other parts of the world) that enlightened support of the extension of the rights of a formerly oppressed minority has not been simply accepted with gratitude, but rather used as a basis for demanding ever more power and autonomy. But among most, the reaction is probably simple puzzlement. Though they do not know it, their attitudes are very much like the pro-British imperialist attitudes so common in Ontario in the nineteenth century, which provoked the rise of French-Canadian nationalism in the first place; attitudes which, in their turn, were possible because of the expansion of the English-speaking empire that had begun two centuries earlier and had been advanced by such military successes as the British conquest of Nouvelle France in 1759–1760. *Plus ça change, plus c'est la même chose.* Secure in their status as monolingual anglophones, such English Canadians can only wonder why such a small number of people should make such a fuss about maintaining what has become, as they think, a relatively unimportant language in the world, and one which is certainly not of any real importance in North America. To them it is clear that in North America English is the language of commercial success, just as it has to be the language of wider communication in the rest of the world. It is the language of public entertainment, the language of the most spectacular scientific and technological accomplishments, the language in which most of the world's printing is done, the language which (so far as they know) is the most widely used in the world. The peculiarities of the Canadian situation may have made Canadian attitudes to English unique in some respects. In their serene assurance about the importance of their language, however, English Canadians are just like most of the rest of the English-speaking world.

Notes

1. Those elements of the vocabulary of Canadian English which are distinctively Canadian or Canadian in origin are presented in *A Dictionary of Canadianisms on Historical Principles*, ed. W. S. Avis (Toronto: W. J. Gage, Ltd., 1967). For the rest, what is known of Canadian English is comprehensively summarized in R. W. Bailey, "The English language in Canada," *English as a World Language*, ed. M. Görlach and R. W. Bailey (Ann Arbor: University of Michigan Press, 1982). I should note that since attitudes to English in Canada have been so little studied, my views are necessarily personal; in addition, since the country varies so much regionally, they are probably biased by my closer acquaintance with the Provinces of Ontario and Quebec than with the rest of the country. In part, my views have been shaped also by my work on the Linguistic Survey of the Ottawa Valley, a research project generously supported since 1976 by the Social Sciences and Humanities Research Council of Canada.
2. Howard B. Woods, "A socio-dialectology survey of the English spoken in Ottawa: A study of sociological and stylistic variation in Canadian English." Unpublished U.B.C. Ph.D. dissertation, 1979.
3. Ian Pringle, "The concept of dialect and the study of Canadian English," *Queen's Quarterly*, **90**, 1 (Spring 1983), 118.
4. Ralph Connor, *The Man from Glengarry*, intro. by S. Ross Beharriell (Toronto: McClelland and Stewart, 1969), p. 182 (originally published 1900).
5. Don Harron, *Charlie Farquharson's Histry of Canada* (Toronto: McGraw-Hill Ryerson Ltd., 1972), p. 62.
6. W. S. Avis, "So eh? is Canadian, eh?" *Canadian Journal of Linguistics*, **17** (1972), 89–104.

Avis shows that, with one possible exception, the uses of *eh?* considered to be typically Canadian did not originate in Canada and are not peculiar to Canadian English.

7. R. W. Burchfield, "Pronounced distinctions," *Times Literary Supplement*, No. 4142 (20 Aug. 1982), p. 900.
8. "Our fighting vocabulary," *The Canadian Magazine of Politics, Science, Art and Literature*, xvii (May, 1901), p. 53. I owe this and a number of the succeeding citations to one of the rare attitudinal studies of Canadian English, Neil C. Hultin's "Canadian views of American English," *American Speech*, **42** (1967), 243–260.
9. W. S. Avis, "Introduction," *Dictionary of Canadian English on Historical Principles*, pp. xii–xv.
10. M. H. Scargill, *A Short History of Canadian English* (Victoria, B.C.: Sono Nis Press, 1977), chap. I.
11. *The Anglo-American*, I (1852), p. 196. I owe this citation to Mr. Hultin's study.
12. The Reverend A. Constable Geikie, "Canadian English," *The Canadian Journal of Industry, Science and Art*, N.S., **2** (1857), 353.
13. Anonymous review of J. A. H. Murray's *The Evolution of English Lexicography, The Canadian Magazine*, XVI (January, 1901), p. 288. I owe this citation to Mr. Hultin's study.
14. Thomas Rolph, *Observations Made during a Visit in the West Indies and a Tour through the United States of America, in Parts of the Years 1832–3; together with a Statistical Account of Upper Canada* (Dundas, Upper Canada: G. Heyworth Hackstaff, 1836), p. 262.
15. V. E. Parvin, *Authorization of Textbooks for the Schools of Ontario, 1946–1950* (Toronto: University of Toronto Press, in association with the Canadian Textbook Publishers' Institute, 1965), pp. 6–46.
16. For example, J. MacMillan of the Ottawa Collegiate Institute "edited" an American textbook, William Swinton's *Campbell's New Language Lessons* (New York: Harper Brothers, 1878) without the author's consent. The editing consisted of deleting such stories as "The Battle of Bunker Hill," substituting Wellington for Washington, London for Chicago, etc., changing the title to *Swinton's Language Lessons*, and otherwise suppressing all references to the original author. See Parvin, p. 52.
17. W. S. Avis, "Canadian English," in Jim W. Corder and Walter S. Avis, *Handbook of Current English, Canadian Edition* (Toronto, Gage Educational Publishing Company, 1979), pp. xvii–xviii. There have been two preliminary studies of Canadian attitudes to spelling, Murray G. Wannamaker, "Who controls writing standards," *English Quarterly*, **9**, 4 (1977), 45–52, and Robert J. Ireland, "Canadian spelling: An empirical and historical survey of selected words," unpublished dissertation, York University, 1979.
18. Geikie, p. 345. See Hultin, p. 251, n. 29.
19. Anon., *Composition and Grammar for Public Schools* (Oshawa: Canadian Watchman Press, 1920), p. 106.
20. O. J. Stevenson and H. W. Kerfoot, *Ontario High School English Grammar* (Toronto: The Canada Publishing Company Ltd., 1935), p. 108.
21. R. J. McMaster, *Developing Your Communication Skills* (Toronto: Longman Canada Ltd., 1978), p. 109.
22. "The death of meaning," Toronto *Globe and Mail*, 9 Sept. 1961, p. 6.
23. Edwin Newman, *Strictly Speaking: Will America be the Death of English?* (Indianapolis, Ind.: Bobbs Merrill, 1974), pp. 32 f.
24. J. C. Tressler and C. F. Lewis, *Mastering Effective English*, Third Edition (Vancouver, Toronto and Montreal: Copp Clark, 1961), p. 54.
25. Norman DePoe, "Speaking of words," *The Ottawa Citizen*, 11 Jan. 1973.
26. Albert H. Marckwardt and Fred G. Walcott, *Facts About Current English Usage*. New York and London: D. Appleton-Century Incorporated, for the N.C.T.E., 1938.
27. Waterston and Beattie, p. 198.
28. *The Gage Canadian Dictionary*, ed. W. S. Avis *et al.* (Toronto: Gage Eductional Publishing, Ltd., 1973), s.v. *will*. Avis was, of course, aware that his recommendations are sometimes entirely a matter of his personal preferences; he acknowledges that fact in his essay prefaced to Corder and Avis, 1979 (see n. 17).

29. H. W. Fowler, *A Dictionary of Modern English Usage* (Oxford: Clarendon Press, 1926), s.v. *none*.

30. See Parvin, pp. 10, 13.

31. J. Sledd and Wilma R. Ebbitt, eds., *Dictionaries and that Dictionary*. Chicago: Scott Foresman and Co., 1962.

32. *Strictly Speaking: Will America be the Death of English?*, p. 32.

33. H. J. Persoon, "On linguistics and the teaching of English," *Indirections*, **7**, 3 (Fall 1983), 49 f.

34. "Languages in contact: A review of Canadian Research," *The Individual, Language and Society in Canada*, ed. W. H. Coons, D. M. Taylor, and Marc-Adélard Tremblay (Ottawa: The Canada Council, 1978), pp. 15–36.

35. The essays in the Coons, Taylor, and Tremblay work mentioned in the previous note provide very comprehensive bibliographic references for such studies.

36. Mann Trofimenkoff's *Dream of a Nation: A Social and Intellectual History of Québec* (Toronto: Macmillan of Canada, 1982) offers extensive and (I think) unbiased analysis of many events insofar as they are relevant to Quebec social and political history. H. Blair Neatby's "A tale of two languages" (*Language and Society*, **1**, Autumn 1979, pp. 24–26) and the accompanying chart "Language over Time" offer a very convenient summary of language legislation and many other measures which affected the status of the official languages between 1867 and 1979; however, there is no room for discussion of other areas of controversy (particularly education) which so often provided the context for language laws and rulings. A recent paper by Denise Daoust, "La planification linguistique au Québec: Un aperçu des lois sur la langue" (*Revue québécoise de linguistique*, **12**, 1 [1982], 9–75), offers an extensive and (to my mind) tendentious discussion of recent Quebec language legislation and its motivation.

37. Clear examples of recent attempts at the suppression of minority languages in France are documented in Frédéric Hartweg, "La situation linguistique en Alsace: un bilan," *Carleton Germanic Papers*, **2** (1974), 1–30, and Lenora A. Timm, "Language treatment in Brittany," *Language Planning Newsletter*, **8**, 3 (Aug. 1982), 1–6.

38. Examples of the kinds of distortions used to justify such policies are documented by William Johnson, "French weren't language victims," *Globe and Mail*, Monday, 4 April 1983, p. 4; "Trotting out a hoary myth," *ibid.*, Wednesday, 13 April 1983, p. 6; "Twisting history to shaft Anglos," *ibid.*, Friday, 15 April 1983, p. 4.

IV: *Attitudes and Usage: English in the World Context*

Introduction

BRAJ B. KACHRU

IN TERMS of the number of its speakers and their demographic distribution, English has already acquired a dominant status as a world language, compelling us to reconsider the traditional definition of the term "speech community." The 300 million native speakers of English are now outnumbered by its 400 million non-native speakers, who are spread over virtually all the continents. The significance of these numbers is open to evaluation, since they provide no clue as to the competence of the users and the extent to which the language is used. However, it is beyond dispute that in its various forms, ranging from pidginized varieties to localized standard varieties, English has acquired vital functional domains as a native language, as a second language, and as a foreign language. The unparalleled diffusion of English is essentially a post-World War II phenomenon.

The papers in this section are primarily devoted to the use of English as a non-native language: as a second language (ESL) or as a foreign language (EFL). It is these uses which have given English the enviable position and strength of a universal language. But such uses of English also pose numerous questions for linguists, sociolinguists, and educators – questions that have been raised in these papers directly or indirectly.

We may conveniently distinguish *institutionalized* and *performance* varieties of English, the first encompassing the regions where English is a second language, and the second the areas where it is a foreign language. Even where English is used as the major second language, this status is recognized in different ways. The Indian Constitution recognizes English as an "associate official language"; in Nigeria, Kenya, and Zambia, it is an important "link" language; and in several other countries, English serves the purpose of an "additional" language. The performance varieties, however, are primarily the foreign language varieties used, for example, in Japan, China, Hong Kong, Thailand, and Egypt. Does this, then, imply that ESL and EFL are static categories that may be applied without qualification to describe the status of English in a region or in a country? On the contrary, the status of English in each region is dynamic: it changes with shifts in attitudes towards English, in language policies, and in the relative power of linguistic pressure groups. Until recently, Malaysia, Pakistan, and Bangladesh were considered ESL countries, but that categorization is now being reconsidered. Indonesia used to be strictly an EFL country, but in recent years the functional domains of English have been increasing in that country and English is slowly acquiring the domains of Dutch. In Central, Northern, and Eastern Europe, one likewise has to be very cautious in using firm labels. As these papers point out, the typology of English as a second or foreign language is merely indicative of tendencies.

The papers focus on several other issues concerning culture-specific and cross-cultural functions. The first relates to the functional domains allocated to English in non-native contexts. These are primarily the domains assigned to a "High" variety, those used for wider communication and status-indication. In Germany, as Görlach and Schröder say, English has "snob appeal," and it is used "even where German equivalents are easily available." In Germany (as indeed in India, Singapore, or Nigeria), "listeners do not resent the use of English words even if they understand them incompletely or not at all." The use of English thus initiates one into a "high caste" with accompanying social privileges and status.

The second issue concerns the variation within the non-native varieties, a pedagogue's nightmare and a variationist's delight. We should separate myth from reality: the homogeneity of localized varieties (e.g. South African, Indian, Singaporean, Malaysian, Lankan) is as much a myth as is the opposite belief that the localized varieties have confusing subsystems with no shared norms of performance among their speakers. There is a cline of proficiency rather than homogeneity. Viewed in sociolinguistic terms, the varieties within a regional variety whether it is endo-normative (based on local norms) or exo-normative (based on external norms) represent a range that includes lects of varying proficiency: acrolects, masolects, and basilects. One sees this variation, for example, in Singapore, Nigeria, India, and the Philippines, where each lect has its domains of use; in such situations linguistic competence entails dexterity in appropriate lectal switching.

Thirdly, there is the still little-understood "love–hate relationship" with English, a clear case of linguistic schizophrenia. Within this intricate relationship, English now seems to have the advantage. In German-speaking and other European countries, English provides, according to Görlach and Schröder, a "neutral ground"; this "neutrality" has favoured the continued use and retention of English, in for example, South Asia and parts of Africa. In Israel, according to Cooper, an earlier attitude of "hostility" toward English has slowly changed to one of "enthusiastic acceptance," which at present is characterized by "hunger" and "indecent passion" for acquiring English. As in Israel, so in other parts of the world it is "never too early to begin instruction in English." In South Africa, Lanham argues that ". . . in the most clearly perceived social meanings recognized by all ethnic groups, English symbolizes the antithesis of the Afrikaner identity." On the other hand, for some Afrikaners, English ". . . still expresses the 'old enemy'." In the new political context the "old enemy" has its uses, and "almost all language shift . . . has been from Afrikaans to English as language of identity." What we see repeatedly is that non-native users of English on the one hand publicly condemn retention and use of English – a linguistic legacy of their colonial past – but on the other hand prefer English to other possible linguistic candidates. The increasing use of English is considered by some to be "too much of a good thing," as Cooper suggests in the case of Israel; however, in spite of this attitude, English continues to spread and to be welcomed.

The fourth issue of language preference is related to the previous one: a language is used for what it does for a person, as an individual, or as a member of a speech community. Nationalism, or ethnocentrism might compel some to discard English, but the advantages of using English persuade many to be realistic and to acquire the language. In India, Malaysia, and English-speaking Africa, it is therefore common to see vehement nationalists and anti-English enthusiasts send their own children to English-medium schools with the ultimate ambition of having them accepted for higher education in a Western university. The slogans of linguistic chauvinism seem to have specific consumers in mind, and they need not include one's kith and kin.

The fifth issue (significant for sociolinguistics) is the development of new English-based codes in situations of language contact and cultural contact. One manifestation of such contact, discussed by Rickford and Traugott, is the English-based pidgins and creoles that are found in (among other places) Nigeria, Papua New Guinea, and Surinam. The other is code-mixing and code-switching with English, referred to by Kachru and others. Such mixing and switching has brought about the Englishization of major world languages and literatures, resulting in both linguistic and literary innovations which raise challenging issues for linguistic description and lexicography.

The sixth point relates to the development of what have been broadly termed "non-native English literatures", "contact literatures," and "new English literatures." In specific areas, cover terms such as "Indian English literature" or "African English literature" are generally used for such literatures. This writing introduces new stylistic, literary, aesthetic, and cultural dimensions to a literature which used to be essentially British or American. The term "literatures in English," suggested by Indian critic C. D. Narasimhaiah, seems to capture this pluralistic global creativity in English. This aspect is another unprecedented phenomenon connected with the universalization of English.

The seventh issue involves attitudes toward non-native innovations in English at the lexical, grammatical, and discoursal levels. In some countries, for example Germany, such nativization is not yet attitudinally recognized; we see this in the claim of Görlach and Schröder that ". . . there is no nativization of English in Europe, the teaching and usage norm being derived from outside the respective countries."

These five papers pose many other crucial and provoking questions. One might, for example, ask: What are the implications of the internationalization of English for redefining the English-knowing speech community? In what sense has English now moved from the Judaic-Christian and European norms to what may be considered essentially non-Western cultural and aesthetic norms? What are the implications of such new experimentation and creativity for our understanding, appreciation, and teaching of "literatures in English"? How are the norms of intelligibility for English to be defined now that English has acquired various culture-specific and region-specific norms? And, how does one interpret the time-honored term "native speaker" of English? Educators and researchers cannot ignore these questions, for the cross-cultural and international uses of English demand new concepts, new types of research and research methodology, and new teaching strategies. And, equally important, these issues are central to a clearer understanding of the functions of, and attitudes toward, the English language of today.

Essentially, the questions are not new: they have been encountered in the earlier diffusion of such languages as Latin, Sanskrit, Persian, and Arabic, and more recently, in the spread of French, Spanish, and Portuguese. What is unprecedented in the case of English is that for the first time in recorded history, the issues affect so many cultures, regions, language groups, and individuals.

Chapter 1

Institutionalized Second-Language Varieties

BRAJ B. KACHRU

WHATEVER vagueness one at first associates with the term *second*-language varieties of English as opposed to *foreign*-language varieties slowly diminishes when one assesses the international uses of English in geographical, historical, attitudinal, linguistic, and sociolinguistic contexts. The term *second*-language varieties acquires more meaning once the world varieties of English are further seen in terms of their functional distribution and localized formal characteristics. Who are the second-language users of English? Internationally, the users of English are viewed from three perspectives: that of a native user for whom English is the first language in almost all functions; that of a non-native user who considers English as a foreign language and uses it in highly restricted domains; and that of a non-native user who uses an institutionalized second-language variety of English. I am concerned here with the last group, which must ideally be separated from those who use English as a foreign language. The two non-native groups differ in their acquisitional settings, in their motivations for learning English, and in their reasons for its nativization.[1]

These non-native varieties of English have alternatively been labeled "interference" varieties since in such second- or foreign-language varieties there is a clear linguistic and cultural interference from what may be termed the first language(s) and culture(s) of the user. The term "institutionalized" varieties generally refers to the varieties used by second-language users to distinguish them from the "performance" varieties of English, used essentially as foreign languages. This distinction is useful in understanding the context for the use of English in a particular region, and for planning the strategies for teaching. The terms are not vital, but understanding the underlying shared and non-shared characteristics of these two types of varieties is important. (See, for example, Kachru and Quirk 1981, and Kachru ed., 1982.) The institutionalized second-language varieties have a long history of acculturation in new cultural and geographical contexts; they have a large range of functions in the local educational, administrative, and legal systems. The result of such uses is that such varieties have developed nativized discourse and style types and functionally determined sublanguages (registers), and are used as a linguistic vehicle for creative writing in various genres.[2] We find such uses of English on almost every continent, for example, in Nigeria, Kenya, the Republic of South Africa, and Ghana in Africa; Bangladesh, India, Pakistan, and Sri Lanka in South Asia; and the Philippines, Singapore, and Malaysia in Southeast Asia.

211

The number of foreign-language and second-language users together adds up to 300 to 400 million, depending on whose figures one accepts.[3] Whatever the exact figures, this is a historically unprecedented phenomenon of language spread. When we add to this figure almost 300 million native speakers, we get 700 million users of English around the world. This figure puts English numerically among the most widely used world languages: Chinese, Hindi-Urdu, Russian, and Spanish.

But these figures are not mere numerical indicators. They also convey the message that the non-native users of English have given a wide geographical distribution to this language. English has acquired a variety of intranational and international functions across cultures and languages, and has gained the unprecedented status of a universal language. What was until recently a "colonial alien language" is now being used and spread by the former colonial subjects. The roles which linguistic visionaries foresaw for an artificial international language have slowly been assumed by English. As the statistics show, those who use English as their second language now outnumber the users of Australian (13 million), Canadian (13 million), British (55 million), American (182 million), and New Zealand (3 million) varieties. By their geographical distribution, numerical strength, and varied uses of English, the second-language users have made English, as it were, a window on the world.

But the spread of English in its various incarnations has not been an unmixed blessing – at least in the opinion of some. The more localized "unEnglish" uses English acquires, the more varieties of new (non-native) English come into existence. Cynics and purists see a sign of disintegration in the modification of English by alien users of the language: they seem to foresee the same fate for English which, for example, Latin met in Europe.

Is this attitude linguistically and pragmatically sound? Has the English language really fallen on hard times, especially on foreign shores in the mouths and writing of those who use it as their second language? We might gain some insights into the sociolinguistic issues by exploring two perspectives on second-language varieties. First, there is the attitude that second-language users manifest toward English in its various native and non-native models, and toward the innovations which are deviant from British or American English. Second, there is the attitude of native speakers of English toward these varieties.

The term *linguistic attitude* is used here in a broad sense, One might reveal such an attitude by using what may be termed *attitude-marking modifiers* for a variety of English (e.g. *Babu* English, *Indian* English, *cheechee* English, *Singapore* English, *Nigerian* English), or toward a variety within a variety, or toward non-native innovations in pronunciation, vocabulary, usage, discourse, and style types.

As is well documented, there are no authoritative codifying agencies such as language academies with the power to prescribe norms for using English as a second language. The codification is more in the sense of a preferred model, the preference being determined by such considerations as historical accident of exposure to a particular model, political colonization, geographical proximity, and attitude toward a variety. Who are the regulators of the norm? In the case of English, such regulators have been indirect and very subtle: dictionaries, pedagogical manuals, preferred models on television, radio, and in other media, and expressed social attitudes toward a particular manner of language use.

In earlier periods, both in Britain and in the U.S.A., organized efforts for codification have invariably failed.[4] But that failure has not deterred the messengers of linguistic doom from foretelling linguistic disintegration. In every generation such Cassandras arise who express concern about the decay of English among the native or non-native users, recent examples being Edwin Newman, and (for teaching English internationally) Clifford Prator.[5]

For English it is possible to choose between an idealized exo-normative model and an institutionalized endo-normative model. An exo-normative model refers to a native model (e.g. American or British) for emulation and teaching. On the other hand, an endo-normative model provides a local educated variety as the model for teaching and learning (e.g. by and large in India and Nigeria). The division is not always clear-cut: one finds coexistence of the two, and a wide range of variation between the accepted norm and the actual linguistic behavior.

In the history of attitudes towards second-language varieties we find several overlapping stages (see Kachru 1982). One first notices non-recognition of the localized variety, in the period of an "imitation model." This is followed by an extensive diffusion of local varieties of English, with varying degrees of success in teaching an exo-normative model. The third stage shows less discrepancy between the norm and the behavior: the localized (educated) norm is recognized by contextualizing the teaching materials to fit the local sociocultural situations, by recognizing the intranational uses of English, and by accepting local creative writing in English as part of national writing, as is certainly happening, for example, in Nigeria, Kenya, India, Singapore, and Malaysia.

I shall term these stages as *internal* within the speech community that uses English as a second language. Attitudinally, however, a second-languge user seems to stand between a rock and a hard place; the internal attitude is only one aspect of the picture. It is equally vital to investigate the attitude of native speakers toward the users of second-language varieties, or toward a particular second-language variety. Such attitudes provide fascinating sociolinguistic data.

Native speakers have traditionally viewed non-native innovations in (and nativizations of) English with ambivalence. Nativization has essentially been seen as *deficiency*, not as *difference*, as has been discussed with illustrations in several studies (for example, Kachru, 1982, especially chapters 3 and 20). Nativization must be seen as the result of those productive linguistic innovations which are determined by the localized functions of a second-language variety, the "culture of conversation" and communicative strategies in new situations, and the "transfer" from local languages.

There may also be other reasons for such innovations – for example, acquisitional limitations, inadequate teaching, and the lack of a consistent model for practice. There has been, furthermore, a subtle political reason: the desire to establish and maintain "language distance." The colonizers insisted on not teaching their language too well to "non-ingroup" Asians or Africans, the underlying idea being that the colonizers' code, if shared equally with the colonized, would reduce the distance between the rulers and the ruled. At the same time, the inevitable nativization of English by the brown and black sahibs (as the English-knowing natives were called) did not go unnoticed by the colonizers and provided a storehouse of hilarious linguistic anecdotes to be related in the "white only" clubs. In South Asia, the mythical "Babuji" became the source of such linguistic entertainment. The second-language user never seemed to win in this see-saw of attitudes. If he gained "native-like" linguistic competence he was suspect; if he did not gain it he was an object of linguistic ridicule.

The above discussion gives us some idea about the complexity of the issues. I shall now discuss manifestations of the attitude of second-language users toward models of English, toward functions of English, and toward linguistic innovations.

Traditionally, the main acquisitional models for English have been the educated British and American varieties. In order to contextualize the discussion, let me take the specific example of India. India has the longest tradition of teaching English as a second language, and the Indian variety of English is used in a number of domains of language function. In a 1976 survey two types of reactions concerning the preferred model have been reported (Kachru, 1976, especially pp. 229–234). One is the ranking of faculty preference for a model; a second is graduate students' attitudes toward various models of English, and their ranking on a scale of preference (see Tables 1 and 2 below). The survey was based on written questionnaires administered to 700 Indian students enrolled in Bachelor's and Master's degree courses in selected urban and rural universities and colleges, 196 teachers of English in selected universities and colleges, almost all holding graduate degrees in English, and 29 heads of departments of English. In Tables 1 and 2 the "scale of preference" or "preference rating" indicates the preference in terms of choosing a particular model out of three possible models (i.e. American, British, and Indian).

Perhaps more revealing (than Tables 1 and 2) is the graduate student's

TABLE 1. *Indian Faculty Preference for Models of English for Instruction*

Model	Preference		
	I	II	III
American English	3.07	14.35	25.64
British English	66.66	13.33	1.53
Indian English	26.66	25.64	11.79
Don't know		5.12	

"self-labelling" of their own English (see Table 3). It is generally believed that only a generation ago the gap between linguistic behavior and perceived norm was much wider. At that time, one would have hesitated to label one's own English "Indian," but by 1976 the picture was different, and it is still changing.

TABLE 2. *Indian Graduate Students' Attitude Toward Various Models of English and Ranking of Models According to Preference*

Model	Preference		
	I	II	III
American English	5.17	13.19	21.08
British English	67.6	9.65	1.08
Indian English	22.72	17.85	10.74
Don't care		5.03	
"Good" English		1.08	

TABLE 3. *Indian Graduate Students' Self-labeling of the Variety of their English*

Identity-marker	%
American English	2.58
British English	29.11
Indian English	55.64
"Mixture" of all three	2.99
Don't know	8.97
"Good" English	0.27

A study by Shaw[6] includes the preference of Singaporeans, Indians, and Thais for the variety of English they should learn to speak (see Tables 4 and 5).

But before drawing any far-reaching conclusions, one must note that the attitude toward British English may simply be explained in historical terms. British English provided a perceived norm, though actually *Indian* English has always been used in the subcontinent. It is true that empirical studies on this aspect of English use are lacking. However, the asides by educators of localized varieties provide further significant attitudinal clues. Bamgboṣe (1971, p. 41), discussing the teaching of English in Nigeria, says that "the aim is not to produce speakers of British Received Pronunciation (even if this were feasible). . . . Many Nigerians will consider as affected or even snobbish any

TABLE 4

Preference for models of English

	Singaporeans	Indians	Thais
British	38.3	28.5	49.1
American	14.4	12.0	31.6
Australian	.6	.3	.3
Own way	38.9	47.4	3.5
Others	7.8	11.8	15.5

TABLE 5. *Comparisons of Percentages choosing Native and Non-native Standards*

	Present			Future		
	Singaporeans	Indians	Thais	Singaporeans	Indians	Thais
Native	47.0	30.6	34.5	53.3	40.9	80.9
Non-native	53.0	69.4	65.5	46.7	59.1	19.1

Nigerian who speaks like a native speaker of English." Similarly, in Ghana, Sey (1973, p. 1) warns us that if an educated Ghanaian speaks the Received Pronunciation of England he "is frowned upon as distasteful and pedantic." In the Ghanaian context, as elsewhere in Africa, an educated localized variety does not mean "the type that strives too obviously to approximate to RP."

In South Asia the position of Sri Lanka (Ceylon) is not much different from that of India, as we see in the study by Passé (1947, p. 33). He observes that,

> It is worth noting, too, that Ceylonese [Sri Lankans] who speak "Standard English" are generally unpopular. There are several reasons for this: those who now speak standard English either belong to a favoured social class, with long purses which can take them to English public schools and universities, and so are disliked too much to be imitated, or have rather painfully acquired this kind of speech for social reasons and so are regarded as the apes of their betters; they are singular in speaking English as the majority of their countrymen cannot or will not speak it . . . Standard English has thus rather unpleasant associations when it is spoken by Ceylonese [Sri Lankans], . . .

This observation was made four decades ago. Today, in independent Sri Lanka where Singhala has a dominant position, an RP-sounding Singhala would be less acceptable, as has been indicated by Kandiah (1981) and other researchers.

The countries I have cited so far have been under the political domination of Britain. Let us now take the case of the Philippines, which has been under political control of the U.S.A., and where even now that influence continues. Llamzon (1969, p. 15) observes that "Standard Filipino English" is generally used, and it is "the type of English which educated Filipinos speak and which is acceptable in educated Filipino circles" (see also Llamzon, 1983).

One can go on adding to this list other areas where institutionalized second-language varieties of English have developed: Singapore, Malaysia, and Puerto Rico to name just three.[7] This list of countries makes one thing very clear: the attitudinal conflict between indigenous and external norms is slowly being resolved in favor of localized educated norms. This move is motivated more by pragmatic considerations than by a desire for linguistic emancipation. The trend is very clear, and there is a lesson in it.

Another aspect of second-language use reveals the attitude toward the functions and status of English in what may be termed utilitarian, intimate, and cultural domains. In a sense, these domains are related to what Quirk *et al.* (1972) call the "vehicular load" of English. This preference for English in various domains has contributed to the spread of the language, and to its retention after the end of the colonial period. It is unconsciously (and not-so-unconsciously) believed that English has an alchemy which "authenticates" a function in which it is used (see Kachru, 1984). That is why it became the language of anti-British campaigns in Africa or Asia where it is used to foster the revival or development of nationalism. It is also a preferred medium for technology and science. Let me illustrate this phenomenon by providing appropriate data from two studies, those of Fishman *et al.* (1977) and of K. Sridhar (1982).

In Fishman *et al.* (1977) we find that the use of English as a tool (or instrument) for science, technology, and other disciplines was "endorsed by the largest number of students (61%) as being the most important reason for studying English in Israel." This clearly is in consonance with an earlier study by Kachru (1976) for India. Cooper and Fishman in the above study assert that

> Not only did the students appear to value knowledge of English, they displayed favourable attitudes toward English vis-a-vis other languages. When asked to rate the suitability of each of five languages for each of twenty uses, English received the highest average rating on eight uses, including science, oratory, international diplomacy, philosophical treatises, and light verse. For two additional uses, novels and poetry, English received the highest average rating along with French. Thus English was the language most commonly viewed as most suitable for contexts associated with high culture and science. It was, however, also given the highest average rating for a more popular culture item, folk songs. English was even given the highest average rating for talking to babies, perhaps on the grounds that it is never too early to begin instruction in English.

Table 6 cites the reasons given by Israeli students for the study of English.

Let us now turn to the Dravidian language speakers in the south of multilingual India. Tables 7 and 8 show the functional distribution of Hindi, English, and other languages in South India.

In the non-Hindi South of India where Hindi is not the mother tongue, English is the preferred language in social interaction and professional contexts. The pan-Indian preference becomes clearer in Tables 9 and 10. Attitudinally, therefore, English is high on the language hierarchy.

The third aspect of language attitude involves the reaction of second-language users toward linguistic innovations in non-native institutionalized varieties. In several studies (e.g. Kachru 1981), the distinctiveness of, for example, American, Australian, or Canadian Englishes has actually been claimed on the basis of such localized innovations. The reaction of the users of British English toward such variations and innovations was not always one of

TABLE 6. *Reasons for the Study of English in Israel*

Reason	%
1. To read textbooks assigned in universities or other institutions of higher learning	61.4
2. To get along when abroad	47.4
3. To become broadly educated	47.4
4. To pass matriculation examination	42.1
5. To read English-language books for pleasure	36.8
6. To get a job which pays more	19.3
7. To gain friends among English-speaking people	14.0
8. Yields personal satisfaction	10.5
9. To begin to think and behave as Americans do	5.3
10. To learn about foreign points of view about Israel	3.5
11. To know tourists better	1.7
12. To know English-speaking immigrants better	1.7

Source: Fishman, Cooper, and Conrad, 1977.

TABLE 7. *South Indian Students who Use Mother-tongue, English, and Hindi/Urdu in Social Interaction (%)*

Domain	Language	Regularly	Rarely
Family	English	15	29
	Mother Tongue	87	1
	Hindi-Urdu	3	54
Friends	English	42	8
	Mother Tongue	53	12
Neighbors who can speak your language	English	17	24
	Mother Tongue	65	6
	Hindi-Urdu	4	48
Friends and relatives, during weddings, etc.	English	24	15
	Mother Tongue	71	3
	Hindi-Urdu	5	47
Teachers	English	57	3
	Mother Tongue	24	26
	Hindi-Urdu	2	57
Strangers on the bus	English	47	11
	Mother Tongue	35	11
	Hindi-Urdu	5	48
Office and bank employees	English	57	8
	Mother Tongue	26	17
	Hindi-Urdu	2	49
Political and technical discussions	English	42	8
	Mother Tongue	41	12
	Hindi-Urdu	4	50
While visiting another state in India	English	64	6
	Mother Tongue	17	27
	Hindi-Urdu	15	32

Source: K. Sridhar, 1982.

TABLE 8. *Employees who Use English, Mother Tongue, and Hindi-Urdu in Professional Contexts in South India (%)*

Domain	Language	Regularly	Rarely
Friends	English	33	6
	Mother Tongue	66	3
	Hindi-Urdu	25	6
Colleagues and supervisors	English	64	3
	Mother Tongue	31	19
	Hindi-Urdu	16	7
Subordinate staff	English	22	25
	Mother Tongue	48	14
	Hindi-Urdu	30	5
Customers who speak mother-tongue	English	38	9
	Mother Tongue	45	13
	Hindi-Urdu	27	6
Customers who don't speak your language	English	74	1
	Mother Tongue	5	25
	Hindi-Urdu	14	14

Source: K. Sridhar, 1982

TABLE 9. *Use of English in the Reading of General Literature*

Type of material	Always	Rarely	Frequently	Never
Newspapers and magazines	70.74	5.03	23.40	.40
General reading	63.94	6.12	28.84	.10

TABLE 10. *Use of English in Personal Interaction*

Interaction with	Often	Rarely	All the time	Never
Family	50.34	28.97	9.11	8.29
Friends	49.65	10.6	40.81	.27
Teachers	27.75	3.35	67.48	.13

Source: Kachru, 1976.

acceptance. Such innovations were considered signals of language decay, language corruption, or language death at the hands of those who were not in touch with the "real genius" of the language. Later, this attitude was extended to the English of non-native users.

What is meant by a linguistic innovation? A linguistic innovation is one result of nativization of English (Kachru 1982, p. 7), which in turn is the result of the new ecology in which a non-native variety of English functions. We see the influence of new linguistic, cultural, and social ecology in the *Americanness* or *Australianness* of English in the U.S.A. and Australia, respectively. It is in this ecology that the innovations acquire their communicative "meaning." Such innovations are not only lexical but also involve distinct culture-bound strategies for writing personal or official letters, invitations, obituaries, newspaper reports, and other discourse types. As one travels in the English-using world one encounters such regional innovations in the form of local borrowings, calques, translations, and in the 'mixing' of elements of English with local languages or vice versa. To the local English-using population such items are part of their linguistic repertoire and come to them as naturally as do *bull-frog*, *turkey-gobbler*, and *eggplant* to the users of American English. In various regions of Africa an outsider wonders what the following items mean: *kloof* 'ravine, valley'; *kraal* 'enclosure'; *aardvark* 'anteater'; *khang* 'cloth wrapper'; *sufuria* 'cooking pot'; *okrika* 'secondhand clothing'; *okyeame* 'headspokesman'; *penin* 'elder'; *dunno drum* 'a type of drum'; *give kola* 'offer a bribe'; *cry die* 'wake, funeral rites'; *throw water* 'offer a bribe'; *barb* 'haircut'; *head tie* 'head scarf'. One has the same reaction when one notices in spoken or written English in various parts of Asia innovations such as *kampong* 'a small settlement'; *makan* 'food'; *tiffin-carrier* 'a carrier for snack or lunch'; *ahimsa* 'non-violence'; *nose-screw* 'a decorative gold or silver ornament for the nose used by women'; *waist-thread* 'a ritualistic thread tied around the waist'; *Himalayan blunder* 'a big blunder, serious mistake'; *military hotel* 'non-vegetarian hotel'.

These innovations certainly are not pan-African or pan-Asian; these are localized and serve a communicative need in a region of South, West, East Africa, or of South and Southeast Asia. In some cases they have a specific connotation for a religion or community as have *caste mark* and *forehead marking* to the Hindu society, and *communal question* (*-riots*, *-harmony*, etc.) to the relations between Hindus and Muslims. These innovations and their semantic extensions or restrictions are, therefore, indicative of acculturation of English in new sociocultural and linguistic contexts and reflect its acceptance as a vehicle of non-native social norms and ecological needs. One might ask: Who is to judge the appropriateness and acceptance of such innovations? The actual non-native user or an idealized native speaker? The answer is not easy.

The reactions to such non-native innovations in institutionalized second-language varieties are deeply linked to linguistic attitudes. If the fundamental linguistic attitude is puristic, all innovations seem to signal decay. One tends to ignore the new cultural, social, and pragmatic contexts in which the language is embedded.[8] Each generation produces (perhaps well-meaning) linguistic alarmists whose concerns are sincere but unrelated to the pragmatics of a living language.

Lexicologists have generally demonstrated a more pragmatic language attitude which takes into consideration the non-English context, the need to use contextually appropriate lexis, and above all the importance of language as a vehicle of communication (see Kachru, 1980).

The nativized innovations in second-language varieties of English cannot be lumped together as *mistakes*; there is a difference between what may be called a mistake and a *deviation*. From a native speaker's viewpoint both entail non-native uses, but there is an important linguistic, contextual, and pedagogical difference between the two, as I have explained elsewhere (Kachru, 1982, chap 3; p. 45):

> A "mistake" may be unacceptable to a native speaker since it does not belong to the linguistic "norm" of the English language; it cannot be justified with reference to the sociocultural context of a non-native variety; and it is not the result of the productive processes used in an institutionalized non-native variety of English. On the other hand, a "deviation" has the following characteristics: it is different from the norm in the sense that it is the result of the new "un-English" linguistic and cultural setting in which the English language is used; it is the result of a productive process which marks the typical variety-specific features; and it is systemic within a variety, and not idiosyncratic. There is thus an explanation for each deviation within the context of situation.

Why are deviations an essential part of the context of second-language varieties of English? Answering that question leads us to a digression concerning the new contexts in which English is used and the relationship between language form and function. It entails viewing the use of English in institutionalized second-language varieties from a different perspective. How have such formations been viewed earlier? Again, let us consider the attitudinal history toward the South Asian variety of English. What is true of this variety is generally true of other institutionalized varieties of English as well. The attitudes typically refer to nativization of the following types: lexical or collocational changes, stylistic innovations (e.g. code-mixing), functional varieties, and lastly, responses to the development of non-native English literatures, and to the thematic and stylistic nativization displayed in such texts.

The responses are of four broad (and not mutually exclusive) groups: the *descriptivists*, the *purists*, the *cynics*, and the *pragmatists*. I shall discuss briefly the approaches of each group.

The descriptivists did not involve themselves with attitudinal evaluation of a variety and the innovations in it. Their studies primarily accounted for regional phonetic, lexical, and grammatical characteristics. One group of descriptivists was interested from a lexicographical point of view, while another looked at such innovations purely in terms of contact of two or more languages. An applied lexicographer's goal is well accomplished in the monumental work of Henry Yule and A. C. Burnell entitled *Hobson-Jobson*, and the earlier contact between English and South Asian languages is discussed by the German linguist Hugo Schuchardt (1842–1927). The latter group included structuralists and phoneticians – the structuralists as we understand them in the post-Bloomfield American paradigm, especially as applied to language pedagogy.

The lexicographers worked in two areas: They compiled collections of essentially local (e.g. South Asian) borrowings into the localized functions of English, and they recorded some semantically nativized English lexical items. In addition, they provided purpose-specific lexical lists: these were the precursors of what later became known as English for special purposes (ESP), and they were very useful to colonial administrators dealing with alien languages and cultures (e.g. Brown, 1852; Carnegy, 1877; Roberts, 1800; Stocqueler, 1848; Yule and Burnell, 1866; and Wilson, 1855).[9] The linguists, like Schuchardt, studied Indian English as a case of language contact and language change.

The line between descriptivists and prescriptivists has been a very fine one (especially in language teaching). When these two were blended, the result usually was linguistic purism. Once we talk of purism we invariably encounter an underlying norm. The combination of descriptivism and purism is evident in Goffin (1934), Whitworth (1907), and a long tradition of grammars specifically produced for the second-language learner. In its more extreme form we find this position espoused by Prator (1968; for a response to it see Kachru, 1976). The cynics are cynical about the status of the localized varieties and of the non-native innovations. They are aware of the use of localized non-native models in education, the media, and administration, but are hesitant to consider such models 'standard' for a region. With regard to the non-native literatures in English they are not sure whether such literatures belong to the local literary traditions.

Finally there are the pragmatists or functionalists who see language as part of a semiotic system in which various innovations and deviations are related to language function and change. Even the users of the transplanted first-language varieties had to wage a series of battles to establish their distinct identities, as in, for example, the United States or Australia.

A functionalist, then, sees an institutionalized second language as a living and changing system, naturally acquiring new identities in new sociocultural contexts. The context provides "meaning," and as the cultural and linguistic contexts change the language acquires new meanings. In new contexts, therefore, new *uses* and *users* of English have developed appropriate linguistic tools. I shall give below the observations of two Indian linguistic realists, one an educator and linguist, P. E. Dustoor, and the other a creative writer, R. K. Narayan. Dustoor has made an apt observation on this phenomenon:

> Our mental climate will always foster plants that do not flourish in England or America: and such plants, just because they are somewhat exotic, add to the charm of a garden. All lovers of English will, therefore, encourage them to grow in the world-wide garden of English. It is only the weeds, which spring up whenever ignorance, carelessness, or pretentiousness infects the air, that need to be pulled up by the roots (Dustoor, 1968; p. 126).

Narayan is more forthright:

> We are not attempting to write Anglo-Saxon English. The English language, through sheer resilience and mobility, is now undergoing a process of Indianization in the same manner as it adopted U.S. citizenship over a century ago, with the difference that it is the major language there but here one of the fifteen listed in the Indian Constitution. (Quoted in Press, 1965, p. 123.)

In functional terms, then, the institutionalized second-language varieties are part of the linguistic repertoire of the uses. English is one linguistic tool among many, as we have seen above in Sridhar's study with reference to allocation of domains. One important domain is that of literary creativity, the results of which include *Indian* English literature, *African* English literature, and *Malaysian* English literature, to name only three. These are new, not yet fully studied facets of English in a world context.

The spread of English – especially of its institutionalized varieties – has other dimensions which are directly related to language attitude. For example, consider the question of linguistic identity and language nationalism. The use of English by its non-native users as one linguistic tool among many such tools raises interesting questions: Does one necessarily lose one's cultural identity by using a non-native second language? Can one preserve one's identity and yet use a second language in intimate, professional, and cultural domains? The answer depends on how one interprets history. A pragmatist might respond affirmatively to both of these questions, and history does support such a response in the cases of South Asia, West Africa, and parts of Southeast Asia. But, then, this is a controversial question, on which there are opposing views.[10]

Once national identity is associated with a second language, the question of preserving an external norm becomes difficult. We have seen this in the Nigerian novelist Chinua Achebe's attitude toward the Africanization of English and in the Indian novelist Raja Rao's attitude toward the Indianization of English, and we find it in a Singaporean diplomat's attitude when he says:

> ... when one is abroad, in a bus or train or aeroplane and when one overhears someone speaking, one can immediately say this is someone from Malaysia or Singapore. And I should hope that when I'm speaking abroad my countrymen will have no problem recognizing that I am a Singaporean. (Quoted in Tongue, 1974, pp. 7–8.)

In the purists' view perhaps English is internationally in disarray, going through a process of decay. In reality, however, English is acquiring various international identities and thus acquiring multiple ownerships.

In the second-language varieties this acquisition of new identity sometimes occurs by design. In the foreign-language varieties, it generally is not so conscious. It is, however, difficult to say exactly when it is conscious and when it is unconscious. One has to accept the fact that humans have a way of blending the language with functions, and thereby creating a new linguistic ecology. English has been going through this process since at least the seventeenth century. The reassurance of the British linguist J. R. Firth is still, therefore, very relevant and meaningful. He specifically addresses the question of international uses of English and says (Firth, 1956, p. 97):

> "the study of English" is so vast that it must be further circumscribed to make it at all manageable. To begin with, English is an international language in the Commonwealth, the Colonies and in America. International in the sense that English serves the American way of life and might be called American, it serves the Indian way of life and has recently been declared an Indian language within the framework of the federal constitution. In another sense, it is international not only in Europe but in Asia and Africa, and serves various African ways of life and is increasingly the all-Asian language of politics. Secondly, and I say "secondly" advisedly, English is the key to what is described in a common cliche as "the British way of life."

These words are worthy of attention at a time when the interplay of language attitudes, especially concerning English, demands pragmatism and linguistic realism.

Notes

1. A detailed discussion of several aspects of the second-language varieties of English can be found in Smith, ed., 1981, Kachru, ed., 1982, and Kachru, 1983.
2. For references see S. N. Sridhar, 1982.
3. See, for example, Gage and Ohannessian, 1974, which primarily gives the enrollment figures, and Strevens, 1982. See also Kachru, 1981.
4. See, for example, Heath, 1977 and 1980, Finegan, 1980, Baron, 1982.
5. Newman (1974 and 1976 [1980]) have already been discussed widely by the media. For attitudes toward non-native varieties, see, for example, Prator, 1968, and my response to him in Kachru, 1976.
6. See Shaw, 1981. The survey was conducted "among final year Bachelor degree students in three locations: (1) Singapore, Republic of Singapore; (2) Hyderabad, India; (3) Bangkok, Thailand. The students in each group were from the fields of English literature and teaching, engineering, and business/commerce. Over 825 students from twelve universities and colleges participated in the study. There were 170 students from Singapore, 342 from India, and 313 from Thailand (108). The participants in the survey were asked to complete the sentence "I think that we should learn to speak English . . .' They had the following choices, (1) like the British; (2) like the Americans; (3) like the Australians; (4) in our own way; and (5) like educated non-native speakers from other countries (Shaw, 1981, p. 119). Table 5, as Shaw says (p. 120), ". . . compares the totals of the figures given for these two types of standards in the descriptions given by the students of the present English language situation as they see it, and their estimate of how they would like to see the situation develop."
7. For descriptions of such second-language varieties of English see, for example, Bailey and Görlach, eds., 1982; Kachru, ed., 1982 and 1983; Pride, ed., 1982; and Smith, ed., 1981.
8. See Kachru, 1976 and later, collected in Kachru, 1983. See also Kachru, ed., 1982, and Smith, ed., 1981.
9. These studies were specifically about South Asia; see Kachru, 1980.
10. These questions have been discussed in detail in Kachru, 1984. For a historical perspective on the attitudes toward American English and language controversy, see, for example, Baron, 1982, Daniels, 1982, and Heath, 1977.

References

BAILEY, RICHARD W. and MANFRED GÖRLACH (1982) *English as a World Language*. Ann Arbor: University of Michigan Press.

BAMGBOṢE, AYỌ (1971) "The English language in Nigeria." In *The English Language in West Africa*, edited by J. Spencer. London: Longman.

BARON, DENNIS (1982) *Grammar and Good Taste: Reforming the American language*. New Haven: Yale University Press.

DANIELS, HARVEY A. (1982) *Famous Last Words: the American language crisis reconsidered*. Carbondale: Southern Illinois University Press.

DUSTOOR, PHIROZE EDULJI (1968) *The World of Words*. Bombay: Asia Publishing House.

FINEGAN, EDWARD (1980) *Attitudes Toward English Usage: The history of a war of words*. New York: Teachers College Press.

FIRTH, JOHN RUPART (1968) "Descriptive linguistics and the study of English." In *Selected Papers of J. R. Firth, 1952–1959*, edited by F. R. Palmer. London: Longman.

FISHMAN, JOSHUA A., ROBERT L. COOPER, and ANDREW W. CONRAD (1977) *The Spread of English: The sociology of English as an additional language*. Rowley, MA: Newbury House.

GAGE, W.W. and S. OHANNESSIAN (1974) "ESOL enrollments throughout the world". *Linguistic Reporter* (Reprinted in *English Teaching Forum*, July 1977.)

GOFFIN, R.C. (1934) *Some Notes on Indian English*. S.P.E. Tract No. 41. Oxford: Clarendon Press.

HEATH, SHIRLEY B. (1977) "Language and politics in the United States." In *GURT*, 1977, edited by M. Saville-Troike. Washington, D.C.: Georgetown University Press.

HEATH, SHIRLEY B. (1980) "Standard English: biography of a symbol." In *Standards and*

Dialects in English, edited by T. Shopen and J. M. Williams. Cambridge: Winthrop Publishers.

KACHRU, BRAJ B. (1976) "Models of English for the Third World: white man's linguistic burden or language pragmatics?" *TESOL Quarterly*, **10**, 221–239.

KACHRU, BRAJ B. (1980) "The new Englishes and old dictionaries: directions in lexicographical research on non-native varieties of English." In *Theory and Method in Lexicography: Western and non-Western perspectives*, edited by Ladislav Zgusta, pp. 71–101. Columbia, S.C.: Hornbeam Press.

KACHRU, BRAJ (1981) "American English and other Englishes." In *Language in the USA*, edited by Charles A. Ferguson and Shirley B. Heath, pp. 21–43. New York: Cambridge University Press.

KACHRU, BRAJ B., ed. (1982) *The Other Tongue: English across cultures*. Urbana: University of Illinois Press.

KACHRU, BRAJ B. (1983) *The Indianization of English: the English language in India*. New Delhi and New York: Oxford University Press.

KACHRU, BRAJ. B. (1984) "The alchemy of colonial Englishes: social and functional power of non-native varieties." In *Language and Power*, edited by Cheris Kramarae, Muriel Schulz, and William O'Barr. Beverly Hills: Sage Publications.

KACHRU, BRAJ B. and RANDOLPH QUIRK (1981) "Introduction." In *English for Cross-cultural Communication*, edited by Larry E. Smith, pp. xiii–xx. London: Macmillan.

KANDIAH, THIRU (1981) "Lankan English schizoglossia." *English World-wide: A journal of varieties of English*, **2** (1) 63–81.

LLAMZON, TEODORO A. (1969) *Standard Filipino English*. Manila: Ateno University Press.

LLAMZON, TEODORO A. (1983) "Essential features of new varieties of English." In *Varieties of English in Southeast Asia*, edited by R.B. Noss, pp. 92–109. Singapore: SEAMEO Regional Language Center.

NEWMAN, EDWIN (1974 and 1976) *Edwin Newman on Language: Strictly speaking* and *A Civil Tongue*. New York: Warner Books, Inc., 1974 and 1976. [Paperback edition, 1980.]

PASSÉ, H.A. (1947) "The English language in Ceylon." Ph.D. dissertation. University of London.

PRATOR, CLIFFORD (1968) "The British heresy in TESL." In *Language Problems of Developing Nations*, edited by Joshua A. Fishman, Charles A. Ferguson, and Jyotirindra Das Gupta, pp. 459–76. New York: John Wiley and Sons.

PRESS, JOHN, ed. (1965) *Commonwealth Literature: Unity and diversity in a common culture*. London: Heinemann.

PRIDE, JOHN, ed. (1982) *New Englishes*. Rowley, MA: Newbury Publishers.

QUIRK, RANDOLPH, S. GREENBAUM, G. LEECH, and J. SVARTVIK (1972) *A Grammar of Contemporary English*. London: Longman.

SCHUCHARDT, HUGO (1980) "Das Indo-Englische." *Englische Studien*, 15, 286–305. [English translation in Pidgin and creole languages; selected essays by Hugo Schuchardt, edited and translated by Glenn G. Gilbert. London and New York: Cambridge University Press.]

SEY, K. A. (1973) *Ghanaian English: An exploratory survey*. London: Macmillan and Co.

SHAW, WILLARD (1981) "Asian student attitudes towards English". In *English for Cross-cultural Communication*, edited by Larry E. Smith, pp. 108–122. London: Macmillan.

SMITH, LARRY E., ed. (1981) *English for Cross-cultural Communication*. London: Macmillan.

SRIDHAR, KAMAL K. (1982) "Functional distribution of Hindi vis-a-vis other languages in South India." Paper presented at the South Asian Languages Roundtable, at Syracuse University, 20–23 May 1982.

SRIDHAR, S.N. (1982) "Non-native English literatures: context and relevance." In *The Other Tongue: English across cultures*, edited by Braj B. Kachru, pp. 291–306. Urbana: University of Illinois Press.

STREVENS, PETER. (1982) "World English and the world's Englishes – or, whose language is it anyway?" *Journal of the Royal Society of Arts*, 5311, CXXX, pp. 418–431.

TONGUE, R. K. (1974) *The English of Singapore and Malaysia.* Singapore: Eastern Universities Press.

WHITWORTH, GEORGE C. (1907) *Indian English: An examination of the errors of idioms made by Indians in writing English.* Letchworth, Herts: Garden City Press. [Later edition, 1932, Lahore].

Chapter 2

"Good Usage" in an EFL Context

MANFRED GÖRLACH AND KONRAD SCHRÖDER

Introduction

Central and northern Europe is one of the regions in the world where the number of non-native speakers of English is particularly high. The following account is based on material from German-speaking countries, but seems to be fairly representative for some neighbouring areas as well: Belgium, the Netherlands, and the Scandinavian countries (and possibly Poland and Czechoslovakia at least until 1945) have seen similar trends in English language teaching and the functions of English – though German has itself always been an important foreign language in North and East Europe, and has thus competed with English; and multilingual states such as Switzerland, Belgium or Finland have always given priority to the languages spoken on their territories – in education, even if this fact is not always reflected in daily life. Frequently English is also considered useful as "neutral ground" for conversation among speakers of different languages, especially in cases of language conflicts.

However, much work remains to be done before the EFL (English as a Foreign Language) situation in the Germanic-, Slavonic- and Romance-speaking countries in Europe can be adequately described and compared. It is, however, certain that the EFL problems of (Central) Europe are very different from those of South America, Africa or Asia, and it is doubtful whether, for many aspects, the range within EFL countries is not wider than the often hazy distinction (if applied to individual cases) between EFL and ESL (English as a Second Language) countries. Applying the term "EFL" to Europe in its accepted meaning, one can have no doubt that *all* countries in Europe (outside Britain and Ireland) fall into this category – not even Malta being excepted. This means that there is no "nativization" of English in Europe, the teaching and usage norms being derived from outside the respective countries.[1]

1. The Historical Perspective

The objectives for learning English in Continental Europe were utilitarian until at least 1765, when there began a pre-romantic veneration of English *belles-lettres*. Unlike French, which from about 1570 was studied for the sake of oral (rather than written or printed) communication and which was widely taught by native speakers, English was acquired by a professional elite and emphasis was laid on written comprehension and translation. Teachers of English were mostly non-native speakers with an academic background, who might have been to England for a year or two after graduating from university. From 1800 onwards, the prevailing method in classical *and* modern language teaching was grammar-translation, inspired by the neo-humanism of the founders of the state grammar schools, who insisted on the development of advanced reading proficiency and the art of translating into the mother-tongue of scientific and literary works. Oral English was considered to be of little practical use since direct contacts with Britain or the United States were few. In spite of a common veneration of Shakespeare and the English Romantic poets, the pronunciation of English did not receive much attention. This was at least partly due to the fact that English phonetics and prosody seemed to defy "scholarly" description (modern phonetic transcription did not exist before the late 1880s). English Studies ("Anglistik") developed into an academic discipline after 1872, when it split off from the historically oriented subject of Germanic philology. Anglistik was largely confined to the study of early periods of the language, and therefore it is no surprise that many of the earliest professors of English philology could not speak the language properly. They had received their training at grammar schools, where modern languages were not widely taught and where Latin-oriented methodology prevailed, fused with the prescriptive tradition of eighteenth-century English grammarians such as Lowth.

Until about 1880, then, "good usage" in a grammar-school context meant an artificial variety of written English, often clumsy and hypercorrect in the attempt to follow literary models closely: an English with too many latinate constructions, -*ing* forms and standardized idioms. After 1880, as a result of changes in the economic and political status of both British and American English, the teaching objectives gradually changed. The post-1871 colonialism of the German Reich together with Germany's increasingly important position in world trade, required school leavers whose knowledge of English was not restricted to translating Shakespeare, but included oral comprehension, a certain fluency in everyday conversation, and the ability to read newspapers and write simple letters. After 1900, not only was spoken English taught as well as written, but also more stress was laid on modern texts, literary and non-literary, and on the teaching of English life and institutions. Nevertheless, the Latin-oriented concept of "grammatical correctness" remained more or less intact, and its tradition unbroken, right into the 1970s, when the new model of "communicative competence" took over. For example, the distinction between *will* and *shall* continued to be rigorously hammered into pupils' heads well into the 1950s, and the intricacies of gerund constructions still tend to be seen as the touchstone of the student's mental maturity.

The decline of French as an international language led to a shift to English as the first foreign language in several European countries after World War I. In Germany, Bavaria was the first state to introduce English as the first foreign language in 1923, but a general change from French to English did not take place until 1936, when the Nazi government gave preference to English for racial reasons (claiming a natural friendship based on blood relations) and political reasons. In more recent times, since the teaching of English became compulsory for *all* pupils in some European countries, the predominance of English has caused some concern. The undoubted pragmatic usefulness of English has been said (Weinrich 1981) to leave little motivation for the learning of other modern languages (the incentives for the learning of Latin are somewhat different). Such a development is in obvious contrast to what politicians have tried to achieve for a unified Europe ever since the foundation of the first supranational institutions: a diversification that would give room in education to all the major languages of the community (Zapp, 1979; Christ, 1980, pp. 71–76). Also, the congruence of individual motivation and educational facilities has favoured English to such a degree that there is already a serious shortage of learners of French, Spanish, and Italian (and other languages) needed by industries and the administration (Christ, 1980, pp. 90–91).

There can be no doubt that, before 1945, British English was the only accepted standard in the official English language teaching curricula in Central Europe. After World War II, however, the scene quickly changed: in the four Occupied Zones of post-war Germany, the first foreign language was the language of the respective occupying power. American English became admissible at least in the American Zones of Germany and Austria. Exchange programmes for pupils and teachers helped to strengthen the American English influence, and the regional services of the American Forces Network created, in the minds of many pupils in the areas it reached, a distinction between "bad" English (the British variety taught at school in the morning) and "good" (useful and progressive) English (the American pop music variety spoken in the streets in the afternoon). At the same time, English began to be introduced into secondary technical schools (*Volksschulen*, for children aged 10–15) and thus became the most integrative factor in "secondary education for all." This new movement, out of reach of the influence of the gymnasium (the traditional academic secondary school) created its own teaching objectives: English was to be taught strictly as an international language, without one-sided emphasis on Britain, and as a means of every-day communication. Literature was considered less important, as was the teaching of the cultural background. The post-1960 gymnasium curricula decree that either the British or the American standard should be followed (especially in pronunciation) and that any form of "mid-Atlantic" should be avoided, even when a change of teachers means that pupils are exposed to different standards.

2. Objectives for Learning English Today: Some Latest Developments

The present scene is characterized by two main developments against a background of change in educational and politico-linguistic theory. On the one hand, the view that grammatical correctness cannot be the supreme objective of English language teaching, especially if English is to be learnt by everybody and as an international language, has led to a new approach to pupils' errors and mistakes, an approach backed by applied linguistics (error analysis) and by the psychology of foreign language learning, which has shown that learners proceed via incomplete grammatical systems. To be able to communicate successfully – even if not always grammatically correctly – has become the ultimate goal (and "communicative competence" the key-word) for schools that aim at mutual intelligibility rather than overall correctness, and that have borrowed from social psychology the idea that world-wide understanding implies the ability to speak (and write) to one another without fear and, in most cases, with recourse to a very limited proficiency in the target language. The approach, though it has been ridiculed in various contexts, has had a profound effect both on the teaching of English as the only foreign language in secondary technical schools, and on the development of new teaching materials. Through these it has also strongly influenced the teaching of English in evening classes for adults. One of the central and politically most stirring arguments for the teaching of English to the less able is, in fact, that through contact with a second language these learners can develop their mental faculties in general and improve their communicative range in particular. Good usage is, of course, still being aimed at, but the mastery of it or its constituents is not of central importance.

The second new development, contrary to some extent and yet complementary in part, is the rediscovery of British English as the idiom of a "neighbouring culture." The idea has sprung from the current image of a united Europe in which the individual regions should keep their cultural and linguistic identity as well as they can in order to avoid the dangers of the melting-pot. A multilingual Europe can only be preserved if neighbouring languages and cultures are studied in addition to international languages. To learn English merely as an international language over a period of six to nine years is not desirable; instead, British English and British culture should be taught, the one through the other, right from the beginning, as an example of another national variety of European culture and civilization. This approach implies foreign language studies in depth on a grammatical and also on a historical basis. Yet it has its points of contact with the approach discussed above: Even if they do not succeed linguistically, pupils following a course constructed along these guidelines will lose, through the contact with a second variety of European culture, some of their ethnocentric beliefs. Good usage, within this approach, certainly matters a great deal, but it is not the sole determining feature of success.

Apart from these main currents, there have been a number of smaller changes in the 1970s and the early 1980s. Thus, more stress has been laid on the receptive skills, especially on listening comprehension. Tapes, cassettes, and records have opened up new horizons in the area of modified standards as well as African or Asian varieties of English. The growing interest in Commonwealth literature adds a new touch. Of course the liberal use of different varieties and standards in English language teaching has its dangers. The result, with many learners, is an odd mixture of speech levels and an uncontrolled "Mid-Atlantic," an artificial jargon acceptable neither to the educated Briton nor to the educated American.

Nevertheless, a poll of English language teachers in Central Europe would probably show that the great majority consider "good usage" to be the kind of English used by an educated Englishman in his formal and semi-formal social contacts and within his own family. Of course, what has been called "kind of English" here comprises several varieties, which would have to be distinguished. And here the real trouble begins.

3. Attitudes and Evaluations

There are several indications of the popularity of English in Central Europe:
1. Inquiries held among students in various European countries show a stable preference for English, because of its usefulness and popularity (Schröder, 1981, p. 66).
2. The influence of English on other European languages is far-reaching. Contrastive studies investigating this phenomenon are urgently needed to assess its influence on the major European languages at both the spoken and printed levels, and within the various social groups and in specific registers. Not only would the results probably reveal national characteristics and a clearer concept of how this interference works, but they would also show the common core of international English in use throughout the region. Impressionistically, its influence is less strong in the Romance languages (even though the French have felt called upon to legislate against *franglais*), and is particularly obvious in German (mainly in the form of loanwords). The fact that its influence is found in East Germany, too, shows that it is not alone the enforced teaching of English but, rather, its popularity, especially in its American form, that accounts for the widespread knowledge of the language. Even though these forms of interference are not welcomed by school authorities, language academies, puristic writers, and other word-watchers, there is obviously no way to stem the flood.

In fact, English loanwords are already affecting the phonological structure of German, since it is prestigious to pronounce them in a form close to English: specimens like *Teenager*, *Sex*, *Jazz* (earlier /jats/) or *Thriller* (usually /sr-/) have added new phonemes and combinations. On the other hand, the morphology and syntax of German appear to be much less affected. Most striking is the coinage of quasi-English words and phrases fabricated from English lexical material: *Twen* 'person aged 20–29'; *Dressman* 'male model'; and even East German *Intershop* 'shop where goods can be bought with western (= international) currency' (Viereck 1980, 1982).
3. Registers such as the language of the media, and especially of advertising, show an increased use of English words (though not of coherent texts), even where German equivalents are easily available. Therefore their use must be ascribed to "snob appeal," and it has in fact been shown that readers or listeners do not resent the use of English words even if they understand them incompletely or not at all (Viereck 1980). Even if there were greater efforts to keep the German language "tidy," it is easy to predict that such language planning would have little effect in 1984. (In post-war Germany, this can be partly explained by the positive estimation of cosmopolitan attitudes, and the

negative evaluation of nationalistic attitudes; such tendencies have never been strong in Austria or Switzerland.)

In Western Europe, English is apparently here to stay, because the majority of the population sees a need for it, and is motivated to learn it. Although the opinion expressed by Denison (1980, p. 5) will be regarded as exaggerated by some, it is shared by many – not only by those who are concerned about the future of individual European languages.

> With regard to the role of English in Western Europe, a stage has now been reached, for a growing proportion of the population, in which a diglossia situation is rapidly approaching or already exists. The time is opportune, therefore, to begin to examine the developing scene in the light of studies in societal plurilingualism.

Note

1. Compare with this paper an article written fifty years ago by one of the most renowned teachers of English in Continental Europe in his time: "Standards of English in Europe" by R. W. Zandvoort, *American Speech*, **9** (1934), 3–10.

References

CHRIST, HERBERT (1980) *Fremdsprachenunterricht und Sprachenpolitik*. Stuttgart: Klett Cotta.
DENISON, NORMAN (1980) "English in Europe, with particular reference to the German-speaking area" In *Europäische Mehrsprachigkeit*. Festschrift Mario Wandruszka. Tübingen: Niemeyer, pp. 3–18.
LOVEDAY, L. ed. (1982) *The Sociolinguistics of Learning and Using a Non-native language*. Oxford: Pergamon.
SCHRÖDER, KONRAD (1981) "Eine Sprache für Europa?" In *Wort und Sprache*. Berlin: Langenscheidt, pp. 62–69.
VIERECK, WOLFGANG, ed. (1980) *Studies on the Influence of the English Language on German*. Tübingen: Narr.
VIERECK, WOLFGANG (1982) "The influence of the English language on German". *Amerikastudien/American Studies*, **27**, 203–215.
WEINRICH, HARALD (1981) "Fremdsprachen in der Bundesrepublik Deutschland und Deutsch als Fremdsprache". In *Wort und Sprache*, pp. 70–85.
ZAPP, FRANZ-JOSEF (1979) *Foreign Language Policy in Europe*. Brussels: European Cooperation Fund.

Chapter 3

Fantasti! Israeli Attitudes Towards English

ROBERT L. COOPER

ABOUT twenty years ago, many new immigrants were arriving in Israel from former French colonies in North Africa. The Israeli Ministry of Education decided to teach French to the immigrants' children rather than English, normally the first foreign language studied by Israeli pupils. The Ministry took this decision because many of the immigrants' children already knew some French. Inasmuch as it would presumably have been easier for them to excel in French than in English, it was thought that the teaching of French would ease their integration into their new school environment. Contrary to expectations, this decision aroused an outcry among the new immigrants. They felt insulted. They saw this action as demeaning to their children. They demanded that their children be taught English not French, even if English proved to be harder to learn. Their demand was met. This anecdote, told by Raphael Gefen, Chief Inspector of English at the Israeli Ministry of Education, is a good example of the force of Israeli attitudes towards English.

That these attitudes have not changed over the past twenty years can be seen from an article by Susan Bellos which appeared in the 18 December 1981 issue of *The Jerusalem Post*. The article, entitled "Too much of a good thing," concerned the "indecent passion for more and more English instruction in the schools." Several anecdotes in the article reflect the Israeli population's "hunger for English":

1. A school decided to stop teaching English to 17-year-old students who had difficulty with school learning on the grounds that the time spent on English instruction could be more profitably devoted to instruction in basic Hebrew, the primary language of the country. The pupils refused to attend classes until the English lessons were reinstated.

2. Chief Inspector Gefen suggested to a group of vocational school principals whose pupils both study and work that English be dropped from the curriculum. The principals told him that if English were dropped, their pupils wouldn't come to school at all.

3. A teacher at a community center in Jerusalem hoped to enrich the Hebrew of a group of semi-literate women. She was told that the women were only interested in "English conversation."

Brief Historical Background

Israeli attitudes towards English have not always been so positive. When

Palestine was a part of the Ottoman Empire, ruled from Constantinople, its chief language of communication with the outside world was French. Thus when the British took control of Palestine in 1917, relatively few of the local inhabitants knew English. Thereafter, the position of English changed dramatically. In 1922 it became the first of the territory's three official languages – English, Arabic, and Hebrew – named in that order in the Proclamation of the King at his Council. In cases of a contradiction between the English version of an official order, announcement, or form and that of the Arabic or Hebrew version, the English version was controlling. With the British Mandate's financial support of Jewish public schools, in which Hebrew was the medium of instruction, came the imposition of English as a compulsory school subject from the fifth grade through high school, a policy which has remained more or less intact until the present day.

Initially welcomed by the Jews as liberators and as sponsors of a national home for the Jews in Palestine, the British came to be seen as colonial oppressors. Attitudes towards the English language reflected this change in attitude towards the British. When, five years before the end of the Mandate, the British demanded that English be taught for five hours per week rather than four in the fifth and sixth grades, Jewish teachers opposed the proposal. At one point they even suggested that any foreign language *other* than English be taught. Some young Jews refused to speak any language but Hebrew and opposed their English lessons, a decision which they later came to regret.

Israel gained its independence in 1948, but hostility to English continued during the first few years of the State. In the first year of independence, Israel's parliament, the Knesset, voided that part of the 1922 Proclamation of the King at his Council that referred to English. Thus Hebrew and Arabic but not English remained as official languages, although the right (as distinguished from the obligation) to use English for governmental purposes was apparently not affected. The Knesset's official gazette, for example, continues to be published in English. English continues to be taught as the first foreign language.

By the late 1950s the Jews appeared no longer to regard the English language as a symbol of colonial oppression. For one thing, relations with Great Britain had improved. Secondly, English was the national language of Israel's great and good friend, the United States of America. Third, the world's largest concentration of Jews lived in North America: the language known by more of the world's Jews than any other was neither Hebrew nor Yiddish but English. Finally, English became, after the Second World War, the world's most important international *lingua franca* or language of wider communication, the language most likely to be used by people who wish to communicate with one another but who do not share the same mother tongue.

Factors Promoting English as a Language of Wider Communication

The emergence of English as the world's most important language of wider communication is attributable to several factors. First, it was imposed throughout the vast empire of Great Britain, which usually ruled its colonies long enough for the language to take root there. Most of these colonies were linguistically diverse: their inhabitants did not share the same mother tongue. Colonial administration created both the need for a local *lingua franca*, as peoples who were formerly separated came into increasing contact with one another, and the opportunity to learn one – English. English became the chief language linking the local elites with one another. (Other languages learned outside school, such as Swahili in much of British East Africa, spread as local *lingua francas* among the masses.) And of course English also became the chief language linking the indigenous elites with the rest of the world. The addition of these new recruits to English, in turn, made English even more attractive as a language of wider communication: the more people who know a language, the more useful it becomes as a *lingua franca*.

A second factor promoting the use of English as a language of wider communication has been the importance of English-speaking countries as markets in world trade. The sociologist Stanley Lieberson points out that among the leading countries in world trade, nine are countries in which English is either an official language or was an official language in colonial times (Australia, Canada, India, Malaya, New Zealand, South Africa, the United Kingdom, and the United States). These accounted for more than one-quarter of the world's imports in 1974. In contrast, the leading French-speaking countries (Belgium, Canada – included for both English and French – France, and Switzerland) accounted for only about 15 percent, which was the second highest figure for a language block. Although the importance of English-speaking countries as a world market has in fact declined from its position in the pre-First World War period (when they accounted for about one-third of all imports), Lieberson reminds us that there was a tremendous expansion of world trade after the Second World War. This expansion was far greater than the increase in the production of either manufactured goods or unmanufactured commodities. Thus international trade became increasingly important to national economies. Even though English-speaking countries declined in *relative* importance as a world market, there was an *absolute* increase in the intensity of commerical interactions with them.

There appears to be, in fact, a relationship between the use of English within a country and the importance of English-speaking markets for that country's exports. This can be seen from an analysis carried out a few years ago. Each of approximately 100 countries in which English is *not* spoken natively by a substantial proportion of the population was rated according to the degree to which it used English domestically (as the first foreign language taught, as a *lingua franca* within the country, etc.). This overall domestic usage was then compared to the percentage of the country's exports sent to the United States. Nations which sent a relatively high proportion of their exports to the United States tended to have a higher domestic English-usage index than nations which sent a relatively small proportion.

The importance of English as a language for international trade creates economic incentives for learning it. These incentives can be seen in Israel from a survey of help-wanted advertisements in the 1973 Hebrew press. Ten percent of all the jobs which were surveyed mentioned English as a job requirement. For some job categories, this percentage was much higher. One-quarter of all clerical jobs, for example, specified English. In contrast, a survey of help-wanted advertisements in the *New York Times* for about the same period showed that fewer than 1 percent of the jobs surveyed mentioned a foreign language as a job requirement. The negligible economic importance of foreign-language proficiency in the United States is not due to any lack of interest in exports. On the contrary, exports are vital to the American economy. However, most customers of American exporters can use English because English has become for most countries the chief language of international trade.

A third factor promoting the use of English as a language of wider communication has been the scientific and the technological superiority of the United States after the Second World War. The pre-eminent role of the United States as a creator of and a market for science and technology has made it increasingly difficult for persons to pursue a career in science or applied science without a working knowledge of English. Not only has knowledge of English increasingly become a prerequisite for work in science and applied science, but also more people have entered scientific careers as the importance of science and of its commercial and military applications has increased. Thus even more people have had to learn English than if the importance of science and technology had not expanded. In Israel the relevance of a knowledge of English for careers in science and technology can be seen from the fact that, in 1973, 84 percent of the books in Israeli medical libraries were in English.

The growth of Israeli statehood coincided with the growth of English throughout the world as a language of wider communication. Therefore, even had Israelis continued to be hostile towards English as a symbol of colonial domination, they would probably have continued to learn it anyway. As the psychologist John Macnamara pointed out, the Irish had no love for the English, but nonetheless by the middle of the nineteenth century most of the Irish had abandoned the Irish language for English, after centuries of English economic and political domination. The Israelis did not abandon Hebrew, of course, which remains the principal language of everyday life, but substantial numbers have learned and continue to learn English as their chief language of wider communication.

Measuring Attitudes

There are numerous ways to assess people's attitudes towards a referent – whether the referent is a candidate for political office, an ethnic group, or a language. However, all procedures can be classified into either one of two categories. One can either ask people questions designed to elicit their attitudes towards the referent or one can observe people's behavior with respect to the referent in the conditions of everyday life. One can, for example, ask immigrants if they are in favor of supporting the use of their mother tongue for cultural activities or one can invite immigrants to an evening of cultural activities conducted in their mother tongue and see how many come to it. There are advantages and disadvantages to both approaches.

Asking people what they think is usually the more straightforward procedure. One can ask many questions of many persons and can thereby build up a reliable description of what people *say*. But sometimes what people say does not reflect their true attitudes. People may not want publicly to express views which are socially unacceptable. Others with socially unacceptable views may fool themselves into thinking that their attitudes are different from what they really are. Others say what they think will please the investigator. Still others may not really know what they think, having not considered the topic before.

While observations of people's actual behavior may sometimes give a truer picture of their attitudes towards a referent than their statements about it, at other times observed behavior may not reveal underlying attitudes. People's everyday behavior is influenced not only by their attitudes but by other factors as well, and sometimes these other factors are so powerful that attitudes can have little influence. For example, even during the period when Israeli attitude towards English was at its most hostile, Israeli behavior towards English continued, by and large, as before. Israelis continued to study English and to use it because they had no viable alternative. Another problem in the use of systematic observations of behavior in order to infer attitudes is that we are less able to judge important characteristics about the people observed. We are not always sure whom we are observing.

Because of the problems inherent in each of these approaches, it is usually best to gather information by means of both. To the extent that the results obtained thereby overlap, we can be more confident in our conclusions. With these qualifications in view, let us turn to expressed attitudes and systematically observed behavior with respect to English in Israel.

Expressed Attitudes

When Israelis are asked to rate the social prestige of the languages spoken in Israel, Hebrew and English are ranked at the top. The Israeli psychologist Simon Herman found that there is a high correlation between the social prestige of various immigrant groups in Israel and the social prestige of their mother tongues. American, British, Canadian, and South African immigrants (called "Anglo Saxons" by veteran Israelis) are generally accorded high prestige, and their language is highly rated as well.

One group of largely middle-class high-school students in Jerusalem was asked, in the 1970s, to rate the suitability of Arabic, English, French, Hebrew, Russian, and Yiddish for each of twenty functions. English received the highest average rating for eight uses, including science, oratory, international diplomacy, philosophical treatises, and light verse. For two additional uses, novels and poetry, English was tied with French for first place. Thus English was the language most often viewed as most suitable for contexts associated with science and high culture. It was, however, also given the highest average rating for a more popular culture item, folksongs. English was even given the highest average rating for talking to babies, perhaps on the grounds that it is never too early to begin instruction in English.

With respect to stereotyped notions about languages' characteristics – expressed by adjectives or expressions such as *rich, musical, precise, logical, pleasing to the ear* – these high-school students gave English very high ratings in comparison with the same five languages. Here, however, English shared top honors with French, whose average rating was slightly higher than that of English.

The same high-school students were asked to indicate which of twelve reasons for studying English were among the three most important to them. Three types of reason were listed: instrumental reasons (for example, to read textbooks assigned in universities or other institutions of higher learning), integrative reasons (for example, to gain friends among English-speaking people), and reasons of personal satisfaction (for example, to read English-language books for pleasure). Instrumental reasons were the overwhelming favorites, on the average chosen eight times as frequently as integrative reasons and twice as frequently as reasons of personal satisfaction. Clearly, these students chose practical reasons as the most important ones for learning English. As the late Wilfred Whiteley once observed, "it is worth remembering that the desire to learn another's language springs only very rarely from a disinterested wish to communicate with one's fellow humans."[1]

In addition, the students were asked to rate the importance of English proficiency and the importance of Hebrew proficiency for attaining each of thirty-two goals whose personal importance they had previously rated (for example, having interesting work to do, making a good impression on other people). The importance of language skills was judged to be greater for the more highly valued goals, and English and Hebrew were seen as roughly equal in importance for the promotion of these goals. These findings suggest that the students strongly valued their knowledge of English. Of all the attitude measures employed with these students, the only ones which were related to the students' actual proficiency and usage of English were the ratings of the importance of English for the attainment of personal goals. Those who viewed English as helping them reach valued goals knew it better and used it more than those who viewed it as less important.

On the basis of the survey of these students – which in terms of the number and variety of questions asked is probably the most extensive language attitude survey carried out in Israel to date – it seems that middle-class Israeli high-school students view English positively. They regard it as very suitable for high culture and science, and their stereotyped views of it are positive, not to say romantic, but their incentives to learn it are largely instrumental or practical.

Systematic Observations of Behavior

What can we learn about attitudes towards English from systematic observations of people's behavior? In one study, people were approached randomly on a busy street in a middle-class neighborhood near downtown Jerusalem and asked for directions in English. One purpose was to see how many passersby could respond in English. (About 60 percent of the people approached responded in fluent English, but this is a higher percentage than one would find in the country as a whole.) A second purpose was to see what reactions the passersby would have to being addressed in English. Almost no one seemed surprised to find someone asking for directions in English, and this was true whether or not the questioner was a native speaker of English. Most people tried to be helpful, with about four-fifths showing positive or very positive attitudes. Only a tiny fraction showed signs of rejection. Most of the people addressed appeared anxious to display their knowledge of English. (Fluent English tends to be a marker of social class, with middle-class persons knowing it better than working-class persons on the average.) Most of the people addressed probably considered the questioners to be tourists, as the questions asked were ones which were likely to be asked by tourists. When the questioners became involved in longer conversations and said that they were new immigrants, a frequent reaction was "Don't you know any Hebrew?", reflecting Hebrew's status as the *lingua franca par excellence* for use by Israelis with each other. Favorableness of attitude towards being approached in English was related to the passerby's knowledge of English. Those with greater proficiency tended to show more favorable attitudes.

These pedestrians' attitudes towards English can be contrasted with attitudes towards Yiddish, as revealed by the following encounter observed by the author. In a crowded stationery shop in downtown Jerusalem a few years ago, a middle-aged man asked the shopkeeper for an item in Yiddish. From his dress, it was clear that the customer was a pious, ultra-conservative Jew. Many of the communities to which such persons belong believe that Hebrew is a sacred language to be reserved for prayer and that consequently it is a profanation to use Hebrew for ordinary everyday secular purposes, such as buying pencils in a shop. Another customer, a middle-aged woman, turned sharply to him and said, in Hebrew, "Speak Hebrew!" It is extremely unlikely that the use of English would have provoked a similar outburst. A customer who used English with the shopkeeper would have been assumed to be either a tourist or a new immigrant who did not yet know Hebrew. The Yiddish speaker, on the other hand, because of his orthodox religious background, could be assumed to know Hebrew.

Attitudes appear to discourage the use of languages other than Hebrew and English in public. On the same street on which people were approached in English and asked for directions, other pedestrians on the street and customers in the shops that lined the street were observed speaking to one another and to the shopkeepers. A record was kept of what languages were spoken. Naturally, most of the speakers used Hebrew. However, the language heard next most often was English – about six times as frequently as German and about eight times as frequently as Yiddish, the languages heard next most often. Almost all the people overheard speaking English spoke it natively whereas about half of those overheard speaking Hebrew spoke it with a foreign accent. (Large-scale immigration after the establishment of the State has meant that a large proportion of today's Hebrew speakers in Israel do not speak the language natively.) While a substantial number of persons were observed speaking English on the street, only a few customers were observed speaking English to the shopkeepers, although most of the shopkeepers knew English. Thus to the extent that this street is representative of middle-class urban neighborhoods, it appears that attitudes towards English permit its use in public by native speakers with one another but not with native speakers of other languages if both speakers know Hebrew. The rule seems to be: speak Hebrew in public unless you are a native speaker of English, in which case you may speak English if the other speaker is also a native speaker of English.

Positive attitudes to English can also be seen from the results of an experiment, by Yisrael Weintraub, on the influence of language on persuasion. One might expect that messages are more persuasive in the listener's mother-tongue than in a foreign language. Weintraub's study tested this assumption. He played two tape-recorded messages to university students who were native speakers of Hebrew. One message cited educational and psycho-logical research to support its argument, whereas the other message cited the Bible in support of its position. Both messages were recorded by the same speaker, a native speaker of Hebrew who spoke English with a Hebrew accent. Half the students heard the first message in English and the second message in Hebrew, and half the students heard the first message in Hebrew and the second message in English. As judged by the students' responses to the messages, the message appealing to educational and psychological research was more persuasive in English than in Hebrew whereas the reverse was true for the message appealing to Biblical sources. The fact that English is the pre-eminent language for science and technology – most of the reading required of Israeli university students is in English – may have given English a persuasive advantage over Hebrew for the domain of science, at least within the context of this experiment.

Legislation for the "Protection" of Hebrew

Three language laws were submitted to the Knesset in 1980. The ostensible purpose of these bills was, in the words of Moshe Shamir, one of the sponsors, to "erect a barrier against foreign-language domination," which poses a "danger to the society's linguistic and spiritual independence." There was no doubt that the foreign language in question was English.

Among other things, the bills would have required the use of Hebrew in contracts, signs, advertisements, menus, consumer packaging, government documents, international agreements, and warranties and instructions for the use of consumer goods. The use of other languages would have been permitted in addition to Hebrew, however, and the non-Jewish sector of the population would have been excluded from these provisions. One bill would have required all foreign-language films shown at cinemas and on television (most are in English with Hebrew subtitles) to be dubbed into Hebrew. Another bill would have prohibited the use of foreign words in contracts or advertisements if a parallel Hebrew expression exists.

These bills testify to the threat which some Hebrew-language purists see in the use of English for certain public purposes. Motivating their concern has been the peppering of Israeli Hebrew speech with English terms (some examples: *aktivi, optimi, fantasti, sentimentali, optsia, konflikt, sanktsia*). These bills aroused little interest, however, and the Knesset's term expired before they could be brought to a vote. The public, apparently, was unconcerned.

Concluding Remarks

Attitudes towards English among the Jewish majority in Israel have changed from hostitlity, during the conclusion of the British Mandate and during the first years of independence, to enthusiastic acceptance. There appears to be a genuine desire to learn English at all socio-economic strata. This chapter has given examples of Israelis' positive attitudes towards English and has attempted to explain them. Some of these examples also demonstrate that although English terms continue to enter everyday spoken Hebrew, English poses no threat to the status of Hebrew as a symbol of Jewish statehood and as the normal language of everyday life for the Jewish inhabitants of that state.[2]

Notes

1. Wilfred Whiteley, *Swahili: the Rise of a National Language*. London: Methuen, 1969, p. 13.
2. This chapter has been based on the following sources: Susan Bellos, "Too much of a good thing," *The Jerusalem Post Magazine* (*The Jerusalem Post* supplement), 18 Dec. 1981, p. 6; L. F. Brosnahan, "Some historical cases of language imposition," in John Spencer, ed., *Language in Africa*, Cambridge: Cambridge University Press, 1963, pp. 7–24; Robert L. Cooper, "A framework for the study of language spread," in Robert L. Cooper, ed., *Language Spread: Studies in Diffusion and Social Change*, Bloomington: Indiana University Press, 1982: Robert L. Cooper and Joshua A. Fishman, "A study of language attitudes," in Joshua A. Fishman, Robert L. Cooper, and Andrew W. Conrad, eds., *The Spread of English: the Sociology of English as an Additional Language*, Rowley: Newbury House, 1977, pp. 239–276; Robert L. Cooper and Fern Seckbach, "Economic incentives for the learning of a language of wider communication: a case study," in Joshua A. Fishman, Robert L. Cooper, and Andrew W. Conrad, eds., *op. cit.*, pp. 212–219; Joshua A. Fishman, "Bilingual attitudes and behaviors," in Joshua A. Fishman, Robert L. Cooper, Roxana Ma *et al., Bilingualism in the Barrio*, Bloomington: Research Center for the Language Sciences, Indiana University Press, 1975, 2nd edition, pp. 105–116; Joshua A. Fishman, Robert L. Cooper, and Yehudit Rosenbaum, "English around the world," in Joshua A. Fishman, Robert L. Cooper, and Andrew W. Conrad, eds., *op. cit.*, pp. 77–107; David L. Gold, "An introduction to English in Israel," *Language Problems and Language Planning*, Vol. 5 (1981), pp. 11–56; Simon N. Herman, "Explorations in the social psychology of language choice," *Human Relations*, Vol. 14 (1961), pp. 149–164; Stanley Lieberson, "Forces affecting language spread: Some basic propositions," in Robert L. Cooper, ed., *op. cit.*; John Macnamara, "Attitudes and learning a second language," in Roger W. Shuy, and Ralph W. Fasold, eds., *Language Attitudes: Current Trends and Prospects*, Washington: Georgetown University Press, 1973, pp. 36–40; Elizabeth Nadel and Joshua A. Fishman, "English in Israel," in Joshua A. Fishman, Robert L. Cooper and Andrew W. Conrad, eds., *op. cit.*, pp. 137–167; Yehudit Rosenbaum, Elizabeth Nadel, Robert L. Cooper, and Joshua A. Fishman, "English on Keren Kayemet Street," in Joshua A. Fishman, Robert L. Cooper, and Andrew W. Conrad, eds., *op. cit.*, pp. 179–194; Yisrael Weintraub, "The relative influence of languages in persuasive messages," unpublished Hebrew University seminar paper, 1978.

Chapter 4

The Perception and Evaluation of Varieties of English in South African Society

L. W. LANHAM

Introduction

Ethnically, South African society is highly heterogeneous and social and political forces promoting the separation of ethnic groups have, over nearly two centuries, served to magnify racial and descent-group differences and make South Africa (hereinafter SA) of the late twentieth century a deeply divided society. Language and dialect differences are, in consequence, of considerable significance, and attitudes evoked by them, and the social information which varieties of English convey, are extremely complex. Varieties of English used and distinguished by members of the society are:

(a) White, mother-tongue English in three main accents (dialects in some degree) and four second-language varieties:
   (1) Extreme South African English (Ext SAE)
   (2) Respectable South African English (Resp SAE)
   (3) Conservative South African English (Cons SAE)
(b) Afrikaans English (Afrik E) of whites who have Afrikaans as mother-tongue.
(c) South African Black English (Bl E) of South Africans with a Bantu language as mother-tongue.
(d) Coloured English (Col E) of the Coloured community of mixed descent who traditionally have Afrikaans as mother-tongue.
(e) South African Indian English (Ind E) of the Indian community in South Africa.

As Labov's early studies (Labov, 1964, 1966) demonstrated, even an ethnically diverse and stratified society shows remarkable consensus in its perception of social information conveyed by varieties of English. In reference-group behaviour, however, which reveals allegiance to social values (hence the attitudes and beliefs of individuals), there is a diversity of response. Labov (1964, p. 84) noted with surprise that "those who showed the highest use of the non-standard forms in their own speech were often among the most sensitive in detecting and stigmatising these forms in the speech of others." In behaving in this way the working class are said to "endorse" middle-class values (Labov, 1967, p. 68), while remaining committed to working-class,

242

"covert" values. What they reveal, therefore, in their "endorsement," is no more than social knowledge – the social consequences of dominant middle-class values. Their true allegiance is to the conflicting covert values of their own class such as masculinity, in-group cohesion and a disdain for the proprieties in social behaviour. There is clear evidence of the same phenomenon operating in SA society; we therefore find a need to separate social information conveyed by language varieties from attitudes directed to those varieties.

In the three main sections which follow we first provide brief descriptions of the forms of English in SA society ((a)–(e), see above) and their speakers, then outline the social meaning conveyed by them, and finally discuss the main attitudes (which include beliefs relating to stereotypes) pertaining to well-defined varieties of English. Our evidence in support of statements made is mainly experimental and empirical and reflects the findings of recent sociolinguistic inquiries; circumstantial evidence and (when sufficiently revealing) anecdotal evidence is occasionally cited and our opinions are offered.

Forms of English in SA

White, mother-tongue speakers of English, mainly of British descent, number about 1,120,000. Most individual accent profiles in the community can be assigned to three accents which have regional and social associations:

(a1) Ext SAE has its origins in the speech of the descendants of the first British settlers in the Cape in the early nineteenth century. It is the most typically local of English speech in SA and its defining variables reflect working-class or lower middle-class accents of the Home Counties at the turn of the eighteenth century and, through contact with the Dutch (Afrikaans-speaking) colonists, a number of phonological, grammatical and lexical borrowings from Afrikaans. Regionally, Ext SAE is associated with the Cape; socially, in the industrial cities, this accent connotes low social status.

(a2) Resp SAE is mainly characterized by pronunciation variables which originate in the English of Natal where British settlement differed from that of the Cape in the time of settlement (mid-nineteenth century) and its social and regional origins in Britain. This society succeeded in remaining close to Britain in mind and behaviour. A high proportion of settlers came from the Midlands and the North, and Resp SAE variables reveal this. Supported by the high prestige associated with "being English," Resp SAE has spread from Natal to upwardly mobile groups elsewhere, particularly in the mining–industrial society of the Witwatersrand.

(a3) Cons SAE is close to standard southern British English and has none of the defining variables of varieties of SAE with any degree of prominence, certainly not any associated with Ext SAE. Socially, Cons SAE has a clear correlation with the highest socio-economic status, mainly among the over-50s who have strong "associations with Britain" (a social variable defined in Lanham, 1982, p. 336).

Since the British occupation of the Cape in 1806, and particularly after the proclamation of 1822 by Lord Charles Somerset (the Governor of the Cape) which made English the only official language, South Africans of Dutch descent (Afrikaners) have been involved in extensive English-Afrikaans bilingualism. Van Wyk (1978) estimated that 83.7 percent of Afrikaners have average to excellent command of English and this percentage adds 1,750,000 to the total number of competent users of English in SA.

(b) Afrik E is a clearly distinguishable accent with significant variables drawn from Afrikaans. Although many South Africans have a low level of sensitivity to the differences between Afrik E and Ext SAE (with its own borrowings from Afrikaans) these are nevertheless real and easily identifiable. The extreme forms of Afrik E are widely encountered in the bilingualism of, for example, low-status government officials who are mainly Afrikaners.

In a calculation based on a recent survey of black SA users of English and Afrikaans (Schuring 1977), I included five and a half million in the "English-using population" in SA (Lanham, 1982, pp. 337 ff.). These tend to concentrate in the larger towns and cities which are "English," i.e. having 65 percent or more whites (according to the 1960 census) who are mother-tongue English speakers.

(c) Bl E is immediately recognized by all in SA society with its prominent pronunciation variables reflecting Bantu-language phonology, idioms and fixed expressions, redefined semantic content, and peculiar grammatical structures. In a century and a half of learning English as a second language, norms peculiar to Bl E have evolved and characterize an acceptable variety of English as a second language.

The Coloured community are predominantly Afrikaans speaking, but Van Wyk (1978), using census figures, estimated that 123,000 now have English as mother-tongue. A major shift in language loyalty (from Afrikaans to English) is currently reported and this is associated with upward socio-economic mobility in the major industrial cities.

(d) Col E is marked by advanced pronunciation variants of more extreme Afrik E and, differentially according to region, advanced variants of certain Ext SAE variables (reflecting contact with English speakers in the Cape over a number of generations). Col E has many borrowings from Afrikaans and has a specially distinctive intonation contour: pitch tends to rise on final accented syllables in statements. Probably because of the strength of Col E as a symbol of Coloured identity and in-group solidarity, even the more formal speech of the well educated has at least the pronunciation variables that characterize this stigmatized variety of English in SA society. Most South Africans encounter Col E in colloquial form in which English and Afrikaans are mixed and code switching proceeds at a bewildering rate.

The Indian community in SA numbers some 387,000 and almost all are competent users of English. The growth-rate of English as home language in this community (calculated as almost 13 percent by Watts, 1976) means that the entire population will be mother-tongue users of English by 1990.

(e) Ind E of older, less well-educated generations has many of the pronunciation variables which characterize English in India. However, these features have become considerably less prominent in younger generations, particularly those who are well educated. This shift towards the more standard, less obviously Indian, accent is noteworthy for the fact that the model adopted is not an obviously local variety of English; it is not even Natal English – the majority of Indians live in Natal and have from an early age extensive exposure to the English of white Natalians.

Social Information Conveyed by Varieties of English

Experimental evidence supports a claim that, in spite of differences amounting to those between subcultures, the two main divisions in white SA society perceive the same social information conveyed by varieties of English in SA, and probably have the same sensitivities in recognizing the linguistic variables which define them. Macdonald (1975) reports on an experiment in which she explored the extent to which different sectors of white SA society were prepared to associate vignettes of social behaviour as realizations of specific social values, with the main accents of white society. She used four accents: British Received Pronunciation, Resp SAE (admittedly poorly defined in the speaker used), Ext SAE, Afrik E. Her subjects included English and Afrikaans-speaking respondents in Johannesburg and they were entirely uniform in making the following three significant responses: the speaker of Ext SAE was identified as "not a leader, uneducated, unsophisticated, gregarious and physically strong"; the speaker of RP was sophisticated, cultured, and well educated; no difference in stereotype was evoked by Afrik E and Ext E and the same social and personal attributes were ascribed to both.

In the most clearly perceived of social meanings recognized by all ethnic groups, English symbolizes the antithesis of the Afrikaner identity, and the ideology and values associated with Afrikaner nationalism. In the white, and probably the Indian communities, this social meaning is probably cancelled when the speech is obvious Ext SAE or Afrik E. Specifically in reference to Afrikaner attitudes and perceptions of the social information conveyed by English, I have written:

> For some Afrikaners, socially remote from English South Africans, English in some sense still expresses the "old enemy." More generally, however, English symbolically rejects the Afrikaner and his cause, and in these terms white society is of a common mind in the symbolic content of language choice. The Afrikaner can be said to see in English the betrayal of true South Africanism and the white man's mission in southern Africa. (Lanham, 1982, p. 346.)

Continuing with the examination of the symbolic content of varieties of English for white South Africans, we note empirical evidence which reveals the stereotypic associations of Ext SAE and Afrik E: in an experiment using the matched guise technique, Penn and Stafford (1971) found remarkable unanimity among female university students associating Ext SAE with lowest-status occupations and Cons SAE with highest-status occupations. In relating social meaning to social values, I have suggested (Lanham and Macdonald, 1979, p. 56) that Ext SAE expresses the covert values (in the sense used by Labov, 1966) of the society; in essence: masculinity, independence, physical toughness, a disdain for the proprieties, and a commitment to the typically SA identity.

Resp SAE, I have suggested (Lanham and Macdonald, 1979) expresses the informal standard in South African English connoting high social status and sophistication (but probably not "correctness' which is still reserved for more obviously British English). Resp SAE conveys this to those who lack sensitivity to the fine detail of British norms in behaviour and speech. In an experiment determining the perceptions of the various sectors of the society of the defining, prominent variables of Resp SAE, we found (Lanham and Macdonald, 1979) that this accent is highly valued by, in ascending order of approbation: old (over 50) white Cape females; young white Witwatersrand females; young Jewish females. Those who reject this meaning are mainly Natalians (from where Resp SAE originates and where it is recognized as "local" speech) and high-status respondents of recent British descent elsewhere.

Cons SAE and standard southern British English, which few locally born South Africans can distinguish, have uniformly through white SA society the highest prestige and express the formal standard in the sense of high social status and correctness in language use. Macdonald (1975) identified the following stereotypic associations of this accent revealed in her research: sophistication, high social status, leadership and authority, good education.

We turn now to the social information conveyed by English to black South Africans. To them it presents a clear stereotype according to Vorster and Proctor's (1976) research. Using a matched guise technique with black university students, they opposed English to Afrikaans in certain social attributes and a number of non-pejorative personality traits. They found:

> The English stereotype is not seen as taller or stronger than his Afrikaans counterpart, but he is much better looking, has a higher-status job, is more likeable, more sociable, and kinder. In short, then, the English stereotype is of a "nice" person, whereas the Afrikaans stereotype could be of a "strong" person (p. 108).

Schuring (1977) analysed the results of the Human Sciences Research Council survey of the knowledge and use of English and Afrikaans by black South Africans. It is possible to extrapolate from this inquiry the social meaning of English for blacks: prestige and a passport to higher education which carries implications of economic advantage and political power. Edelstein (1972) found that 88.5 percent of black parents in Soweto desired English as the language in which they wanted their children educated. The association between English and educational advancement is clear and, although now rejected as the sole or even the major cause for the Soweto riots of 1976, the fact that blacks cite the demand for English in education as the cause for the riots is evidence enough of their sensitivities relating to English.

Ind E does not appear to convey much social information to SA Indians and the advance of English in the Indian community should not to be taken as evidence of English as the expression of the SA Indian identity or of group solidarity. Indians keep up the struggle to retain their cultural identity and their traditions, but are overwhelmed in the predominantly white society in which they seek acceptance and live out their economic lives. English is highly valued in the Indian community; it is the medium of education in Indian schools and this is readily accepted and promoted, but we believe that the motivation for acquiring English is largely pragmatic – Indians have to make their way in an English-speaking world. The comparatively rapid receding of prominent Ind E pronunciation variables indicates that this manner of speech does not have an integrative value. To members of the white SA community, caricatures on stage and radio associated with extreme Ind E suggest such stereotypic properties as occupations as street vendors and small shopkeepers eager to bargain rather than sell, ingratiation and obsequiousness. Mann (1963) found, however, that whites rated Indians as friendlier, more hard-working and thrifty and as making better use of opportunities than themselves.

In a substantial sociolinguistic study of Afrikaans in the Coloured community, Klopper (1976) confirmed the extensive English-Afrikaans bil-ingualism reported for this community and the code mixing and switching referred to above. Col E is so clearly delineated in the perception of white South Africans, and the conflation of it with Coloured Afrikaans so commonly recognized, that Klopper's findings can be taken as valid for English also. Klopper's findings generally support comments I have made elsewhere:

> Coloured English, on the other hand, seems to be cultivated and to symbolize group identity and solidarity. Its use supports the social image of the "South African Cockney" and some of the positive attributes associated with the traditional Cockney. White society is aware of this image and demonstrates some affection for the stereotype, while nevertheless stigmatizing Coloured English strongly in terms of overt values. The Coloured community, particularly in the Cape, has long occupied a low socio-economic stratum, and the need to reinforce "covert values" in group norms is compelling even in adult life. The extent to which Coloured English represents defiance and rejection of the power structure in South African society needs to be studied and, because of recent political events, might be stronger today than it has been in the past. (Lanham, 1982, p. 348.)

Klopper's report does emphasize, however, the clear socio-economic stratification of Coloured society and the strong tendency of the upper class to disclaim identity with the lower class and reject its norms of behaviour. Klopper's evidence shows that the extreme form of Coloured speech and behaviour conveys as much stigma for Coloured society as it does for white South Africans. It is, nevertheless, cultivated as an expression of covert values of the society and its alienation from, and rejection of, the white society.

Black South Africans have a clear perception of their own English as distinct from other varieties of English, but little sensitivity to differences in the latter. This is discussed below in reporting on the only empirical study of black attitudes and perceptions relating to varieties of English.

Attitudes to English

We turn now to positive and negative attitudes of major social significance in terms of the motivations that promote them. The attitudes can be taken as being held by comparatively large numbers of South Africans and statements made about them are supported by empirical evidence.

Probably the most obvious of attitudes in the wider society is allegiance to

English as a denial of the ideology and values associated with Afrikaner nationalism. This attitude might be realized in behaviour such as a refusal to accept Afrikaans in any form of public and official communication and in the media, and the patronizing of only English-speaking institutions. Van der Merwe *et al.* (1974, chap. 2) demonstrate that the English-Afrikaans confrontation marks the deepest division in white SA society. According to the evidence provided by their survey "home language provides the key to most of the internal differences within the elite group, be they attitudinal or otherwise." They continue: "Ethnic background, religious preference and political preference [i.e. ideological allegiance in the specifically South African sense] are strongly differentiated." Those who hold positive attitudes to English by virtue of this motivation would certainly include the 48 percent of Schlemmer's (1976) sample of white English speakers who chose to be called "English South Africans" (or "British"), specifically not "South Africans". These in turn include his "anglophiles" defined as "people who perceive themselves as English-speaking South Africans as opposed to South Africans and identify with international Anglo-Saxon culture" (p. 108). The anglophiles are said to show the "greatest resistance to Afrikaans."

The attitude *vis-à-vis* Afrikaans discussed in the previous paragraph extends across ethnic groups. The 123,000 members of the Coloured community who claim English as mother-tongue have at some time or another undergone a language-loyalty switch implying a rejection of whatever Afrikaans symbolizes. The unknown number of upwardly mobile Coloured families recently reported to have switched to English as mother-tongue may be evincing the same attitude, possibly linked to English as a symbol of social prestige. One suspects that the switch to English does demonstrate a motivated rejection of Afrikaans because there is a movement afoot to counter this switch in language loyalty, with Coloured leaders proclaiming that "It (Afrikaans) is, after all, our language."

Connotations of prestige as motivation for positive attitudes to English as such (i.e. not to the prestige accent, see below) are evident mainly among second-language users of English. Black South Africans have a "love and esteem" for English in the words of E. Mphahlele, a prominent black South African writer. Evidence of this attitude is found in the rejection by black South Africans of the title "English-as-second-language" when applied to their qualifications. At least one South African university has abandoned this title for a degree for this reason. Those who were affronted by the former title, together with many black teachers, simply say: "English is a second first language for us." The motivation of blacks in acquiring English nevertheless remains instrumental rather than integrative. Very few families have English as home language. Schuring (1977) summarized his findings by giving the most obvious of his conclusions as:

> For black South Africans between 15 and 54 years of age, English has greater prestige while Afrikaans has greater utility value (*pragmatiese waarde*). [My translation from Afrikaans; p. 66.]

Schuring's findings do make it clear, however, that in the black South Africans' affinity for English at the present time, prestige is linked with the value of English as an international medium for higher education. The association between English and black attitudes to education has been made clear in the reasons for the Soweto unrest in 1976 and developments in education following that event.

In a recent inquiry into black South African perception of, and attitudes to, English accents in SA society, I used a group of forty-five primary school teachers from Transkei (at least 10 years of schooling and 2 years of college, and wide exposure to white society). One important finding was that, apart from Bl E which 100 percent identified correctly, there was a remarkably low level of ability to identify and distinguish other accents. Forty-one per cent identified a particularly obvious variety of Afrik E as American English; 25 percent said it was the "English of England." British RP was identified by 80 percent as the English of SA. Resp SAE was said to be the "English of England" by 48 percent; as American English by 23 percent; 23 percent said it was the English of Afrikaners.

In questions relating to the social status and occupation of each of the four speakers, Resp SAE was most highly valued, followed by British RP. In this regard, Bl E was negatively evaluated (by 57 percent), obviously reflecting attitudinal norms of the wider society. In response to the question as to which form of English should be taught to black children, 49 percent of those responding to this question chose British RP and 26 percent Resp SAE (which 48 percent had associated with Britain).

Attitudes of the Afrikaans-speaking population towards English are complex and best interpreted as a love–hate relationship. Hate stems from the promotion of Afrikaans as a symbol of the Afrikaner cause and sense of nation, and the long struggle against British domination. This attitude has been apparent from the end of the last century and there is evidence that it hardly existed before then (Lanham and Macdonald, 1979, pp. 9 ff). Until then, English (i.e. the language, not necessarily the speakers) carried connotations of *geleerdheid* (good education) and social prestige for Afrikaners; these connotations appear to underlie whatever "love" there is for English today.

Hauptfleisch (1977) analysed data from the Human Sciences Research Council Languages Survey (HSRC LS) of 1973 covering language use and attitudes among white South Africans. He reported that 25 percent of the 18–24 age-group of Afrikaners would like to be taken as English in the company of English speakers and 58 percent of this group feel that the ability to speak English is prestigious. Of interest are the contrary attitudes of the 55-plus age-group; only 7.5 percent wish to be taken as English speakers. Van der Merwe *et al.* (1974, chaps 2 and 10) in their study of white elites note that Afrikaners acquiring the highest socio-economic status in the industrial cities make up the majority involved in the trend to anglicization; that is the threat to the Afrikaner cause clearly recognized and combatted by the Church and the Nationalist Party. Hauptfleisch (1979) studied cases of language-loyalty switch in the HSRC LS sample of 1607 persons and found that: "Almost all language shift . . . has been from Afrikaans to English as language of identity" (49 cases against 3 switching from English to Afrikaans).

Attitudes relating to what white English speakers recognize as the standard are of particular interest because they run quite contrary to those prevailing in Australia whose English origins, traditions, and form of English are closest of all Commonwealth countries to those of SA. I have provided strong empirical and circumstantial evidence of the fact that "near-British-English" represents the standard (in the sense of correctness and high social status) for the influential sectors of the English-speaking SA; conversely, obviously local speech is non-standard and strongly stigmatized (Lanham and Macdonald 1979). Supporting this claim as to the identity of the standard variety, is the strong pressure of public opinion on the South African Broadcasting Corporation (a government body with a monopoly on radio and television broadcasting) preventing the main newscasts and serious drama being presented in obviously local accents. The success of their efforts can be gauged from the comments of John Simpson, the BBC's southern African correspondent:

> Listening to the radio is like switching on the BBC Home Service in the days before Suez . . . the accents of the English services are impeccably upper middle-class. It's only when people are interviewed that you hear authentic South African being spoken – the accent, after all, of the majority of whites here. (*Johannesburg Star*, 16 April 1973).

In a commentary on SA English, Partridge (1971) remarked cynically that "the English-speaking population . . . is touchy only in its uncritical reverence for the Received English pronunciation." British English, or what is perceived as such, remains the "voice of authority" and the model of correct English enshrined in the hearts of most influential English-speaking South Africans. (In Lanham and Macdonald, 1979, sections VII, VIII, socio-historical reasons are adduced for this.) English-speaking whites do, however, accept both a formal (near-British-English) and an informal standard (Resp SAE). Those in SA society without sensitivity to the fine detail of British speech and behaviour adopt the latter as model and positive attitudes to it have been found experimentally (Lanham and Macdonald, 1979, section V).

Those committed to "near-British-English" by virtue of its expression of the standard, hence those most likely to accept its speakers as a reference group, are difficult to define in usual demographic terms. (SA has no white working class, but class divisions exist. The differentials are, however, not easy to name.) Perhaps this group is best defined negatively: they are the majority of white mother-tongue English speakers who do not subscribe to the "SA tradition in social values." I see the SA tradition in social values as the present-day reflection of the frontier tradition of the nineteenth century (Lanham and Macdonald, 1979). The adherents to this tradition are therefore close to the world-view and values of the typical Afrikaner: they value the South African identity, independence, and masculinity; they are patriotic, gregarious, strongly conforming to in-group norms, and have adulation for sport and sportsmen. In sum, these amount to the covert values of the society and for this reason positive and negative attitudes to near-British-English are an individual as well as a group response. For example: some young, upper-class males, identified by all criteria relating to the "British tradition in social values," give clear indication in their speech as having adopted "typical local man" as reference group by flaunting Ext SAE in formal and informal situations.

English as first or second language has pre-eminence in SA society in its communicative power and importance; social approbation far outweighs disapprobation. Negative attitudes to English are located mainly in the Afrikaans-speaking population among those who retain the animosities fostered in the period of advancing Afrikaner nationalism. For them the *taalstryd* (language battle) still rages.

References

EDELSTEIN, M.V. (1972) *What do Young Africans Think?* Johannesburg: Institute of Race Relations.

HAUPTFLEISCH, T. (1977) *Language Loyalty in South Africa.* Vol. 1: *Bilingual Policy in South Africa – Opinions of White Adults in Urban Areas.* Pretoria: Human Sciences Research Council.

HAUPTFLEISCH, T. (1979) *Language Loyalty in South Africa.* Vol. 3: *Motivation to Language Use: Opinions and Attitudes of White Adults in Urban Areas.* Pretoria: Human Sciences Research Council.

KLOPPER, R.M. (1976) Sosiaal Gestratifiseerde Taalgebruik in die Kaapstadse Kleurlingge- meenskap – 'n Fonologiese Ondersoek. Unpublished thesis. University of Stellenbosch.

LABOV, W. (1964) "Stages in the acquisition of standard English." In: R. Shuy (ed.), *Social Dialects and Language Learning.* Champaign, Ill.: National Council of Teachers.

LABOV, W. (1966) *The Social Stratification of English in New York City.* Washington, D.C.: Center for Applied Linguistics.

LABOV, W. (1967) "The effect of social mobility on linguistic behaviour." *International Journal of American Linguistics*, Part II, **33**, 58–75.

LANHAM L.W. (1982) "English in South Africa." In *English as World Language*, edited by R. W. Bailey and M. Görlach, pp. 324–52, Ann Arbor: University of Michigan Press.

LANHAM L.W. and C. A. MACDONALD (1979) *The Standard in South African English and its Social History.* Heidelberg: Julius Groos.

MACDONALD, C.A. (1975) An investigation of the responses to four South African English dialects, and of the values esteemed by white South African university students. Unpublished dissertation. University of the Witwatersrand, Johannesburg.

MANN, J.W. (1963) "Rivals of different rank." *Journal of Social Psychology*, **68**, 11–28.

PARTRIDGE, A.C. (1971) In: Potgieter, D.J. (ed.), *The Standard Encyclopedia of Southern Africa*, Vol. IV. Cape Town: Nasou.

SCHLEMMER, L. (1976) "English speaking South Africans today: Identity and integration into the broader national community." In: A. de Villiers (ed.), *English-speaking South Africa Today.* Cape Town: Oxford University Press.

SCHURING, G.K. (1977) *'n Veeltalige samelewing*, Deel 2. *Afrikaans en Engels onder swart mense in die RSA.* Pretoria: Human Sciences Research Council.

VAN DER MERWE, H.W., ASHLEY M.J., CHARTON, N.C.J., and HUBER, B.J. (1974) *White South African Elites.* Cape Town: Juta.

VAN WYK, E.B. (1978) "Language contact and bilingualism." In L. W. Lanham and K. P. Prinsloo (eds.), *Language and Communication Studies in South Africa: Current issues and directions in research and inquiry.* Cape Town: Oxford University Press.

VORSTER, JAN and PROCTOR, LESLIE (1976) "Black attitudes to 'white' languages in South Africa: A pilot study." *Journal of Psychology*, **92**, no. 1, 103–108.

WATTS, H.L. (1976) "A social and demographic portrait of English-speaking white South Africans." In A de Villiers (ed.), *English-speaking South Africa Today.* Cape Town: Oxford University Press.

Chapter 5

Symbol of Powerlessness and Degeneracy, or Symbol of Solidarity and Truth? Paradoxical Attitudes Toward Pidgins and Creoles

JOHN R. RICKFORD AND ELIZABETH CLOSS TRAUGOTT

I. It don't take you nowhere. It don't do good to a person . . . If one can pick up, you know, good English, you know, you see, he can spread it among his children . . . But if you start with the different kind of Creole language on them, you know, you'll make them go out the wrong side.

II. . . . yuh gat to larn fuh larn yuh, yuh own language, yuh know . . . Abee na waan dem Englishman teachin an ting da no mo, man. Dem ting da mus' done ". . . you have to learn your, your own language, you know . . . We don't want those English people's teaching and so on any more, man. Those things must end."[1]

Introduction

The stigma associated with non-standard language varieties in general is associated *par excellence* with pidgin and creole varieties, which are even more divergent from the standard language than the average non-standard dialect in Britain or the U.S.A., and which tend to be spoken by people of the "wrong" ethnic background or social status. As has often been noted, the importance of a language derives from its users. The consequences of this relationship have been pointed out by Dell Hymes for attitudes to pidgins and creoles:

> Because of their origins, however, their association with poorer and darker members of a society, and through perpetuation of misleading stereotypes – such as that a pidgin is merely a broken or baby-talk version of another language – most interest, even where positive, has considered them merely curiosities. Much of the interest and information, scholarly as well as public, has been prejudicial.[2]

Like other non-standard varieties, however, pidgins and creoles have also been viewed as symbols of truth and reality, and embraced as signals of solidarity. These positive attitudes are not always as visible on the surface as the negative ones, and are certainly reported less often in the literature. One early report, however, is the following from Hall:

> For the normal, unpretentious Haitian, use of Creole is the symbol of truth and reality, and French is the language of bluff, mystification, and duplicity.[3]

In the following pages we will explore the paradoxical combination of negative and positive attitudes which are found in communities where pidgin and creole varieties of English are spoken, beginning with general attitudes reflected in newspapers and literary works, and continuing with the more specific attitudes which the application of sociolinguistic survey techniques have revealed. First, however, we need to say a few words about what pidgins and creoles are.

Pidgins, Creoles, and Creole Continua

While the identification of a pidgin or a creole is often a matter of considerable debate among linguists,[4] initial working definitions such as the following will serve. A pidgin is nobody's native language. It arises in situations such as plantation life, trading, or military operations, where speakers of several mutually unintelligible languages come together, usually as social subordinates to a socially dominant minority who speak yet another language. In such situations, a new "mixed" language may develop for basic communication. Its vocabulary is usually drawn primarily from the prestige language of the dominant group, while its grammar retains many features of the native languages of the subordinate groups. The prestige language which supplies the bulk of the vocabulary is the one which is usually thought of as being "pidginized"; hence "pidgin English" rather than "pidgin Yoruba" or "pidgin Twi" for the pidgin emerging from contact between English traders and African slaves from a variety of language-backgrounds. It is as if the vocabulary provides the basic material, and pidginization refers to the techniques of working it into a usable garment. These techniques in turn depend on the ways of putting material together with which the subordinate groups are accustomed (i.e. the grammars of their native languages), plus some "universal" principles of reduction or simplification which speakers seem to draw on the world over when trying to communicate across linguistic barriers. Furthermore, the dominant group may change over time, as it so often did in the African-Caribbean slave trade, and this may result either in a full-scale change-over in the source of the vocabulary, or in a sprinkling of words from the languages of each of the groups which were formerly in control. In Guyanese Creole, for instance, the vocabulary is largely English-derived, but the residue of past colonial shifts in power is represented by words like *paaling* "fence" (from Dutch), *cabane* "hut, makeshift bed" (from French), and *pikni* "child" (from Portuguese).

Pidgins have typically developed in situations with slaves or other large work-forces from widely differing ethnic communities (as in the Caribbean, or in Hawaii), but they have also developed as the language of communication among traders, and even for general everyday affairs in multilingual countries, as in modern Nigeria, where West African Pidgin English is widely used, and Papua New Guinea, where Tok Pisin, otherwise known as New Guinea Pidgin English, is spoken by the majority of the population. In communities such as Nigeria or Papua New Guinea, the pidgin has become highly stabilized and developed, and functions as a *lingua franca* or general language of communication. Indeed, from the fifties, Tok Pisin has been one of the three main vehicles for communication in Papua New Guinea (formerly called New Guinea) for the House of Assembly: English, Tok Pisin, and Hiri Motu (a pidginized local language). English is used primarily for communication outside Papua New Guinea, while Tok Pisin is used for internal affairs. It has been used extensively for broadcasting and the press, and thus enjoys considerable positive evaluation, particularly over the native languages, of which there are a large number for so small an island, most of them mutually unintelligible. It is claimed that there are some 700 languages for a population of little over $2\frac{1}{2}$ million, and these languages belong to two different language groups: Austronesian and Papuan.[5]

When she did field work in New Guinea in the early seventies, Gillian Sankoff found that pidgin was often the norm not only in contexts where people from different regions were together, but also among people of the same area. Here, translated, is one conversation she recorded on the subject:

A. Even people from the same area don't speak their native language. They don't allow it, saying "Only Pidgin's all right." . . . If we speak our language when you're around you might say, "Hey, those two women must be mad at us or saying something bad about us two". So we don't like it, it's forbidden.
B. I think after a long time, there won't be any more Tok Ples (native languages), just Pidgin and English.

Frequently, pidgins serve limited functions, especially in their early stages. Except in a few unusual cases like Tok Pisin, they may be inadequate in the size of their lexicon, the complexity of syntactic structure, and range of styles for the range of uses to which native languages are put. When, as in the case of the slave-trade, transmission of the language from one generation to another is impossible or nearly so, a nativized pidgin, or "creole," may arise, largely developed by children of the pidgin speakers, a process which has been discussed extensively by Derek Bickerton in *Roots of Language*. This creole is a language with significantly greater lexical, syntactic, and stylistic possibilities than the pidgin, and capable of serving the range of functions which native use requires. However, in situations like that of Tok Pisin where the pidgin is used extensively for a wide variety of purposes, the grammar of adults may show the complication of grammatical machinery associated with a nativized pidgin or creole.[6]

When the creole does not coexist with the standard form of the language from which it draws most of its vocabulary, the creole will develop relatively independently, as it has in the case of Sranan, the creole of Surinam. Here the creole has a basically English-derived lexicon (remarkably well preserved after only sixteen years of English colonization between 1651 and 1667) with some Dutch (the colony belonged to the Dutch, except for two brief periods, between 1667 and 1946). When the creole continues to coexist with the standard form of the language from which it draws most of its vocabulary, however, we usually find progressive "decreolization," producing a continuum of varieties intermediate between the creole and the standard poles.[7]

Attitudes in the Mass Media

Within creole-speaking communities, the view of the creole publicly aired in the mass media has typically been one of self-deprecation, with educators and public officials (some never having spoken the creole themselves, others trying to conceal their association or competence) leading in the attack. One common charge is that the creole is not a real or legitimate language, this claim deriving from the erroneous but frequently-asserted claim that it has no grammar or is merely a mangled version of the standard. One example is provided in the following remarks about Sierra Leone Krio made at the turn of the century by L. J. Leopold, Principal of the Educational Institute in Sierra Leone:

> The Sierra Leone patois is a kind of invertebrate *omnium gatherum* of all sorts, a veritable *ola podrida* [sic] collected from many different languages without regard to harmony or precision: it is largely defective and sadly wanting in many of the essentials and details that make up and dignify a language. It is a standing menace and a disgrace hindering not only educational development but also the growth of civilization in the colony.[8]

Lest it be thought that such negative views are characteristic only of days long past, Guyanese Home Affairs Minister Stanley Moore is said to have "dubbed Creolese as a vulgar, rough and ready mode of expression," according to a 1981 newspaper account.[9] The reference to vulgarity here represents another cluster of negative views associated with creoles. The category-mistake of identifying prestigious language varieties with high morals and non-prestigious ones with low morals is age-old and by no means restricted to attitudes toward pidgins and creoles (cf. George Bernard Shaw's *Pygmalion*), but it finds a particularly ready outlet among some deprecators of these languages.

A third tendency is to view the creole as a symbol of social and political degradation (the attitude highlighted in our title), to the extent that it becomes a "pernicious and insulting idea" to advocate its introduction in any form in the public school system.[10] This particular attitude derives not only from the present-day associations of the creoles with "poorer and darker members of a society," but also from its historical associations with slavery, and with attempts to keep slaves subjugated by preventing them from becoming educated and informed. For instance, one Guyanese newspaper editorial written in the sixties advocated the upholding of standard English in the schools and society as a kind of trophy of war, wrested from the imperialists who had sought to deny slaves and ex-slaves the right to learn, live, and speak as those in power did.

The preceding quotations all come from newspapers, and represent one way in which the press can give us evidence of local attitudes: by direct quotation of attitudes, whether reported or printed in the form of editorials and letters to the editor. But there is another, more subtle means by which newspapers and other media give us information about attitudes: by the kinds of material which they choose to represent in creole versus standard. Comic and racy materials are often stereotypically rendered in the creole: the comic-strips, cartoons, and gossip-columns of newspapers, for instance, or the joke-shows of radio and TV. Straight reporting and editorializing about serious subjects is, by contrast, almost invariably in standard English.

Attitudes in Literature

Like non-standard dialects, pidgins and creoles have traditionally been used to inject comedy into a story, to present a pathetic character, or at best to suggest the folkways of the people who speak them. This is the kind of attitude that we can infer from such writings as Daniel Defoe's *Colonel Jacques* (about a Virginian who uses pidgin English), and Harris's *Nights with Uncle Remus* (where Daddy Jack, a former African slave, speaks a variety fairly close to Gullah, a creole still spoken in parts of South Carolina, Georgia, and Texas). Even writers like Ambrose Gonzales, who collected many Gullah tales in the 1920s and fictionalized them, in the preface to *The Black Border: Gullah Stories of the Carolina Coast*, speaks of the "grotesqueness" and "laziness" of the Gullah language, which he labels "jungle-talk."

Recently, however, more and more writers have been using pidgins and creoles in a different way – as a vehicle for the presentation of the cultures and rich communities in which these languages flourish, often as the voice of reality, truth, and genuineness in a world otherwise largely destructive (the colonial world) or corrupt (the go-getting, often fraudulent world of post-colonial governments). Some writers have come to use it as the sole vehicle of short stories and poems. Among them are Julia Peterkin who writes of South Carolina and Gullah speakers, Samuel Selvon (for example, *Ways of Sunlight*, 1957, set in Trinidad), Edward Brathwaite, who writes of Barbados, R. O. Robinson and Louise Bennett, whose works are set in Jamaica.[11] Especially conscious of the negative attitudes toward creole, Louise Bennett rightly points out that English has always been a mixed language in this impassioned plea against the suppression of the creole:[12]

BANS O' KILLING

So yuh a de man, me hear bout!
Ah yuh dem sey dah-teck
Whole heap o' English oat sey dat
Yuh gwine kill dialect!

Meck me get it straight Mass Charlie
For me noh quite undastan,
Yuh gwine kill all English dialect
Or jus Jamaica one? . . .

Yuh wi haffe get de Oxford book
O' English verse, an tear
Out Chaucer, Burns, Lady Grizelle
An plenty o' Shakespeare!

Wen yuh done kill "wit" and "humour"
Wen yuh kill "Variety"
Yuh wi haffe fine a way fe kill
Originality! . . .

Wit, humor, originality, poignancy, all these are functions to which the pidgin or creole may be put in literature. Above all, the multiplicity of languages and language varieties in a pidgin or creole-speaking society and the importance for survival to be able to command a range of styles often becomes a theme in itself. An amusing example can be found in Selvon's *An Island is a World*:

"I say, awful hot weather we're having, isn't it?" Ranjit, schooled for five years in the usual opening sentences about the weather English people use when they get together, had forgotten that Trinidadians don't really give a blast if it's hot or cool. He sat and crossed his legs, pulling up his trousers from the knees to preserve the seams. He spoke with a pseudo-Oxford accent.

Jennifer typed him at once in her mind, as she had typed all the others. The way they all spoke was ridiculous. It might have sounded all right in England; here in the house it always sounded pretentious, as if they were no longer Trinidadians but tourists paying the island a visit.

She decided to give him the usual treatment. "I ain't notice dat it making hot", she said to him in a flat voice, "must be how you just come back."[13]

A particularly elaborate portrayal of different attitudes to a pidgin (in this case West African Pidgin English) can be found in Chinua Achebe's novel *A Man of the People*. A novel about the corruptness of African politics in general, it is also about the politics of language, its abuse, and its potential. The corrupt and ridiculous minister attempts to speak primarily in "pure" English or sometimes in West African Pidgin English, never his native tongue, which he despises. On the occasions when he does use the pidgin, he exploits it as a way of "reaching the people" whom he pretends to love (but only uses to get votes), or in mimicking them. At the same time, the voice of common sense is expressed by his bodyguard and others who speak the pidgin in making interpretive and evaluative comments. The Minister, in other words, uses the standard language as a vehicle of self-promotion, and also of "bluff, mystification, and duplicity"; the association of standard language and morality is called into question. The bodyguard, on the other hand, uses the pidgin to express what he perceives as truth and reality; here morality and the non-standard language are linked. The pidgin is used in other ways too, most especially as the vehicle of intimate joking and excitement.

As an author, Achebe himself is in a double bind – for him English is of course the vehicle for international and even national success (the many languages spoken in Nigeria have almost inevitably allowed English to remain as the language of the educated, even after independence). He has therefore attempted to develop a distinctly African idiom for the English he writes, a literary language with its own characteristics and its own prestige, dependent on, but not wholly the same as, the British English of the former colonialists.[14]

In short, many writers seek to delineate "a possible alternative to the European cultural tradition which has been imposed on us and which we have more or less accepted and absorbed, for obvious historical reasons, as the only way of going about our business."[15] This alternative is multilingual, and language plays a key role in it; depending on who uses it and in what context, the pidgin or creole may be an object of ridicule, or the only true way in which to express the richness of the human condition, the only vehicle of creativity, or the only hope for escape from colonial oppression.

Attitudes in the Villages and Towns

We have dealt so far with the attitudes toward English pidgins and creoles conveyed in the mass media and in literature, but both of these tend to be avenues of expression for only a minority (albeit a powerful and influential one). What about the attitudes of the men and women who live in the towns and villages where pidgins and creoles are spoken, and who rarely have either opportunity or inclination to express themselves in the media? Their attitudes tend to be less well known or written about, but they can be gleaned from three kinds of evidence: the popular reaction to materials in pidgin or creole, anecdotal reports of conversations with individuals, and sociolinguistic surveys conducted with socially and ethnically stratified groups.

The popular reaction to materials in pidgins and creoles is typically far more positive than the mass-media sentiments reported above might have led one to suspect. In the Caribbean, for instance, folklore and music (e.g. calypso and reggae) making use of the creole have always been popular, and *The Harder They Come* – a recent Jamaican film with creole dialog and English subtitles – was a box-office hit. In Papua New Guinea, the popularity of the evangelical publication *Wantok* soared after it began carrying the adventures of the Phantom translated into pidgin (a sample dialog is, *Fantom, yu pren bilong me* "Phantom, you are a true friend of mine"). And in Hawaii, a recent illustrated glossary of the local pidgin English, entitled *Pidgin to da Max*, had gone through six printings for a total of 80,000 copies within its first four months of publication, this in a total Hawaiian population of only 950,000. Its back cover, with a picture of a plump mother-figure saying reproachfully: *How many times I tol' you . . . NO TALK LI' DAT!!* mocks the conventionally-reported attitudes towards pidgin-creole varieties, as does the commercial success of this book and similar ventures elsewhere.

Anecdotes about individually expressed attitudes can be very revealing, but they provide quite unsystematic and sometimes conflicting evidence. On the one hand, individuals are quoted as expressing negative attitudes similar to those of the "big guns" in the media (as exemplified by the quotation at the beginning of this paper). On the other hand, often somewhat more positive reactions are reported. For instance, Fanakalo, a creole language in Zimbabwe whose vocabulary is about 24 percent English, 70 percent Nguni (mainly Zulu), and 6 percent Afrikaans,[16] has reportedly been described by Sir Harry Johnston as an "ugly and stupid jargon," and the South African mining industry apparently wants to replace it in the mines with English or Afrikaans. But as Luis Ferraz, to whom we are grateful for the preceding information, also noted:

> However, my last informant, a hotel waiter in Johannesburg, told me that Africans had no dislike for Fanakalo. On the contrary, he said, if I were to be walking down the street and asked for some water in Fanakalo, they would give it to me very gladly.

Sociolinguistic group surveys provide more systematic and reliable evidence on native-speaker language attitudes, but these are few and far between as far as pidgin-creole speaking communities are concerned. Donald Winford, who recently administered a survey questionnaire to 112 trainee teachers in Trinidad, reported that in the response to a set of questions about the appropriateness of Trinidadianese in education and the media:

> . . . we once more find no unanimously held set of values about the language of Trinidadians. The hostility of a few to Trinidadianese is matched by the hostility of a few to "correct English" . . .[17]

In Guyana, Rickford recently conducted a Matched-Guise survey with twenty-four villagers evenly divided between the lower-income Estate Class (cane-cutters and other laborers) and the lower middle-class-income Non-Estate Class (shopkeepers, clerks, and skilled tradesmen).[18] In the Matched-Guise technique, respondents are played samples of different speech varieties, and asked to evaluate the speakers in each case. The samples, however, are actually produced by one or more speakers recurring in the guise of different varieties, and the different evaluations are therefore attributed to the stereotypes attributed to each variety.[19] Rickford found that there was unanimity among the respondents in so far as they associated more standard speech with better jobs, and more creole-like speech with less prestigious jobs. But the two social classes tended to disagree on the nature of the association, with the Non-Estate respondents believing that the more standard speech itself contributes to one's getting a better job, and the Estate respondents feeling that the association merely reflects the way things are, the characteristic speech of the *status quo*. Moreover, in their evaluations of Matched Guise "speakers" on a friendship scale, the reflected attitudes of the two groups diverged even more, with the Estate Class respondents warming most to the distinctly creole "speaker," and the Non-Estate respondents warming to him least. These results agree in part with studies in other communities which indicate that non-standard varieties often have a high affective or solidarity value, but they demonstrate further that the solidarity ratings cannot be predicted on the basis of assumptions regarding the standard or non-standard varieties as such, but on the usage of the respondents themselves. Herein lie some keys to the conflicting attitudes which we sometimes find when we step out of the mass media into the streets: the extent to which the pidgin-creole varieties are positively evaluated depends partly on the kinds of people we ask and the kinds of dimensions that we tap.

Conclusion

While we have discussed attitudes to pidgins and creoles largely without regard to the effect of political changes, it must be emphasized that pidgins and creoles owe their existence to political situations. What they have in common is a mixed society which is normally highly stratified, and in which the majority normally have little access to a standard language. But the nature of the mix and the reasons for lack of access may be very different in different communities. Necessarily, changing attitudes depend heavily on these differences. For example, in Papua New Guinea, limited access to the native languages is a function of the mountainous terrain, and the small number of speakers of any one language. The exceptionally positive attitude toward Tok Pisin can be attributed in part to the fact that it was never the language of slavery. Although indisputably a product of colonialism, it is nevertheless a language that has developed in (former) New Guinea, and is not as markedly foreign as English. As a result, it can well serve for many Papuans as the symbol of the new nationalism.[20] A very different reason for positive attitudes to the creole can be found in Belize. Creole English, which in this case is associated with slavery, was for long held in contempt, but has recently become a target of "refocusing" of interest, as against the originally more prestigious Spanish, in reaction to the threat of a Guatemalan take-over.[21] Yet another context for refocusing can be found in the linguistic rebellion against colonialism and European or middle-class values that has led to the popularity of "Dread Talk," or Rastafarian speech among young Jamaicans.[22]

To be a pidgin or creole speaker means to live in a multi-dimensional sociolinguistic world, and it therefore inevitably means to live with paradoxes. But the particular mix of these paradoxes will continually shift according to the changes in the socioeconomic and political situation.

Notes

1. Speaker I is "Oxford," a retired car-driver, speaker II is "Reefer," a militant cane-cutter, both recorded by Rickford in Cane Walk, Guyana, in 1975. See John R. Rickford, "Standard and non-standard language attitudes in a Creole continuum," *Society for Caribbean Linguistics, Occasional Paper 16*, Trinidad, 1983, p. 3 (also forthcoming in Nessa Wolfson and Joan Manes, eds., *Language of Inequality*, The Hague, Mouton).

2. Dell Hymes, ed., *Pidginization and Creolization of Languages*, New York, Cambridge University Press, 1971, p. 3.

3. Robert A. Hall, *Pidgin and Creole Languages*, Ithaca: Cornell University Press, 1966, p. 133; cf. also Karl Reisman, "Cultural and linguistic ambiguity in a West Indian village," *Afro-American Anthropology: Contemporary Perspectives*, ed. N. E. Whitten and J. F. Szwed, New York, Free Press, 1970, p. 40, on similar attitudes in Antigua.

4. For some major works on pidgins and creoles, see Derek Bickerton, *Dynamics of a Creole System*, New York, Cambridge University Press, 1975, and *Roots of Language*, Ann Arbor, Karoma, 1981; Dell Hymes, ed., *Pidginization and Creolization of Languages*, New York, Cambridge University Press, 1971; Albert Valdman, ed., *Pidgin and Creole Linguistics*, Bloomington, Indiana University Press, 1977; Albert Valdman and Arnold Highfield, eds., *Theoretical Orientations in Creole Studies*, New York, Academic Press, 1980.

5. Cf. Gillian Sankoff, "Political power and linguistic inequality in Papua New Guinea," and "Multilingualism in Papua New Guinea," *The Social Life of Language*, Philadelphia, University of Pennsylvania Press, 1980; S. A. Wurm and P. Mühlhäusler, "Attitudes towards New Guinea Pidgin and English," *New Guinea and Neighboring Areas: a Sociolinguistic Laboratory*, ed. S. A. Wurm, The Hague, Mouton, 1979.

6. For the development of Tok Pisin Creole, cf. Gillian Sankoff and Suzanne Laberge, "On the acquisition of native speakers by a language," *The Social Life of Language*, Philadelphia, University of Pennsylvania Press, 1980. According to some definitions, Tok Pisin itself would be a creole because of its extended repertoire.

7. John R. Rickford, "What happens in decreolization," *Pidginization and Creolization as Language Acquisition*, ed. R. W. Andersen, Rowley, Mass., Newbury House, 1983.

8. *Sierra Leone Weekly News*, 19 Jan. 1901, quoted in Leo Spitzer, "Creole attitudes toward Krio: an historical survey," *Sierra Leone Language Review*, V (1966), p. 41.

9. *Sunday Chronicle*, Guyana, 15 Feb. 1981, p. 4.

10. Vera Johns, *Kingston Star*, Jamaica, cited in Frederic G. Cassidy, "Teaching Standard English to speakers of Creole in Jamaica, West Indies," *Report of the Twentieth Annual Round Table Meeting on Linguistics and Language Studies*, ed. James E. Alatis, Washington, D.C., Georgetown University Press, 1970, p. 208.

11. For a sketch of the history of pidgins and creoles in literature, see Loreto Todd, *Pidgins and Creoles*, London, Routledge and Kegan Paul, 1974; also Robert B. LePage, "Dialect in West Indian literature", *Journal of Commonwealth Literature*, VII (1969), 1–7; Jean D'Costa, "The West Indian novelist and language: a search for a literary medium," *Papers from the Third Biennial Conference of the Society for Caribbean Linguistics*, Aruba, 1980; Mary Hope Lee, "Ethnographic statement in the Nigerian novel with special reference to

pidgin," *Readings in Creole Studies*, ed. Ian F. Hancock *et al.*, Ghent, Belgium, E. Story-Scientia, 1979.

12. Excerpted from Louise Bennett, *Jamaica Labrish*, with notes and introduction by Rex Nettleford, Sangsters Bookstores, Jamaica, 1966, p. 218–219. Reprinted by permission of Sangsters Bookstores.

13. Samuel Selvon, *An Island is a World*, London, Allen Wingate, 1955, p. 34, cited in Stephen A. Bernhardt, "Dialect and style shifting in the fiction of Samuel Selvon," *Papers from the Third Biennial Conference of the Society for Caribbean Linguistics*, Aruba, 1980.

14. For fuller discussion, see Elizabeth Closs Traugott and Mary L. Pratt, *Linguistics for Students of Literature*, New York, Harcourt Brace Jovanivich, Inc., 1980, pp. 386–389.

15. Edward Brathwaite, *Jazz and the West Indian Novel*, quoted in Marina Maxwell, "Towards a revolution in the arts," *Savacou*, II (1970), p. 19.

16. A. L. Epstein, "Linguistic innovation and culture on the Copperbelt, Northern Rhodesia," *Readings in the Sociology of Language*, ed. Joshua Fishman, The Hague, Mouton, 1968.

17. Donald Winford, "Teacher attitudes toward language varieties in a Creole community," *International Journal of the Sociology of Language*, VIII (1976), 45–75.

18. Rickford, 1982, *op. cit.*

19. Wallace Lambert, "A social psychology of bilingualism," *The Journal of Social Issues*, XXIII (1967), 91–109.

20. Wurm and Mühlhäusler, *op. cit.*

21. R. B. Le Page, "Theoretical aspects of sociolinguistic studies in Pidgin and Creole languages," Valdman, *op. cit.*

22. Mervyn Alleyne, *Comparative Afro-American*, Ann Arbor, Karoma, 1980.

V: *Reactions: Personal and Professional*

Introduction

SIDNEY GREENBAUM

THE papers in this section are written by persons professionally concerned with the English language. They represent different viewpoints; creative writing, literary criticism, dialectology, linguistics, stylistics, language education, rhetoric, and composition.

In addition to their other professional roles, Morton Bloomfield and Donald Davie are college teachers of English literature. They are probably representative of literature teachers in expressing strongly conservative views about the use of the English language. Bloomfield argues the case for a prescriptivist approach to usage questions. Writing also from the point of view of a poet, Davie urges that students be taught to write correct, clear, and elegant English. More liberal views are presented by Raven McDavid and Susan Miller. As a dialectologist, McDavid is an expert on variation in the English language of the United States. He explains what one needs to do if one wants to become informed about usage. Writing as an administrator, teacher, and researcher concerned with the teaching of freshman college composition, Miller reflects on the current literacy crisis in the United States. She emphasizes the danger for the teaching of writing in making a sharp distinction between basics (correctness of language) and composition (organization of writing directed to a specific readership for a specific purpose).

The final three papers deal directly with the formal teaching of English in the United States. Writing on the situation in the elementary school, Jerrie Scott and Geneva Smitherman assess the effect of teachers' unfavourable attitudes toward the language of their students, particularly those belonging to minority groups; they propose strategies for changing the attitudes. Baird Shuman discusses several areas in which public attitudes impinge on the teaching of English in the secondary school: the teaching of grammar and teaching about language in general, the treatment of students who speak non-standard dialects or who are bilingual, censorship of the language of literature, calls for a return to the basics, and minimum competency tests. James Sledd draws on a long career in college teaching to comment on the low standards of student writing in the colleges. His paper includes detailed criticism of a highly popular writing manual for college students.

Chapter 1

The Question of Correctness

MORTON W. BLOOMFIELD

A LANGUAGE has to reach a certain degree of sophistication and respect by its users before its speakers begin to worry about correctness[1], but once that stage is completely reached, as it was with English in the last part of the eighteenth century, fierce debate often ensues about what is acceptable and what is not. In the English-speaking world today, there are two groups on opposing sides in this debate: the prescriptionists, who issue pronouncements on what is "correct" and who are generally opposed to change, and the permissivists who are ready to accept new expressions – and even worse in the eyes of the prescriptionists – to violate some of the traditional rules of English grammar and to confuse the meanings of certain words (or what are assumed to be their meanings, sometimes wrongly). The prescriptionist–permissivist quarrel is largely confined to the English used in writing and to people conscious of language and its use.

Prescriptionists have widespread popular support among the educated and those who consider themselves educated. It is the basic language philosophy of most intellectuals, of those who hold positions of importance in society, of the large number of members of society who aspire to those positions. These people speak and write a variety of English which belongs for the most part to the literary tradition of England and America. They tend to use in speech and especially in writing a more rule-bound variety of English and what they think to be a more traditional variety of English – the best known dialect of English.

Strictly speaking, everyone has a unique dialect, while understanding dialects of other English speakers and occasionally using them. In writing, however, there are fewer distinctions. We roughly divide language into dialects on the basis of general similarity. Social dialects are often forces of social cohesion, creating group loyalties and contributing to a group's sense of specialness and, in some cases, superiority.[2] Some of these groups, like rock musicians and adolescents, disregard "correctness" and favor innovations; others, like writers and intellectuals, dislike innovation and emphasize "correctness." The differences reflect more general differences between radical and conservative attitudes. Support for change in language tends to accompany a desire for political change.

Those who speak a variety of English that tends to be traditional attempt to maintain their mode of writing, and to some extent speaking, by appealing to the notion of "correctness." Most people, and especially the traditionalists, when they think about their language at all, think of it as fixed and unchanging.

Some believe that the standard for all languages, except for vocabulary, was fixed by Latin grammar once and for all, a legacy of an educational system that once stressed the importance of Latin. Most, however, are not even aware of the fact that language – especially their own – has a history.

Our first formal training in language presents it dogmatically. We are corrected by parents, relatives, teachers, and older children who hear our "errors." In school we are taught "rules of grammar" (when grammar is taught at all) and some exceptions to the rules. Many students, in fact, learn what rudiments of grammar they know when they study a foreign language and there, too, teachers emphasize correct usage. Language is usually taught as either right or wrong (as it probably should be for most children in the early years) and, by early adolescence, we have normally developed a fixed repertoire of language structures and a relatively fixed vocabulary. We therefore tend to think of language as fixed, unless we deliberately change our speech as part of a rebellion against our education, parents, or social class.

Prescriptionists have occasionally won battles. The -*ing* [ɪŋ] pronunciation ending of the present participle, largely because of its spelling, won out over the -*in* [ən] ending prevalent in the nineteenth century. School teachers who knew little of the history of the language and of the reasons for its traditional spelling succeeded in reinstating the current educated pronunciation. But prescriptionists usually lose because language is not fixed; its structure changes through time. Words and phrases fall out of favor; new words and phrases enter the vocabulary; and words extend their meaning to keep up with changes in the world of events.

Language change is not the same as change in the world of nature. There, objects are destroyed or transformed. In language, words or phrases are reconstructed and only rarely drop completely out of use; the system is renovated to ensure its continuity and its functioning. A language which does not change dies. Latin, for example, is kept alive by the Vatican through a Commission that recommends usage changes to keep pace with changes in contemporary life. The Language Academy of Israel does the same with Hebrew so as to maintain the modern form of Biblical Hebrew. Because modern Hebrew, unlike modern Latin, is a spoken language, it is less dependent on its "authority" than Latin is; but both committees have a difficult task preserving language standards.

Living languages, like all human creations and indeed like human beings themselves, are subject to change, and English, especially in the United States, seems to be more vulnerable to pressures than most Western languages. Why this should be is a complex question. For one thing, there is no established authority – no Academy – which watches over the language as there is in France, for example. For another, English speakers, especially in the United States, no longer have a tradition of strictness in the teaching of English. Third, the United States lacks an hereditary upper class, which tends to be conservative. Finally, the American tradition of an open society and its stress on individualism contribute to the willingness of Americans to consider, if not readily accept, change.

The good-usage problem is greatest in written, not oral, language. A number of shibboleths of usage apply only to punctuation, to rather fine points of syntax, and to words and phrases which are rarely used in conversation.

Once we recognize that language inevitably changes, we are confronted with the conflict between change and stability. Should we struggle to hold the line? Should we worry about correctness? If we hold the line, where should we hold it? These questions have exercised speakers of English since the mid-nineteenth century, and Americans in particular have taken them to heart.

The focus on "usage" as the arbiter of correct English started in the late seventeenth century. The *OED*'s first reference to the use of the term as a linguistic criterion is dated 1697 in an essay by Defoe. Many eighteenth-century writers and scholars, including Samuel Johnson, Robert Lowth, Joseph Priestly and George Campbell, employed the term. Only Priestly gets full marks for consistency from modern historians of the language. The others pay tribute on occasion to usage but do not adhere to the principle consistently. We can trace their laxness to the fact that "usage" was not reasonably defined until the twentieth century. It tended earlier to mean "usage of the educated class."

As knowledge of language accumulated and fewer linguistic scholars believed in the literal truth of the Bible and in particular the story of the Tower of Babel, the way was opened for the notion of good usage as the criterion of correctness and by the first quarter of the nineteenth century it became widespread. But as the number of "usage" supporters increased, so did the number of prescriptionists.[3]

In recent years, however, permissivists in particular have flourished. They have pointed out that language must accommodate contemporary trends, must be flexible and responsive to human change. The vast majority of them, however, do not ascribe to the "anything goes" school. Jeremy Warburg, who wrote an essay on "Notions of Correctness" at the end of Randolph Quirk's *The Use of English* (London: Longmans, 1968) and who strongly attacked the prescriptionist position, writes (p. 358):

> This is not, of course to say that we should have no standards, anything goes, whatever is is right; only that we should have realistic, helpful [standards].

All serious students of our language, even those who attack prescriptionists, will probably agree that by employing usage as the criterion of correctness one does not mean that there are not certain usages which should be favored over others in particular situations. Everything does not "go." Yet most linguists do not think that this point needs emphasizing. What they think needs emphasizing is the danger of prescribing. They want those concerned about language use to share their confidence that "usage" alone is enough to answer our questions about choice of words, tone, grammatical rules, and so forth.

The permissivists are mainly professional linguists but include, as we have indicated above, people who tend to resist restraints of any sort. Serious linguists are deeply aware of the inevitability of change in language: Change is everywhere and especially in language, they argue. Their acceptance of the inevitability of change induces many of them to ignore attitudes that stress correctness in language.[4] The fact that language changes does not, however, require us to speed up the process.

The criterion of usage *per se* is not terribly useful for most purposes when one is faced with a choice of alternatives or when one wonders what the usage is. What we still need is a careful analysis of the term. In our list of criteria we have to include audience, good taste, common sense, and social context. In effect, we must recommend to some extent a prescriptionist modification of usage.

A sensible prescriptionist view should not maintain that language is static. Language should not be rigidly fixed according to the arbitrary preferences of the late seventeenth-century, eighteenth, and early nineteenth-century grammarians and literary figures. Nor must it be based on the rules of Latin grammar. Good usage means appropriate usage and allows for an educated level of English as much as for a level which denies rules beyond the simple criterion of being understood.

Prescription to some degree is normal in all languages. A prudent prescriptionism is justified not only by human nature but also by the social dimensions of language.

Noam Chomsky, who has revolutionized modern linguistics, wrote in 1966–1967 that "a concern for the literary standard language – prescriptivism in its more sensible manifestations – is as legitimate as an interest in colloquial speech.[5] In a later and extremely important article, "The case for Prescriptive Grammar,"[6] Geoffrey Nunberg has presented the case for modified prescription with force, linguistic sophistication and elegance, claiming that "linguists have often been as uncritical in their condemnation of prescriptive grammar as others are in its defense" (p. 31). Nunberg stresses that the relatively new subject of sociolinguistics should, and to some extent does, take prescriptivism seriously, even when these specialists disapprove of it. Nunberg repeatedly emphasizes the complexity of the problem and stresses the symbolic importance of the few "rules" which prescriptionists highlight.

A sensible prescriptivism assumes a verbal universe in which there are still values and magic. If language is only a tool for communication as the traditional wholehearted supporter of usage maintains, then perhaps we should all agree with him that "anything goes." But modern theorists of philosophy such as Austin and of linguistics such as Firth have shown that language is more than a system for communicating information. Literary authors and critics have always emphasized the magic of words, and in recent years they have made us conscious of it more than ever. Our greatest present-day writers, not to mention the large number from the past, display the power of language. Joyce, Yeats, Eliot, Stevens, and others have shown us what magic can be in words.

As Nunberg writes, "The tradition of prescriptive grammar embodies a set of linguistic values that are anything but superficial or illegitimate, and which cannot be explained away by facile references to prior class values or amateur theorizing about what is 'logical.' " Nunberg has here presented the heart of the case for a reasonable prescriptivism. We must recognize that the so-called scientific approach to language is not enough to understand its power and significance. Nunberg has presented a strong argument for the recognition of some kind of prescriptivism, based upon the "scientific" principles of sociolinguistics. As a humanist, I recognize and accept the scientific and objective attitude to life as well as to language, but I wish to go further.

If we take a lax attitude towards tradition in language, we are denying the role of value in writing and to some extent speech. We are denying the freedom of an educated group or of those who wish to enter that group to speak in the way it speaks and to write in the way it writes, a freedom allowed by the "anything goes" school to every other group. This school may seem to be striking a blow for freedom, for equality, for revolution. But what they allow to every other language group – the freedom to use English as it wishes – they deny to educated men and women or to those who wish to enter that group. An attempt to restrict the freedom of certain groups in their desire to use traditional varieties of language would severely limit the ability of speakers and writers of English to express certain distinctions easily which are of importance to them.

The determination of the facts of usage is by no means a simple matter. To rely completely on usage can lead into a morass of confusion. There are signs that some linguists are beginning to recognize this, and to acknowledge that it is necessary to study prescription in order to understand actual use and even more to understand attitudes towards a language by its speakers and writers. The variety of choice offered us by language forces upon us decisions about usage. If we follow the "anything goes" principle we are displaying a contempt for language and especially our own language. A system that lacks values or is not based upon values is not worthy of support, though the values need not be based upon metaphysical and eternal principles. Social cohesion demands values.

The attempt to "educate" the English-speaking public into paying no attention to traditional educated standards (even if some of them are the creation of nineteenth-century grammarians) has been in progress for the past hundred years at least, although the process has accelerated in the past fifty years. Its success has not been notable. Educated people as a whole still worry about "correct" English.

The people who run things in the world generally accept certain usages as "correct" or even superior, and this situation is going to last for a good while, if not forever. To refuse to educate young people to use the variety of language used by the dominant figures in society will in practice be harmful to them. Furthermore, to deny the existence of a general acceptable standard is to make communication more difficult, especially written communication. There is and will always be a tension, however slight, between certain popular usages and what is considered "standard" usage. Sensitive speakers and writers will always be to some extent anxious about what is called for in particular cases. They will want an answer.

Deep down in many human beings, even if they can't articulate their feelings, is a concern for values, a feeling that certain ways of writing and speaking are better than others. A desire for "correctness" in certain contexts is found in the languages of all cultures that have long literary and scientific traditions. Nor is it limited to written cultures. As I have personally experienced, oral cultures such as the Zulu and Xhosa cultures, which until the past century had no written traditions, have strong feelings that certain ways of saying something are better than others. The tradition of "high style" is by no means confined to written traditions. The need for correctness may be a human illusion, but it answers to a deep need for richness of expression and clarity of distinction. Good usage reflects something basic in human beings, perhaps the need to make distinctions. For values depend upon distinctions.

Irrational prescriptionism is to be condemned, but the recognition of values in linguistic modes of expression demands tolerance of traditional attitudes towards "good usage." Some battles will be lost, but they are worth fighting for. Linguists as scientists may have more important concerns, but linguists as educated human beings must themselves recognize the need for value in language – the freedom to say "well" or "badly written." Most of them write well, in a way that educated people consider to be well. They should not complain if teachers and parents wish their charges to be imbued with a desire to write well. Not only have teachers and parents the right to do so, they also have the duty to do so.

Prescription, then, must rely upon usage appropriate to the social context, the audience, and the purpose of the communication. It should not be considered merely useless fussiness or reactionary fogyism.

Notes

1. For English (and possibly other Western European languages), this stage first appeared in the late seventeenth century. It was not until deep in the next century, however, that non-English speakers (especially the French) became aware of the importance of learning English. Until that time the great figures of English science thought and wrote in Latin. Even as late as Newton's time, Latin was the usual method of scientific communication for Englishmen and Europeans. English was not considered a major language by its neighbors until the mid-eighteenth century. The change in their attitude raised the prestige of English in the eyes of the English speakers.
2. This paper does not discuss geographical dialects, for which "correctness" is usually not an issue.
3. Notable strict American prescriptionists before the First World War were George P. Marsh, Richard Grant White and Ralcy Husted Bell. These were opposed by Fitzedward Hall and others. (See A. McTibbetts, "Were nineteenth-century textbooks really prescriptive?", *College English*, **27** (1965–66), 309–315.)
4. For one reasonably balanced view of a professional linguist, see Charles Carpenter Fries, *The Structure of English: An Introduction to the Construction of English Sentences* (New York: Harcourt, Brace & Co., 1952), pp. 5–7.
5. See Chomsky's "Reply" to Ronald Wardhaugh's "A comment on Noam Chomsky's 'The Current Scene in Linguistics': Present directions" in *College English*, **28** (1966–67), 468.
6. As far as I know, not published yet. I possess a draft long copy of a version which was presented in shortened form at N-Wave IX, Ann Arbor, on 31 October 1980. In *College English*, **15** (1953), 33–37, an article of mine "The problem of fact and value in the teaching of English" was published which with a somewhat different emphasis (on pedagogy and education) than in this article, argued that some role must be given to prescription in education and that "The aim of education is not a linguistic question" (p. 34).

Chapter 2

Some Audibility Gaps

DONALD DAVIE

"SOME audibility gaps" is an expression that I made up on the model of that expression with which we have all become familiar over the last several years – *credibility gap*. Though this expression is indeed familiar, I'm not sure that I understand it. At all events I'd be hard put to it to define it. If we say that a certain administration suffers from a credibility gap, do we mean only that most of us either can't or don't believe what the spokesmen of that administration say? But if that is all we mean, why do we need the portentous polysyllable *credibility* followed by the no less portentously harsh monosyllable *gap*? So far as I can see, the only function of the new expression is to introduce a technological metaphor; in speaking of credibility gap, I think we take gap as something which in the right circumstances an electrical spark might jump across. The effect therefore is to remove such matters as truthfulness and trust from the realm of morals into something which, apparently, we find more manageable – that is to say, the realm of electrical engineering. Or consider this scrap of dialogue: "Have you read Billy Budd?" "No, I've never been exposed to Melville." *Exposure* – here surely is once again a metaphor from technology, in this case from radiotherapy. If so it has some alarming implications: for instance that literature is dangerous unless administered in carefully limited dosages; also that only a strictly limited part of the anatomy (that is to say, by analogy, of the personality) is involved in what otherwise may be a lethal transaction! As soon as we think about it, we realize that not all the metaphors involved in these newfangled expressions are technological. For instance an American poet questioned recently by an interviewer replied to a question by saying not "I have forgotten" or "I don't remember" but "My memory's short-term on that." Here the metaphor appears to be financial: memory is something loaned to us by some psychological bank, and the loan may be long-term or short-term. Or one hears: "When I'm in a learning situation . . ." Here the metaphor may be called behaviorist: the implication is that the speaker finds himself in the classroom because of circumstances beyond his control, not in consequence of any act of choice or volition on his part.

Thus you will perceive that in calling my essay "Some Audibility Gaps" I am being ironical, if not sarcastic. The expression is itself an example of that which I mean it to point toward – that is to say, of the situation in which some of us say things which others of us just cannot hear. For instance a student says "When I'm in a learning situation . . ."; and I reply "You mean, when you want to learn something?" Well, no, that *isn't* what he means, not exactly; and so I have misheard him. Or again: "Do you often read poetry?" "No, I haven't been much exposed to it." Which was not what I meant; and so *he* has misheard *me*.

At any rate I think it might be useful to describe from personal experience three areas in which I find that such "mishearings," such audibility gaps, are particularly common. The first of these involves my being a British poet who has American readers. In *Thomas Hardy and British Poetry* (1972) I maintained that British poetry and American poetry, while still on speaking terms, were no longer on *hearing* terms; that American readers for the last twenty years if not longer have no longer been hearing the voice of British poetry; and that, vice versa, British readers have only pretended that they could hear the voice of American poetry, at least since the coming into favor of William Carlos Williams. Among people who have taken notice of this little book of mine, some – both British and American – have agreed with this contention; others – again, British and American – have vehemently denied it. Not surprisingly I think better of those who have agreed with me. However that may be, it seems that people have no difficulty in envisaging the possibility of an audibility gap between different bodies of users of the English language. The second area in which I find such a gap is in my relations as a British poet with my *British* readers. I must be careful here, for I do not want to seem to whine about having been neglected and/or misunderstood. On the contrary I have had good luck, perhaps better luck than I deserve: a sufficient measure of respect and esteem was accorded to me quite early in my writing career, and this has been sustained. My point is a different one: that, alike among those who applaud my poetry as among those who denigrate it, there was until very lately a general misunderstanding of what I was trying to do in my poems. I would put it more precisely still: an inability to believe that I really meant in my poems precisely what I said in them. This I put before you only as a personal and very modest instance of what we all know from the history of poetry, and the life records of poets much more illustrious than I: that it appears normal for a poet's public, even the most assiduous and well-disposed part of that public, to take twenty-five or fifty years (in my case it seems to be about twenty-five, so in that too I am lucky) to "catch up" with the poet, literally to hear what it is he is trying to say. And the third area where mishearings are common is the area which I share with all of you – the relations of a teacher with his students, whether the students be British or American. I should like to suggest that all these audibility gaps are analogous, so that thinking about any one of them may help with the others.

I foresee already two objections that may be raised. In the second and third of the cases I have cited, it may be said that I am dealing with another gap that we have heard a lot about – the famous, not to say tedious, generation gap. I would answer that the generation gap (insofar as that expression too has any function beyond introducing an inappropriate technological metaphor into matters of human relations) is only a special instance of what I have called mishearings. And the first case that I cited – that of a 50-year-old American reader mishearing a 50-year-old British poet – shows that the audibility gap can come about by distance in space as much as by distance over time. The second objection that may be raised is weightier. It may be objected that I am being merely fanciful in presenting as a gap in audibility what is really a gap in comprehension. You may say to me that I don't really mean that others don't *hear* me – only that they don't understand what they hear. But this I would deny. The case of British poets read by Americans, or American poets read by the British, is here again illuminating. By saying that we have difficulty hearing one another across the Atlantic, I mean just that: the tempo and the shape of the syllables as they come from an American mouth according to normal American pronunciation habits is in and by itself alienating and estranging for the ordinary British hearer. (And of course vice versa.) So it is, I suggest, in the difficulties that we experience as teachers in trying to communicate with many of our students. It is not a matter of our using unfamiliar words – or familiar words in unfamiliar senses (though of course that happens, and every teacher learns early in his career to guard against it); but it is, I think, the emphasis, in particular very often the earnestness, with which we say certain crucial words like *poetic*, or *imaginative*, or even *modern*. Thus, in these exchanges also, what intervenes to prevent full communication is very often such simply audible qualities as tone, cadence, speed, forcefulness, and distinctness of enunciation. For instance, when I reply to the imaginary student "You mean you want to learn something?" I believe this is heard by him as an act of aggression, a "put-down." My own experience suggests that mere clarity of enunciation (whether actually heard, or implied from print by the exigencies of meter and cadence), mere succinctness and directness of grammatical ordering, is heard, by my readers and my students alike, as a *threat*. (What dismays the undergraduate, one may say, is the *directness*; what throws the graduate is the succinctness!)

*   *   *

If this is the situation in which we find ourselves time and again, the question of course is what we must do about it. And in the first place I take it for granted that we cannot simply go along with it. In our several capacities as poet or teacher or whatever, but simply as humane people living and working in a technological culture, we cannot tolerate these innovations in language which convert into something like an electrical circuit considerations of truthfulness and trust, parental care and filial obligation, or the mutual respect and cooperation which we all know to be involved in any transaction that can be called from one point of view *teaching* – or from the other end *learning*. And yet have we not all of us tolerated from students, and even perhaps in ourselves, expressions like *feedback*, *input*, and *exposure* (to literature)? It is no wonder if we have. For we no less than our pupils are subject to a daily and hourly bombardment of language from innumerable sources which characteristically, though by no act of choice on the part of anyone involved, transform human and moral transactions into technological or financial or behavioristic terms. We are ourselves infected with the disease that we try to cure, and in that way our situation is desperate. Nevertheless I take it for granted that the effort of diagnosis and cure must be sustained by each of us. It is easy indeed, once one begins to think along these lines, to discern sinister aspects to words which at first glance seem innocuous. Consider only the word *technique*. In a technological world, to speak of *verse-technique* has inevitable dangers, since it cannot help but suggest to some of our students that the tricks of the trade of writing verse are techniques in just the same sense as the tricks learned by a racing motorcyclist, or a television anchorman. It would be a counsel of quixotic perfection to try to eliminate the word *technique* from our vocabularies in the classroom; but it would do no harm perhaps for us to use *technique* and *technical* markedly less often than we do. Or consider even that expression so beloved of educators and college administrators – *writing skills*. *Skill* is obviously a more humane word than *technique*. And yet the very plural form, *skills*, belies what most of us know to be the truth of the matter when we consider in all seriousness how good writing comes about. We all either know from our own experience, or else devoutly believe, that good writing, whether in verse or prose, is the product of the total personality concentrated and attentive to what needs to be said. In other words a paragraph of good prose is not assembled from parts like a good automobile engine. It does not come about by the application at one point of a particular skill (say, punctuation) and at another point of a quite another skill (say, imagery). And however necessary it may be in a session with a particular student writer (those sessions in which we all now spend so much of the time that we thought we should spend in teaching Shakespeare or Henry James) . . . however necessary it may be, I say, to analyze the writer's problem under separate heads, into categories that seem distinct, we ought always if we can to emphasize that ultimately what is asked of him, and what he should ask of himself, is on the contrary a singularly unified act of total attention.

It will be apparent by now that I take it for granted that in both of my functions – as poet and as English teacher – my stance must be *conservative*. It is my fellow poets, rather than my fellow teachers, who find this hard to swallow. In the rhetoric which has enveloped and attended the practice of poetry, indeed of *writing*, for the past hundred years and more, the dominant and most fervently advanced metaphor has been the one in the originally French expression – the *avant-garde*. It is the metaphor of the poet, the writer, as the explorer, the pioneer, the breaker of new ground. Conditioned by this without our being aware of it, how we find our pulses quickening, our spirits rising, even now, when we are told that such and such a writer is working at or beyond the frontiers of current linguistic practice! "Breaking new ground" is still thought to be one of the most glorious accolades that we can bestow on a writer: for him or her to be "unprecedented" is thought to be a high compliment, one of the highest. In fact this is just one instance of the time lag, the audibility gap, between a poet and his readers, including those readers who are poets as he is, though younger. For W. H. Auden through the last twenty-five years of his life was insisting that on the contrary the place of the responsible poet, in the second half of the twentieth century, is not on the imperial frontiers but on the ramparts of the beleaguered metropolis; not in the steppes or prairies of infinite possibility, but within the city where properly civic language and conduct can no longer be taken for granted. When the barbarians are already within the gates, the place of the poet is not with the avant-garde, but on the contrary within the ranks of the rear guard, determined, if the worst comes to the worst, to sell his life dearly.

When I speak with my colleagues in the teaching profession, this asser-tion – that our function is nowadays necessarily defensive and conserva-tive – is on the whole readily accepted. And yet, among English teachers also, are not words like *innovative* or *forward-looking*, even that tired old warhorse *progressive*, still taken to be words of good omen? When we write recommen-dations for our ex-pupils, or imagine others writing recommendations for ourselves, are not words like *innovative* and *forward-looking* still thought to carry with them a plus sign? If not we ourselves, then the administrators who judge us and control us, need to learn that innovative and forward-looking colleagues are precisely what we have had all too much of and can do without for the foreseeable future. Here too we see the hand of technology: the new and improved model is what the technologist can and must look forward to. But in the arts there is in that sense no progress at all: who ever improved on Thomas Wyatt's model of the English lyric, or on Montaigne's model for the essay, or on Cervantes's model for prose narrative? Our concern must be not to lose touch with, nor to slip too far back from, those monuments in our past; the administrators over us, and the students at our feet, find it equally difficult to conceive how this can be, and to adjust to our point of view from the one which the rest of our society loudly and insistently takes for granted.

We must press this point even further and say that our function must be not just conservative but positively reactionary. To take a specific instance: when the Episcopal church largely abandons the use of the King James Bible and the Book of Common Prayer, or when (a slightly different but firmly related case) the Roman Catholic church largely abandons the Vulgate and the Latin Mass, there may or may not in either case be a good sociological or devotional reason for the change; but in both cases, different as they are, the decisions have compounded the difficulties that face us as teachers of English language and literature, a language and a literature intimately dependent on the Latin and Romance cultures of European Christendom. I hate to foresee a time in which the Book of Common Prayer has to be prescribed as an essential background text for courses in literature as far removed in time as Shakespeare's plays and Eliot's *Four Quartets*. And yet we must recognize that that time is only just around the corner. Indeed one or two among us might make a modest fortune here and now by preparing, in advance of the event, an annotated edition of the Book of Common Prayer for use by undergraduates majoring in English. Surely all of us, Christian and non-Christian alike, must be appalled by the prospect of having this monument of our common literary heritage thus relegated to the category labelled *college texts*.

I should like to probe a little further what is meant by defining the audibility gap as a time lag – between the poet and his readers, between the teacher and his students. Because in the arts there is no question of *progress*, because there is no question of considering William Carlos Williams as a new and improved model of Ben Jonson, or Sylvia Plath as in any way an "advance" upon Emily Dickinson, it follows that we are running on a circular track. And thus when we as teachers (or as writers) get too far ahead of our students (or our readers), we are overtaking them from behind. We are in fact, in the precisely accurate language of long-distance runners, *lapping* them. We come abreast of them once again, having however completed at least one circuit of the track more than they have. And surely every teacher recognizes this experience when he listens to his students, just as every writer recognizes it when he reads his reviewers. It is the experience of being agreed with all too readily, of having our contentions approved out of a survey of the evidence much less exhaustive than the survey we have conducted for ourselves. Take merely as one instance the matter of colloquial language in poetry: if we have convinced ourselves, out of a survey of poetry in English since Chaucer, that the spoken as opposed to the written language is indeed a necessary standard by which to judge poetic dictions from Chaucer's day to our own, how are we to deal with the student (or the reviewer) who will enthusiastically endorse our contention, having however taken note of no poetic practice earlier than Charles Olson's? The temptation is flagrant, and I daresay we have all succumbed to it: we give that student an A, we take that reviewer out to dinner, But all the time we know guiltily that the arguments for an "aureate," a noncolloquial, diction for poetry are powerful, and have been powerfully advanced by distinguished and sincere individuals throughout recorded history; and, whereas we may have met and wrestled with and finally to our own satisfaction vanquished their arguments, we know very well that our students (or our readers) have *not* met with those arguments and, we suspect, wouldn't be able to rebut them. Any intellectual position is praiseworthy according to the energy that has gone into arriving at it and sustaining it, according to (we may say) how many circuits of the track the runner has made; and an intellectual position may be identical with ours, and yet may be privately regarded by us with a certain contempt because we know that it has been arrived at too easily. And thus we know that there can be no shortcuts in the study of literature, even as we are compelled, by our vocations as teachers (or as poets), to construct such shortcuts and to recommend them.

In this situation what recourse do we have, if we are to preserve our self-respect, except to be once again curmudgeonly conservatives? If we judge that our students by and large are incapable of coping with anything like the range of relevant literature from the past (much of it not in English), then I suppose we have the duty to make them aware of this, and to tell them that their judgments about literature in general will carry weight only when backed by much more reading than at the moment they are capable of. This is not what students like to be told. And we all want to be popular teachers, to be liked or loved by our students. (Quite apart from the fact that for the administrators who decide on our promotions and our career prospects, a *popular* teacher and a successful teacher amount to the same thing.) And so, as usual, what duty demands of us is something that goes against the grain of our natural impulses and wishes, and indeed against our worldly prospects.

To conclude these disconnected remarks, I want to return to a point that I made earlier: the gaps that we are talking about are in the first place not gaps in comprehensibility but in *audibility*. It is not so much that we don't understand one another as that we don't hear one another (and *therefore* don't understand . . .). On the one hand this means that we need to emphasize in our classrooms, far more than most of us do, how a poem does not even *exist*, as a subject of study or an occasion for enjoyment, until it is "given to the air" as a sequence of sounds and rhythms shaping time, carving or moulding the time which it takes to be read aloud. So long as the poem exists before us only as a sequence of black marks on a white page, it does not truly exist, it is not genuinely present. And accordingly no time in the classroom is so little wasted as when a student is forced to read aloud – and if necessary to reread more than once – the poem on the page before the class, and this as a necessary *preliminary* to any explication of it or commentary upon it. I would go further and say that the same holds for any carefully written prose also – a paragraph of Dickens or Faulkner. To insist on this often (it should be an absolute rule, but I admit that I fail to make it so myself) is a very chastening and disconcerting experience for the teacher as well as the student. The student who is most adept at explicating a poem is among the least able to enunciate it. Moreover the experiment shows very disconcertingly just how wide the Atlantic is – as no one can doubt who has heard, as I have, the tongues of British students trying to do justice to a page of Faulkner or a poem by Ransom or Stevens. On the other hand there is no alternative to the student's doing it *for himself*; and if after repeated trials he manages what is at best a poor performance, I believe we have to let it go at that. If his reading conveys in the end a certain shapeliness of rhythm, even though it certainly wasn't the rhythmical shape in the ear of the writer as he wrote it, we must be grateful for that – and it's a great deal more than a lot of our students can manage. Hearing practiced or professional readers on disc or tape doubtless has its educational uses, but it is no substitute for the student's being forced to perform himself; and the polished assurance of the professional reader may have the bad effect of aggravating a student's inhibitions about giving voice himself.

In any case I suspect that the need for voice, for audibility, clear enunciation, goes far beyond this special, though very important, matter of reading literature aloud. I bow to those of you who have much more experience than I have in the matter of teaching remedial English composition, when I suggest that students would learn a lot from being forced to *say aloud* some of the shapeless lumps of language which they have committed to paper under the illusion, or in the hope, that they are reasonably elegant English sentences. If their own voices stumble and choke, or if they run out of breath, while reading aloud their own writings, do they not experience for themselves, without their teacher having to tell them, much of what is wrong with their writing? I would go further, and say that we fail our students if we pass without comment things they say in conversation, when those things are gabbled or mumbled or eked out with meaningless gestures and interjections. If they have something to say, should they not be made to say it clearly and deliberately? Their vocabularies may be limited – for present purposes, that is not the point; but they should be obliged to treat with respect and deliberation such vocabulary as they have. I say "with *respect*" – and that is crucial. We, like our students, are constantly bombarded by voices that treat our language without any respect, as we see clearly from the spendthrift gabble with which they spill our words upon the air. I mean of course the newscasters, advertisers, disc-jockeys, and anchormen (those for starters): these are the *gabblers*. But almost worse, for our purposes, are their mirror image: the *mumblers*. When a society with good reason begins to suspect the too glibly fast-talking articulate, it swings to the other extreme and begins to esteem as the only honest individuals the professionally *in*articulate. This has already spilled over into poetry: from William Carlos Williams (a genuine poet, but also the first *professionally inarticulate* poet known to history) there has stemmed a whole school of poets, already into its second or third generation, which, implicitly in its unpunctuated practice and at times explicitly in its theoretical pronouncements, is vowed to the discrediting of the subject-verb-predicate structure of the English sentence, a structure which is held to be in and of itself fraudulent, to be emasculating a reality of perception "by field" – a reality to which the distinction of noun from verb is unknown. This is predominantly but by no means exclusively an American phenomenon: in particular the theorists of the school come as often from the Sorbonne or Frankfurt-on-Main as from New Haven, Connecticut, or Austin, Texas. If these people – practitioners and theorists alike – could be in good conscience dismissed as faddish and talentless opportunists, our problem with them would be relatively simple. But that is not the case: on the contrary some of the people who write this way and out of this conviction are among the most earnestly dedicated and gifted writers now at work – as we might expect, since their dedicated mumblings are an inevitable and not dishonorable reaction against the professional gabblings which infest the mass media. And this puts us all in a bind. The young scholar who has spent his Sunday eloquently justifying Charles Olson's distrust of the subject-verb-predicate structure, on Monday morning finds himself schizophrenically attempting to implant into a freshman just the structure that the teacher has so lately, and quite sincerely, disavowed. This is a case of "lapping": to disavow the subject-verb-predicate structure is quite another thing when one knows what it is one is disavowing from rejecting it when one is still entirely innocent of it. And yet there are historically demonstrable reasons for assigning positive values in our culture to "innocence"; and all of these work upon us powerfully to persuade us that our students have in their innocence as much reason for rejecting sentence structure as we in our jaded experience may suppose we have, after reading the latest pronunciamento from Frankfurt or Paris. We think, or we persuade ourselves, that our students hear us when we inveigh againt discursive reason in favor of some allegedly superior, nondiscursive reason implemented by literature; but of course we deceive ourselves – they think that they hear us, and we think so too – but they do not because they have not been round the track as many times as we have.

For that matter I think that very few of us have circled the track enough times to make up our minds firmly on such a momentous matter, affecting the very fabric of the language we have inherited, which is in our keeping. I think that very few of us – whether we are poets or story-tellers, or critics, or teachers – have really thought through what we are doing when we lightheartedly malign discursive reason, and propose to jettison the grammatical structures which embody that reason in our language. I do not myself go along with the poets who go to work in this way, any more than with the critics and theorists who seem to endorse them. But however that may be, I'm quite sure that our students do not have the right to justify their own inarticulateness as more honest than our articulateness, their mumbling as more heartfelt than our clarity. In fact few of our students do this, because few of them know about these sophisticated arguments. But some students are already cloudily aware of them, and in any case it is only a matter of time before they become aware of the writers whom I call professionally inarticulate among whom, let me say again, are to be found poets as earnest and as gifted as William Carlos Williams, Charles Olson, George Oppen. And so the situation is that by no means all of our distinguished literature works upon its readers so as to support what most of us would agree to regard as the minimal principles of good writing. A student who modeled his prose style on the critical essays of William Carlos Williams could hardly receive an A from any of us.

I must conclude without finding even a crumb of comfort for any of us. The audibility gaps exist, and they are likely to get worse rather than better. I can only reiterate that I think those gaps can be closed not by technology, not by gimmickry in teaching methods or teaching materials, but only (as always) by sympathy, vigilance, and above all conviction, in us as teachers.

Chapter 3

A Linguist to the Lay Audience

RAVEN I. McDAVID, JR

I SPEAK on usage out of my own experience. Though officially a linguist, I often think of myself as a layman who happened to become interested. In high school I was diffident about English; but it became my college major because I had a superb teacher of freshman composition. Although I studied Old and Middle English and Gothic during my work toward a doctorate in Milton, I had no systematic training in the structure and history of the language. My interest in usage arose from exposure to various regional and social dialects, in a variety of situations, including camp meetings and campaign speakings. My first teaching was in Charleston, South Carolina, notorious in the South for its aberrant vowels; my father's work as an industrial lobbyist introduced me to various local uses and functional varieties. Then, by a happy misadventure, in 1937 I was a post-doctoral visitor at a Linguistic Institute and not only attended Sapir's lectures but – as an informant interviewed for the Linguistic Atlas – discovered what I wanted to do. With some encouragement from H. L. Mencken and Hans Kurath, I have spent the last 45 years trying to learn enough to do it. The books I mention, however many, are some that contributed to this self-education. They are recommended as part of the self-education of others, who may go only part of the way or much further. In the process I have endured enough patronizing by academic wiseacres to be sympathetic with the hillbilly and the swamp rat and others of various levels and degrees; from them, in my field interviews, I learned much of the richness of American culture as expressed in American English – a richness beyond the comprehension of those who would become arbiters of usage.

But realization of this richness does not make it easy to speak to the generality. One must be aware of both public expectations and his own limitations; he must know that his audience is largely unfamiliar with the technical language that he takes for granted; above all, he must treat his subject with humor and grace, keep his temper, and resist the temptation to wax devastatingly clever.

Everybody has opinions, even prejudices, on some details of the language he uses; linguists have no built-in immunity. Differences in the acceptability of particular details, or whole varieties, of language are recognized in almost every society. Paradoxically, they become most important in open societies that boast of removing traditional class distinctions: as mass production makes material luxuries – or facsimiles difficult to detect – accessible to everyone, a demand arises for intangible marks of prestige, more easily attained and recognized than skill at the piano or familiarity with the works of Aristotle. In the Renaissance, conduct books suggested the need to conform to the usage of the established orders; through the eighteenth century, grammarians and orthoepists (teachers of pronunciation) prospered by helping the rising middle classes to perform; as economic and educational opportunities have multiplied, so have the numbers of these practitioners. Edwin Newman and John Simon are the heirs and assigns of Richard Grant White and Sherwin Cody, offering pat solutions to problems demanding years of attention. They probably do less damage, in the long run, than those who profit from American anxiety every election year, but their popularity makes it hard for the serious student of language to get a hearing.[1] It almost seems that the layman expects to be told that there is something wrong with his grammar and usage – an expectation that can curdle the social relations of anyone associated with the teaching of English.[2]

Teachers of English, themselves, are uneasy about usage. After a nationwide study, sponsored by the MLA and the NCTE, Marjorie Daunt of London reported to a 1936 professional meeting that there were three possible attitudes: indifference, assurance, and anxiety; of the thousands of American teachers she had interviewed, none was indifferent, and the only assured were two maiden ladies of Charleston, South Carolina.[3] Even 50 years ago the teaching corps was largely recruited from the lower middle class – a group seeking in the profession a road to social status, and itself most uneasy about language. Since then teaching has become more onerous, as schools divert their attention from education to public entertainment (especially competitive athletics), social panaceas, and simple custody – keeping adolescents off the job market and out of jail. There is little time for serious reading or for practice in composition; although regular themes should be assigned as early as the second grade, many who hold high-school diplomas have never written connected prose and some have never learned to read; efforts to establish reasonable standards for advancement are frustrated by the orthodoxy of social promotion.

Nor do teacher-training programs provide adequate understanding of language. It is often recommended that all teachers dealing with language should have serious training in the structure and history of English; for practical as well as humanistic reasons they should also master a linguistic system other than their own – what they will expect of students who normally use another language or a non-standard dialect. Yet few American undergraduates take a foreign language, and the program of the undergraduate English major rarely has a linguistic requirement.

The melancholy question *quis ipsos custodes custodiet?* can be asked of the faculties who produce the English majors who teach in the schools. Even in the most respectable universities, the Ph.D. in English is no longer expected to have a knowledge of Old and Middle English or of contemporary linguistic variety; like foreign languages for undergraduates, such requirements were brushed aside in the 1970s, partly in a search for "relevance," partly in the hope of turning out more doctorates to handle the putatively expanding student population. Even some of the most distinguished ornaments of such departments rarely have solid basis for their usage judgments; many echo the hue-and-cry of the lynching posse that took out after the Merriam *Third*; others are mesmerized by such popular cults as transformational grammar or so-called Black English.[4] A linguist seriously concerned with usage is at best a lonely person on an English faculty.

Nor, fashions being what they are, does he get too much help from fellow linguists. Theoreticians – for whom *data* is the most obscene four-letter word – ignore the problem. Serious interest in usage is largely confined to dialectologists and lexicographers. Though these groups are far from dominant among linguists, they appeal to the intelligent laity largely through their very concern with data. Though the United States has not developed the regiment of active volunteers who contributed so much to the original *Oxford* and the *English Dialect Dictionary*, it has a large potential audience for data on usage among businessmen, lawyers, and newspaper people who work with the living language – probably more extensively than university faculties – and who are glad to hear from someone who will speak with knowledge and humor and clarity. The linguist must be able to communicate with this group.

A linguist discussing usage should first admit his own limitations. Every judgment of usage rests on incomplete knowledge; the full record for any form would include all the linguistic and social contexts in which that form has been used, and with what intentions and effects. A look at a dictionary will find some errors, but more omissions and incomplete statements. Very few list *panamax*, a noun attributive indicating the size of cargo vessels ("maximum size for the Panama Canal"); they inadequately define the pejorative *wimp*, and give no clear hint of its origin, though it became an issue in the 1982 campaign for governor of Illinois. Not till 1958 did anyone publicly comment on *clout*, a Chicago political term meaning "access to power"; *Ausländer* often misinterpret it as meaning power itself. Only recently did I encounter *longneck*, a term used by some Chicago topers for what is commonly called a *long* (or *tall*) *drink*, such as a *highball* or *collins*. *Snuck* as the past tense of *sneak* is often labeled a dialect relic; actually it is a recent innovation, favoured by the younger and more sophisticated and patterned after such earlier innovations as *stuck* and *dug*. An attentive person will encounter linguistic forms and meanings never met before; linguists are no exceptions. They can make shrewd guesses, but they should admit they are guessing.

A linguist should also recognize his linguistic prejudices, and acknowledge that the prejudices of others are just as legitimate. I find it physically impossible to use *gay* in the current modish use "homosexual." Like other linguists, I am aware of the acute if sometimes irrational sensitivity about national or cultural epithets; brought up to avoid them, I probably use as few as anyone, though I recorded them in quantity in my field work. No one knows all the terms that may give offense; often a once-acceptable term takes on the offensive aura of older forbidden words. In 1980, Jay McMullen – husband of Chicago's Mayor Jane Byrne – dismissed President Carter as a *cracker*, a term often as offensive to white Georgians as *nigger* to black ones. Knowing that in upland South Carolina *hoosier* is a byword for mountain uncouthness, a few degrees more offensive than *hillbilly*, I hesitate to use it to someone from Indiana, though I know it has been disinfected in that state (it is still a fighting word in St. Louis). Some of my prejudices may seem quaint, such as my distaste for *kid* as a synonym for *child*; I find it extremely distasteful when applied to graduate students. If blacks resent *mammy* as perpetuating a stereotype, they may be amused to learn that in parts of the South *mammy* and *daddy* were once used by whites only as terms of respect for elderly blacks. Knowing the background and the extent of use for terms one dislikes will not make them acceptable, but it may make us less nervous about them. However unlikely I am to use *kid*, I recognize it as part of normal present-day American English, if sometimes overworked. One must recall Winston Churchill's retort when chided about recognizing Stalin – whose record he had condemned – as an ally: "I do not like the Honourable Member from Ebbw Vale [Aneurin Bevan], but since he is a member of this House I am bound to recognize him."

To cope with ignorance and prejudice, after realizing they exist, the linguist should recommend the kinds of professional experience that have made him competent to discuss usage. Laymen rarely have reason or time to prepare themselves as deeply, but the quality and direction of preparation should be the same.

First, attention to the language as it is used: Who says what to whom, on what occasions and with what effects? When do words or pronunciations or grammatical forms trouble us? Can we dissociate the language from the person using it? How do we react when familiar words are used in unfamiliar senses? Sometimes these new senses are so explicitly defined that they displace the old: in 1576 the French political philosopher Jean Bodin offered a generalized definition of *sovereignty*, hitherto used only about monarchs; it is now the prevalent one. Nuclear physics has provided new meanings for *fission* and *fusion*; mishaps in nuclear power plants have alerted us to the ominous possibilities of *meltdown*. Changes in the rules and tactics of sports, sometimes under pressure from television and other sources of revenue, yield new terms, such as *tiebreaker*, a scoring device in tennis to end a set lest the match extend into the traditional time for *situation comedy*, itself a neologism.

One should also recognize actual usage in grammar and pronunciation as well as in vocabulary. From an older tradition, perhaps, I am uncomfortable when I hear the final syllables of *yesterday* and *tomorrow* pronounced with the full vowels of *day* and *go* rather than the reduced vowels natural to me; but millions of educated Americans use them, including the younger generation in my own family. I learned to say *he persuaded me to go*, with the infinitive, but only *he convinced me (that) I should stay*, with a noun clause. Now the two verbs pattern the same way, and *he convinced me to stay* goes unnoticed in educated speech. Some would assert peculiar ethnic identity for structures old in the language: the appositive pronoun with a noun subject (but see *thy rod and thy staff they comfort me*, in the King James version of the 23rd Psalm), or the inverted order of direct questions in indirect ones, as *they asked him would he run for Congress* (found in the language before Chaucer). Neither of these structures is usual in formal expository prose, but they are natural in educated speech. An alert observer will find the range of educated usage broader then even "liberal" grammarians sometimes recognized: once Fries (1940, p. 10) rejected the rhyming of *catch* and *fetch* as uneducated, but the evidence is otherwise.

Besides being generally attentive, the person who wants to be informed about usage should read widely, especially such kinds of expository prose as essays, history, and political commentary. Some of the best works about language are also good models of usage, such as Mencken's *The American Language*, Hall's *Linguistics and Your Language*, Pyles's *Words and Their Ways in American English*, and Quirk's *The Use of English*. Since the study of language has established itself as a science, there have probably been fewer readable works in the field than there were in the nineteenth century, and most observers feel that British linguists write better than their American counterparts. When one's reading reaches this stage, it begins to need direction: popularity is a treacherous guide. One should look at *Publications of the American Dialect Society* (PADS), *American Speech*, and the *Journal of English Linguistics* (*JEngL*). Reviews in the last two indicate the status of particular works; since everybody seriously concerned with English usage has written for these journals at one time or another, a reader will gain some idea of the style and interests of the contributors. Some articles have considerable importance in revealing the climate of opinion in which judgements of usage are uttered: an article in the fifth volume (1971) of *JEngL*, on the first stage of the controversy over the Merriam *Third*, shows (1) that the hostile reception of the *Third* by American journalists and literary critics antedated not only the official publication date but the date when copies were available for examination; (2) that this reception was prompted by the official publicity of the Merriam Company, which drew attention to features that could be misunderstood, misinterpreted, and misrepresented.

One should also examine the more important reference works which treat usage: dictionaries of various sorts, reference grammars, histories of the language, and usage guides. For inquiring readers a most important interpreta-tive work is *Dictionaries and THAT Dictionary*, by James Sledd and Wilma Ebbitt, published at the height of the controversy over the *Third*. It not only offers a selection of the arguments for and against the editorial policies of the *Third*, but indicates the place of the *Third* in the history of English dictionaries – something that Merriam had slighted in its publicity. Especially valuable are the sections dealing with the "Emperor of Dictionaries" (as Mencken called it), the *Oxford*; those interested in the problems and personalities involved in editing the *Oxford* (and by implication, other large-scale reference works) can find an intimate discussion in *Caught in the Web of Words*, by K. M. Elisabeth Murray, granddaughter of its first editor.

One who reads dictionaries should pay particular attention to the introductory material. Though it is more copious and better written in some works than in others, it always prevents misunderstanding of the significance of labels, the pronunciation key, and the order in which meanings and alternate pronunciations are entered. The *Oxford*, the Merriam, and the *Webster's New World* follow a historical order; other dictionaries arrange meanings by present-day frequency. Readers accustomed to one order may be confused by another: in a 1978 case involving smuggling of marijuana, the defense suggested that in the absence of the commodity the defendants could have been dealing in wild tobacco, since the first meaning listed in the *Third* and its 1934 predecessor was "a kind of wild tobacco grown in Sonora, Mexico," and would have tried to assert that this was the most common meaning (they lost; later research indicates that the first Merriam sense lacks evidence). Frequently it is asserted that the first pronunciation indicated for an entry is *ipso facto* "preferred;" a more accurate statement is that any pronunciation included and not stigmatized by an adverse label is part of educated usage. Indeed, no dictionary has given the full range of educated pronunciations, as was found in the preparation of Kurath–McDavid (1961).

Many reference dictionaries are designed to give more intensive coverage of a regional usage or the usage of a period than the *Oxford* could provide. Most of these are modeled on the *Oxford*, with the range of meaning shown by illustrative citations and the definitions being shorter than those in general dictionaries like the Merriam. The most significant of these are the *Dictionary of American English* (1938–1944), the *Dictionary of Americanisms* (1951), the *Dictionary of Canadianisms* (1967), the *Dictionary of American Regional English* (1985–), and the *Historical Dictionary of American Slang* (in progress). The *Dictionary of Newfoundland English* (1982), the *Dictionary of Prince Edward Island English*, the *Dictionary of Australian English* (the two last in progress), and the *Dictionary of Jamaican English* (1967; 2nd ed., 1981) not only offer insights into cultures far different from mainstream America but often correct enthusiastic generalizations about particular forms.

One interesting type of dictionary is the usage guide, which has no general standard. It is highly personal, both in the kind of knowledge its editor brings to the task and in its tendency to reflect the prejudices of the editor. Rarely is the editor knowledgeable about the history and structure of the language; probably the best American work is still George Philip Krapp's *Comprehensive Guide to Good English* (1927); although its attitude is sometimes rather conservative, it reflects a lifetime of experience with everything from Old English poetry to the history of American English; it was the most useful work consulted for Kurath–McDavid (1961), in recognizing variant pronunciations extant in standard usage. No recent competitor shows as much knowledge of the language or general good sense (for a comparison, see Creswell, 1975). Several recent works were deliberately designed to counteract the pernicious liberalism of the Merriam *Third*; especially horrible is Morris and Morris (1975).

An interesting study of usage, whose method is still valid though both the linguistic and the social data have changed, is Fries (1940). It exemplifies the principles on which good studies of usage are based, and which are explicitly set forth as the rational for the current massive study by Quirk and his associates. Using holograph letters written to a government agency by petitioners (therefore on their best linguistic behavior), about whom there was evidence on education and occupation and social standing in their communities, Fries was able to set up social categories on non-linguistic evidence. Then he set down the variants – inflections, function words, word order – used by each social class, especially contrasting "Standard English" and "Vulgar

English" on each point at issue, and using this evidence to draft a practical program for teaching. Few details of grammar unequivocally set off "Standard" from "Vulgar" usage; in fact, some of the shibboleths in the textbooks, such as *those kind of people*, were found only in the letters of the educated. Much more important were differences in fluency, facility, and versatility; the letters of the "Vulgar" showed less variety and smaller vocabularies, a conclusion reached in many subsequent studies. Four decades old, with evidence dating from World War I, Fries (1940) is not a picture of contemporary usage, but it remains an important model. Anyone seriously interested in usage differences must read the first four chapters and the concluding one.

Another type of systematic investigation is represented by the regional linguistic atlases and works derived from them. In designing these American surveys in 1931, Hans Kurath departed from the European tradition of linguistic geography, which had concentrated on the speech of uneducated villagers. Like Fries, he chose to study three principal classes of speech (while conceding that the intensive study of social differences in even the smallest communities demanded a much more intricate classification): folk, common, and cultivated. He realized, like many before him, that no single variety of educated spoken American English has prestige comparable to Southern British Received Standard or Parisian French; furthermore, directions of linguistic change may be suggested by the group between the folk and the cultivated, which is sometimes nearer to the usage of one end of the spectrum, sometimes nearer to that of the other – depending on the history and social structure of the community. For each informant there is detailed evidence on genealogy and personal experience; the length of the interview provides further evidence on the social class of the informant. Actual usage may run contrary to expectations and handbook judgments; *hadn't ought* from aristocratic Yankees and *might could* from aristocratic Southerners must be entered in the register of informal cultivated usage.[5]

Like Fries (1940), or any usage study, each of the American regional surveys presents data recorded at a particular time. American usage – complicated from the beginning by the fact that no regional or local variety is drawn from a single variety of British English and that almost every variety has been leavened by contacts with speakers of other languages – reflects traditions of geographic and social mobility, of industrialization and urbanization and general education. In the half-century since the regional investigations were begun with the *Linguistic Atlas of New England* (Kurath et al., 1939–1943), these traditions have continued to affect standards of usage, though not the same way in every community. The mechanization of agriculture and the decline in rural population have made obsolete a large part of the vocabulary familiar to those interviewed in the 1930s. Changes in pronunciation and grammar have generally been less drastic, but can be noted: few natives of New York City now have the same vowel in *oil* and *earl*; few natives of Charleston have the same vowel in *ear* and *air*. Everywhere there is a tendency toward pronouncing *Mary* and *merry* and *marry*, *hoarse*, and *horse*, with the same vowel, and *wail* and *whale* with the same initial consonant. These trends are discovered in various ways, especially in new broad-gauge studies; in parts of the South the investigators for Cassidy's *Dictionary of American Regional English* are finding that forms once generally used at the time of the *Atlas* interviews are now socially restricted. But this does not mean that one can disregard the older investigations; like the census records of a generation ago, they provide baselines against which changes in regional and social patterns can be assayed.

Such baselines are important in evaluating recent sociolinguistic studies. Many of the best known of these have been undertaken in response to *cris de coeur* from harried school systems, seeking solutions for impossible problems – notably the striking differences from local educated usage in the speech of new arrivals from the South or from Latin America. These studies are generally *ad hoc*, rarely utilizing scholars who have previously made systematic studies of language variety. Consequently, the description of the speech of a particular problem group (say, blacks in the District of Columbia) is rarely balanced by evidence on the speech of whites in areas where black influence is unlikely, such as eastern Kentucky, Maine, or Newfoundland; the search for historical roots in West African languages, pidgins, and Caribbean creoles is rarely balanced by equally careful examination of the roots of American English in the British Isles. To take a modest example, the participle *gwine* "going" is traditionally associated with blacks; but in the 1930s it was also recorded in northeastern New England and in Oxfordshire. Regrettably the evidence from the primary evidence is not always accessible, and some of the interpretative studies, like Atwood (1953), are now out of print. Even when accessible, the elegant primary studies require special knowledge. Until a new and more comprehensive overview is presented, the interested person – linguist or layman – must at least start with Carroll Reed (1977), Kurath (1972), and various essays by Harold Allen, Cassidy, Albert H. Marckwardt, Lee Pederson, and others.

Dialectology is an outgrowth of historical linguistics; the geographical and social dimensions of usage cannot be studied apart from the historical. Fries and others have emphasized how London English, which underlies all varieties of present-day educated usage, was itself the product of dialect mixture, and that many of its forms were brought in from the north of England, such as *they*, *their*, *them*, *she*, and *are*. In teaching the history of the language we cannot assume a linear development from Late West Saxon to present-day Received Standard. The former yields one regional variety of Middle English, and the earliest texts from London show striking differences from the usage of Chaucer. Thus writing an introductory reference history is a complicated task; possibly the most useful is Baugh and Cable (1978), revision of a dependable work with considerable emphasis on the cultural history manifested in the linguistic. A good rule of thumb in judging new works in the field is to discount claims for revolutionary novelty. But some appreciation of history is needed to realize that the now stigmatized multiple negative was once acceptable, and that forms we use naturally like the present passive participle (*Our new house is being built*) were once deplored as inelegant.

Histories of the language, even as detailed as Baugh and Cable (1978), are bound to be overviews. Persons concerned with the history of particular details of usage must look deeper – sometimes in special studies, such as those Fries undertook on *shall* and *will* and other problems, oftener into the historical reference grammars. The four best of these have been written by Continental scholars, a Dane and three Hollanders: Jespersen, Poutsma, Kruisinga, and Visser. If none is complete, if each overlooks or misinterprets some of the evidence, they are but human; as scholars they would welcome addenda and corrigenda. All of them set forth plentiful data, from which their conclusions are derived.

Until very recently, there was no reference grammar of present-day English comparable in quality to the historical grammars. The need has now been supplied by Quirk *et al.* (1972). Buttressing the *Grammar* are dozens of related studies, which one can examine as time and interest permit. What distinguishes these works from nearly all predecessors and contemporaries is the recognition that English usage is complex and many-dimensional, and must be based on data objectively gathered and analyzed; the method of each related study is carefully described. In the introduction to one of the larger related works, Svartvik and Quirk (1980), two principles are set forth: (1) no person has full mastery of the whole repertory of styles for any language; (2) usage cannot be accurately studied by intuition and introspection, however fashionable such shortcuts may be. If Quirk is – as many believe – the most distinguished student of the English language ever to arise in Britain, he will leave in his *Grammar*, and in the Survey of English Usage out of which it arose, an unchallengeable legacy, like that of Murray in the *Oxford English Dictionary*. It is derived from long traditions of examining the language for what it is rather than for what one would like it to be, though wishes and expectations of the user are part of the record of usage, especially when those wishes and expectations are at variance with the objective data.

It is not accidental that the preparation of a linguist for making judgments of usage should resemble the kinds of experience Quirk has brought to the Survey and the *Grammar* – childhood familiarity with regional varieties, association with people outside academic life (in his case, the RAF), an understanding of history and lexicography, and a realization that however elegant may be one's theories, they are always accountable to the data, the language itself. However little one may match Quirk's general knowledge, the principle remains the same: all who would speak about usage should recognize their own limitations and prejudices, should learn to observe carefully, should read widely, and should be aware of the amount of good work that has been done in dictionaries of various kinds, linguistic atlases, histories of the language, and historical grammars.

Having achieved a modest amount of knowledge about language variety in general and about variety in English in particular, what should the linguist then do? There are three ways in which he needs to employ this knowledge: in speaking to the laity, in advising teachers (and prospective teachers such as his students), and in his own work.

When the laity raise questions, a linguist should remember that these questions are complex and need careful and temperate answers. He should accept social expectations as inevitable, but try to put those expectations in the proper perspective. Harry Truman disturbed sensitive souls in Washington by injecting *manure* into his informal political comments; Mrs. Truman reminded those souls of her long struggle to persuade him to use a word as dignified as *manure*. A Charlestonian who uses *ain't* informally among his social peers would never use it in a formal speech, let alone in writing. And however important some point may seem today, it may be less important tomorrow. Perhaps the greatest service the linguist can render the laity is to encourage intelligent curiosity; to this end he should always be looking for readable books and articles to recommend to those who ask questions.

In dealing with teachers, a linguist should realize that though an objective concern with language is an ideal, the elementary classroom – in fact, almost any classroom except that where the language is being studied scientifically – is not the best place to pursue it. If in one sense, as viable linguistic systems, all natural varieties of language are equal, in the practical world some are more equal than others. The use of some linguistic forms may interfere with the reception of the message they convey; it is fine to speak about creative imperatives, but for most people creative writing is a spare-time luxury. Most of what most of us write most of the time is designed to convey specific messages to influence thinking or behavior, even on so low a level as correcting a mistake by the shipping clerk. A linguist should realize that for English – or any other language – there is a body of acceptable usage, fairly well agreed upon, and that the range of acceptability is more restricted in writing than in speech. To be sure, the purpose of courses in composition is to develop ease in communicating in a tolerable range of styles; and the writing of connected prose is far more important than drill on minutiae of usage. Neverthless, everyone who writes connected prose should be aware of the amenities of educated writing, and the teacher should expect the students to observe those amenities. Yet in dealing with those amenities, the teacher should learn to distinguish the important from the trivial. In the 1950s a freshman instructor at Western Reserve complained that all semester she had been vainly trying to get her charges to write *somebody's else* rather than *somebody else's*; even if her judgment had been correct (and it wasn't) the problem was minor.

Finally, the most important obligation of a linguist is toward himself. He should never assume a pose of infallibility but always be willing to learn. He should shun the quick retort, the temptation to expose the ignorance of others, especially the ignorance of those who have no way of knowing better. Even when dealing with the arrogant and the pretentious, he should avoid retorts that may lead to long and fruitless controversies; a linguist seriously concerned with his profession has more than enough to do in setting his own data in order. The pundits-at-large have nothing more important to do than make noises; in controversies with them the serious linguist loses even if he wins the point at issue. It is well to remember the caution Hans Kurath gave to a colleague: "Honest work will always be honest work, and the maunderings of a fool will always be the maunderings of a fool – and sooner or later people will tell the difference. . . ." However little one may feel Kurath's optimism, a linguist should not be an evangelist about his work – though by precept and perhaps by example he may enlarge the frontiers of knowledge and lighten the darkness of ignorance. It is his business to learn as much as he can about the use of language, that most human form of behavior, and to let others see – as Mencken tried to do – that his kind of study is not only amusing and interesting but important.

Notes

1. That popularity is a poor guide in other fields is illustrated by an experience of T. S. Eliot at a women's club in Detroit in 1938. When he invited questions after his lecture, the first was "What kind of car do you drive?" Nonplussed, he responded, "A Ford. Why do you ask?" "Our Mr. Guest drives a Cadillac."
2. See Baron (1982, p. 226). Mostly in good-natured jest, the public relations staff at the University of Chicago, aware of my interest in American English, would signal my approach by calling out, "Here he comes! Watch your grammar!" To get natural interviews in the field, I found it advisable to identify myself as a historian or folklorist – anything but an English teacher.
3. One of these was probably my first-grade teacher, who conducted a small private school in Greenville in 1918–1919, when family obligations took her away from her distinguished private school in Charleston.
4. One of my distinguished colleagues, in rhetoric and literature, insists on a conflict between "grammar" and "structural linguistics," and repeatedly calls for a dictionary listing the words he doesn't use.
5. Kenyon (1948) shows that "informal" usage is not inferior to "formal," but another modality, and that one must recognize a formal substandard, as when *I done gone* is replaced by *I have went*.

References

The following list of references, drawn chiefly from works mentioned in the text, are suggestions for further reading. Further reading may be suggested by the bibliographies in Finegan (1980), McDavid (1979, 1980), and Mencken (1963). The reader should remember, however, that reading is no substitute for informed observation, and that in the long run everyone is responsible for his own judgments.

ATWOOD, E. BAGBY (1953) *A Survey of Verb Forms in the Eastern United States.* Ann Arbor: University of Michigan Press.

AVIS, WALTER S. *et al.* (1967) *A Dictionary of Canadianisms on Historical Principles.* Toronto: W. J. Gage.

BARON, DENNIS E. (1982) *Grammar and Good Taste: Reforming the English language.* New Haven and London: Yale.

BAUGH, ALBERT C. and THOMAS CABLE (1978) *A History of the English Language,* 3rd ed. Englewood Cliffs, New Jersey: Prentice-Hall.

CASSIDY, FREDERIC G. (1985–). *Dictionary of American Regional English.* Cambridge, Massachusetts: the Belknap Press of Harvard University.

CASSIDY, FREDERIC G. and ROBERT LePAGE (1967) *Dictionary of Jamaican English on Historical Principles.* Cambridge, England: Cambridge University Press.

CRAIGIE, SIR WILLIAM and JAMES R. HULBERT (1938–1944) *A Dictionary of American English on Historical Principles.* Chicago: University of Chicago Press.

CRESWELL, THOMAS J. (1975) *Usage in Dictionaries and Dictionaries of Usage.* PADS 63-4. University, Alabama: University of Alabama Press.

EAGLESON, ROBERT *et al.* (in preparation) *Dictionary of Australian English.*

FINEGAN, EDWARD (1980) *Attitudes toward English Usage: The history of a war on words.* New York: Teachers College Press.

FRIES, CHARLES C. (1925) 'The periphrastic future with *shall* and *will* in Modern English', PMLA 40.963–1024.

FRIES, CHARLES C. (1940) *American English Grammar*. New York: Appleton-Century-Crofts.

HALL, ROBERT A., JR. (1960) *Linguistics and Your Language*. Garden City, New York: Anchor.

JESPERSEN, OTTO (1922–1949) *A Modern English Grammar*, 7 vols. Heidelberg: Winter.

KENYON, JOHN S. (1948) 'Cultural levels and functional varieties of English.' *College English*, 10, 31–36.

KRAPP, GEORGE PHILIP (1927) *Comprehensive Guide to Good English*. Chicago: Rand McNally.

KRUISINGA, ETSKO (1925–1932) *A Handbook of Present-day English*, 4 vols. Groningen: Noordhoff.

KURATH, HANS (1972) *Studies in Area Linguistics*. Bloomington, Indiana: Indiana University Press.

KURATH, HANS and RAVEN I. MCDAVID, JR. (1961) *The Pronunciation of English in the Atlantic States*. Ann Arbor: University of Michigan Press, 1982: reprint University of Alabama Press.

KURATH, HANS *et al.* (1939–1943) *Linguistic Atlas of New England*. 3 vols., bound as 6. Providence: Brown University for the American Council of Learned Societies, 1972: reprinted, 3 vols., New York: AMS Press.

LIGHTER, JONATHAN and BETHANY DUMAS (in preparation) *Historical Dictionary of American Slang*. New York: Random House.

MCDAVID, RAVEN I., JR. (1979) *Dialects in Culture: Essays in general dialectology*, ed. William A. Kretzschmar, Jr., University, Alabama: University of Alabama Press.

MCDAVID, RAVEN I., JR. (1980) *Varieties of American English: Essays selected and introduced by Anwar S. Dil*. Stanford, California: Stanford University Press.

MATHEWS, MITFORD M. (1951) *A Dictionary of Americanisms on Historical Principles*. Chicago: University of Chicago Press.

MENCKEN, H.L. (1919) *The American Language*. New York: Knopf.

MENCKEN, H.L. (1936) 4th edition.

MENCKEN, H.L. (1945) Supplement One.

MENCKEN, H.L. (1948) Supplement Two.

MENCKEN, H.L. (1963) One-volume abridged edition: the fourth edition and the two supplements, edited with new material by Raven I. McDavid, Jr., with the assistance of David W. Maurer.

MORRIS, WILLIAM and MARY MORRIS (1975) *Harper Dictionary of Contemporary Usage*. New York: Harper & Row.

MURRAY, SIR JAMES A.H. *et al.* (1882–1928) *Oxford English Dictionary*, 12 vols. Oxford: the Clarendon Press.

MURRAY, SIR JAMES A.H. (1933) *Supplement*, ed. C. T. Onions and Sir William Craigie.

MURRAY, SIR JAMES A.H. (1972–) *Second Supplement*, ed. R. W. Burchfield.

MURRAY, K.M. ELISABETH (1977) *Caught in the Web of Words*. New Haven: Yale.

POUTSMA, HENDRICK (1914–1929) *A Grammar of Late Modern English*, 2 pt. in 5 vols. Groningen: Noordhoof.

PRATT, TERRY K. (in preparation) *Dictionary of Prince Edward Island English*.

PYLES, THOMAS (1952) *Words and their Ways in American English*. New York: Random House.

QUIRK, RANDOLPH (1968) *The Use of English*., 2nd ed. London: Longman.

QUIRK, RANDOLPH, SIDNEY GREENBAUM, GEOFFREY LEECH, and JAN SVARTVIK (1972) *A Grammar of Contemporary English*. London: Longman.

REED, CARROLL E. (1972) *Dialects of American English*. Cleveland: World. 1977, 2nd ed., revised. Amherst, Massachusetts: University of Massachusetts Press.

SLEDD, JAMES H. and WILMA R. EBBITT (1962) *Dictionaries and THAT Dictionary*. Chicago: Scott, Foresman.

STORY, GEORGE *et al.* (1982) *Dictionary of Newfoundland English*. Toronto: University of Toronto Press.

SVARTVIK, JAN and RANDOLPH QUIRK (1980) *A Corpus of English Conversation*. Lund: Gleerup.

Visser, Fredericus Theodorus (1963–1973) *An Historical Syntax of the English Language*, 3 vols. in 4. Leiden: Brill.

Webster's Third New International Dictionary (1961) Springfield, Mass.: G. & C. Merriam.

Wells, J.C. (1982) *Accents of English*, 3 vols. Cambridge, England: Cambridge University Press.

Wright, Joseph (1898–1905) *English Dialect Dictionary*, 6 vols. London: Frowde.

Chapter 4

Between the Lines

SUSAN P. MILLER

YOU might assume that people whose teaching and research are devoted to written composition get together fairly often to commiserate, and that such gatherings occur more frequently these days. Most people who give the matter any thought acknowledge the difficulties inherent in teaching composition under any circumstances, but lately a "literacy crisis" attributed to various causes (e.g. new grammars that suddenly rather than thoughtfully replaced familiar pedagogy) is nationally recognized. But when I describe recent professional responses to this literacy crisis not as gatherings of scholars and teachers pointing red pens at enemies of standard writing, but instead as groups thoughtfully pondering the special and particularly troublesome status of writing in America today, I may seem to portray us as passive or unconcerned about the quality of written discourse. This is not so, but we nonetheless find ourselves assenting only partially to what appears to be new public support for our task and disagreeing – but only partially – with public views of the crisis in written language.

Let me explain.

Academic as well as public complaints about the "writing crisis" tend to fall into two groups. For instance, in a poll I recently conducted at the University of Wisconsin-Milwaukee, faculty most often identified two "student writing problems" as most troublesome: *basics* (mechanics, grammar, spelling, syntax) and *composition* (focus, organization, purpose, clarity, brevity, readability). In general, this rough but overwhelmingly agreed-upon identification of student problems coincides with the identification that a broader public makes. The current decline of writing ability in those who must write on the job is also frequently categorized in terms of *basics* and *composition*. These are generally perceived to be the discrete problems of two groups who write in professional and business settings – those who write as recorders and archivists of others' ideas, and those who write to create and convey new ideas that become part of the written context for action that may define a profession, a business setting, and ultimately our culture.

The first group – secretaries, word processors, clerks, or administrative assistants of one and another title – must primarily be familiar with accepted conventions of Edited American English. When these workers do not "write" accurately, they present bad images not so much of themselves as of the organization or institution they work for. They become human embodiments of broken wheels, clogged pipes, and "technical difficulties beyond our control." Like beginning college students who bring down faculty and community wrath on high schools, or like high-school students who provoke the same ire against pre-secondary education, people who "write" primarily to promulgate and display other people's ideas are expected by their readers to produce an accurate surface, what we in fact call the *surface features* of written discourse.

As an administrator of large writing programs for entering college students, I have become most familiar with charges of failure in this quality of writing. Written texts, perceived as graphic representations of prior thought are – as speech is not – relatively permanent objectifications of facts and ideas. They cannot easily be qualified, recast, or restated to assure their communicative effectiveness. Written language preserves and is conservative. Its conventional practices enable it to stand for and stand in for its author or its intent. A law, a contract, a letter, a newspaper, an advertisement, a personnel file, or the minutes of a meeting must accurately re-present past actions and make clear future commitments. Those responsible for displaying these explicit and implicit actions through written language are important functionaries in any literate society. The scribes who recorded Charlemagne's diplomatic correspondence and read it aloud in another court assured that illiterate king and his time of our recognition.

We agree, therefore, with public and academic complaints about basics, although our compulsion is not primarily to preserve a fixed and standard written code but rather to allow written language itself to retain its documentary function. We nag poor spellers, mark sloppy citations of research sources, or complain that students who speak them fluently "do not know what a sentence is" without embarrassment or constraint, despite questionable predictions that computers and visual media will replace writing in a new cultural setting. Our rain falls on the just and the unjust – the humanities student as well as the young engineer – not because we think that everyone should be an English major, but because we know that accuracy, attention to detail, and pride of craft represent and sustain literate civilization. It is fussiness itself, not only our particular fuss, that we charge ourselves with preserving.

But there are, you have noticed, problems with this point of view. That "writing" should be only, or even primarily the study of the functionary, the scribe, the writing technician, is hardly satisfactory. What about purpose, organization, clarity, and focus? What about *writing*?

It is not only academics, nor even especially academics who teach writing, who notice the sharp disparity between the bright, alert, curious, intelligent, creative student – or lawyer, doctor, and executive – and his or her wooden, mindless, wordy, disorganized prose. Business and government today spend fairly large sums setting up continuing education programs within which consultants attempt to make institutional writing readable. While the National Assessment of Educational Progress repeatedly demonstrates that pre-college writers are no less in control of *basics* now than ten years ago, expanding corporate government, and university-level writing programs all attest to a writing problem of another sort. More and more of the statements that functionaries and machines can (or cannot) record in a standard written form do not make sense.

Thus my qualification of our assent to public attitudes toward writing. If we disagree only partially with complaints about the quality of written language, we must also limit our agreement with common placements of the problem only in relaxed language standards. I must instead argue that the general division, or categorization, of writing problems is not a simple identification of two kinds of problems, but in effect a complicated and contradictory perception. *Basics* and *composition* have become two poles; the tension between them is the writing crisis we thoughtfully ponder.

I can most directly demonstrate the nature of this overlooked contradiction by exploring the implications of the word *basic*, which is most generally taken to mean something learned before it is used or practiced. It follows for most people inside and outside academe that writing should be mastered *before* students come to college, or certainly *before* they proceed to specialized work in pre-professional programs. It was this principle that in 1898 motivated C. C. Thach (whose report was echoed in the Harvard Board of Overseers Report the following year and reads uncannily like recent *Time* and *Newsweek* essays on the current decline of adult literacy) to state that:

> It is difficult to believe, at times, that many of the writers of college entrance papers are English-speaking boys. In the most mechanical points of execution – in handwriting, spelling, punctuation – a large number are deficient to an appalling degree. They have no vocabulary; words do not appeal to them, or have for them the least significance. . . . Unity or coherence of thought is seldom exhibited. Long chains of unrelated ideas are tacked together in a slack-rope sentence. . . . Paragraphing is seldom attempted, unless after the fashion of one student who systematically indented in lines in blocks of five.

Now whether students can "read and write" before they come to college, or could do so in the past, the deeply rooted opinion that writing is something one properly learns before applying it poses a curious logic that those who teach writing find problematic, not only because its validity would make their endeavors at best always remedial. The example of "doing research" will perhaps best explain what I mean.

When a high-school student is assigned the task of a "report," be it book report or collecting some facts about, let us say, the Civil War, that student is learning new and important *basics* about the world of written discourse. He or she is first of all coming to know that libraries have systematically arranged resources about "history," "war," "military tactics," "the American South," "slavery," and a long list of other such relevant categories. Additionally, the student is being encouraged to survey this material to learn about *basic* reference sources – the *Encyclopedia Brittanica*, for instance. And the student is also learning, usually for the first time, that books contain authoritative information; only rarely will the sources disagree about "the facts," and students only rarely will know when they do.

The high-school student, then, will accomplish "research" by finding, reading, and reporting what books – often only encyclopedias and the resources of a small high-school library – say. A report that the teacher likes may be a compilation of quotations from sources. To the student (and to the evaluating teacher), finding out what the Civil War was all about is the point; when, where, who, how, and perhaps why make up the substance of a good report.

Obviously, this sort of "research" won't do in college or in business. A college-level teacher of either history or research techniques expects not only more, but also different, content in a research project about the Civil War. The teacher of research in an English Department will, if he or she believes that the student should be able to "read and write" before entering college, find it frustrating to have to elaborate and explain how to "read" the biases, intentions, and general etiology of a particular book about the Civil War. The teacher will find it unfathomable that the student who claims to have done research in high school will not know that accurately citing the author, date, and publisher of an opinion is essential in academic discourse. But the student does not yet know that *the* book is only one of many similar books. Its economic explanation of the Civil War may oppose another's argument from cultural history; its author may have repudiated its conclusions in a later publication; its publisher may be known for publicizing fairly shallow, decidely right-wing or leftist cases. So "simple" matters – paraphrase, citations, or using books to support *your* case rather than only "to report" what books say – are beyond the student, however well he or she read and wrote in high school.

It might be argued that intensive instruction in high school could accelerate this progress and genuinely prepare students to be able college researchers *before* college or prepare the high-school graduate to write reports in a business setting. For exceptional students, this is surely true. But because most students learn to understand multiple perspectives, to mediate among arguments, and to assume public rather than personal points of view only at about age 17, the idea that they would be able composers of research *before* entering college is largely unrealistic. They are ready to learn to compose their own cases using other sources, but they will not have already learned to do so.

Most important, my own and others' research shows that all writers tend to lose control of the surface features of writing when they write for new audiences, in new contexts, in new formats, and about new topics. The belief that people learn to write *before* applying the basics thus becomes highly questionable. Even adapting to a new medium – the electronic typewriter, the word processor, or the dictaphone – will dislocate the formerly able, formerly "correct" writer, at least temporarily. But whether the medium is new or familiar, each of us can re-create our vaguely anxious hesitations at any age when we must compose our first publishable writing outside of school, our first letter outside the company, our first report to a lawyer or the IRS.

Consequently, we could multiply indefinitely the brief example of the problem of focusing, organizing, and elegantly shaping written research about the Civil War in a new, collegiate setting. No more than the best swimmer at the local pool can navigate the Chesapeake, be on an Olympic team, or consider attempting Diana Nyad's open-water feats can an unpracticed writer accomplish what someone experienced in a particular discourse context achieve. Even to argue, "surely they can learn to *spell* and remember it" is to forget that in the new collegiate or professional setting, the writer must learn new content and new strategies for making a point, must identify the issues that are important in this context, and must learn new formats, styles, and registers. Spelling is the last thing on anyone's mind. Except the impatient reader's. No one would argue that impatient reader out of the right to the courtesy of readable, conventional, corrected prose – only out of a simple view that the "parts" of writing are sequentially mastered for all time. Understanding that they are not will not appease the impatient reader, but will alert writers to watch for their own new inabilities in newly demanding writing.

But the idea that writing is something learned *before* its practice nonetheless controls both its public and its academic images. Even those who teach writing yield to the temptation implicit in thinking that *basics* only precede *composition*, and that they are merely two different, rather than inextricably mixed, problems. They search for ways to teach people to be "writers" as though they would be able to find the keys to one-shot, permanently effective, attractively boxed programs that could substitute "training" for development. Instead of explaining to students at any level, whether in schools or in new "development" programs in business, that their writing will always be subject to the entire spectrum of writing problems and that its composition as well as its editing will mirror their ease and comfort with a particular human situation, teachers – understandably, if unfortunately – try to find ways to get writing over with. They are schooled to "hunt down errors," not to understand them; they look for tricks and authorities to improve products rather than descriptions of the complicated processes that result in provisional mastery of both basics and composition. Such teaching divides writing skills from writing – from history, literature, and philosophy, for instance – to make the statement that such writings are different not in purpose but in *kind*, that they are "privileged," esoteric, and unquestionable as the results of a particular writer's intentions. It encourages students to learn writing as a technique, not as a potential source of public impact and/or power they must account for in a long history of other writings.

It is clear, then, that public and academic ideas interact to further complicate the relation of *basics* to *composition*. While both realms require writers to produce focused, organized, clear, meaningful composition, both also are under the spell of technological mythologies rooted in our century's respect for (and popular misunderstanding of) science and empiricism. Consequently, the "something" I have been referring to as learned *before* has become specified in both spheres as a skill. "Skill" of course originally meant "ability," but the word now connotes a knack, trick, or bit of information that can assure success in any performance. Skills are the components of mental technologies – once "in place," they "work." Skills blur, rather than show a clear connection between *basics* and *composition*.

In education at all levels, the skills mentality has produced a nomenclature for writing that is ludicrously at odds with the human difficulties inherent in the act of composition. Writing is "diagnosed," treated with "prose paramedic" methods, "profiled," and "assessed" or "measured." It is assigned according to number of words, format, or "mode" rather than purpose. It is organized by "models" like the "inverted funnel," praised for having an "argumentative edge" whose ideas are "nutshelled." One textbook was recently promoted as "teacher-proof," and others "program" learning in "modules."

The point to protesting these inorganic metaphors in this context is not that they represent inhumane trappings, but that they provide people learning to write for themselves with essentially useless substance about composition. That is, while our entire culture complains of unreadable prose that is not written by a person who has something to say and a particular reason for saying it, such educational practices suggest that writing may be accomplished apart from its author, readers, and communicative purpose.

This attitude is subsequently returned to educators, in the person of the student who thinks writing is a highly technical skill whose mastery is both beyond possibility and irrelevant to life. Students are themselves the public who have come to see writing as but one of many specialized skills that is in no way more central to their lives than any other. They have, after all, had to master a number of literacies. They can often make and always interpret films, and are unself-consciously familiar with conventions like split screens that only recently required thoughtful interpretation. They can often program computers, read statistical data, and visualize charts or graphs that quantify qualitative statements. They are then genuinely surprised to learn, if they do, that written language contains and defines their civilization, or that its mastery will be required not as a *basic*, nor even as a *skill*, but also as *composition*. When asked independently to form and shape ideas into particular and effective documents suitable for public communication, they are at a loss.

But students, after all, may yet be required to learn both *basics* and *composition*. Their opposition or education blurring into one impossibly technical skill is of less consequence than the prevalent public anxiety that allows writing to be thought of almost as a foreign language. Because it is so common to focus on the concept of correctness – and the difficulty of achieving it – as the hallmark of powerful, cultivated writing, the public's anxieties disproportionately cloud their abilities to judge the purpose of written communication – their own as well as others'. While everyone is willing to agree that "writing is important," everyone is equally capable of being alienated from both the reading and the accurate composition of it. The burdensome image of "writing" therefore intimidates, dangerously, our good sense about thoughtless, mindless, or intentionally misleading prose.

Examples abound. None of us think that the following sentence makes a clear point:

> Pursuant to the recent memorandum issued August 9, 1979, because of petroleum exigencies, it is incumbent upon us all to endeavour to make maximal utilization of telephonic communication in lieu of personal visitation.

Any one of us can better understand:

> As the memo of August 9 said, because of the gas shortage, try to use the telephone as much as you can instead of making personal visits.

But any one of us has read such sentences and been willing to believe that the people who wrote them were powerful, had "good" educations, and could write. Pompous diction is not, unfortunately, so often associated with pomposity as it is with "good," or "school" or "English teacher" writing. Big words and stilted sentences signal to us not that the person writing knows what he or she is talking about, but rather that the writer has clout and is well connected within a structure we must obey.

Such writing wastes the time of the writer, costs business, government, and the public unnecessary sums in time for reproduction, and keeps many readers from looking closely for the meaning of written communication. It is expensive, not only in dollars, but also in the human costs of unnecessary distance between people who have "petroleum exigencies" in common.

But writing need not be primarily pompous to be dangerous. This sample from an actual recall letter can illustrate:

> In addition, your vehicle may also require adjustment service to the hood secondary catch system. The secondary catch may be misaligned so that the hood may not be adequately restrained to prevent hood fly-up in the event the primary latch is inadvertently left unengaged. Sudden hood fly-up beyond the secondary catch while driving could impair driver visibility. In certain circumstances, occurrence of either of the above conditions could result in vehicle crash without prior warning.

If the company wanted to tell millions of people owning a particular car that they were in danger of an accident because of a design error, it would begin, perhaps, with: A problem with the design of your car may cause an accident. But if the company wants to save money, reduce its liability, and blur the entire problem, it writes (notice *it*, not Mr. Edsel or Mr. Coronado) to distract, tire, confuse, and insofar as possible obscure the issue. Such writing "sounds" technical; it "sounds" purposeful. It is "correct." But no one wrote it and no one hopes that anyone will read it. And no one will read it who is willing to be intimated, put off, or overwhelmed by writing that decomposes rather than composes a relation between writer, reader, and purpose.

Both of these examples illustrate the usually overlooked danger to the public from the public willingness to believe that "writing" is well executed if its spelling, grammar, and vocabulary appear to embody what Tom Wolfe has called "the right stuff." By valuing propriety over meaning, our culture conspires to separate both reading and writing from life, where they in fact may cause accidents.

We have not collectively appropriated the written language. On the one hand, we become impatient with education (in the person of the English teacher) telling us that writing, unlike speech, depends on conventions that must be adhered to because they embody statements we will be responsible for when we are not present, at a later time. We mistrust conventional correctness, associating it with phoney posturing rather than with nurturing carefulness. But on the other, we do allow a phoney correctness – in its broadest definition as pomposity, wordiness, and obfuscation – to tyrannize our good sense. We do not demand that government, corporations – even educators – make written sense, reply to writing by writing ourselves, or read carefully between the lines. We allow a false sense of hierarchy to keep us from the available, powerful medium that sustains and controls much of our lives. The points implicit in each of my explanations – that both *basics* and *composition* are inextricably and variously linked to specific people in specifically motivated situations and that people of any age never divorce writing (or reading) from their motivations, from experiences with a particular kind of medium, from audience, from outcomes, or from anxieties – should be taken not as another English teacher's prodding, but as an invitation to full participation in the written fabric of our culture.

The causes of our separation from our written language as well as of *basics* from *composition* and their results have long, deep roots in American sociology and politics, where writing well rather than correct or "received" pronunciation determine social and economic mobility. It might be argued that pitting appropriate phoney correctness and the *basics* against *composition* preserves an inevitable – some would say necessary – separation of functionaries from professionals, of workers from management. You know, I am sure, arguments that separate the kind of literacy some students "need" from the sort that others do. But in a real sense, this separation has finally caught up with us all. By treating writing as a technique rather than as a potential source – for good and ill – of power and impact, education has placed ideas about power, impact, and excellence in writing beyond the realm of the ordinary. Mirroring the public it serves, education separates the vocational and technical skill of writing from the authoritative personal power of writings – history, economic theories, philosophy, religion, literature. And it thereby, if paradoxically, helps overwhelm the development of clear, effective, public voices in the elite whose supposed access to full literacy cannot, it turns out, be taken for granted. Both the functionary and the powerful, the reader and the writer, are inadvertently crippled in a world of texts where the importance of making sense in writing is never fully explored.

This is to say, of course, that an education in only "grammar and mechanics," or even additionally in forms, formats, and formulas that make up measurable "skills," leaves us unable to operate within the changing world of documents we have made. While it is clear to anyone alive since the Second World War that any education must not be "training," but rather an ability to *retrain* oneself to adapt to cultural transformations, this clarity has not shaped attitudes toward writing. The public demands that writing be a fixed, standardized code and wants to know *the* right form for a memo or report, *one* way to document research, the *correct* vocabulary for a particular field. Rules rather than principles tend to control both the surface and the substance of writing. The idea of writing is lost in our unnecessary alienation from pen and paper, and we compose, read, and fuss over surfaces rather than raising issues and making points, proposing and recording complex meanings. The more "literate" we have become, the less literate we are.

No other society arose so directly from the power of a people to write for itself. The Bill of Writes might have been the better name for the document that preceded the Declaration of Independence, the Constitution, and the Federalist Papers. A shipment of books – not of well-born faculty – founded Harvard College. No other society has shared its originating power so widely among all citizens. But for those of us who attempt to continue this tradition, the inability to foster both strong *and* acceptable written voices in new generations has become a complex problem perhaps never elsewhere experienced.

It is on these grounds that those of us who profess writing thoughtfully ponder the contemporary writing crisis. Even our functional and necessary equivalent of Charlemagne's scribe will be called upon for complex tasks of analysis, interpretation, media management, and self-protection in a world of print and printouts we may not yet have imagined. Neither visual nor sound recordings will replace or even compete strongly with writing as a way of generating and documenting the social, economic, and political management of this society. Yet the however minimally "educated" are increasingly overwhelmed by writing, its victims rather than its competent and imaginative cohorts. Consequently, while we agree, we also disagree – but only partially – with descriptions of a writing crisis more essential and serious in its implications than most people consciously realize.

For Further Reading

BOLINGER, DWIGHT. *Language: The Loaded Weapon.* London and New York: Longman, 1980.

MILLER, SUSAN. "Rhetorical Maturity: Definition and Development." In *Reinventing the Rhetorical Tradition*, pp. 118–127. Ed. A. Freedman and Ian Pringle. Rpt. Champaign, Illinois: National Council of Teachers of English, 1981.

SHAUGHNESSY, MINA. *Errors and Expectations.* New York: Oxford University Press, 1976.

STUBBS, MICHAEL. *Language and Literacy: The Sociolinguistics of Reading and Writing.* London: Routledge & Kegan Paul, 1980.

WHEELER, THOMAS C. *The Great American Writing Block.* New York: Viking Press, 1979.

WILLIAMS, JOSEPH. *Style: Ten Lessons in Clarity and Grace.* Chicago: Scott, Foresman & Company, 1981.

Chapter 5

Language Attitudes and Self-Fulfilling Prophecies in the Elementary School

JERRIE SCOTT AND GENEVA SMITHERMAN

LARGELY as an outgrowth of the social movements of the 1960s, a good deal of public attention has been directed toward the educational failure of minority and "disadvantaged" students. In daily newspapers, one often finds tables, similar to those used in academic research reports, that provide comparative data of test scores received by Anglos, Afro-Americans, Hispanics, and lower social-class students. The Self-Fulfilling Prophecy thesis, advanced by Rosenthal and Jacobson (1968) primarily for an academically oriented audience, has been discussed so widely that most anyone can provide the corollary colloquial explanation: "what you expect is what you get." Far less public attention has been directed toward the information that has been most beneficial in demystifying the nature of the Self-Fulfilling Prophecy. Such information stems largely from studies of language attitudes and their relationship to teacher expectations and student performance. Not only have these studies greatly enhanced our understanding of problems confronting minority students in the schools, this work has also provided new insights into the role that public attitudes towards language play in shaping the school culture.

Perhaps the most disturbing conclusion that has emerged from studies of language attitudes in the schools is that the social structure of the schools seems to replicate the social organization of American society. Simply stated, the Have's perform well, and the Have-Not's become educational failures. The critical question is whether this social structure is to be attributed solely to the students or whether the schools play a role in shaping the social structure. In his discussion of the school's role, Rist notes:

> It appears that the public school system not only mirrors the configurations of the larger society, but also significantly contributes to maintaining them. Thus the system of public education in reality perpetuates what it is ideologically committed to eradicate – class barriers which result in the social and economic life of the citizenry (1971, p. 108).

Rist's conclusion is drawn from a study conducted during the time when the general public was concerned about educational inequities, a time when desegregation plans were being initiated and compensatory education programs were being implemented to address the needs of minority students.

Currently, more emphasis is placed on raising educational "standards." Yet, there are many who are concerned about how this new educational focus will affect the social structure of the schools. For example, in the February 1983 issue of the *Advocate*, a monthly publication of the Florida Teaching Profession–National Education Association (FTP–NEA), the guidelines proposed for raising school standards were criticized for their failure to consider the needs of disadvantaged students and minorities. Similarly, the FTP–NEA contends that the new proposals are a threat to basic educational principles:

> ... it [the report of the Governor's Commission on Secondary Schools] concentrates on the achievement of excellence, which is commendable, but does so in such a way that the school system could become elitist, leaving many of Florida's students without assistance, and violating the principle of free, public education for all children (p. 3).

Whether one focuses on problems relevant to eradicating educational inequities or elevating educational "standards," there is still concern over whether the school system can change without perpetuating "what it is ideologically committed to eradicate."

Now that a significant body of research has been done on the social barriers that exist in the schools, it should be possible to address educational problems so that all children will benefit from the educational process. This paper begins with a brief summary of viewpoints that emerged from studies of language attitudes. Our intent is to demonstrate how frequently, how unconsciously, and sometimes how unwisely, we use language cues to evaluate others. At a more specific level, research has provided new insights into the mechanisms by which class barriers are formed and maintained in classrooms and the effects that class barriers have on the performance of minority students. The second part of the paper describes factors that influence the social structure of the classroom and the performance of minority students. Our intent is to de-mystify the events that make the Self-Fulfilling Prophecy a reality in the classroom. In the third and final section of this paper, we examine ways that attitudinal problems can be addressed in the schools. Again our discussion draws heavily on research findings, but attention is also given to attempts to apply research findings to problems in the schools. Special attention is given to the highly publicized King Federal court case in Ann Arbor, Michigan.

Language Attitudes

Of the conclusions that have been drawn from studies of language attitudes and education, five are of special importance to this discussion:

1. Associations are made between speech patterns and one's social status and ethnic group affiliation.
2. Associations are made between speech patterns and the personal qualities of the speaker.
3. One's personal evaluational reactions to speech are a stereotyped version of his/her attitudes toward the users of that speech.
4. Teacher expectation of a pupil's academic performance has a sometimes "unwitting" yet significant influence on the actual performance of that pupil.

ET–K

5. The school strongly shares in maintaining the organizational structure of society.

Before discussing the five points above, it is useful to describe the methodology of researchers on language attitudes. Rather than asking people if they use speech cues to evaluate others, a segment of taped speech is played and people are asked to evaluate the characteristics of the speaker. The characteristics to be evaluated are presented on a rating form, consisting of pairs of opposite traits, selected on the basis of the associations being investigated. Characteristics may include features having to do with language, e.g. standardness vs. non-standardness; with personality traits, e.g. honesty vs. dishonesty; or even with academic potential, e.g. least vs. most likely to succeed, and the list goes on. The features are placed on a scale of, say, one through five, allowing for a wide range of possible responses. Although most people make associations between speech patterns and characteristics of a speaker, they either are not consciously aware of this tendency or do not readily admit that they make these associations. Perhaps people feel that morally the practice seems unjust, or intellectually it seems unsound. In any case, the method described above makes it possible to elicit data on people's impressions in an indirect and systematic manner, which is attested to by the consistency with which different researchers attained similar results. This technique reveals another important point about attitudes towards language: attitudes are often formed unconsciously and communicated unintentionally.

Regarding the first of the five conclusions, several studies have shown that correct identification of race (or ethnicity) can often be made on the basis of speech samples (Bryden, 1968; Shuy, 1969; Lambert and Tucker, 1969). Similarly, though less often, correct identification of socio-economic or social status can also be made on the basis of speech samples, as reported in studies by Putnam and O'Hern (1955), Harms (1961), and Ellis (1967). Still other studies have shown that there is a connection between judgments about ethnicity (or race) and social class (Williams, 1970a; Naremore, 1969).

As evidence of our tendency to associate speech patterns with ethnicity and social class, it is interesting to consider examples from everyday experiences. In telephone conversations, for example, one may find that an unknown caller can be identified according to race. As with everything else, however, we sometimes err; nevertheless, mistaken identity is as informative as correct identity. An excellent example of mistaken identity was reported in a recent issue of *Newsweek*. The article, "What's wrong with Black English," was written by a Black college sophomore as a plea, we think, for Blacks to learn standard English. The author tells of her experience apartment hunting. After calling various rental offices, she was immediately invited over, but upon entering the establishment, she was immediately turned down. This case of mistaken identity is informative.

> The thinly concealed looks of shock when the front door opened clued me in, along with the flustered instances of "just getting off the phone with the girl ahead of you and she wants the rooms." When I finally found a place to live, my roommate stirred up old memories when she remarked a few months later, "you know, I was surprised when I first saw you. You sounded white over the phone." Tell me another one, sister (Jones, 1982, p. 7).

Beyond telling us that associations are made between speech and race, this case also illustrates one of the ways in which language is used in the general society to maintain a segregated system.

There is yet a deeper message in the article. One might wonder, for example, why the writer urges Blacks to learn standard English. Obviously she had been rejected, though fluent in standard English. As "soulful" as Black English is, she notes:

> Studies have proven that the use of ethnic dialects decreases power in the marketplace. . . . it hurts me to hear black children use Black English, knowing that they will be at yet another disadvantage in an educational system already full of stumbling blocks. . . . And what hurts most is to be stripped of my own blackness simply because I know my way around the English language (p. 7).

The deeper message here is that the person whose language is too rigid to communicate both within the community and in the dominant society is likely to be caught in what Smitherman has called the "push–pull syndrome," pushing toward mainstream language and culture and at the same time pulling toward the warmth and comfort of the family and home language and culture (Smitherman, 1977). The contradiction has posed a continuing dilemma for many Blacks as well as members of other non-mainstream groups.

Just as the research on associations between speech and race or social class gives explicit corroboration to what most people know implicitly (i.e. through "common sense"), the research on associations between speech and personal traits makes a similar powerful point (Holmes, 1968; Hughes, 1967; Williams, 1970a; Guskin, 1970; Fleming, 1970). Although most people pay little conscious attention to this practice, it is quite common. A question such as "did she/he sound friendly?" is likely to elicit a response, though the respondent may not be able to describe the particular features of speech that make one sound friendly. Writers often make use of this practice in their attempts to depict certain qualities of characters. In Daniel Keyes' novel, *Flowers for Algernon*, Charlie Gordon, the protagonist, undergoes brain surgery; his intelligence changes from moron to genius and back to moron. Keyes uses language to depict Charlie's progress from moron to genius.

As Moron: I had a test today. I think I failed it and I think maybe now they won't use me. . . . His name is Burt. I fergot his last name because I don't remembir so good (p. 1).
As Genius: When [the mouse, Algernon] found himself moving along the unfamiliar path, he slowed down, and his actions became erratic: start, pause, double back, turn around and then forward again, . . . (p. 216).

As an exercise, one might try to determine the specific differences between Charlie's language as a moron vs. his language as a genius. Based on what is known from research, writers may be more concerned with creating a stereotype than with matching a systematic group of language features with a particular personal trait. From the two samples above, we could make the general observation that Charlie the Moron pronounced words differently and used shorter sentences and smaller words than Charlie the Genius. So, our general impression of Charlie is based on rather general characteristics of his language, along with certain stereotypes we might have formed about people of high and low intelligence. And indeed, this line of reasoning is in keeping with the view expressed in the third conclusion, known among researchers as the stereotyping hypothesis.

The stereotyping hypothesis, as articulated by Williams (1970b), holds that people's reactions to speech are a generalized version of their attitudes toward the speaker's reference group. Williams, leading researcher in the area of language attitudes, conducted a series of studies to test the stereotyping hypothesis, reasoning that:

> (1) Speech types serve as social identifiers. (2) These elicit stereotypes held by ourselves and others (including ones of ourselves). (3) We tend to behave in accord with these stereotypes and thus (4) translate our attitudes into social reality. That is, we perpetuate or again reaffirm those distinctions of social structure stored in our stereotypes and manifested in our actions (p. 383).

This line of reasoning sheds light not only on the processes involved in stereotyping but also on the relationships between teachers' expectations and students' performance and between teachers' expectations and the social structure of the schools. Note that while speech cues may serve to initiate the stereotyping behavior, the stereotypes themselves stem from generalizations about the social group rather than the individual speaker. Expectations of the speaker are thus based on stereotypes about the social group. We tend to treat others according to how we think they will or should behave. Behavior becomes a critical factor in explaining the events that make self-fulfilling prophecies a reality in society and in the classroom. Through our behavior, we communicate to others what we expect of them. Whether these others act in accordance with our expectations or not, we may perceive them as doing so. Depending on the status and roles of ourselves and these others, our perceptions of them can help shape their expectations and perceptions of us as well as of themselves.

The school setting accords a high status and a dominant role to the teacher; consequently, teacher attitudes play an important role in shaping students' expectations and perceptions of themselves as well as of the teacher. Social reality is revealed in the classroom in terms of teacher attitudes, the role that teacher attitudes play in shaping teacher expectations, and the influence that teacher behavior has on student performance. Studies concerned with these factors led to the fourth and fifth conclusions.

Rosenthal and Jacobson studied teacher expectations; the Self-Fulfilling Prophecy thesis emerged from that study. Briefly, Rosenthal and Jacobson shaped teachers' expectations of children by describing the children as "spurters." Though randomly selected from the total student body, the group described as spurters showed significantly higher gains in their performance than other students for whom no descriptions were offered. The results of the study suggest that teacher expectations influence student performance. Emphasis in this work is placed on teacher expectations as input and student performance as outcome. Obviously other intervening factors need to be considered: how teacher expectations are communicated to students; how students and teachers interact in the classroom; and how each of these factors influences the social structure of the classroom.

The conclusion that the school shares in maintaining societal structure was deducted from research that sought to analyze the process by which expectations influence the classroom experience for the teacher and the student. In this latter work, social criteria were shown to play an important role in teachers' decisions about how to group students in different groups and in the type of interaction patterns between teachers and students perceived as "high" and "low" achievers. To the extent that social criteria are used to guide educational decisions, the school culture can be predicted to perpetuate the social structure of society.

Unfair though it might seem, the general public expects teachers' attitudes toward the learning potential of all students to be positive, regardless of children's social class, race, or ethnicity. The public's expectations are not always fulfilled, in large measure because school personnel may not be consciously aware of the subtle ways in which attitudes toward language influence the learning environment, and, therefore, the social structure of the classroom.

Social Structure and Classroom Barriers

Teachers react to language cues and form expectations about the performance of others in much the same way that other people do. Depending on the kind of pre-professional or in-service training a teacher has had, negative attitudes toward low prestige varieties of language and negative stereotypes toward non-mainstream groups may have been reinforced by educational theories. For instance, the ideology of compensatory education validates the practice of using language patterns of lower socio-economic groups to evaluate academic potential by advancing the notion that the language of the lower social class is cognitively deficient. Though the language deficit hypothesis has been refuted on linguistic grounds (Labov, 1970) and on educational grounds (Baratz and Baratz, 1971), its basic principles are still expressed in much of the literature used in teacher education programs. In devising compensatory education programs, an elaborate list of labels emerged to describe minority students: culturally deprived, language deficient, economically disadvantaged, etc., each rationalized on the basis of students' language "deficiencies," their low social class status, or their environmental and cultural "deprivations". In the implementation of compensatory education programs, clever grouping schemes were devised, using social rather than academic criteria for assessing student learning potential. Based on the premise that the minority child's home environment ill prepared her/him for equal participation in the school culture and recognizing that the school culture was based on middle class norms, compensatory education programs attempted to prepare the student to be middle class, thereby preparing the student for the school culture. But most importantly for our discussion here, teachers may react to the language of minority students more negatively than the general public, precisely because of their continued exposure to educational theories/hypotheses that sanction negative reactions to lower socio-economic groups and to their language.

From this vantage-point, it is possible to see that in much the same way that

Rosenthal and Jacobson shaped teachers' expectations of a randomly selected group of students by describing them as "fast learners" and "spurters," the ideology of compensatory education helps shape teachers' expectations of any randomly selected group of minority students by labelling them as "deficient." Just as the language deficit theory links language structure to thinking abilities, teachers often employ this same practice as a rapid, "theoretically sound" measure of student academic potential. In a pedagogy founded on the premise that minority students must imitate the language patterns and language behaviors of middle-class children in order to benefit from instruction in the schools, teachers could very well be expected to model their instructional programs and their teaching styles accordingly. And when teachers follow compensatory education guidelines for grouping students, the so-called ability groupings in the classroom may be little more than social-class groupings. From the research on language attitudes in the schools, we now know that language attitudes, teachers' expectations, teachers' performance, and the social structure of the classroom all too often reflect the ideology of compensatory education.

Concerning teachers' attitudes toward the language of minorities, researchers tell us that some language patterns and language behaviors of students systematically elicit favorable responses from teachers (Rist, 1971):

Language Patterns —Standard English pronunciation, in particular the absence of stigma-
tized features, such as "den" for "then";
—Standard English grammar, most notably standard usage of subject
verb agreement rules, such as "he walks" rather than "he walk";
—Length of sentences: longer sentences are preferable to shorter ones;
—Absence of pauses in speech, a feature presumably associated with
fluency.
Language Behavior—Initiating statements in class;
—Appearing confident in speech;
—Giving directions/demands to other students;
—Speaking for the class, e.g. "we want to color"

Almost any educator will agree that the characteristics above do not provide sufficient data on which to evaluate a students' academic potential. Yet when information about how teachers assess academic potential is indirectly elicited, the above characteristics have been shown to play an important role in that assessment. These are the speech cues which, according to Williams (1970b) serve as social identifiers. Moreover, they elicit stereotypes, and the stereotypes help to shape teachers' expectations of students. If teacher expectations influence student performance, then we need to be concerned about the factors that intervene between what teachers think and what students do.

Rist set out to discover the factors that were most critical in the teacher's development of expectations for various groups and to determine how differential expectations are manifested in the classroom. Of special impor- tance to his study was the grouping pattern of students. Rist found that four criteria were used to group students: (1) physical appearance; (2) interactional behavior, both among students themselves and with the teacher; (3) use of language within the classroom; and (4) social factors, e.g. financial status of family, educational level of parents, marital status of mother, number of siblings. Concerning teacher expectations as reflected in the ability groupings of the classroom, Rist concluded that "attributes most desired by educated members of the middle class became the basis for her [the teacher's] evaluation of the children" (p. 81). More specifically,

> Highly prized middle-class status for the child in the classroom was attained by demonstrating ease of verbalization in Standard American English; the ability to become a leader; a neat and clean appearance; coming from a family that is educated, employed, living together and interested in the child; and the ability to participate well as a member of a group (p. 81).

Rist's explanation makes two points vividly clear; (1) teacher expectations are reflected in the grouping patterns; and (2) teacher expectations are based upon social, rather than educational, criteria. What's more, students can generally tell you which groups they are in, no matter how the group names are coded; those identified as "fast learners" can generally provide a list of their strengths, while those identified as "slow learners" can tell you their weaknesses. The point here is that the mere existence of expectations, or prophecies, does not mean that they will be fulfilled. There is "a greater tragedy than being labelled as a slow learner, and that is being treated as one" (Rist, p. 107).

There are, concludes Rist, four stages in the fulfillment of negative expectations, each having to do with student-teacher interaction in the classroom. They are:

> The student came into the class possessing a series of behavioral and attitudinal characteristics that within the frame of reference of the teacher were perceived as indicative of failure. Second, through mechanisms of reinforcement of her initial expectations as to the future performance of the student, it was made evident that he was not perceived as similar or equal to those at the table of fast learners. In the third stage, the student responded to both the definition and actual treatment given to him by the teacher which emphasized his characteristics of being an educational failure. Given the high degree of control oriented behavior directed toward the slower learner, the lack of verbal interaction and encouragement, the disproportionally small amount of teaching time given to him, and the ridicule and hostility, the child withdrew from class participation. The fourth stage was the cyclical repetition of behavioral and attitudinal characteristics that led to the initial labeling as an educational failure (1971, p. 104).

The implication here is that in kindergarten, the level described by Rist, children are socialized to maintain the status of their parents. They are grouped according to their social status, and the groups are treated differently in both the quality and quantity of instruction they receive. This pattern continues after kindergarten, except that teachers beyond kindergarten also have school records on which expectations may be based. Research shows that the move from high to low group occurs more frequently than the move from low to high group. Further, research also shows that test results, which are used to aid in the grouping of children, often do not provide accurate assessments of the capability and achievement levels of minority students. Certainly, students do not change their status enough to keep the cycle of failure from repeating itself, as teachers at other levels are as much affected by the practice of evaluating academic potential in terms of social criteria as the kindergarten teacher.

To further explain the mechanism of self-fulfilling prophecies, specific behaviors that communicate positive expectations to students have been identified. As reported by Dworkin and Dworkin:

> Extensive research shows that teacher interaction with students perceived as low achievers is less motivating and less supportive than interaction with students perceived as high achievers. Research also tells us that high achievers receive more response opportunities and are given more time to respond to questions. When high achievers do have difficulty, teachers tend to delve, give clues, or rephrase the question more frequently than with low achievers (1979, p. 712).

Some of these same interaction patterns are included in Kerman's "Classroom Interaction Model":

Strand A: Response Opportunities – equitable distribution, individual help, delving, and higher level questions.
Strand B: Affirm-correct, praise, reasons for praise, listening, accepting feelings
Strand C: Personal regard – proximity, courtesy, personal interest and compliments, touching, (1979, p. 717).

All teachers were reported to have practiced the above interactions more frequently with high achievers than with low achievers. Obviously behavior is easier to control than attitudes. And indeed, when teachers consciously used with all students those behaviors which they had unconsciously used with "fast learners," they communicated their high expectations to students. Of course, both the slow and fast learners showed significant gains in patterns of growth (Kerman, 1979).

Through research and a bit of common sense, the events that make the Self-Fulfilling Prophecy a reality in the classroom have been de-mystified. While it is true that teacher expectations are often fulfilled by students, we now know that the critical intervening variable is behavior. It is therefore appropriate to modify the adage "what you expect is what you get," to "what you expect and what you give is what you get." There is much here to suggest that the Self-Fulfilling Prophecy can work for, rather than against, minority students, now that we know more about what the schools must give. Likewise, the social structure of the school need not reflect the social organization of society and certainly should not, now that we know more about the mechanisms by which the school "perpetuates what it is ideologically committed to eradicate – class barriers which result in inequality in the social and economic life of the citizenry" (Rist, p. 108). But what must the schools do in order to eradicate the social barriers that impede the fulfillment of its stated goals?

Change

Negative attitudes toward language in the schools need to be changed; about this there can be no doubt. These attitudes are, however, difficult to change for several reasons, four of which can be readily deduced from the discussion above.

First, teacher attitudes reflect societal attitudes, including society's language attitudes. In fact, some scholars have argued that one of the main roles of schools is to preserve the social structure of society. As we have pointed out, the schools may perpetuate social barriers, but to do so is to be in conflict with the stated goals of the schools.

Second, negative attitudes toward the language of low prestige social groups are sanctioned by educational theories which are highly respected by school personnel. Indirectly, the traditional methods of teaching English have left educated Americans with strong prejudices against the use and users of English patterns that deviate from standard English. And more directly, the underlying principles of recent educational theories have left teachers, at best, with low expectations of minority students' academic success and, at worst, with the firm conviction that they cannot teach students who suffer from the so-called environmental and cultural deprivations of their home. Ironically, the conceptual framework of compensatory education masked as the savior of Blacks and other non-mainstream groups provides theoretical justification for practicing the kinds of behaviors that research has shown to be most damaging to the learning environment of non-mainstream students.

Third, it is difficult to change negative attitudes toward non-mainstream varieties of English because attitudes are often formed unconsciously and communicated unintentionally. Although teachers may exchange information about the inadequacies of children's language, few are consciously aware of how their evaluations of a child's language influence their expectations of the child, grouping of children, their interaction with children and the content and style of instruction. Even fewer are aware that somehow negative attitudes are communicated to their students.

Fourth, we cannot directly observe attitudes, making it difficult to assess attitudinal changes. As suggested by the research, attitudes are communicated through our behavior. Like the wind, attitudes can be felt but not seen.

In view of the four points above, we offer as a general principle the view that attitudinal changes must be approached in a systematic way. Following Scott (1980), we propose three mechanisms for approaching attitudinal changes: (1) The need for more information about language in general and language variation in particular; (2) The need for changes in behavior; and (3) The need for a more balanced assessment of student academic potential.

As with any change, we must first recognize the need for change. This recognition comes often through an expansion of our knowledge base. Perhaps no other strategy for changing attitudes toward language has been used more widely than in-service training. This approach was used by the Ann Arbor School District in response to a court mandate which emanated from the widely publicized *King* case (see Scott, 1981; Smitherman, 1981; Labov, 1982). Because this case directly called for the application of current information about the language and cultural patterns of a low prestige group to the school setting, it is useful here to review those aspects of the case which bear directly on our discussion.

In July 1979 the case of *Martin Luther King Junior Elementary School Children vs. Ann Arbor School District Board* was heard before Federal Judge Charles C. Joiner. The plaintiffs, parents of eleven Black children, charged school officials with denying their children equal educational opportunities by failing to help the children overcome language barriers, a violation of U.S.C. 1703:

> No state shall deny equal educational opportunity to an individual on account of his or her race, color, sex, or national origin, by . . . the failure by an educational agency to take appropriate action to overcome language barriers that impede equal participation by its students in its instructional program.

Although many people believed that the purpose of *King* was to determine whether Black English was a language or a dialect, the intent was actually to determine whether or not the language system – Black English – used by the eleven children constituted a barrier in the educational process and whether the schools had taken appropriate action to help youngsters overcome these barriers. Expert witnesses testified that the language barrier was not based on students' complete inability to understand different varieties of English. Rather, the language is a barrier in the educational process because of the stigma attached to it, the lack of respect given to it, and the lack of knowledge about it. All of the above have been shown to lead to damaged self-concepts of students, low expectations of student performance, and sometimes to inappropriate placement of students, e.g. into speech pathology and learning disabilities classes. As we have noted throughout, social criteria are also used to group children, and instruction for groups perceived as low achievers differs both quantitatively and qualitatively from instruction received by students perceived as high achievers.

The courts found it appropriate to require the Ann Arbor School District Board to ". . . take steps to help its teachers to recognize the home language of the students and to use that knowledge in their attempts to teach reading skills in standard English" (Memorandum and Opinion, 1979, p. 4, in Smitherman, 1981).

In response to the court order, Ann Arbor devised an In-Service Training Program for teachers. As outlined, the Program was to provide information in three areas: (1) teacher attitudes relevant to the sociological aspects of language and non-standard dialects; (2) teacher knowledge concerning, for example, language structure, including structural patterns of Black English, and language acquisition; and (3) teachers' skills relevant to language assessments and the application of information about Black English to teaching the language arts. Based on the authors' experiences with in-service training programs, we know that after being exposed to information such as that outlined in Ann Arbor's Educational Plan, school personnel tend to agree that negative attitudes toward the language of low-prestige groups should be changed. By providing this kind of information, we can fulfill one essential step in our systematic approach to attitudinal changes.

The next step involves monitoring behavior that communicates negative attitudes to students. As indicated by Kerman's research (see above), it is possible for teachers to change their interactional patterns with students, but the change will not be automatic. Instead, in Kerman's study, behavior monitoring was practised by small groups or teams, who met on a regular basis to discuss their observations, evaluations, and progress. As the second step in our systematic approach to attitudinal change, we are suggesting a behavior-oriented task, which can be carried out best in teams, in short, behavior modification for teachers. As teachers change their interactional patterns with students, students will change their responses to teachers and ultimately their performance in the classroom.

The final and third step in our approach to attitudinal change involves the careful monitoring of evaluative statements made about students, particularly those students who have been persistently unsuccessful in school. Evaluative statements help to shape teachers' expectations of students. It is quite easy to accumulate a long list of negative evaluations of those students perceived as failures. It is more challenging to balance the negative evaluations with positive ones. It is unfortunate, but true, that for students perceived as failures, neither teachers, parents, nor the students themselves know anything of the students' strengths. Consequently, each is likely to concentrate on correcting the students' weaknesses to the exclusion of building on their strengths. The technique of building on strengths, referred to by Scott as the "Balanced Data Bank", is made easier after: (1) teachers have been exposed to information such as that described in step one; and (2) teachers have modified their interactional patterns so as to elicit more positive reaction from students, as described in step 2. While the former provides a sounder knowledge base, the latter provides more positive experiences with students. Knowledge and experience combine to provide an important characteristic of effective schools. As reported in a recent study of effective schools for poor Black children, one of the important characteristics of the effective schools was that "school personnel transmitted the expectation that every child *will* learn" (Glenn and McLean, 1982, p. 154). (Emphasis added.)

Analysis and follow-through, as suggested in this paper, should go a long way toward making school the societal leader that it should be, rather than the follower that it has been.

References

BARATZ, S. and J. BARATZ (1971) "Early childhood school intervention: The social science base of institutional racism." In *Challenging the Myths: The Schools, The Blacks, and The Poor. Harvard Educational Review*, Reprint Series No. 5, pp. 111–132.

BRYDEN, J.D. (1968) "On acoustic and social dialect analysis of perceptual variables in listener identification and rating of Negro speakers." Bureau of Research, Office of Education, HEW Project No. 7-C003.

DWORKIN, N. and Y. DWORKIN (1979) "The legacy of Pygmalion in the classroom." *Phi Delta Kappan*, June 1979, pp. 712–715.

ELLIS, D.S. (1967) "Speech and social status in America." *Social Forces*, **45**, 431–437.

FLEMING, J.T. (1970) "Teachers' ratings of urban children's reading and performance." Paper presented at AERA Conference, March 1970.

FLORIDA TEACHING PROFESSION–NATIONAL EDUCATION ASSOCIATION. "Governor's Commission Report Calls for Dangerous Changes in School Standards." *Advocate*, Vol. 9, No. 6, Feb. 1983.

GLENN, B. and T. MCLEAN (1982) *What Works? An Examination of Effective Schools for Poor Black Children*. Cambridge, Mass.: Center for Law and Education, Harvard University.

GUSKIN, J. (1970) "Social perception of language variations: Black dialect and expectations of abilities." Paper presented at AERA Conference, Mar. 1970.

HARMS, L.S. (1961) "Listener judgments of status cues in speech." *Quarterly Journal of Speech*, **47**, 164–168.

HOLMES, M.B. (1968) "Interaction patterns as a source of error in teachers' evaluations of head start children." Final Report, Office of Economic Opportunity, Aug. 1968.

HUGHES, A.E. (1967) *An Investigation of Certain Sociolinguistic Phenomena in the Vocabulary, Pronunciation, and Grammar of Disadvantaged Pre-School Children, Their Parents, and Their Teachers in the Detroit Public Schools*. Diss., Michigan State University.

JONES, R. (1982) "What's wrong with Black English." *Newsweek*, 27 Dec. 1982, p. 7.

KERMAN, S. (1979) "Teacher expectations and student achievement." *Phi Delta Kappan*, June 1979, pp. 716–718.

KEYES, D. (1966) *Flowers for Algernon*. New York: Harcourt Brace Jovanovich, Inc.

LABOV, W. (1970) *The Study of Nonstandard English*. Urbana, Illinois: National Council of Teachers of English.

LABOV, W. (1982) "Objectivity and commitment in linguistic science: The case of the Black English trial in Ann Arbor." *Language in Society* (Fall 1982).

LAMBERT, W.E. and G. R. TUCKER (1969) "White and Negro listeners' reactions to various American English dialects." *Social Forces*, **47**, 463–468.

NAREMORE, R.C. (1969) *Teachers' Evaluational Reactions to Pupils' Speech Samples*. Diss., University of Wisconsin.

PUTNAM, G.N. and E. O'HERN (1955) "The status significance of an isolated urban dialect." *Language*, **31** (part II), 1–32.

RIST, R.C. (1971) "Student social class and teacher expectations: The self-fulfilling prophecy in ghetto education." *In Challenging the Myths: The Schools, The Blacks, and The Poor. Harvard Educational Review*, Reprint Series No. 5, pp. 70–110.

ROSENTHAL, R. and L. JACOBSON (1968) *Pygmalion in the Classroom*. New York: Holt, Rinehart and Winston.

SCOTT, J. (1980) "The King Case: Implications for educating Black youth." In Mary Hoover, ed., *Conference Proceedings of Black English Conference*. Jacksonville: Edward Waters College.

SCOTT, J. (1981) "Black language and communication skills: Recycling the issues." In *Black English and the Education of Black Children and Youth*, ed. Smitherman. Wayne State University Center for Black Studies.

SHUY, R. "Subjective judgments in sociolinguistic analysis." *Monograph Series on Languages and Linguistics*. Washington, D.C.: Center for Applied Linguistics.

SMITHERMAN, G. (1977) *Talkin and Testifyin: the Language of Black America*. Boston: Houghton Mifflin.

SMITHERMAN, G., ed. (1981) *Black English and the Education of Black Children and Youth: Proceedings of the National Invitational Symposium on the King Decision*. Detroit: Wayne State University Center for Black Studies Press.

WILLIAMS, F. (1970a) "Psychological correlates of speech characteristics: On sounding 'disadvantaged.'" *Journal of Speech and Hearing Research*, **13**, 472–488.

WILLIAMS, F. (1970b) "Language, attitude and social change." *In Language and Poverty*, ed. F. Williams. Chicago: Markham Publishing Co.

Chapter 6

English Language in the Secondary School

R. BAIRD SHUMAN

THE public at large has strong attitudes about language and these attitudes affect broadly the whole secondary school English curriculum. Members of literate, print-oriented societies predictably have stronger opinions about the teaching of their native tongues than they have about the teaching of other school subjects. This is because, regardless of their own educational attainment, they have a fairly comprehensive practical knowledge of their own language, no matter how non-standard their native dialect may be. They have mastered the grammatical forms of the languages they speak, although they may, even as adults, not be able to identify by name the grammatical forms they use and understand with ease – infinitive phrases, conditionals, absolutes, predicates, participles, and subjunctives in contrary-to-fact conditions such as, "If I were you. . . ." By the time they enter school for the first time, many people have working vocabularies of 3000 to 7000 words, while some few know at age 5 or 6, 20,000 or more words.[1] By the time they enter high school, their vocabularies have usually doubled and they readily understand complicated grammatical constructions and a variety of dialects divergent from their own.

In the United States, familiarity with language and an ability to use it effectively shapes the attitudes everyone has about English instruction other than language at the secondary level, most notably the teaching of literature and composition. This chapter considers three major areas in which public attitudes toward language impinge upon the teaching of English in secondary schools: (1) the place of grammar and language instruction; (2) the treatment of students who speak non-standard dialects or who are bilingual; and (3) the teaching of literature. It also considers two recent movements, back-to-basics and competency testing, that reflect public attitudes toward language and toward the secondary school teaching of English.

Should We Teach Grammar?

If Gallup's pollsters were to ask a representative sampling of people the question, "Should grammar be taught in secondary school English classes?", one can assume that a healthy majority would answer affirmatively. Gallup's usual random sampling includes people from many walks of life and people from all kinds of educational backgrounds, ranging from those who have not completed the eighth grade to those who have pursued graduate training to the doctoral level or beyond. A typical sampling would include plumbers, electricians, secretaries, English teachers, teachers of other subjects, editors, scientists, professional linguists, and maybe even some old-fashioned philologists. One might reasonably ask, then, "Why all the fuss? Everyone knows that grammar is a necessary part of English instruction."

Alas, the rub is that the key word in the poll, *grammar*, has, like many other words, different meanings to different people. To some, *grammar* is a set of complicated and immutable rules through whose mastery people learn to write and speak "correctly"; to others *grammar* is concerned with the structure of language, with how words are put together to form sentences and with how sentences are put together to form paragraphs; to still others, *grammar* describes how language is used and makes no judgments about correctness or incorrectness as long as meaning is conveyed.

When English grammar began to be taught formally in the eighteenth century, it was modeled on Latin grammar, and this arrangement caused problems with which educators still deal today. English, a Germanic language, does not correspond consistently in all its particulars to Latin, a Romance language.

Traditional grammar, which is still taught with considerable vigor in many secondary schools, may forbid English sentences to end with prepositions, This is a holdover from Latin, in which it was clearly impossible to place a preposition in the terminal position in a sentence because all prepositions had to have objects. The very word *preposition* means "placed before." While prepositions in English must have objects, people sometimes fail to realize that some words look like prepositions – *up*, *with*, *out*, *around*, etc. – but function as other parts of speech in some contexts.

Up is a preposition in the sentence, "The adventurers moved *up* the Amazon"; however, *up* serves a quite different grammatical function in a sentence like, "This is the bond money the accused arsonist put *up*." In the latter case, *up* can be viewed either as part of the verb – *put* is different from *put up* or *put up with* – or as an adverb. What it is called is less important than how it functions in a sentence. Clearly in the latter sentence, *up* requires no object and it cannot be legitimately regarded as a preposition. Neither can it reasonably be subjected to the rules governing the use of prepositions in traditional grammar. Similarly, in Latin infinitives cannot be split – how can one split *amāre*? – and English has been saddled with this needless grammatical prohibition since the eighteenth century. What was impossible in Latin is quite possible in English. Rules of Latin grammar cannot be applied across the board to English usage, and where such applications are attempted, in many instances inconsistency and confusion follow.

Few high-school English teachers are thoroughgoing traditionalists, structuralists, or transformationalists. Rather, they teach a combination of grammatical approaches in their classes. The traditional classification of parts of speech, for example, is useful to high-school students, because if they know it and other traditional terminology, they have a vocabulary with which to discuss their writing. A knowledge of the generation of various kinds of sentences from a kernel sentence will open for students the important world of sentence combining, which is one of the most useful and practical legacies of the transformational-generative movement. A structural understanding of how words function in sentences can reveal to students something about the dynamics of their language.

To the non-grammarian, the terms *correct grammar* and *incorrect grammar* are perfectly acceptable – *he don't* is incorrect; *he doesn't* is correct. To the modern grammarian, the terms *correct* and *incorrect* have only limited meaning – *he don't* communicates as clearly as *he doesn't*; in some situations, the latter term is socially preferable, but as a communicative device used to convey meaning it is neither more or less effective than the former term, except, perhaps, to the extent that the non-standard form might divert the listener's or reader's attention from *what* is being said to *how* it is being said. *He don't*, as a spoken form uttered in some language environments, is indeed more standard than *he doesn't* and probably diverts listener attention less than the standard form.

Language Instruction

Secondary schools cannot abrogate the responsibility of teaching students about the structure of language (how language operates), about the mechanics of expression (spelling and punctuation, for example), and about appropriate usage (varieties of English and the conventions of the language). Students whose mechanics and usage are inappropriate to given situations have a handicap. They need to be taught about levels of usage and about appropriateness rather than about "correctness" and "incorrectness." They need to be aided in developing a sensitivity to language that will enable them to function in a variety of social and vocational contexts. Language study should be less a moral pursuit than a scientific pursuit if it is to benefit students to the utmost.

The study of language is inherently interesting, and teachers who capitalize on this interest will serve their students well. Students who are set to work compiling a dictionary of, let us say, twenty terms related to space travel or computer technology or heart surgery will learn more about language operationally than they will ever come to know as passive learners with their grammar workbooks open to the fill-ins on subject-verb agreement. Students who are asked to keep track of the kinds of people who say "ain't" and the kinds of people who say "isn't" or "aren't" will learn much more about "ain't," "isn't," and "aren't" as verbs plus a negative than students who are told such lies as, "*Ain't* isn't in the dictionary" or "Educated people never use *ain't*."

Students who are encouraged to gather information about language as modern linguists do and to observe from people and printed sources around them how language is actually used are likely to find the pursuit interesting and will consider it more honest than traditional grammar instruction. Also, in writing up their findings, such students will enhance their own facility with the language. Students learn more about usage and mechanics of expression through a teacher's careful grading of their written work and through subsequent conferences about their written work than through direct classroom instruction. Therefore, teachers must demand written reports and must grade them in such ways as to give students the individual instruction they need about the usage and mechanics in their own papers. Student writing will be vigorous and honest only if it has a strong subject base. Language investigation can provide such a base.

Because the public at large may not understand assignments unlike those they were given as students, it is the role of teachers to try to enlighten concerned parents about new methods of teaching language, usage, and mechanics. Some laypeople may be so ingrained in their prejudices that they will be unyielding; however, their intransigence should not cause any teacher to abandon a legitimate pedagogical strategy that has been well thought out and carefully planned. English teachers, working in concert and communicating with such other professionals as English supervisors and college faculty members, must be regarded as the experts in their classrooms and in their own subject. As long as they work in accordance with the best current research-supported methodologies of their profession, they must be permitted to teach in ways which not all laymen will understand or support. Administrative support and understanding are the underpinnings of effective teaching at any level, so administrators must be kept informed about the reasons that given methods of language instruction are used in their schools.

Dialects

As society has moved steadily to include Blacks, its most prevalent racial minority, and other smaller minority groups in the mainstream of American life, considerable attention has been directed toward the study of Black English and bilingualism. Ways are being sought to reach all dialect speakers in the schools, Black or otherwise, who may experience an initial disadvantage when they find themselves in learning situations that pre-suppose their ability to handle the dialect in which textbooks and standardized tests are written and which teachers typically use in their classroom presentations.

The landmark King decision, rendered in 1979 by U.S. District Judge Charles W. Joiner, has broad implications for teachers at all levels. Eleven students in the Martin Luther King Junior Elementary School in Ann Arbor, Michigan, sued the Ann Arbor School District Board, contending that because they were users of Black dialect at home, they did not have the equal opportunity guaranteed them under the Constitution. The finding of the court was that the children, indeed, did not have equal access to the tools of learning that their white classmates had, and it decreed that the School District Board (1) find ways of heightening teachers' awareness of language differences; (2) provide teachers with a means of learning the features of non-standard Black dialect; and (3) seek ways of using the teachers' newly gained knowledge to devise means of teaching more effectively students who are non-standard speakers of English.[2]

This decision was precedent-setting, and its effects will be felt for generations to come. The precedent set here applies not only to Black children or to elementary school children, but to all students whose language background sets them apart and limits their access to materials and environments that would enhance their learning.

Only in the last three decades has much been done to study Black English as a legitimate form of English,[3] grammatically consistent and predictable. Much work remains to be done in studying other dialects.[4] William Labov and others collaborated on remarkably interesting studies during the 1960s[5] pointing to the fact that one's degree of literacy is not *per se* related to one's intellectual ability. Their sociolinguistic findings were compelling to those who read them, but did little to change public attitudes about language in either the Black or White community.

The handicaps experienced by speakers of Black dialect who tried to learn reading from books written from the standpoint of middle-class White America have been amply documented through the last two decades. Attempts have been made to help Black children overcome some of their basic communication problems by using reading materials with them that are more in keeping with both their language and experience.[6] However, the Black community has been far from unanimous in approving such tactics and has suggested that their use will simply remove Blacks further from the mainstream of American society and make it more difficult for them to compete effectively in the work world they eventually must enter. Attempts to use bidialectal primers in the public schools of Washington, D.C. were met with great resistance from Black parents who insisted that their children had to learn Standard English if they were to enter the work world without stigma.[7] Certainly such parental concern is understandable. Black children must ultimately know and use standard English if the cycle of poverty is to be broken.

Teachers' attitudes toward Black English were assessed in an extensive survey by Orlando L. Taylor.[8] He found that with the exception of those teaching first grade, teachers – many of them Black – were almost equally divided about the status of Black English. Only first-grade teachers gave it overwhelmingly positive marks. Secondary school teachers, particularly those at the ninth grade level (where the sample was too small to be really meaningful), tended to be more dubious about Black English than elementary school teachers did. Taylor also found that teachers with 6–10 years of experience had more reservations about Black English than did those with more or less experience.

The attitudes of teachers, particularly of English teachers, toward Black English are particularly relevant in assessing public attitudes toward it. Presumably secondary-school teachers of English are better trained in language than is the broader population. That half of this group had reservations about the status of Black English reveals the sort of resistance that linguists and school administrators have encountered in their attempts to bring about public recognition of the clearly established fact that Black English is a legitimate, consistent dialect of English, in some ways more logically defensible than the more prevalent dialect. The social acceptability of saying, "I got three brother," is not established even when one comes to the realization that the terminal -*s* on *brothers* is redundant in Standard English because *three* has already, quite clearly, indicated the plurality of the statement.

In many instances, white regional dialects are tolerated in schools much more easily than Black regional dialects are. This is because the regional dialect is the prevailing dialect of the power élite in the community in which it is used. For example, in the southeastern United States, the "might can/could" construction ("I might can have your car ready by five o'clock") is much less likely to be corrected in English classes than is an expression in Black English that deviates from the norm of Network Standard English ("Every time we phone her, she don't be there"). In written English, however, because it is more formal, both regional usages would likely be noted as items to be corrected.

Bilingualism in the United States

The United States has been more aware of bilingualism in the past quarter of a century than at any time in her past history. The waves of immigrants who came to our shores in the nineteenth and early twentieth centuries from Europe and the Orient had two immediate priorities: (1) to gain economic self-sufficiency and (2) to learn the English language and, thereby, to become integrated as quickly as possible into American society. Such are still the highest priorities of some recent immigrants into the United States; however, in many parts of the country, in both rural and urban areas, Spanish has become a dominant language, and many children enter public schools with little or no knowledge of English.

In such instances, the major question is whether instruction in substantive areas should be offered in English or in the native tongue. Some advocate that the native tongue be used initially, but only as a transitional language until the student can function productively in English. The problem is complicated because students from non-English speaking backgrounds do not necessarily enter school in an English-speaking community in the primary grades. Many family members of non-English-speaking families first enter schools that use English as the medium of instruction when they are of secondary-school age. Others feels that students who are not taught in their native tongues will lose their bilingualism and with it much appreciation of their non-English cultures.

Americans are chauvinistic about their language. Even when they are travelling abroad in foreign-language environments, they expect people to speak it. Many resent having tax money spent to offer students instruction in their school subjects in any language other than English.

It is estimated that 28 million Americans are non-native speakers of English and that of this group, about 10 percent speak no English. Between a quarter and a half million children of school age speak not enough English to be functional in the language either as speakers or as listeners.[9] In 1974, in the case of *Lau vs. Nichols*, the United States Supreme Court went on record as saying that equality of educational opportunity does not exist for students who cannot function in the English language and for whom the schools fail to offer instruction in the native tongue. This decision sent shock waves through the educational community and enraged much of the citizenry whose public attitude toward language idealized the whole melting-pot philosophy of the nineteenth and early twentieth centuries. Legislation was passed requiring that any school district with concentrations of non-native speakers offer instruction in substantive areas in the native language. This legislation was largely ignored by most school districts, except where large concentrations existed of speakers of a specific foreign language such as Spanish, German, Polish, or a Native American language such as Cherokee or Navajo. Most of the relevant legislation enacted in the past decade has either been repealed or ignored as unworkable. School districts usually deal with problems relating to non-English speakers on an *ad hoc* basis.

Even Americans who recognize the advantage of being bilingual or multilingual often resist becoming so. They are used to being citizens of a large, economically influential country. The basic American attitude toward foreign language acquisition and toward dealing with non-English-speaking students ranges from an attitude of indifference to one of outright hostility. Some parents of students from non-English-speaking environments discourage bilingualism and insist that English be spoken at home.

Language Attitudes and the Teaching of Literature

It is doubtful that public attitudes toward the English language intrude upon any area of the secondary school English curriculum more than upon the teaching of literature. Literature teachers are assailed from both the left and the right, and often their sole solution seems to be to teach only from vapid literature anthologies or to teach books that are so antiseptic as to be valueless in providing a legitimate literary experience for young readers.

Liberals have been responsible for curtailing the use and circulation of *Huckleberry Finn* because of its use of the word *nigger*; *Merchant of Venice* because of its unfavorable depiction of Shylock, a Jew; and numerous books that contain sexist language such as *policeman, fireman, chairman*, and *cleaning woman*.[10] The Moral Majority and others who are less far to the right have howled with indignation about profanity, slang, and informal usage in books. Even such commonplace oaths as *hell* and *damn*, which must be used if one is to record human speech accurately and depict it realistically, have been responsible for public outcries. Probably no recent book has evoked more widespread ire than Salinger's *Catcher in the Rye*. Ronald LaConte surveyed English Department heads about this book and found that fully 70 percent of those responding considered *Catcher in the Rye* not to be suitable for use in their departments,[11] this despite the fact that the book's protagonist is essentially a quite moral youth and that its value as a high-school reading has been defended by such savvy critics as Wayne Booth, Donald J. Foran (significantly a Jesuit priest), Eugene McNamara, and Clinton W. Trowbridge. The major cause for objecting to *Catcher in the Rye* has had to do more with the use of a single, oft-repeated scatological word than with the book's moral content.

Hans Guth's contention that "great literature is typically more searching, revealing or disturbing than literature designed to confirm existing standards"[12] seems unassailable. Such literature must present the verisimilitude of real discourse, and much of the discourse, by the very nature of challenging literature, will be discourse uttered under the pressure of strong emotions. A major purpose of exposing students to literature is to provide them with the opportunity to experience worlds apart from their own. The inhabitants of these worlds – and, in reality, of their own day-to-day worlds – do not speak a purified, sterilized language. However, many critics of school literature programs demand that quality literature be replaced by literature that has little relationship to the real world or to the students reading it.

Lee Burress points to one of the most serious problems facing the schools today when he writes, "Critics both of right and left destroy the essence of literature by reducing literature to whatever dimension by which they measure it. To go through books to collect all the bad words, whether racist or sexist or profane, is to destroy books."[13] More importantly, though, to do what Burress objects to is to destroy learning by making important information inaccessible to students.

It should be noted that narrow attitudes toward language have been responsible for the banning of five major dictionaries from the public schools of Texas, strictly on the grounds that those who were making the decisions objected to some of the words and definitions in those dictionaries.[14] Burress cites a National Council of Teachers of English survey taken in 1977 indicating that "obscene or bad language was by far the most common objection stated in efforts to censor 145 books."[15] The public attitude toward the English language assumes a new dimension in the light of such a finding!

Opposing Burress we find some like Janet Egan, who writes, "By removing sexist language from our schools and by *the indoctrination of our boys and girls with equality, sex role reversal, 'career' and sex education* (i.e., population control, contraception, abortion, etc.) which our schools do, we break the females [*sic*] natural tendency to desire marriage and have babies"[16] (Egan's italics). Egan, who also objects to profanity in literature, has led a crusade in Wisconsin to control what may be taught in literature classes, and her objections to the problems posed by the use of almost any quality literature are so strong and diverse that, were they heeded, English teachers would be best advised to teach no literature at all in their classes.

The National Council of Teachers of English has attacked the problem of dealing with censorship in all of its major journals and in several other publications, one of which, *The Students' Right to Read*,[17] has been revised and updated through the years and is particularly useful. James E. Davis' excellent book, *Dealing with Censorship*,[18] is the most recent NCTE publication on the topic.

Back to Basics

People often romanticize their school experience and exaggerate their school accomplishments. Someone who proclaims stridently, "When I went to school, you didn't get a diploma if you couldn't read and write," may be correct in this proclamation. However, the proclamation omits some important details. For example, in 1900 all secondary-school students were literate. If they were not, secondary schools were closed to them. Most high-school graduates could get into college. At the turn of the century, only 10 percent of all teenagers went beyond eighth grade. High-school graduation requirements in most states were identical to college-entrance requirements.

As increasing numbers of young people began to attend and be graduated from secondary schools during and after World War I, drastic curricular revisions had to be made to accommodate those who were not on the college preparatory track. Some of the adjustments made then, often under pressure, may now seem excessive to us, although at the time they were put into force, they seemed justifiable. A strong reaction to an educational system the public had come to view as permissive and ineffective was precipitated in 1957 when the Russian launching of Sputnik wounded American technological pride in such a way that it could be healed only by our becoming competitive with the Russians in the exploration of space.

With leadership from the White House, Americans determined to strengthen their educational system, which they saw as the first and most necessary step they could take to surpass the Russians. Through the first half of the 1960s, school curricula, first in mathematics, the sciences, and foreign languages and later in social studies and English, were made more rigorous. The National Defense Education Act (NDEA) of 1958 helped promising young people to become teachers and ran countless institutes so that in-service teachers could sharpen their skills. Master of Arts in Teaching Programs, many of them aided substantially by generous grants from the Ford Foundation, were instituted at about the same time in many major universities. The public outcry for quality in education was heeded as whole academic disciplines were being redefined and restructured for presentation to secondary school students.

This period saw the first major back-to-basics movement on a national level. Optimism ran high in educational circles. Teachers were in demand. Educational funding was easily obtained. Students, many of whom had not previously been challenged by school, were now beginning to rise to the challenge of having heavier academic demands placed upon them. This situation persisted essentially until the end of the decade in which it began, and vestiges of it linger still.

More recently a vocal public, perhaps alarmed by a sense of frustration at its inability to deal with a world that is changing cataclysmically, has called with almost hysterical vigor for a return to basics. Such cries often are unaccompanied by any real definition of what is basic, but laymen who support the movement have expressed displeasure and concern because high-school graduates are unable to read, spell, write, speak coherently, and perform simple mathematical operations. Many critics of the schools blame this sorry state on secular humanism, on values education, on sex education, and on driver education. These critics would do away with the frills and teach "what students need to know."

Ignored in most of the arguments in favor of back-to-basics is the fact that the country's high schools are graduating each year hundreds of thousands of students who perform well in the so-called basic skills. The indictment against public education is usually a sweeping one, too sweeping, indeed, to be

ET–L*

logically acceptable. Nevertheless, hundreds of school districts have rushed back to what they consider the basics. Susan Skean points out, "The Back to Basics approach to the problems of public education is simplistic at best . . . minimum skills are supposed to be the tools students employ in their daily activity. They are refined by their constant use. To focus on them alone is to miss the point."[19] In a similar tone, Robert Donmoyer reminds one that Ernest Boyer, President Carter's Commissioner of Education, promoted the slogan "Access to Excellence" in advancing the President's educational program, but then focused the official concern of his office on functional literacy and a return to basics.[20]

Donmoyer makes a salient point when he notes the back-to-basics supporters of the 1960s "were concerned about skill development, but that was primarily so that students would have access to subject matter."[21] The problem with the present back-to-basics craze is that it is in some quarters narrowly focused and is inextricably intertwined with the competency movement in education.

Competency Based Education

Responding to widespread public complaints that many high-school graduates had not achieved basic skills of literacy prior to graduation, most of the fifty states began in the late 1970s to move toward broad programs to test for minimum competencies. By 1979, thirty-five states had legislated programs, and others have followed suit in the intervening years. Robert Ebel writes, ". . . the demands [for minimum competency testing] come from the public and from legislators speaking for the public. They come from disappointed employers, from disappointed parents, even some disappointed students."[22]

Because one's use of language, whether spoken or written, is much more public usually than one's use of a subject like mathematics, the secondary school English curriculum has been criticized more than most for not teaching students basic skills. Skills are, after all, basic to competency in all subjects, but the public is less able and therefore less likely to judge student skills in a foreign language, in the social studies, or in the sciences than it is in English.

Ebel is strong in his support for minimum competency testing of students: "Minimum competency testing will not cure all the ills of contemporary education, but it will do much to correct one of the most serious of those ailments: It will help to restore concern for the cognitive development of young people to the highest priority in the mission of the school."[23] However, Ebel is perhaps deluding himself at least partially in this contention. Writing of the emphasis on basics, Donmoyer cautions, "The current movement's concern for adequacy and functional literacy . . . may lead to the ignoring of students who are already academically adequate and who may require subject matter focus and the expectations of excellence that were central concerns of the earlier [1960s] era."[24]

Certainly it seems legitimate to test students at various points in secondary school to make sure that they are in possession of the minimum competencies that might reasonably be expected of someone in a particular grade. However, teachers and administrators must constantly remind themselves that they are testing for *minimal* competencies. In a typical secondary school, nearly all students taking the tests should be expected to receive acceptable grades on them, and administrators have to be ready to defend to the public such wholesale passing of the tests. The tests are not to be confused with entrance examinations to a college or university. They focus considerable attention on such survival skills as balancing checkbooks, reading and writing simple directions, interpreting reasonably simple maps and diagrams, and filling out forms. Such skills are necessary for anyone who is to function in modern society. If schools teach to these relatively simple tests to the exclusion of more complex subject matter, then the testing program will have succeeded only in diverting the school from its major educational task, that of leading students as far into the world of ideas as each can go.

Afterword

This chapter has dealt with some areas of the secondary school English curriculum that seem most affected by public attitudes toward the English language. Many concerned with education have addressed these matters in one way or another – scholars in the field, teachers, administrators, school boards, groups of parents, publishers, and others deeply concerned with the education of the nation's youth. At the moment, the overall situation in secondary-school English is diverse, complicated, confusing, and, quite sadly, so polarized that one often wonders whether one side is hearing the other at all.

Public concern with education is essentially healthy, but public domination of specialized curricular areas can have highly deleterious outcomes and can severely damage if not totally subvert the broad educational mission of the schools. Freedom guaranteed by the First Amendment to the Constitution cannot be withheld from students without endangering these freedoms for all men and women in this country. If schools are to remain vital, productive institutions, they must preserve for their students the right of access to the broadest possible range of ideas, certainly not with the thought that students will adopt unquestioningly all of the ideas to which they are exposed but with the firm conviction that directed exposure to these ideas will enable them to function as intelligent, productive, and articulate citizens.

Notes

1. Isidore Levine, "Quantity reading: An introduction," *Journal of Reading*, **15** (May 1972), 256–57, claims that "at age five [the typical child's] vocabulary will range from 3,000 to 7,000 words depending on the education of those he converses with daily." On the other hand, the College Examination Board's *Freedom and Discipline in English: Report on the Commission on English* (New York: College Entrance Examination Board, 1965), p. 23, contends that "even at the age of 4 or 5 [a child] has a vocabulary that may run as high as 24,000 words."
2. The case of *Martin Luther King Junior Elementary School Children, et al., vs. Ann Arbor School District Board* (Civil Action No. 7-71861) is the subject of a volume edited by Geneva Smitherman, *Black English and the Education of Black Children and Youth: Proceedings of the National Invitational Symposium on the King Decision* (Detroit: Wayne State University, 1981), and has been the subject of many articles, among the strongest of which is Elaine G.

Wangberg's "Nonstandard speaking students: What should we do?" *The Clearing House*, **55** (Mar. 1982), pp. 305–307.

3. See, for example, J. L. Dillard, *Black English: Its History and Usage in the United States* (New York: Random House, 1972); William Labov, *Language in the Inner City* (Oxford: Basil Blackwell, 1972); and David Sutcliffe, *British Black English* (Oxford: Basil Blackwell, 1982).

4. Some work has already begun on considering dialects other than the dialects of Black English. Ricardo L. Garcia's "Toward a grammar of Chicano English," *English Journal*, **63** (Mar. 1974), 34–38, and Nila Banton Smith's "Cultural dialects," *The Reading Teacher*, **29** (Nov. 1975), 137–41, are both aimed at teachers. However, no concerted attention to dialects other than Black and written primarily for teachers has yet emerged.

5. William Labov, P. Cohen, Clarence Robins, and J. Lewis, *A Study of the Non-Standard English of Negro and Puerto Rican Speakers in New York City: Report on Co-operative Research Project 3288*, New York: Columbia University, 1968.

6. William Stewart and the Education Study Center in Washington, D.C. produced several bidialectal readers.

7. See Dorothy S. Strickland and William A. Stewart, "The use of dialect readers: A dialogue," in Bernice E. Cullinan, ed., *Black Dialects and Reading* (Urbana, IL: National Council of Teachers of English, 1974), pp. 146–151.

8. Orlando L. Taylor, "Teachers' attitudes toward Black and nonstandard English as measured by the language attitude scale," in Roger W. Shuy and Ralph W. Fasold, eds., *Language Attitudes: Current Trends and Prospects* (Washington, D.C.: Georgetown University Press, 1973), pp. 174–201.

9. Dorothy Waggoner, "Non-English language background persons: Three U.S. surveys," *TESOL Quarterly*, **12** (1978), 247–59.

10. See James E. Davis, ed., *Dealing with Censorship* (Urbana, IL: National Council of Teachers of English, 1979), pp. 19–22 and 24–27 for a full list of books that have been found objectionable in some secondary schools.

11. Ronald T. LaConte, "The English department chairman – selector or censor?" *The Leaflet*, **68** (May 1969), 40–47.

12. Hans P. Guth, *English Today and Tomorrow* (Engleside Cliffs, NJ: Prentice-Hall, 1964), p. 23.

13. Burress, p. 19.

14. See Edward B. Jenkinson, "Dirty dictionaries, obscene nursery rhymes, and burned books," in Davis, pp. 2–13.

15. Burress, p. 17.

16. Janet Egan, "Equality," in *Public Schools and the First Amendment* (Bloomington, IN: Indiana University's School of Continuing Studies, 1982), p. 48.

17. *The Student's Right to Read* (Champaign, IL: National Council of Teachers of English, 1962). Revised in 1972 by Ken Donelson and again, under the title *The Student's Right to Know*, in 1982 by Lee Burress and Edward B. Jenkinson.

18. See Davis, *supra*. See also John P. Frank and Robert F. Hogan's *Obscenity, the Law and the English Teacher* (Urbana: National Council of Teachers of English, 1965) and John Hove's *Meeting Censorship in the Schools: A Series of Case Studies* (Urbana: National Council of Teachers of English, 1977).

19. Susan Skean, "Back to basics: A personal response," *English Journal*, **70** (Sept. 1980), 82.

20. Robert Donmoyer, "Back to basics now and 20 years ago – A comparison of two movements," *Educational Leadership*, **36** (May 1979), 556.

21. Donmoyer, p. 557.

22. Robert L. Ebel, "The case for minimum competency testing," *Phi Delta Kappan*, **59** (April 1978), 546.

23. Ebel, p. 549.

24. Donmoyer, p. 557.

Chapter 7

Layman and Shaman; or, Now About that Elephant Again

JAMES SLEDD

IT IS a truth universally acknowledged that when a society of pedagogues addresses itself to the educated layman, the society is in want of public favor. English teachers have never been the public's darlings; and today there is more than usually widespread suspicion that those who can't write teach, that those who can't teach teach teaching, and that those who can neither teach nor write teach the teaching of writing. It is therefore understandable that the educated layman seldom reads addresses to the educated layman from the National Council of Teachers. Since I am too old, moreover, to profit greatly from even the most skilful washing of the public brain, and since I am temperamentally incapable of following a party line, I have assumed that in comparative privacy I may approach my subject in my own way, sidling crabwise. I have invented no new devices for deceiving credulous foundation-men, have mastered no jargon fit for unintelligible answers to insignificant questions, and claim nothing much for my remarks but that they are not based on "empirical research." Instead they reflect a third-generation academic's amused, bemused experience of studying and teaching for almost 50 years in major departments of English and linguistics in Europe, Asia, and the United States. Offended colleagues (my most likely audience) will no doubt suggest that what to me is common sense is in fact the maundering of senility. I hope they will not forget to mutter "anecdotal."

The Use of English in the Defluent Society

Will America be the death of English? Have we lost our paradigms? Must we by God stand firm, with Dwight Macdonald, against the verb *enthuse*? I am not enthused by such querulous crusades. As readers of the present volume should by now have learned, the death of standard English has been mourned in an uninterrupted wake for some 400 years, or roughly since both written and spoken standards became common subjects for discussion; and the most profitably mournful of the presently distressed, the Educational Testing Service and the College Entrance Examination Board, have acknowledged that "that there are no reliable comprehensive measures yet of the comparative competence of today's youth with yesterday's."[1] Hence at least one of yesterday's youth, when asked if there is indeed a literacy crisis or if the language still endures on Simon's rock,[2] is tempted to reply that since literacy is acquired and not innate, each generation is a literacy crisis but that English will be dead only when children have ceased to learn it. A glance at the map of the English-speaking world, or a few moments' observation of adolescent females, will alleviate all fears of that contingency.

Yet the exposure of a false diagnosis does not prove the patient's health. The world's most popular language will certainly survive, presumably without great and rapid structural change; but it is quite conceivable that the proportion of speakers and writers who are capable of certain specialized and traditionally valued *uses* of the language will decline or has declined already. In considering such possibilities, both those who affirm and those who deny must make educated guesses. My guess is that the uses of English which I was taught to value are not the uses which the world most values now. Though I cannot say that the students I have known write either better or worse than students wrote in 1880, 1900, or 1920, I do know that the majority of my victims at every level, from entering freshmen to candidates for the Ph.D., have always written badly (by my standards) and still do. I will refrain from the exhibition of specimen monstrosities to support this limited agreement with the crisis-criers, since I intend to trot out the monsters when I turn from students to their teachers. Instead, I will report the results of just one of several small experiments which I have made since 1940 and will suggest, by quoting Authoritative Sources, that those results are typical.

I made the experiment in January of 1962 at Northwestern University, where the emphasis in the composition course was predictably on literature, not composition. I had provoked a teapot tempest by complaining, in a letter to the editor of the *Chicago Tribune*, that even graduate students in English couldn't write ("by my standards" is always understood) and that the freshmen whom they taught weren't likely to learn. In preparation for a subsequent interview with another newspaper, I decided to make sure that my own inept students were representative, not freakish. With that intent, I collected and examined eight small sets of papers which had been written by Northwestern freshmen for eight different instructors in Northwestern's Freshman English course during the previous two years. My little sample of some forty or fifty papers was as fair as I could make it by careful choice from a well-stocked charnel. Most of the papers chosen had been written outside of class to meet regular assignments, and some had been revised and rewritten after conferences between students and instructors. I should add that most freshmen at Northwestern, like most graduates there, were probably well above the national average.

I drew three conclusions, all of them supported by the monstrous evidence which I have no space for here and which anyhow would be familiar to all teachers and to some despairing parents. (1) The freshmen were still uncertain of correct spelling and punctuation, neither skilled nor resourceful in the choice of words; and they often mangled English sentence-structure. (2) Despite their ineptitude, they were given relatively little practice in writing in their composition course, sometimes producing less than ten typed pages during a quarter. (3) Most instructors paid relatively little attention to punctuation, spelling, grammar, or diction. One instructor had thought it right to give an *A* to an exam in which I found the following misspellings: *trarnish* (for *tarnish*), *tranish, to* (for *too*), *satarical, refering, sarcasam, forbiding, virtous, awarness, Ceasar* (repeatedly; the student was writing about Shakespeare), *triumpherate, wellfare, alliagence, appoligise, grievestruck,* and *prepetuate.* That instructor didn't care though his student had scant knowledge of the parts and relations of mildly bookish English words. Talking about half-comprehended literature (*triumpherate* is ignorance in the nude) was at least more fun than birthing grubby papers.

Though my banal conclusions neither made friends nor influenced people at Northwestern, they were amusingly seconded in April of 1964, when a Commission on the Humanities made the *Report* which led to the establishment of a National Humanities Foundation (actually christened the National Endowment for the Humanities). In that *Report*, the spokesmen for the Modern Language Association acknowledged that "a majority of college students do not speak, write, or read their own language well. Graduate instructors who direct master's essays and doctoral dissertations are shocked at the extent to which they must become teachers of 'hospital'. English. Yet we are aware that many of these candidates are already engaged in part-time teaching of freshman English. If they cannot recognize and correct their own egregious errors, what is happening to the end-products of their teaching?"[3]

Though no experiment is needed to answer that one, for the sake of conviction through overkill I will cite the responses to a questionnaire which I directed to the faculty of the University of Texas at Austin in the spring of 1975. Of 1365 respondents, less than 4 percent were willing to say that undergraduates in their fields wrote "well" or "very well"; about one-third chose the answer "adequately"; and the remaining 63.8 percent described their undergraduates as writing "rather poorly" or "very poorly." The favorite objects of condemnation were poor organization and unsupported assertion, followed rather closely by bad grammar and diction, bad punctuation and spelling. The many voluntary comments were lugubrious: "Students can neither write nor speak their native language well"; "Very few can communicate intelligibly on exams or in papers"; "They cannot think, cannot write, cannot read"; "In fact, we need refresher help for faculty." Yet the noisy grieving didn't indicate general willingness to remove the causes of the grief: 28.5 percent of the grievestruck respondents admitted that in their own courses, required writing influenced the students' grades only slightly or not at all. Among some of the local engineers, the catchword is that "the documentation of engineering isn't engineering."

Students at UT Austin – the subjects of those noisy complaints – are not children of poverty. In 20 years at UT, I have not seen a "basic writer" like the young Black veteran at Austin Community College who told his teacher in 1973 why he "became a paratoop." "It was something I want to do," he wrote, "and you just don't fine people, Who like to Jump out of airplane everyday." No, our students are not the poor and ignorant, the desperately struggling whom open admissions have brought into "higher" education. On the contrary, our students are likely to come from affluent families, families which by America's present standards are relatively well educated. In a freshman class of mine as the 1970s ended, 12 of 22 students (the whole class numbered 27) were willing to state their fathers' annual incomes; even then the average was $32,000. Two-thirds of the fathers and over half of the mothers of the 22 respondents were at least college graduates, and 10 fathers and 4 mothers were reported to have had graduate or professional training.

Yet writing made no real part of their lives. Of those same prosperous professionals and white-collar workers and their spouses, most didn't write at all, according to their children, and such writing as they did was altogether practical, for business not for pleasure. With their children the story was naturally the same. All of the students were from the upper half of their high-school classes, nearly all from the upmost quarter; and 21 of the 22 responded that their grades in high-school English had been either *A*'s or *B*'s. Inability to write well (by standards such as mine) had never cost them anything they really wanted. They had written mainly in English courses, not much in other classes; and outside of school, if they wrote anything, it was mainly personal letters. For the 13 students who knew and reported their scores on the College Board's English Composition Test, the average was 452, which in more demanding universities would have put them into the bonehead course.

Such students read, I have found, no better than they write, for the English-teachers' emphasis on literature has had no better results than their de-emphasis of composition. In my sophomore literature class in the fall of 1981, 28 of 35 students said that they had never lost anything they really wanted because they didn't read poetry, and many had difficulty with any serious text, whether poetry or prose. Of my freshmen in the spring of 1982, only a few can read mildly intellectual prose with confidence, and none say that they read poetry for fun, though they sometimes burble about the beauties which they find in the howled laments of musical groups. They are much like the graduating senior, a prospective *teacher* of reading, who openly complained two years ago that I had been unrealistic in my demands on my class in English grammar because I had expected them to read a college-level textbook.

I do not wish to invite misrepresentation, which will come soon enough unasked. America will not be the death of English, and we have no more lost our paradigms – the basic structure of our language – than John Connally lost his virility or his virulence when he confused the two, to the horror of Douglas Bush and *The American Scholar*.[4] When the Wise Men of Gotham worry about the state of English usage, they are sometimes worrying about nothing more significant than the distinctions of social class which are marked – or used to be marked – by socially graded synonyms; and the distinctions among those synonyms *have* to be arbitrary, because if the distinctions were really significant for communication everybody would learn them naturally, without expensive tuition, and then the distinctions would no longer allow anybody to think himself superior to everybody else.

But there may be more serious reasons for concern than the confusion of *disinterested* and *uninterested*, *infer* and *imply*. Our use of our language reflects the state of our world, the values which our world has taught us. My students, who I think are typical, do read and write badly, by my standards, because the world has given them no desire, no motive, to read or write as ancients like me believe they should. Our state-supported schools, which inevitably support the state, cannot undo what society has done; but the disappointment of unrealistic expectations brings criticism, from both journalists and academics, to which the schools have not made the needed hard reply.

That reply is simple. So long as our society tolerates the rule of the Big Greedy and accepts greed as its favored motive, only those teachers and teachings which serve cupidity will be respected by the cupidinous; and the young, who use language quite effectively for the purposes which make sense to them in their part of the greedy world, will remain indifferent to traditional definitions of good reading and good writing. Most of my undergraduate students have only the most limited knowledge of the traditional language of literature and intellectual discussion. They don't understand why I value that knowledge. On their strange planet, there may be no good reason why it should be valued.

When the Blind Lead the Blind

That pedagogues should turn arguments about the good, the true, and the beautiful into squabbles over language-attitudes is a more valid criticism of the educational system than allegations of a "literacy hoax": pedagogues as a group must ultimately share the values of the encompassing society, and veteran members of the professional organizations of English-teachers know that The Profession serves mainly The Profession. Of the middle class ourselves, and sometimes only recently admitted to that class, we offer our students no higher motive for their use of standard English than "upward mobility in the mainstream culture." We've made it (we say) to steak; we're moving up (we hope) from steak to lobster; and we talk of drawing our students upward with us when in fact we can't keep that promise but ourselves are slipping down from country fried to 'possum and sweet potatoes. Because we too are infected, we deal badly with the social ills which have prompted the hysteria about linguistic decay and galloping illiteracy. We attack our critics' language-attitudes because we are afraid their criticism will cost us money.

The Profession's own knowledge and use of the English language has drawn some heavy fire, partly because, as I've suggested, most English-teachers have been trained to teach literature only (at the most exalted levels, they have preferred not to teach at all). Though in the colleges and universities there has been a shift toward composition in the past 10 or 15 years, the change has in general been unwilling, prompted by the hard fact that enrollment in literature courses has substantially declined; and most departments of English, as departments, have been indifferent or even hostile to language-study and ignorant of its results. Their graduates typically lack the knowledge to frame rational standards of linguistic choice.

My evidence is again from sad personal experience. At the University of California (Berkeley) in the late 1950s, I came to realize that a good many of my graduate students misused the language painfully when they wrote examinations and that they knew rather little about any system of English grammar.

Accordingly, to a class in Middle English I assigned the reading of the grammar in Mossé's familiar *Handbook*,[5] and while the reading was being done, I gave lectures explaining some of the grammatical terms involved. I then gave a little quiz, asking for definitions or explanations of the four terms *case, grammatical gender, inflection,* and *mood*.

I still have the resulting papers, dated 26 March 1959; and from a two-page horror-sheet which I then mimeographed, here are four specimens, one for each of the four terms:

> case of a part of speech indicates the relationship of time of the action – present, past, future etc.
> grammatical gender – occurs when the gender of an article, pronoun, adjective, etc is determine by the word which it modifies or refers to.
> *Inflection*: An inflected language is one where the substantives reflect the various states of the verb, as to number, gender, case and tense.
> *Mood* . . . . There are three moods in modern English (imperative, subjunctive and   ). . . .

From that class, 19 of 32 papers had at least one definition which I marked for possible citation.

When I moved to Northwestern in the autumn of 1960, I decided to repeat my California experiment. With a class in Modern English grammar for juniors, seniors, and graduates, I spent several weeks discussing my own *Short Introduction*.[6] A week before the examination, I told the class that the questions would be limited to the glossary of grammatical terms in that book, and the questions which I actually set were very simple. The first, for example, was to name the traditional 8 parts of speech. Nine of the 44 students couldn't name them; 5 confused mood with tense; 4 confused mood with voice; 2 confused case with number; 33 gave at least one answer so bad that I preserved it. Of the 9 students who couldn't name all 8 parts of speech, one was a member of our own staff who got as high as 6 but couldn't remember the verb. As good an example as any was an explanation of the term *grammatical gender*: "this applies to traditional conjugation of verbs and refers to the number, the tense, and the person of the verb."

I don't see how students like those can read or teach any history or description of any language intelligently; and if majors and graduates in English can make such blunders in one of the best of American universities, then the average college student must be completely baffled by any serious discussion of his language, since he lacks the vocabulary to talk about it. I have got similar results wherever I've tried my experiments.

For one more instance, I will cite a little questionnaire which my Old English class at Northwestern answered anonymously in the spring of 1962. The 16 respondents were a distinctly superior group. All were graduates, 14 of them in their second graduate year; 8 had taught Freshman English at Northwestern in the fall quarter of 1961; with one possible exception, all those who had not yet taught English intended to teach it; and the total number of courses in literature which the 16 had taken was at least 250 and possibly 300.

What did those amiable, cooperative, and intelligent students know about the English language? They hadn't had much chance to learn, since to 250 or even 300 literary courses the corresponding total for courses in the language was just 18; and as usual the students had no linguistic vocabulary. Because the Graduate Club had asked me to speak on the place of syntax and usage in the freshman course, I asked the class what it understood by the terms of the invitation. One very intelligent answer began, "The terms *syntax* and *usage* used in reference to a freshman English class would have very little meaning for me." Such ignorance, however, did not restrain the students' powerful feelings about the relevance of the two subjects to teaching freshmen. Advocates and opponents of strong emphasis on syntax and usage seemed about equal in number, but my favorite answer reflected what I suspect was a prevalent condition: "I have had more strong feeling than definite opinion about *syntax* and *usage* in freshman English."

The most disturbing answers came in response to the questionnaire's fourth question, in which I asked the students to "comment on syntax and usage" in five sentences. Four of the five were ungrammatical sentences which I had taken from examination papers in my grammar course in the fall quarter; the fifth, which I made up myself, was correct. I was surprised to discover that 8 of the 16 students found fault with it without knowing that I had made it up, and the class was just as unlucky in its attempts to criticize the really faulty sentences.

The last of the five sentences (to illustrate) was this: "Both Chomsky and Lees do not attempt to offer the reader a body of material." I had expected a change to "Neither Chomsky nor Lees attempts . . . ," but the students were too much for me. One dodged the issue by saying that he'd have to think about the sentence; another made no comment on the use of *both . . . and* with a negative; two more found the sentence correct as it stood; a fifth only remarked on "the unusual usage in obviously scholarly writing" (true cynicism, that!), and a sixth (a jester, I hope) proposed the correction, "Neither Chomsky and Lees attempt. . . ."

Of the 80 possible comments by 16 students on 5 sentences, only 60 were actually made. Of the 60, 28 were wrong either in finding an error where none existed or in missing an error that actually was there; only 5 of the 16 students made no such mistakes; 5 went wrong or partly wrong on 2 of the 5 sentences; 1 went wrong on 3, 2 on 4, and 1 gloriously on all 5. I had to conclude that the majority of Northwestern's advanced graduate students couldn't be trusted to recognize mistaken sentences when they saw them or to distinguish good sentences from bad.

There is no point in citing similar results from my classes at UT Austin, though that fish is in the barrel if I should choose to shoot it, and the object of my criticism is not so much our students as it is we their teachers in the colleges. Our indifference or our rash and hostile innovation has undermined the one grammatical tradition which might otherwise have remained in the public schools: under our urging, traditional grammars gave way to structural grammars which gave way to transformational grammars, which gave way. To make matters worse, we have provided neither rational standards for the use of English nor (in many cases) shining examples of it. At the very time when our educational system must and should offer literacy to a swarm of semiliterates, the linguists among us have indoctrinated future teachers with such foolish notions as linguistic relativism, the unsupported and unsupportable assertion that every language is its culture's perfect instrument and that all languages and all dialects are equal in complexity and in value – all different but somehow all miraculously same. Since I have, I think, demolished that assertion elsewhere,[7] I will say nothing more about it now, but will go on to show that too many of such popularizing linguists as have enraged our critics by their relativism and too many of our researchers in composition have invited further rage by their abominable prose.

My favorite target among the popularizing linguists is the group associated with Georgetown University and the Center for Applied Linguistics in Washington, and the two books whose pages I will now casually flip are *Language Attitudes: Current Trends and Prospects*, edited by Roger W. Shuy and Ralph W. Fasold,[8] and *Reactions to Ann Arbor: Vernacular Black English and Education*, edited by Marcia Farr Whiteman.[9] To an unreconstructed fogy, the quality of the writing in those books is an index to the competence of their authors and editors to speak about language-attitudes. For my first ten specimens, from *Language Attitudes*, I give page references and authors' names, so that the editors will not be suspected of composing what they did not correct.

1. Considerable evidence exists that just as research can reveal social stratification of various dialect features, it is also apparent that such stratification also exists in the subjective attitudes that persons have toward the dialects of others. (Shuy and Frederick Williams, p. 85.)

2. Because this dimension is separate from the evaluative dimension, it indicates that complexity is not presumed as neither particularly good nor bad. (S. & W. again, p. 88.)

3. In all, the pattern seems to be that in rating a presumably prestigious form such as British speech, positiveness of rating will correspond with the higher the class level of the respondent. (S. & W., p. 92.)

4. The problematicality of the concept as to its empirical validation has been an impetus to the development of variation theory in linguistics. (David M. Smith, p. 101.)

5. Thus, we see that what has been considered to be, for heuristic purposes, two distinct though interrelated systems are, in fact, interpenetrating. (Smith, p. 109.)

6. . . . it has been found that two major clusters of scales account for the most amount of differentiation of children's speech samples. (Williams, p. 115.)

7. It was found that to the degree that speech samples contained selected nonstandardizations . . ., the more that the same samples were rated as sounding ethnic-nonstandard. (Williams, p. 116.)

8. The videotapes were side views of children whom could be seen speaking but whose utterances could not be lip read. (Williams, p. 125.)

9. In fact, ritualistic insults of mothers and relatives as it occurs in sounding are generally considered taboo behavior. (Walt Wolfram, p. 159.)

10. . . . the examination of verbal activities may be just as important, if not more so, than the examination of linguistic items. . . . (Wolfram, p. 165.)

Though there is more fruit on the *Language Attitudes* tree, my next harvest is from *Reactions to Ann Arbor*, from which I choose just five from a much larger number of horrors:

1. . . . the problem born in the classroom took several years to find nourishment from the disciplines which would help feed it. . . . (Shuy, p. 2.)

2. Mencken's professed intrigue with the language of Appalachia, unfortunately, does not

compensate for the underlying negative attributes also contained in the description. (Wolfram, p. 17.)

3. The inability of a tool to elicit the appropriate data . . . generally indicates that false assumptions underlie its theoretical foundation. (Fay Boyd Vaughn-Cooke, p. 39.)

4. Inherent in these varied programs and approaches is the notion of reading skill development – the progressive/sequential teaching and learning of knowledge, concepts, and principles which facilitate the decoding process, vocabulary development, and comprehension of written materials. (Elizabeth M. Whatley, p. 61.)

5. This discussion is not meant to imply that teachers are inherently deficit in their views. . . . (Shirley A. R. Lewis, p. 86.)

My discussion is meant to imply just that.

There are other documents which thrust themselves upon me in some numbers – a pamphlet from the office of the University of California's Vice-President for Academic Affairs, dated 8 April 1973 and entitled *Teaching of Subject A*; the Winter 1982 issue of *fforum*, the newsletter of the University of Michigan's English Composition Board; the March 1982 newsletter of the Center for Teaching Effectiveness at UT Austin; *et al.* you bet – but I will conclude my exhibition of deformities with five from the *Research in Composition Newsletter* for Spring–Summer 1981, whose only partially numbered pages sometimes can be cited by authors only.

1. As they develop, children gain an ability to internalize their audience. . . . (Marie Wilson Nelson and Ken Kantor, p. 2.)

2. Florio and Clark (1979b) view literacy as "a repertoire of context-related expressive behaviors to a large extent imparted and acquired by means of cultural membership." (Nelson and Kantor, p. 3; but Florio and Clark are the chief culprits.)

3. Donald Graves (1980) argues that "one of the reasons teachers have rejected research information for so long is that they have been unable to transfer faceless data to the alive, inquiring faces of the children they teach the next morning." (Blame Graves, quoted by Nelson and Kantor, p. 5.)

4. . . . this enforces behaviors that are counterproductive to the mastery of adult literacy. Better reader/writers go beyond classroom models and grasp a more dynamic model of literacy. (Patrick Hartwell.)

5. The pre and post tests were evaluated wholistically on a six-point criteria. . . . (James A. Freeman.)

By such a sampling of superabundant evidence, popularizing linguists will be irritated but otherwise unmoved. The popular view among pop linguists is that popular notions of the recent history of English as "decline" or "corruption" are remarkable only "for their strength, pervasiveness, and essential wrongness,"[10] but that judgment is too narrow. Strong and pervasive beliefs about the state of the language, whether they are wrong or right, cannot be dismissed so loftily. The illusions – if they *are* illusions – have deep causes and prompt stubborn actions, and the professional language-planners or mind-adjusters will be frustrated unless they consider both causes and effects as they try to tell the world how the world should talk. It is my contention that the purposes of a society built on greed are necessarily corrupt and that the use of English which serves those purposes will not serve other purposes which I consider better. Pompous opacity is very useful to the mandarin, the self-styled expert whose pretense would be exposed by simple clarity and who cares little or nothing for language informed by an awareness of the traditions of intellectual prose in English; but gobbledygook is bad language because it is determined to bad ends. Discussion of language-attitudes, I must say again, is ultimately moral and political.

Teachers of literature generally write better than linguists or compositionists (that word's not my invention), largely because they have read more that was fit to read; but the morality of the purist is only the morality of a different breed of mandarin. My insistence on awareness of tradition in clear communication is perfectly compatible with the conviction that among the chief abusers of language are those who frustrate communication and threaten identity by insisting that everybody else shall speak and write as they themselves do or as they wish they did, usually in the manner of the social class to which they aspire. To avoid the accusation of choosing only the easiest targets, I will take as my example *The Elements of Style* by Strunk and White, a little book which was a sensation on the Berkeley campus when it first appeared in 1959 and which has since been so widely popular that three editions stand on my shelves, the latest dated 1979. The happy few who cherish it may number millions.

Take away the name of E. B. White, however, and the content of the book reveals itself at once as undistinguished, much of it drawn from William Strunk's plain little text for beginners at Cornell: "Form the possessive singular of nouns by adding '*s*'"; "Do not break sentences in two"; "Omit needless words." White's own contribution would never pass inspection by a competent reviewer without the passport of his name. Especially in the chapter on "misused words," there is much sheer prejudice. White begins that chapter with ritual citation of authorities, including (of course) *The American Heritage Dictionary* and *Webster's Second*[11] and (rather oddly) Roy Copperud's *American Usage*.[12] Amusingly, Copperud's up-dating of his earlier books on style and usage, in *American Usage and Style: The Consensus*,[13] provides evidence that White often follows neither usage nor the judgment of word-watchers.

Thus White individually condemns *to contact, to loan, prestigious, transpire* "to happen," and comparison of *unique*, and follows Strunk in condemnation of *cannot help but, can* for permission, synonymous use of *compare to* and *compare with, data* as a singular, *different than, due to* "because of," *have got* "possess," and initial *however* "nevertheless"; but Copperud's material shows that on all these uses, White's opinion could stand some justifying. A striking instance is *loan*, of which White says (in dubious English), "As a verb, prefer *lend*," while Copperud says flatly, "The idea that *loan* is not good form as a verb is a superstition."

White simply isn't comfortable with history. Sometimes history seems to frighten him: "Never tack -*ize* onto a noun to create a verb" (50); "Not all [nouns used as verbs] are bad, but all are suspect" (54). Sometimes his history is distorted: generic *he*, says White, "has lost all suggestion of maleness" (60); but why then do women rage against it? Sometimes he hopes to guide history's course, as when he urges the use of *that* as "the defining, or restrictive pronoun," *which* as "the nondefining, or nonrestrictive" (59). Even the venerable Strunk did not observe that last injunction, so that repeatedly White must put *that* for a Strunkian *which*. History is undoubtedly a slut, but one doesn't redeem a fallen female by urging her to become a virgin.

But from great precisians one does not expect precision. White confuses the simple terms *gerund* and *participle* (12, 13); he uses *correct* (66) and *standard* (83) to mean whatever he and his approve; and he makes the usual bullying applications of relational terms like *acceptable* (66), *annoying* (45), and *permissible* (7). The timid will no more think to ask who is annoyed or who permits than they will understand such popular impossibles as "Keep related words together" (28) – a rule which *such . . . as* violates, as do correlatives (*both . . . and, either . . . or*), logic's *if . . . then*, pronouns and antecedents, subjects and predicate complements, medial *however* "nevertheless," etc. Sometimes White even makes vagueness a matter of principle (67, 77), as if to say, "We in the inner sanctum know – but we won't tell."

When White does justify himself with reasons and not with his cocked ear or superior taste, his reasons are typically antique but flawed – eighteenth-century arguments from logic, from analogy, from a confusion of the two, for the making or keeping of "useful distinctions" which escape one's readers, against the constant danger of that linguistic chaos of which history records no instances. *Different than* is illogical, he says, because with *differ* we use *from* (44); we shouldn't say *ongoing* (and presumably not *outgoing, outstanding, incoming,* or *upcoming*) because there's no infinitive *to ongo* (54); "*people* is best not used with words of number" (56) because *one people* isn't English; *presently* in its older meaning "currently" should be avoided because we shouldn't risk confusing "now" with the procrastinators' "soon" (57); we should make that useful though un-Strunkian distinction between restrictive *that* and non-restrictive *which*; if mere currency authenticated words, "the language would be as chaotic as a ball game with no foul lines" (52). To apply such criteria generally would make the use of natural languages impossible.

Naturally, then, like other competent writers who have become incompetent grammarians, White is either careless enough or sensible enough to violate his own rules. Sometimes the violation results from careless revision of the venerable Strunk. Strunk wrote, "In especial the expression *the fact that* should be revised out of every sentence in which it occurs."[14] From that one sentence, in the venerable Strunk's much venerated section "Omit needless words," White needlessly made two, the first of them being this: "An expression that is especially debilitating is *the fact that*" (24). He had forgotten Strunk's second sentence following: "*Who is, which was,* and the like are often superfluous."[15]

As a few prized instances will show, the nomothete is often even more dizzyingly antinomian ("12. Do not construct awkward adverbs"):

Reminder: "1. Place yourself in the background."
Violation: "At the close of the first World War, when I was a student at Cornell, I took a course called English 8" (xi; the book's first sentence).
Reminder: "18. Use figures of speech sparingly."
Violation: "*The Elements of Style* . . . seemed to me to contain rich deposits of gold. It was Will Strunk's *parvum opus*, his attempt to cut the vast tangle of English rhetoric down to size and write its rules and principles on the head of a pin" (xi; the book's first page).
Reminder: "Avoid the elaborate, the pretentious, the coy, and the cute" (76).
Violations: "In the English classes of today, 'the little book' is surrounded by longer, lower

textbooks – books with permissive steering and automatic transitions" (xvi). "As a mother of five, with another on the way, my ironing board is always up" (a man's invented example, 14). "*Folks*, in the sense of 'parents,' . . . is colloquial and too folksy for formal writing" (47). Etc.
Reminder: "4. Write with nouns and verbs" (71).
Violation: "Rich, ornate prose is hard to digest, generally unwholesome, and sometimes nauseating. If the sickly-sweet word, the overblown phrase . . ." (72).
Reminder: "17. Do not inject opinion."
Violations: *Passim*.

A more serious fault than White's repeated violation of his own precepts is his equivocation about their nature. Are they simply his own preferences, announced for the curious and perhaps the imitative ("Never imitate consciously" – 70), or do they have some binding force, perhaps from logic, from analogy, or from the consensus of good writers? White never makes up his mind. Of his added fifth chapter, "An Approach to Style," he says in his "Introduction" (xii) that it sets forth his own "prejudices," his "notions of error" and his "articles of faith," and he introduces that chapter as "a mystery story, thinly disguised" (66). He can say, quite truly, that "there is nothing wrong, really, with any word" (77), that "no idiom is taboo, no accent forbidden" (84), and, somewhat less truly, that "the whole duty of a writer is to please and satisfy himself" (85). Even of "words and expressions commonly misused" he can say, with the customary formal bow to linguistic change, that "the shape of our language is not rigid; in questions of usage we have no lawgiver whose word is final" (39).

But those free-spirited intentions are too easily forgotten. By the time the reader reaches Chapter V, the discussions of misuse in Chapter IV have become statements of "what is correct, or acceptable" (66), and the same page which subtitles Chapter V "a List of Reminders" claims for those "reminders" that "they state what most of us know and at times forget." What most of us know is no mystery; and from the proposal on p. xii – "to give in brief space the principal requirements of plain English style," *one* style of many – the crucial adjective has been dropped by p. 69; "*The* approach to style is by way of plainness, simplicity, orderliness, sincerity" (emphasis added). A cockroach, if we are to believe Sinclair Lewis, might pass the test of sincerity, but Shakespeare and Milton would flunk on plainness and simplicity.

In fact, White can be quite as foolishly dogmatic as Wilson Follett[16] or John Simon. His attempts to kill the immortal bogy *finalize* show him in his dictatorial mood. *Finalize*, he assures us, is "a pompous, ambiguous verb" (47), one of "a growing list of abominations" (50), and in the chapter of mysteries there is nothing mysterious about its whole-hearted condemnation:

> *Finalize* . . . is not standard; it is special, and it is a peculiarly fuzzy and silly word. Does it mean "terminate," or does it mean "put into final form"? One can't be sure, really, what it means, and one gets the impression that the person using it doesn't know, either, and doesn't want to know. (83.)

That diatribe is standard rubbish, peculiarly fuzzy and silly. Lots of people don't like *finalize*, because they don't like the culture where it grew; but its form is analogical, its meaning clear in context to anyone who wants to understand.

White is simply taking a trite prejudice out for a good run; and – sadly – it is just such posing which has made him the English-teacher's sage.

English-teachers in the colleges (the teachers that I know best) look up to White because there aren't many people for them to look down on. Speech teachers, maybe, or educationists; but the speech teachers long ago got uppity, and the educationists have got some money and some power because they are better politicians than we are. White exalts the English-teacher's battered ego. He comforts the unhappy flunkies who wish they were Ivy League but aren't, the frustrated essayists, the uncultivated ladies and gentlemen of culture. White shared the great days with Strunk-Chips at old Cornell. He writes with skill beyond an English-teacher's dreams. He is wise, moderate, humorous, restrained yet confident; he dislikes pretentious Dr. Fulsome (English-teachers are never pretentious) and dispraises muckers of all schools but tolerates businessmen and advertisers so long as they keep their place (3, 82, 83); and with all that he is a good outdoor type who rides (43) and shoots (69) and sails (35, 36, 49) and splits his own stovewood (78). The lucky know his like at cottages by the quiet ponds in the tame, expensive woodlands of New England; and White, supremely lucky, knew the venerable Strunk. White's reverence for Strunk invites reverence for him as Strunk's disciple, and reverence draws the reverent reader upward to their pedestal, before which finalizers ought to grovel.

Regrettably, even great masters (Jonathan Swift was one) have gone bonkers when they set out to reform the English language; and White, in his role as a grammarian, is out of his element. His language-attitudes are the attitudes of the typical obstructor of communication, the nit-picking critic who isn't content with his right and duty to discipline himself and who forgets that language can be as much abused by those who listen or read with no desire to understand as it can by those who write or speak without intention to be understood. In matters of language, E. B. White is the vulgarian's master snob, the English faculty's false prophet, all the more dangerous because in other ways he is indeed a minor master.

Layman and Shaman

The sidling crab has reached the following conclusions:

1. There is plenty of concrete evidence for the widespread conviction that the majority of college students don't read or write well enough to live as educated and effective citizens in the world as traditional humanists believe the world should be. The world as it is – the society built on greed – has given them no reasons to learn how.

2. Many teachers of English in the colleges and universities are more concerned with their own advancement than with the cultivation of the traditional arts of literacy through the required course in freshman composition, which does more than any other single course to shape the language-attitudes of their often indifferent students. Freshman composition in the big universities is usually taught by miscellaneous slaveys who themselves have not learned to write well and who have no rationally defensible standards for the

use of English. Too often they share the prejudices of men like E. B. White.

3. Instead of defensible standards and good examples, propagandizing linguists have offered mainly relativism and bad writing.

4. In the minds of such journalists and such segments of the public as concern themselves with these matters, the state of the English language is somewhere between critical and hopeless, and the educational system is no better. When the linguist laughs at the notion "that the quality of English is declining sharply,"[17] the journalist labels all such sceptics "nattering nitwits."[18]

It is my concluding argument that although such reciprocal denunciation is great fun, it never convinces anybody; in the jargon of the Men of Greed, it is counter-productive. The linguists are wrong to dismiss the multiplied complaints that our language has decayed, for even literally absurd complaints reflect both old and new realities of our culture.

As I have said, the notion that English is corrupt has been around since standard varieties of English were first recognized in the writing and speaking of the privileged and powerful in and around London – the language of the dominant and of the functionaries who served them in the metropolitan area. Naturally so; for the real standards of the real world are essentially the creations and instruments of centralized national power, means to boss the bossed for the benefit of the bosses. Even today, real standard English in any nation is more than that, of course. Because for centuries the standard varieties indeed have been the linguistic vehicles of all the activities which the powerful have chosen to regulate, they have been ordered and enriched as other varieties of the language haven't; and to my knowledge just no one has ever proposed that they should not be taught. They *should* be taught, both as facts of public life and as means to students' survival as human beings, but their possible use for liberation does not obscure their origin in dominance. The unceasing complaint that English is corrupt is to some extent the indirect denunciation of the have-nots by the haves. It helps to keep underlings under and even makes them think that they belong there.

Besides this deathless reason for mourning the death of English, more limited causes operate in the United States today. Power has been divorced from traditional culture. The presently dominant are concerned for profit, not pure English, and the rich rednecks laugh when powerless professors criticize redneck language. They may not even hear the criticism; but their laughter or indifference redoubles it and deepens the distrust of the bosses which great numbers of the less prosperous academics share with a big part of the general public.

Humanists on the one hand and technologists and hard and soft scientists on the other are likely to differ in this regard, for the technologists and scientists are rewarded as the rednecks' hired brains, though technological innovation and its social consequences complicate the specification of a real or ideal standard language. Breakneck social change disrupts continuity in the use of English. With TV and "secondary orality" hardly stale in the academic news, teenagers insulated against adult responsibility and adult control are already telling their baffled composition teachers how they converse, compose, and publish with their computers. One gets a vision of human brains so linked to machines in a perpetual flow of unfiltered verbiage that people and machines become always harder to distinguish. An eminent humanist recently ended a thought-experiment by suggesting the possibility of the "suicide of a culture and of a political order based on autonomy, active participation, the capacity of individuals to speak and write."[19]

Those generalizations far outrun any possible demonstration, but so do most beliefs that one must live by. What are called language-attitudes are such beliefs – beliefs about goodness and badness, the beautiful and the ugly, truth and falsehood; and when layman and shaman recognize that the so-called attitudes are in fact beliefs about those qualities as they appear in our use of language, they can also recognize their common need for wider and deeper knowledge of the facts about English, for some system of grammar (it will have to be traditional) with which to organize and state those facts, and most of all for reasoned criteria of linguistic choice. I say *criteria*, in the plural, because complete agreement in a single definition of good English is impossible and even if possible would be unsatisfying because it would certainly be at least partially mistaken.

In reasoning about standards, one must begin with purposes – with whatever it is that good English is good *for*. Officious linguists are likely to "see the language situation in terms of resources to be managed" and to "see language problems . . . as amenable to systematic, 'scientific' investigation";[20] but because people are not "resources to be managed," like livestock, by a non-existent science, and because the typical officious linguist is also a cultural relativist, the visions of American language-planners have often been nightmares like "upward mobility in the mainstream culture." Language change is change in people, and different versions of it reflect different notions of what people are and ought to be.

With the Swift of *Gulliver's Travels*, I still prefer to think that all people, not just the boss yahoos, are at least *capable* of reason, which Milton said is only choosing; and we the people deny our being if we let our linguistic choices be made for us by resource-managers with no grounds for right decision. Because I do believe in the autonomy of active individuals, I stress the function of language as creator and marker of identity; but because the self presupposes the other, and because no society could exist with only a present and not a past and future, to *identity* I add the catchwords of *continuity* and *communication*. Good English is English which does, in the given situation, what a good human being would *want* English to get done there; and the three catchwords of *identity*, *continuity*, and *communication* bring that highly abstract statement a little nearer the concrete.

For the sake of communication in society as it exists, teachers must certainly teach real standard English, the English used by the powerful, even if they dislike both the bosses and their language. Real social pressure will support that teaching and give it some chance of success, yet teachers needn't limit themselves to teaching only the dialect of dominance. Greed has not always and everywhere been society's most hallowed motive; not all presidents have been rapacious rednecks. Concern for the continuity of civilization demands that against all odds teachers should keep the language of literature and intellectual discussion alive in the minds of as many students as they can, "a cultivated language always in touch with actuality but never quite contented with it."[21]

Identity, finally, is most clearly and happily marked by whatever language the individual happens to learn first, the language of family and childhood friends. It is for that reason that none of us should demand of others just the language that we try to use ourselves. "Words and expressions commonly misused" don't often get in the way of communication among people who want to communicate, but to sneer at the only English which the world has allowed somebody else to learn is to sneer at the language which allowed a literal infant to become a realized human being.

I see no genuine reason why layman and shaman should not be able to stand together and stand firm on these real basics, no matter what happens to *enthuse*. Most of all, we should hope for parents and citizens, both laymen and professionals, who will teach the young by their own example to value good reading, writing, speaking, listening; for the young are cagey, and learn what the world in fact believes from what it does.

Notes

1. *On Further Examination* (New York: College Entrance Examination Board, 1977), p. 23.
2. Not Simon called Peter but John Simon, apostle of good English to Manhattan.
3. *Report of the Commission on the Humanities* (New York: American Council of Learned Societies, 1964), p. 138.
4. Douglas Bush, "Polluting our language," *The American Scholar*, **41** (1972), 240.
5. Fernand Mossé, *A Handbook of Middle English*, trans. James A. Walker (Baltimore: The Johns Hopkins Press, 1952), pp. 7–130.
6. James Sledd, *A Short Introduction to English Grammar*. Chicago: Scott, Foresman, 1959.
7. James Sledd, "Linguistic relativism." In *Studies in English Linguistics for Randolph Quirk*, eds. Sidney Greenbaum, Geoffrey Leech, and Jan Svartvik. London: Longman, 1979.
8. Roger W. Shuy and Ralph W. Fasold, eds., *Language Attitudes: Current Trends and Prospects*. Washington, D.C.: Georgetown University Press, 1973.
9. Marcia Farr Whiteman, ed., *Reactions to Ann Arbor: Vernacular Black English and Education*. Arlington, Virginia: Center for Applied Linguistics, 1980.
10. Charles A. Ferguson and Shirley Brice Heath, eds., *Language in the USA* (Cambridge: Cambridge University Press, 1981), p. xxix.
11. William A. Neilson and Thomas A. Knott, eds., *Webster's New International Dictionary, Second Edition*. Springfield, Massachusetts: G. & C. Merriam, 1934. A very useful book for readers with no interest in the language of the living.
12. Roy H. Copperud, *American Usage: The Consensus*. New York: Van Nostrand Reinhold, 1970.
13. New York: Van Nostrand, 1980.
14. William Strunk, Jr., *The Elements of Style* (New York: Harcourt, Brace and Howe, 1920), p. 24.
15. Strunk, page 24.
16. Wilson Follett, *Modern American Usage*. New York: Hill & Wang, 1966.
17. Ferguson and Heath, p. xxix.
18. Melvin Maddocks, rev. of *The Graves of Academe*, by Richard Mitchell, *Time*, 7 Dec. 1981, p. 104.
19. Leon Botstein, "Outside In: Music on language," in *The State of the Language*, ed. Leonard Michaels and Christopher Ricks (Berkeley: University of California Press, 1980), p. 360.
20. Ferguson and Heath, p. xxxviii.
21. James Sledd, "Language differences and literary values," *College English*, **38** (1976), 237.

Index